T0212795

Lecture Notes in Computer Science   **9232**

Commenced Publication in 1973
Founding and Former Series Editors:
Gerhard Goos, Juris Hartmanis, and Jan van Leeuwen

More information about this series at http://www.springer.com/series/7407

Bernd Fischer · Jaco Geldenhuys (Eds.)

Model Checking Software

22nd International Symposium, SPIN 2015
Stellenbosch, South Africa, August 24–26, 2015
Proceedings

 Springer

Editors
Bernd Fischer
Stellenbosch University
Stellenbosch
South Africa

Jaco Geldenhuys
Stellenbosch University
Stellenbosch
South Africa

ISSN 0302-9743   ISSN 1611-3349   (electronic)
Lecture Notes in Computer Science
ISBN 978-3-319-23403-8   ISBN 978-3-319-23404-5   (eBook)
DOI 10.1007/978-3-319-23404-5

Library of Congress Control Number: 2015946997

LNCS Sublibrary: SL1 – Theoretical Computer Science and General Issues

Springer Cham Heidelberg New York Dordrecht London

Springer International Publishing AG Switzerland is part of Springer Science+Business Media
(www.springer.com)

Preface

This volume contains the proceedings of SPIN 2015, the 22nd International SPIN Symposium on Model Checking of Software, which was held August 24–26, 2015, in Stellenbosch, South Africa.

While the earlier meetings in the series focused—not exclusively, but primarily—on the use of SPIN and PROMELA, the scope of recent symposia has been broadened significantly. SPIN now attracts a much wider range of papers around the topic of software model checking, but it retains a healthy balance between theoretical advances and practical considerations.

SPIN 2015 received 27 submissions. Each one was reviewed by three Program Committee members, some of whom consulted with external reviewers. After a thorough and vivid discussion phase, the committee decided to accept 18 papers. Of these, there are 14 regular papers and four tool or new idea papers.

In addition to the presentations of the accepted papers, two invited talks were given by Tefvik Bultan (University of California, Santa Barbara) on "String Analysis for Vulnerability Detection and Repair," and by Shaz Qadeer (Microsoft Research) on "Programming Devices and Services with P." An invited tutorial was given by Michael Tautschnig (Queen Mary University of London) on "CBMC: Bounded Model Checking of Concurrent C Programs."

The volume editors would like to thank all members of the Steering Committee, the Program Committee, as well as the external reviewers for their hard work that led to the selection of this year's program. We are also grateful for the generous support of the National Research Foundation (NRF), grant KIC-97478, the Council of Scientific and Industrial Research (CSIR) through the Center for AI Research (CAIR), Microsoft Research, and the Amazon Development Center Cape Town.

August 2015

Bernd Fischer
Jaco Geldenhuys

Organization

Steering Committee

Dragan Bosnacki	Eindhoven University of Technology, The Netherlands
Susanne Graf	CNRS/VERIMAG, France
Gerard Holzmann	NASA/JPL, USA
Stefan Leue	University of Konstanz, Germany
Willem Visser	Stellenbosch University, South Africa

Program Chairs

Bernd Fischer	Stellenbosch University, South Africa
Jaco Geldenhuys	Stellenbosch University, South Africa

Program Committee

Christel Baier	Technical University of Dresden, Germany
Dragan Bosnacki	Eindhoven University of Technology, The Netherlands
Sagar Chaki	CMU Software Engineering Institute, USA
Alessandro Cimatti	FBK–ES, Italy
Lucas Cordeiro	Federal University of Amazonas, Brazil
Alexandre Duret-Lutz	LRDE/EPITA, France
Matt Dwyer	University of Nebraska, USA
Susanne Graf	CNRS/VERIMAG, France
Alex Groce	Oregon State University, USA
Klaus Havelund	NASA/JPL, USA
Gerard Holzmann	NASA/JPL, USA
Franjo Ivancic	Google, USA
Sarfraz Khurshid	University of Texas at Austin, USA
Shuvendu Lahiri	Microsoft Research, USA
Stefan Leue	University of Konstanz, Germany
Igor Melatti	University of Rome La Sapienza, Italy
Eric Mercer	Brigham Young University, USA
Gennaro Parlato	University of Southampton, UK
Suzette Person	NASA Langley Research Center, USA
Stefan Schwoon	ENS de Cachan/Inria, France
Jaco Van De Pol	University of Twente, The Netherlands
Helmut Veith	Vienna University of Technology, Austria

External Reviewers

Benjamin Hillery
Omar Inverso
Felix Klaedtke
Sascha Klüppelholz
Alfons Laarman
Truc Lam Nguyen

Stefano Schivo
Jan Stückrath
Ashish Tiwari
Anton Wijs
Yu Huang

Invited Contributions

CBMC: Bounded Model Checking
of Concurrent C Programs

Michael Tautschnig

Queen Mary University of London, London, UK
michael.tautschnig@qmul.ac.uk

Abstract. CBMC implements bit-precise bounded model checking for C programs and has been developed and maintained for more than ten years. Only recently support for efficiently checking concurrent programs, including support for weak memory models, has been added. CBMC verifies the absence of violated assertions under a given loop unwinding bound by reducing the problem to a Boolean formula. The formula is passed to a SAT solver, which returns a model if and only if the property is violated.

In the tutorial I provide an overview of the key components of CBMC, underlining its straightforward pipeline. Then a number of examples are presented, including floating point and concurrent programs. CBMC is also amenable to full software systems, such as analysing a SAT solver, and was most recently applied across the entire Debian/GNU Linux distribution.

1 Introduction

The C Bounded Model Checker (CBMC) [2] demonstrates the violation of assertions in C programs, or proves safety of the assertions under a given bound. CBMC implements a bit-precise translation of an input C program, annotated with assertions and with loops unrolled to a given depth, into a formula. If the formula is satisfiable, then an execution leading to a violated assertion exists. By default, satisfiability of the formula is decided using MiniSat 2.2.0 [3].

2 Obtaining CBMC

Bounded model checkers such as CBMC reduce questions about program paths to constraints that can be solved by off-the-shelf SAT or SMT solvers. With the SAT back end, and given a program annotated with assertions, CBMC outputs a CNF formula the solutions of which describe program paths leading to assertion violations. An overview of the system architecture can be found in [7].

CBMC is maintained by Daniel Kroening with patches supplied by the community. It is made publicly available under a BSD-style license. The source code and binaries for popular platforms are available at http://www.cprover.org/cbmc.

3   Selected Recent Applications

While CBMC has won the TACAS Software Verification Competition (SV-COMP) 2014, it is also being applied to full software systems rather than well-defined benchmark settings. CBMC is part of the tool chain analysing the Debian/GNU Linux distribution, as presented in [6]. With our implementation of partial orders [1], CBMC gained support for concurrent systems. Examples of its application include the analysis of asynchronous hardware/software systems [4] and interrupt-driven systems [5].

References

1. Alglave, J., Kroening, D., Tautschnig, M.: Partial orders for efficient bounded model checking of concurrent software. In: Sharygina, N., Veith, H. (eds.) CAV 2013. LNCS, vol. 8044, pp. 141–157. Springer, Heidelberg (2013)
2. Clarke, E., Kroening, D., Lerda, F.: A tool for checking ANSI-C programs. In: Jensen, K., Podelski, A. (eds.) TACAS 2004. LNCS, vol. 2988, pp. 168–176. Springer, Heidelberg (2004)
3. Eén, N., Sörensson, N.: An extensible SAT-solver. In: Giunchiglia, E., Tacchella, A. (eds.) SAT 2003. LNCS, vol. 2919, pp. 502–518. Springer, Heidelberg (2003)
4. Horn, A., Tautschnig, M., Val, C.G., Liang, L., Melham, T., Grundy, J., Kroening, D.: Formal co-validation of low-level hardware/software interfaces. In: Formal Methods in Computer-Aided Design (FMCAD 2013), pp. 121–128. IEEE, October 2013. http://ieeexplore.ieee.org/xpl/freeabsall.jsp?arnumber=6679400
5. Kroening, D., Liang, L., Melham, T., Schrammel, P., Tautschnig, M.: Effective verification of low-level software with nested interrupts. In: Proceedings of the 2015 Design, Automation & Test in Europe Conference & Exhibition, DATE 2015, Grenoble, France, March 9–13, 2015, pp. 229–234 (2015). http://dl.acm.org/citation.cfm?id=2755803
6. Kroening, D., Tautschnig, M.: Automating software analysis at large scale. In: Hliněný, P., Dvořák, Z., Jaroš, J., Kofroň, J., Kořenek, J., Matula, P., Pala, K. (eds.) MEMICS 2014. LNCS, vol. 8934, pp. 30–39. Springer, Heidelberg (2014). http://dx.doi.org/10.1007/978-3-319-14896-03
7. Kroening, D., Tautschnig, M.: CBMC - C bounded model checker - (competition contribution). In: Ábrahám, E., Havelund, K. (eds.) TACAS 2014. LNCS, vol. 8413, pp. 389–391. Springer, Heidelberg (2014)

String Analysis for Vulnerability Detection and Repair

Tevfik Bultan

Department of Computer Science, University of California,
Santa Barbara, USA
bultan@cs.ucsb.edu

Abstract. String manipulation errors in input validation and sanitization code are a common source for security vulnerabilities in web applications. This short survey summarizes the string analysis techniques we developed that can automatically identify and repair such vulnerabilities. Our approach (1) extracts client- and server-side input validation and sanitization functions, (2) models them as deterministic finite automata (DFA) using symbolic fixpoint computations, and (3) identifies errors in input validation and sanitization code by either checking them with respect to manually specified attack patterns, or by identifying inconsistencies in input validation and sanitization operations at the client and server-side. Furthermore, we developed automated repair techniques that strengthen the input validation and sanitization checks in order to eliminate identified vulnerabilities. We implemented these techniques in two tools: Stranger (STRing AutomatoN GEneratoR) and SemRep (SEMantic differential REPair), which are available at: http://www.cs.ucsb.edu/~vlab/tools.html. Our experimental evaluation demonstrates that these techniques are very promising: when applied to a set of real-world web applications, our techniques are able to automatically identify a large number of security vulnerabilities and repair them.

This material is based on research sponsored by NSF under grants CCF-1423623, CNS 1116967, CCF 0916112 and by DARPA under agreement number FA8750-15-2-0087. The U.S. Government is authorized to reproduce and distribute reprints for Governmental purposes notwithstanding any copyright notation thereon. The views and conclusions contained herein are those of the authors and should not be interpreted as necessarily representing the official policies or endorsements, either expressed or implied, of DARPA or the U.S. Government. Part of this research was conducted while Tevfik Bultan was visiting Koç University in İstanbul, Turkey, supported by a research fellowship from TÜBİTAK under the BİDEB 2221 program.

Programming Devices and Services with P

Shaz Qadeer

Microsoft Research, Redmond, USA
qadeer@microsoft.com

Asynchronous programming is essential for building a wide range of important software, such as device drivers, distributed services, embedded systems, and user interfaces. A difficult challenge in asynchronous programming is appropriate handling of the nondeterminism due to concurrency and timing of external input. The P language [3] makes it easier to tackle this challenge. It allows the programmer to specify the system as a collection of interacting state machines, which communicate with each other using events. P unifies modeling and programming into one activity for the programmer. A P program can not only be compiled into executable code but also be validated using systematic testing. The high-coverage testing techniques [1, 4, 5, 6] implemented in P have the capability to generate and reproduce within minutes, race conditions that could take months or even years to manifest in a live system.

P has been used to develop software systems in various Microsoft product groups. Examples include the USB 3.0 drivers that ship with Windows and low-level firmware in upcoming devices. With no change to the programming model and a few changes to the runtime, we have also used P to implement reliable fault-tolerant distributed services. The P system is available open-source at https://github.com/p-org/P.

The P approach to protocol design and implementation is a domain-specific language and a compiler to executable C code. While this approach allows considerable flexibility in the design of the language, it also introduces two barriers to adoption. First, a programmer must learn the syntax and the semantics of P. Second, since it is unlikely that an application can be written entirely in P, she must also learn the explicit foreign-function interface between P and its host language C. As an alternative design, the language P# [2] incorporates features of P as an extension to the C# language, allowing programmers to program mostly with familiar C# syntax and freely mix P# and C# code. The P# system is available open-source at https://github.com/p-org/PSharp.

References

1. Burckhardt, S., Kothari, P., Musuvathi, M., Nagarakatte, S.: A randomized scheduler with probabilistic guarantees of finding bugs. In: ASPLOS: Architectural Support for Programming Languages and Systems (2010)
2. Deligiannis, P., Donaldson, A.F., Ketema, J., Lal, A., Thomson, P.: Asynchronous programming, analysis and testing with state machines. In: PLDI: Programming Language Design and Implementation (2015)

3. Desai, A., Gupta, V., Jackson, E., Qadeer, S., Rajamani, S., Zufferey, D.: P Safe asynchronous event-driven programming. In: PLDI: Programming Languague Design and Implementation (2013)
4. Desai, A., Qadeer, S., Seshia, S.: Systematic testing of asynchronous reactive systems. In: FSE: Foundations of Software Engineering (2015)
5. Emmi, M., Qadeer, S., Rakamarić, Z.: Delay-bounded scheduling. In: POPL: Principles of Programming Languages (2011)
6. Thomson, P., Donaldson, A.F., Betts, A.: Concurrency testing using schedule bounding: an empirical study. In: PPoPP: Principles and Practices of Parallel Programming (2014)

Contents

Invited Contribution

String Analysis for Vulnerability Detection and Repair

Tevfik Bultan[✉]

Department of Computer Science,
University of California, Santa Barbara, Santa Barbara, USA
bultan@cs.ucsb.edu

Abstract. String manipulation errors in input validation and sanitization code are a common source for security vulnerabilities in web applications. This short survey summarizes the string analysis techniques we developed that can automatically identify and repair such vulnerabilities. Our approach (1) extracts client- and server-side input validation and sanitization functions, (2) models them as deterministic finite automata (DFA) using symbolic fixpoint computations, and (3) identifies errors in input validation and sanitization code by either checking them with respect to manually specified attack patterns, or by identifying inconsistencies in input validation and sanitization operations at the client and server-side. Furthermore, we developed automated repair techniques that strengthen the input validation and sanitization checks in order to eliminate identified vulnerabilities. We implemented these techniques in two tools: Stranger (STRing AutomatoN GEneratoR) and SemRep (SEMantic differential REPair), which are available at: http://www.cs.ucsb.edu/~vlab/tools.html. Our experimental evaluation demonstrates that these techniques are very promising: when applied to a set of real-world web applications, our techniques are able to automatically identify a large number of security vulnerabilities and repair them.

1 Motivation

According to the Common Vulnerabilities and Exposures (CVE) repository, web application vulnerabilities form a significant portion of all reported computer security vulnerabilities [8]. Additionally, Open Web Application Security Project (OWASP) compiles a top ten list to identify the most critical security flaws in

This material is based on research sponsored by NSF under grants CCF-1423623, CNS 1116967, CCF 0916112 and by DARPA under agreement number FA8750-15-2-0087. The U.S. Government is authorized to reproduce and distribute reprints for Governmental purposes notwithstanding any copyright notation thereon. The views and conclusions contained herein are those of the authors and should not be interpreted as necessarily representing the official policies or endorsements, either expressed or implied, of DARPA or the U.S. Government. Part of this research was conducted while Tevfik Bultan was visiting Koç University in İstanbul, Turkey, supported by a research fellowship from TÜBİTAK under the BİDEB 2221 program.

© Springer International Publishing Switzerland 2015
B. Fischer and J. Geldenhuys (Eds.): SPIN 2015, LNCS 9232, pp. 3–9, 2015.
DOI: 10.1007/978-3-319-23404-5_1

web applications [10]. According to the OWASP top ten lists compiled in 2007, 2010 and 2013, Cross-site Scripting (XSS) and SQL Injection (SQLI) are always among the top three web application vulnerabilities.

XSS and SQLI vulnerabilities are due to improper input validation and sanitization. Errors in validation and sanitization of user input can lead to vulnerabilities for web applications, and since web applications are globally accessible, these vulnerabilities can be exploited by malicious users all around the world. Different layers of a web application interact through commands that often embed user input and are written in many languages, such as XML, SQL, and HTML. Hence, programs that propagate and use malicious user inputs without validation and sanitization, or with improper validation and sanitization, are vulnerable to attacks such as XSS and SQLI.

2   String Analysis

In order to provide a general framework for eliminating vulnerabilities related to input validation and sanitization we have to address multiple issues, such as, automated extraction of validation and sanitization operations from a given web application, detecting if there is a vulnerability by automatically analyzing extracted string operations, and automatically generating a repair that eliminates the identified vulnerability. During last several years, we worked on various aspects of this problem at the Verification Laboratory of the University of California, Santa Barbara (http://www.cs.ucsb.edu/~vlab/). A summary of the techniques we developed in this domain is provided below.

Automata-Based String Analysis: First, we developed an automata-based approach for the verification of string operations in PHP programs based on symbolic string analysis [12,14,15]. String analysis is a static analysis technique that determines the values that a string expression can take during program execution at a given program point. This information can be used to verify that string values are sanitized properly, and to detect programming errors and security vulnerabilities. In our string analysis approach, we encode the set of string values that string variables can take as Deterministic Finite Automata (DFA). We implement all string functions using a symbolic automata representation (MBDD representation from the MONA automata package [7]) and leverage efficient manipulations on MBDDs, e.g., determinization and minimization. Particularly, we developed a novel algorithm for language-based replacement. Our replacement function takes three DFAs as arguments and outputs a DFA. Finally, we apply a widening operator defined on automata to approximate fixpoint computations [6]. If this conservative approximation does not match any attack patterns (specified as regular expressions), we conclude that the program does not contain any errors or vulnerabilities. Our experimental results demonstrate that our approach works quite well in checking the correctness of sanitization operations in real-world PHP applications. We implemented these automata-based string analysis techniques in a tool called Stranger (STRing AutomatoN GEneratoR) which is available at: http://www.cs.ucsb.edu/~vlab/stranger/.

Computing Vulnerability Signatures: Based on automata-based string analysis, we developed techniques that, given a program and an attack pattern (specified as a regular expression), generate string-based vulnerability signatures, i.e., a characterization that includes all malicious inputs that can be used to generate attacks [11,13]. Using forward reachability analysis, we compute an over-approximation of all possible values that string variables can take at each program point. Intersecting these with the attack pattern yields the potential attack strings if the program is vulnerable. Using backward analysis we compute an over-approximation of all possible inputs that can generate those attack strings. In addition to identifying existing vulnerabilities and their causes, these vulnerability signatures can be used to filter out malicious inputs. Our approach extends the prior work on automata-based string analysis by providing a backward symbolic analysis that includes a symbolic pre-image computation for DFAs on common string manipulating functions such as concatenation and replacement.

Relational String Analysis: String analysis techniques based on standard single-track automata cannot precisely represent relational constraints that involve multiple variables. To address this problem, we developed novel relational string verification techniques based on multi-track automata [18,19]. Multi-track automata recognize tuples of strings by reading multiple inputs concurrently. Value of each string variable is represented as one of the input tracks of the automata, which enables us to represent relational constraints on multiple variables. Using this symbolic representation we are able verify relational properties that involve multiple string variables.

Verifying string manipulating programs is an undecidable problem in general [18,19] and any approximate string analysis technique has an inherent tension between efficiency and precision. We developed sound abstraction techniques for strings and string operations that allow for both efficient and precise verification of string manipulating programs [16]. We first defined an abstraction called regular abstraction which enables us to perform string analysis using multi-track automata as a symbolic representation. We then introduced two other abstractions—alphabet abstraction and relation abstraction—that can be used in combination to tune the analysis precision and efficiency. We showed that these abstractions form an abstraction lattice that generalizes the string analysis techniques studied previously in isolation, such as string length analysis or non-relational string analysis. Finally, we empirically evaluated the effectiveness of these abstraction techniques with respect to several benchmarks and an open source application, demonstrating that abstraction techniques can improve the performance without loss of accuracy of the analysis when a suitable abstraction class is selected.

Handling Operations on String Length: Another interesting class of properties involve relationships among the string and integer variables. The lengths of the strings in a regular language form a semilinear set. Since we use automata to encode possible values of string variables, we can use this observation to encode the lengths of string variables as semilinear sets. Moreover, we can construct automata that recognize these semilinear sets, i.e., recognize the possible lengths of a string variable. We developed techniques that construct length automata that accept the unary or binary representations of the lengths of the strings accepted by string automata [17]. These length automata can be integrated with an arithmetic automaton that recognizes the valuations of the integer variables at a program point. We developed a static analysis technique that uses these automata in a forward fixpoint computation with widening [6], and is able to capture relationships among the lengths of the string variables and the values of the integer variables. This composite string and integer analysis enables us to verify properties that cannot be verified using string analysis or integer analysis alone.

Client-side String Analysis: Client-side computation in web applications is becoming increasingly common due to the popularity of powerful client-side programming languages such as JavaScript. Client-side computation is commonly used to improve an applications responsiveness by validating user inputs before they are sent to the server. We developed string analysis techniques for checking if a client-side input validation function conforms to a given policy [2]. In our approach, input validation policies are expressed using two regular expressions, one specifying the maximum policy (the upper bound for the set of inputs that should be allowed) and the other specifying the minimum policy (the lower bound for the set of inputs that should be allowed). Using our analysis we can identify two types of errors (1) the input validation function accepts an input that is not permitted by the maximum policy, or (2) the input validation function rejects an input that is permitted by the minimum policy. We implemented our analysis using dynamic slicing to automatically extract the client-side input validation functions from web applications, and using automata-based string analysis to analyze the extracted functions. Our experiments demonstrate that our approach is effective in finding errors in input validation functions that we collected from real-world applications and from tutorials and books for teaching JavaScript.

Differential String Analysis: Developers typically perform redundant input validation in both the front-end (client) and the back-end (server) components of a web application. As we mentioned above, client-side validation is used to improve the responsiveness of the application, as it allows for responding without communicating with the server, whereas server-side validation is necessary for security reasons, as malicious users can easily circumvent client-side checks. We developed a differential string analysis technique that (1) automatically extracts client- and server-side input validation functions, (2) models them as DFAs, and (3) compares client- and server-side DFAs to identify and report the inconsistencies between the two sets of checks [3]. Our initial evaluation of the technique is promising: when applied to a set of real-world web applications, our technique was able to automatically identify a large number of inconsistencies in their input validation functions.

Automated Test-Case Generation: Automata-based static string analysis techniques we described above can be used to automatically compute vulnerability signatures (represented as automata) that characterize all the inputs that can exploit a vulnerability. However, there are several factors that limit the applicability of static string analysis techniques in general: (1) undecidability of static string analysis requires the use of approximations leading to false positives, (2) static string analysis tools do not handle all string operations, (3) dynamic nature of the scripting languages makes static analysis difficult. As a complementary approach to static string analysis techniques, we developed automated testing techniques for checking string manipulating code [4]. In particular, we showed that vulnerability signatures computed for deliberately insecure web applications (developed for demonstrating different types of vulnerabilities) can be used to generate test cases for other applications. Given a vulnerability signature represented as an automaton, we developed algorithms for test case generation based on state, transition, and path coverage. These automatically generated test cases can be used to test applications that are not analyzable statically, and to discover attack strings that demonstrate how the vulnerabilities can be exploited.

Automated Vulnerability Repair: Based on automata-based static string analysis, we developed techniques that automatically generate sanitization statements for patching vulnerable web applications [13]. Our approach consists of three phases: Given an attack pattern we first conduct a vulnerability analysis to identify if strings that match the attack pattern can reach the security-sensitive functions. Next, we compute vulnerability signatures that characterize all input strings that can exploit the discovered vulnerability. Given the vulnerability signatures, we then construct sanitization statements that (1) check if a given input matches the vulnerability signature and (2) modify the input in a minimal way so that the modified input does not match the vulnerability signature. Our approach is capable of generating relational vulnerability signatures (and corresponding sanitization statements) for vulnerabilities that are due to more than one input.

Although attack patterns are useful for characterizing possible attacks, they need to be written manually, which means that they may contain errors, and they may not be available for newer attacks. We developed an automated differential repair technique for input validation and sanitization functions that does not require manual specification of expected behavior [1]. Differential repair can be used within an application to repair client and server-side code with respect to each other, or across applications in order to strengthen the validation and sanitization checks. Given a reference and a target function, our differential repair technique strengthens the validation and sanitization operations in the target function based on the reference function. It does this by synthesizing three patches: a validation, a length, and a sanitization patch. Our automated patch synthesis algorithms are based on forward and backward symbolic string analyses that use automata as a symbolic representation. Composition of the three automatically synthesized patches with the original target function results in the repaired function, which provides stronger validation and sanitization than both the target and the reference functions. We implemented these automata-based differential repair techniques in a tool called SemRep (SEMantic differential REPair), which is available at: https://github.com/vlab-cs-ucsb/SemRep.

Model Counting for String Constraints: Symbolic execution has become one of the most widely used automated bug detection techniques. In order to apply symbolic execution to analysis of string manipulating programs, it is necessary to develop constraint solvers that can check satisfiability of string constraints. Our automata-based string analysis techniques can be used to build a string constraint solver. To facilitate this, we developed a string analysis library called LibStranger (available at https://github.com/vlab-cs-ucsb/LibStranger) based on our tool Stranger. In a recent independent empirical study for evaluating string constraint solvers, Stranger was determined to be the best in terms of precision and efficiency for symbolic execution of Java programs [9].

However, for quantitative and probabilistic program analyses, checking the satisfiability of a constraint is not sufficient. In addition to checking satisfiability, it is also necessary to count the number of satisfying solutions. Recently, we developed a string constraint solver that, given a constraint, (1) constructs an automaton that accepts all solutions that satisfy the constraint, (2) generates a function that, given a length bound, gives the total number of solutions within that bound [5]. Our approach relies on the observation that, using an automata-based constraint representation, model counting reduces to path counting, which can be solved precisely. We demonstrated the effectiveness of our approach on a large set of string constraints extracted from real-world web applications. We implemented these techniques in a tool called ABC (Automata Based model Counter for constraints) (see http://www.cs.ucsb.edu/~vlab/ABC/).

3   Conclusion

String manipulation is an important part of modern software systems, and errors in string manipulating code continue to be a significant software dependability problem. Our results demonstrate that automata-based string analysis techniques are promising tools in eliminating software dependability problems that are due to string manipulation.

References

1. Alkhalaf, M., Aydin, A., Bultan, T.: Semantic differential repair for input validation and sanitization. In: Proceedings of the International Symposium on Software Testing and Analysis (ISSTA), pp. 225–236 (2014)
2. Alkhalaf, M., Bultan, T., Gallegos, J.L.: Verifying client-side input validation functions using string analysis. In: Proceedings of the 34th International Conference on Software Engineering (ICSE), pp. 947–957 (2012)
3. Alkhalaf, M., Roy Choudhary, S., Fazzini, M., Bultan, T., Orso, A., Kruegel, C.: Viewpoints: differential string analysis for discovering client- and server-side input validation inconsistencies. In: Proceedings of the International Symposium on Software Testing and Analysis (ISSTA), pp. 56–66 (2012)

4. Aydin, A., Alkhalaf, M., Bultan, T.: Automated test generation from vulnerability signatures. In: 7th IEEE International Conference on Software Testing, Verification and Validation (ICST), pp. 193–202 (2014)

5. Aydin, A., Bang, L., Bultan, T.: Automata-based model counting for string constraints. In: Kroening, D., Păsăreanu, C.S. (eds.) CAV 2015. LNCS, vol. 9206, pp. 255–272. Springer, Heidelberg (2015)

6. Bartzis, C., Bultan, T.: Widening arithmetic automata. In: Alur, R., Peled, D.A. (eds.) CAV 2004. LNCS, vol. 3114, pp. 321–333. Springer, Heidelberg (2004)

7. BRICS. The MONA project. http://www.brics.dk/mona/

8. CVE. Common Vulnerabilities and Exposures. http://www.cve.mitre.org

9. Kausler, S., Sherman, E.: Evaluation of string constraint solvers in the context of symbolic execution. In: Proceedings of the 29th ACM/IEEE International Conference on Automated software engineering (ASE), pp. 259–270 (2014)

10. Open Web Application Security Project (OWASP). Top ten project. https://www.owasp.org/index.php/Category:OWASP_Top_Ten_Project

11. Yu, F., Alkhalaf, M., Bultan, T.: Generating vulnerability signatures for string manipulating programs using automata-based forward and backward symbolic analyses. In: Proceedings of the 24th IEEE/ACM International Conference on Automated Software Engineering (ASE), pp. 605–609 (2009)

12. Yu, F., Alkhalaf, M., Bultan, T.: STRANGER: an automata-based string analysis tool for PHP. In: Esparza, J., Majumdar, R. (eds.) TACAS 2010. LNCS, vol. 6015, pp. 154–157. Springer, Heidelberg (2010)

13. Yu, F., Alkhalaf, M., Bultan, T.: Patching vulnerabilities with sanitization synthesis. In: Proceedings of the 33rd International Conference on Software Engineering (ICSE), pp. 131–134 (2011)

14. Fang, Y., Alkhalaf, M., Bultan, T., Ibarra, O.H.: Automata-based symbolic string analysis for vulnerability detection. Formal Methods Syst. Des. 44(1), 44–70 (2014)

15. Yu, F., Bultan, T., Cova, M., Ibarra, O.H.: Symbolic string verification: an automata-based approach. In: Havelund, K., Majumdar, R. (eds.) SPIN 2008. LNCS, vol. 5156, pp. 306–324. Springer, Heidelberg (2008)

16. Yu, F., Bultan, T., Hardekopf, B.: String abstractions for string verification. In: Groce, A., Musuvathi, M. (eds.) SPIN Workshops 2011. LNCS, vol. 6823, pp. 20–37. Springer, Heidelberg (2011)

17. Yu, F., Bultan, T., Ibarra, O.H.: Symbolic string verification: combining string analysis and size analysis. In: Kowalewski, S., Philippou, A. (eds.) TACAS 2009. LNCS, vol. 5505, pp. 322–336. Springer, Heidelberg (2009)

18. Yu, F., Bultan, T., Ibarra, O.H.: Relational string verification using multi-track automata. In: Domaratzki, M., Salomaa, K. (eds.) CIAA 2010. LNCS, vol. 6482, pp. 290–299. Springer, Heidelberg (2011)

19. Fang, Y., Bultan, T., Ibarra, O.H.: Relational string verification using multi-track automata. Int. J. Found. Comput. Sci. 22(8), 1909–1924 (2011)

Abstraction, Refinement, Translation

ASTRA: A Tool for Abstract Interpretation of Graph Transformation Systems

Peter Backes and Jan Reineke[✉]

Universität des Saarlandes, Saarbrücken, Germany
{rtc,reineke}@cs.uni-saarland.de

Abstract. We describe ASTRA (see http://rw4.cs.uni-saarland.de/~rtc/astra/), a tool for the static analysis of infinite-state graph transformation systems. It is based on abstract interpretation and implements cluster abstraction, i.e., it computes a finite overapproximation of the set of reachable graphs by decomposing them into small, overlapping clusters of nodes. While related tools lack support for negative application conditions, accept only a limited class of graph transformation systems, or suffer from state-space explosion on models with (even moderate) concurrency, ASTRA can cope with scenarios that combine these three challenges. Applications include parameterized verification and shape analysis of heap structures.

Keywords: Abstract interpretation · Graph transformation systems · Parameterized verification · Shape analysis · Tools

1 Introduction

Graph transformation is an intuitive formalism: One begins with a start graph and, by nondeterministic choice, matches and applies transformation rules to it, based on subgraph replacement. We are mainly interested in analysis of the graphs reachable by successive application of rules, to verify safety properties, for example.

One of the applications of graph transformation is modelling parameterized concurrent systems. Reasoning about such systems is hard because the state space is infinite. Hence, abstraction methods are required. In this paper, we present ASTRA, our tool for abstraction of graph transformation systems.

A number of tools are available that use abstract interpretation (each based on a different abstraction) to compute a finite over-approximation of the reachable graphs: AUGUR [7] uses a petri net based abstraction and had success with interesting examples of concurrent systems; it does not, however, support negative application conditions. hiralysis [5] is based on partner abstraction.

This work was partially supported by the German Research Council (DFG) as part of the Transregional Collaborative Research Center "Automatic Verification and Analysis of Complex Systems" (SFB/TR 14 AVACS). See http://www.avacs.org/ for more information.

B. Fischer and J. Geldenhuys (Eds.): SPIN 2015, LNCS 9232, pp. 13–19, 2015.
DOI: 10.1007/978-3-319-23404-5_2

It does offer negative application conditions and can analyze some concurrent systems, but requires input grammars to satisfy some rather restrictive "friendliness" properties. GROOVE [9] has an implementation of neighborhood abstraction, which has no such restriction, supports negative application conditions, but analysis of systems with concurrency leads to state space explosion.

2   Cluster Abstraction

Our tool, ASTRA, implements *cluster abstraction* [3]: We consider each node in the graph (to become the *core node* of a cluster) plus its respective adjacent nodes (to become the *periphery*). We merge two or more adjacent nodes into summary nodes if both their labels and configuration (*spoke*) of edges to the core node are equal. If, by this summarization, two merged nodes disagree on to existence of some edge to a third node, we replace it by a $\frac{1}{2}$ edge. After summarization, we are left with clusters of bounded size, and we eliminate any duplicate cluster by assuming (as a further overapproximation) that there can be any number of concrete instances. An example is shown in Fig. 1. The initial graph is abstracted in this way, and then rule application is lifted to the abstraction.

In this paper we describe ASTRA 2.0. An earlier version, ASTRA 1.0 [2], implemented a less precise precursor to cluster abstraction that assumed all edges in the periphery to be $\frac{1}{2}$.

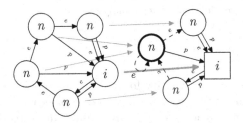

Fig. 1. An example of how a cluster is obtained by abstracting the concrete graph with respect to one specific node (here, the *i*-labelled one). The tool lifts the application of graph transformation rules to this abstraction. We represent node summarization as thick circles, the $\frac{1}{2}$ nodes as dashed lines.

3   Architecture and Usage

ASTRA is a command-line program that expects a start graph and graph transformation rules as input and outputs the clusters from the analysis. When running the analysis, it abstracts the start graph, then enters its main loop. The main loop searches for abstract matches; each left hand side node of each rule is matched against the core node of any cluster from the current working set, and the remaining nodes are matched to a subset of the respective peripheral nodes. In addition, one further cluster with unmatched core node, but matched peripheral nodes is materialized. Those matches are then combined into a partial concretization, with several checks done to rule out cases where no full concretization exists. Not all such cases are detected by the tool; but the result is still a valid over-approximation.

All clusters produced by rule application are added to a temporary set. After each iteration, the tool then, optionally, applies a post-pass reduction step to the temporary set, inspecting it for clusters that can be eliminated or refined. Finally, the temporary set is joined with the working set.

The tool indicates progress as it goes from rule to rule, and from iteration to iteration. After each iteration, the current working set is dumped to disk, which is useful for inspecting the current state of the analysis when running the tool on complex cases that take some time.

The main loop is executed iteratively until the working set remains unchanged, i.e., a fixpoint has been reached. (Given the finite size of the abstract domain, termination is guaranteed, but subject to, like with all abstractions, processor speed and memory size.) The tool then dumps the output to disk, prints statistics and exits. Given the finite size of the abstract domain, termination is guaranteed.

3.1 Input File Format

ASTRA uses the same ASCII-based input file format as `hiralysis` (see [5] Fig. B.1, p. 160), extended by additional application conditions. For example, the constraint `partner(x1)=neg(out,p)` restricts rules to apply only if the node matched by `x1` has no outgoing edge with label `p`.

Consider the following toy case as a running example. The input:

```
nodelabels n,Error,i; edgelabels e,p;
empty; // start graph
create [{x1:n,x2:n,x3:i},
    {(x1,x2):e,(x2,x3):e,(x3,x1):e,(x1,x3):p,(x2,x3):p}];// init
rule [{x1:i,x2:n},{(x1,x2):e}],
    [{x1:i,x2:n,x3:n},{(x1,x3):e,(x3,x2):e,(x3,x1):p}];
rule [{x1:n},{},partner(x1)=neg{(out,p)}], [{x1:n,x2:Error},{}];
```

This example models singly-linked ring buffers into which an unbounded number of nodes are inserted dynamically. One special node is indicated with the label i. New nodes are inserted next to it with a back pointer. Here, we want to use astra to verify the safety property that each node has such a back pointer. We achieve this with the second rule. It uses a negative application condition to generate an error label if a node lacks the back pointer.

As can be seen, the input file format is mainly based on graphs, which are sets of node names, each with a label, and sets of edges (the name being a pair of node names), each with an edge label. The rules specify the subgraph to be replaced and the subgraph by which it is replaced. The node names imply a mapping from the left hand side to the right hand side.

3.2 Command-Line Interface

For our case study, consider the following tool run:

```
$ ./astra -Os -Op test023.gts
  0 [  2/  2] = 100
  1 [  2/  2] = 100
  2 [  2/  2] = 100
done.
6 clusters, 5 matches, 1 active rules,
6 rule applications, 2 iterations
```

The $ indicates the shell prompt; the remaining line is entered by the tool user. In this case, ASTRA is run on the input file of our running example (test023.gts).

In the example, we specify analysis options -Os and -Op, instructing ASTRA to apply a simple peripheral constraint satisfiability check and post-pass reduction, respectively. For our experiments, this proved to be the most practical option set, providing the best speed/precision trade-off. Removing one of the two options lead to drastic decrease in precision, while adding any other lead to merely minuscule gains. Only in specific cases where the analysis would otherwise run into state-space explosion, further analysis options were useful.

Option -n can be used to specify a cutoff iteration after which to prematurely terminate the analysis. This is useful to inspect the intermediate result. Run ASTRA without arguments for further details about the available options.

3.3 Status Report

For each iteration, while running, the current iteration number, current rule, total number of rules and progress (current rule divided by total number of rules) is printed. After finishing the iteration, the number of clusters added and modified (i.e., with peripheral constraints weakened) is printed. Note that clusters added by the initial graph and by rules with empty left hand side are only accounted for in the final statistics printed after the fixpoint has been reached.

3.4 Output File Formats

ASTRA supports DOT (as used by the graph layout tool Graphviz), GML (as used by OGDF and the GoVisual Diagram Editor, respectively), GDL (as used by VCG and its successor aiSee) and GraphML (as used by yEd and yComp, respectively). In addition, the tool supports its own native output format that is similar to the input format.

The output can be loaded or processed with any tool supporting any of those formats. The most common use will be a graph layout tool to inspect the output, but it can as well provide invariants for other analyses, like hiralysis [4].

For our running example, the tool outputs six clusters, visualized in Fig. 2. In addition to the full analysis, we show the intermediate results obtained by using option -n.

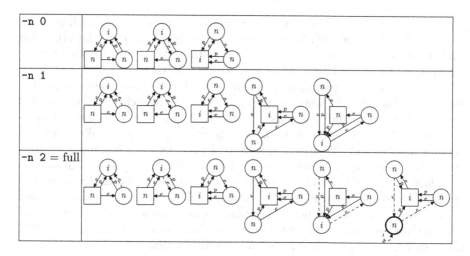

Fig. 2. Analysis results on running example.

These drawings were done by METAPOST, based on an experimental output module built into ASTRA that does primitive circular graph drawing. For common use, aiSee and yEd have proven most useful, especially the organic and hierarchical layout engines.

4   Experimental Evaluation

We already ran the tool on various test cases from the literature in [3], including AVL trees, red-black trees, firewalls, public/private servers, dining philosophers, resources, mutual exclusion, singly-linked lists, circular buffers, Euler walks, and the merge protocol. The merge protocol, our main example, is a distributed car platooning coordination protocol that establishes a logical communication hierarchy on top of the physical communication medium. Analysis of the protocol is hard because of its massively distributed nature, caused by the vast range of topological configurations that may evolve concurrently.

However, all inputs from that case study were written by hand. To demonstrate the robustness of our tool, we apply it to graph transformation systems

Table 1. Benchmark analysis statistics. cl. = clusters, m. = abstract matches, rule app. = rule applications, it. = iterations.

Benchmark	# cl	# m	# rule app	# it.	Time
Synchronous, leader-controlled	22509	75359	36685213	135	9 m 34.200 s
Synchronous, follower-controlled	24957	82569	43679468	144	22 m 30.200 s
Asynchronous,leader-controlled	142326	850889	1006759383	202	13136 m 1.260 s
Asynchronous,follower-controlled	58023	296310	83499253	157	3972 m 37.560 s

generated automatically from higher level models of the merge protocol, specified in the DCS formalism [6,8]. We used the tool dcs2gts [1] to translate the DCS models into graph transformation systems suitable for analysis with ASTRA. We include two new variants, follower-controlled merge.

Synchronous (leader-controlled) merge in our former case study consisted of 402 rules (plus 3 for checking safety properties), the asynchronous version 313 (plus 2). The large number is caused by the fact that many rules are generated from templates that iterate over all node labels. The automatically generated versions use 788 and 835 rules, respectively. In contrast, the number of clusters in the analysis result increased from 873 to 22509 (factor 26) and from 3069 to 142326 (factor 46). This is because the automatically generated version uses intermediate steps to model topology changes. While those steps are serialized by special labels, and thus pose no combinatorial challenge, our analysis shows that the tool does well with all those intermediate configurations absent in the manually created inputs. See Table 1 for the full results.

5   Conclusions and Future Work

We have seen how ASTRA can be used to analyze a simple graph transformation system, modelling insertion of elements into ring buffers. In contrast to related tools, it is not restricted to graph transformation systems of a special form, it supports negative application conditions and it does well when facing models involving concurrency. Our experimental evaluation showed that it is capable of handling very complex inputs generated automatically from higher-level specifications.

Future Work: Our tool already has experimental support for generating an abstract labelled transition system of clusters, but the theory for actually using those with a model checker has still to be worked out. We would also like to provide more powerful application conditions, in particular non-existence of edges between two specific nodes and restrictions on the periphery of a node.

A promising way to considerably speed up analysis is parallelization. The structure of the analysis is very well suited for this and we expect a parallelized version to scale almost linearly.

Acknowledgments. We thank Dmytro Puzhay for assistance with the implementation work and Jörg Bauer-Kreiker for providing his hiralysis test cases. Conny Clausen managed copyright clearance with Saarland University to obtain permission for releasing the tool under a Free Software license. Reinhard Wilhelm provided valuable comments for a draft version of this paper.

References

1. Backes, P.: dcs2gts - An interface between XML-coded DCS protocols and the hiralysis representation of graph transformation grammars. Fopra report, Saarland University, January 2007

2. Backes, P., Reineke, J.: Abstract topology analysis of the join phase of the merge protocol. In: TTC 2010, CTIT Workshop Proceedings, vol. WP10-03, pp. 127–133. University of Twente, Enschede (2010)
3. Backes, P., Reineke, J.: Analysis of infinite-state graph transformation systems by cluster abstraction. In: D'Souza, D., Lal, A., Larsen, K.G. (eds.) VMCAI 2015. LNCS, vol. 8931, pp. 135–152. Springer, Heidelberg (2015)
4. Bauer, J., Schaefer, I., Toben, T., Westphal, B.: Specification and verification of dynamic communication systems. In: ACSD 2006, pp. 189–200 (2006)
5. Bauer, J.: Analysis of Communication Topologies by Partner Abstraction. Ph.D. thesis, Saarland University (2006)
6. Bauer, J., Toben, T., Westphal, B.: Mind the shapes: Abstraction refinement via topology invariants. Technical report 22, SFB/TR 14 AVACS, June 2007
7. König, B., Kozioura, V.: Augur 2–a new version of a tool for the analysis of graph transformation systems. In: Bruni, R., Varró, D. (eds.) GT-VMT 2006, ENTCS, vol. 2011, pp. 201–210 (2008)
8. Rakow, J.: Verification of Dynamic Communication Systems. Diploma thesis, Carl-von-Ossietzky Universität Oldenburg, April 2006
9. Zambon, E.: Abstract graph transformation : theory and practice. Ph.D. thesis, University of Twente (2013)

Refinement Selection

Dirk Beyer, Stefan Löwe, and Philipp Wendler

University of Passau, Passau, Germany

Abstract. Counterexample-guided abstraction refinement (CEGAR) is a property-directed approach for the automatic construction of an abstract model for a given system. The approach learns information from infeasible error paths in order to refine the abstract model. We address the problem of selecting *which* information to learn from a given infeasible error path. In previous work, we presented a method that *enables* refinement selection by extracting a set of sliced prefixes from a given infeasible error path, each of which represents a different reason for infeasibility of the error path and thus, a possible way to refine the abstract model. In this work, we (1) define and investigate several promising heuristics for selecting an appropriate precision for refinement, and (2) propose a new combination of a value analysis and a predicate analysis that does not only find out *which information* to learn from an infeasible error path, but automatically decides *which analysis* should be preferred for a refinement. These contributions allow a more systematic refinement strategy for CEGAR-based analyses. We evaluated the idea on software verification. We provide an implementation of the new concepts in the verification framework CPACHECKER and make it publicly available. In a thorough experimental study, we show that refinement selection often avoids state-space explosion where existing approaches diverge, and that it can be even more powerful if applied on a higher level, where it decides which analysis of a combination should be favored for a refinement.

1 Introduction

Abstraction is a key concept to enable the verification of real-world software (cf. [3,4,14,25]) within reasonable time and resource limits. SLAM [5], for example, uses predicate abstraction [21] for creating an abstract model of the software. The abstract model is often constructed using Counterexample-guided abstraction refinement (CEGAR) [17], which iteratively refines an (initially coarse) abstract model using *infeasible* error paths (property-directed refinement). This technique is integrated in many successful software-verification tools, e.g., SLAM [5], BLAST [7], and CPACHECKER [9]. In the refinement step of the CEGAR framework, Craig interpolation [18,26] is often used to extract the information that needs to be tracked by the analysis [11,22]. Formula interpolation yields for two contradicting formulas an interpolant formula that contains less information than the first formula, but is still expressive enough to contradict the second formula. In verification, we can use information from interpolants over an infeasible error

© Springer International Publishing Switzerland 2015
B. Fischer and J. Geldenhuys (Eds.): SPIN 2015, LNCS 9232, pp. 20–38, 2015.
DOI: 10.1007/978-3-319-23404-5_3

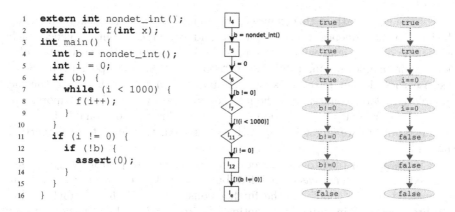

Fig. 1. From left to right, the input program, an infeasible error path, and a "good" and a "bad" interpolant sequence for the infeasible error path

path to refine the abstract model, and iteratively augment the abstraction until it is strong enough so that the specification can be proven.

In order to avoid state-space explosion and divergence during program analysis, we need to keep the precision of the analysis as abstract and concise as possible. Existing approaches that use interpolation to extract precision information from infeasible error paths assign a lot of choice to the interpolation engine, i.e., an infeasible error path might contain several reasons for its infeasibility, some of which might be easier to track than others and thus might be more beneficial for the further progress of the analysis [13]. Our work addresses the choice between different precisions — a concept that we refer to as *refinement selection*.

Figure 1 shows this via an example: For the given program, an analysis based on CEGAR, with an initially empty precision, may find the shown infeasible error path. The infeasibility of this path can be explained independently by the valuations of the variables i and b, as shown by the two example interpolant sequences. In general, and also in this example, it is advisable to track information about boolean variables[1], like the variable b, rather than loop-counter variables, such as variable i, because the latter may have far more different valuations, and tracking loop counters would usually lead to expensive loop unrollings. The given error path of the program can be eliminated from further exploration by tracking the loop-counter variable i, which might force unrolling the loop in further iterations of CEGAR. If we instead choose to track the boolean variable b, then the path can be eliminated and it is guaranteed that the loop is not unrolled. In the next CEGAR iteration, variable i will be added to the precision in order to stop the exploration at line 11. After that, the program is proved correct. In existing work, the decision which variable to track depends solely on the interpolation engine.

---

[1] In the programming language C, a boolean variable is modeled by an integer variable b for which b==0 represents the value *false* and b!=0 represents the value *true* (cf. [2] for a discussion of more fine-grained types for C).

For the error path in this example, we would like the verifier to refine using the interpolant sequence shown on the left, and avoid interpolant sequences such as the one on the right, which references the loop counter. However, interpolation engines cannot distinguish between "good" or "bad" interpolant sequences, because they do not have access to external information such as if a specific variable is a loop counter and should therefore be avoided. Furthermore, the result of an arbitrary interpolation query is not directly controllable from the outside, and thus we might end up with a refinement that leads to divergence of the analysis.

It is possible instead to send several queries to the interpolation engine, each targeted at a different reason of infeasibility, and then choose the result that is expected to be "good" for the further construction of the abstract model. Our previous work introduced the notion of *sliced prefixes* [13] together with an approach to extract a set of such infeasible sliced paths for one given infeasible error path. Each of these infeasible sliced paths can be used for refining the abstract model, and the choice influences the effectivity and the efficiency of the analysis significantly. This work investigates *refinement selection*, yielding the following contributions:

- We present several heuristics for intra-analysis refinement selection, for which we conduct a thorough evaluation that reveals significant effectiveness improvements for both a predicate analysis and a value analysis.
- We define a novel combination of analyses, where inter-analysis refinement selection decides *which* analysis in the combination of analyses is refined.
- We provide an implementation that is publicly available in the open-source software-verification framework CPACHECKER.

Related Work. We categorize the related approaches into approaches that manipulate error paths, interpolation approaches to be implemented inside the interpolation engine, or outside the interpolation engine, approaches based on unsat cores, and combination approaches.

Extraction of Paths. The most related approaches to refinement selection are works that manipulate infeasible error paths. Path slicing [24] is a technique that weakens the path constraints before interpolation by removing facts that are not important for the infeasibility of the error path. This technique produces one infeasible sliced path for one infeasible error path. We need several infeasible sliced paths in order to create a space of choice for refinement selection. Sliced path prefixes [13] is a method that produces a set of infeasible sliced paths, i.e., a set of infeasible sliced prefixes of the original infeasible error path. One of our heuristics (deep pivot location) is similar to counterexample minimization [1].

Interpolant Strength. The strength of interpolants [20] can be controlled by combining proof transformations and labeling functions, so that essentially, from the same proof of infeasibility, different interpolants can be extracted. However, it is not yet clear from the literature how to exactly exploit the strength of interpolants in order to improve the performance of software verification [20,27].

In contrast to our approach, interpolant strength is restricted to predicate analysis, requires changes to the implementation of the underlying interpolation engine, and no available interpolation engine provides this feature.

Exploring Interpolants. Exploring interpolants [27] in interpolant lattices is a technique to systematically extract a set of interpolants for a given interpolation problem, with the goal of finding the most abstract interpolant. Similar to our proposed technique, for a single interpolation problem, the input to the interpolation engine is remodeled to obtain not only a single interpolant for a query, but a set of interpolants. This technique also does not require changes to the underlying interpolation engine, but is restricted to predicate analysis. Yet, this technique could be applied together with refinement selection to generate first the most abstract interpolant for each infeasible sliced path and then select the most appropriate refinement.

Unsatisfiability Cores. Satisfiability modulo theory (SMT) solvers can extract unsatisfiability cores [16] from a proof of unsatisfiability, and there is an analogy between a set of unsatisfiability cores extracted from a formula and a set of infeasible sliced paths [13]. The concept of infeasible sliced paths is more general, because it is applicable also to domains not based on SMT formulas, such as value domains [13]. While SMT solvers typically strive for small unsatisfiability cores [16], this alone does not guarantee a verifier to be effective. It would be interesting to extract several unsatisfiability cores during a single refinement, with the goal of performing refinement *selection*, as proposed in this work.

Combination of Value Analysis and Predicate Analysis. A CEGAR-based combination of a value analysis and a predicate analysis, with refinement of the abstract model in one of the two domains for every found infeasible error path, has been proposed before [11]. However, so far there was no path-based *selection* which domain should be refined: the strategy was to refine first, if possible, the (supposedly cheaper) value analysis, and only refine the predicate analysis if the value analysis could not eliminate the infeasible error path. This analysis may diverge, if the value analysis needs to track a loop-counter variable, for example. The predicate analysis, which might have eliminated the infeasible error path without unrolling the loop, would have not even been considered. With our new approach, we can systematically select the abstract domain that is the most appropriate for refinement, for every single infeasible error path.

2   Preliminaries

Programs, Control-Flow Automata, States. We use basic definitions from previous work [13]. We restrict the presentation to a simple imperative programming language, where all operations are either assignments or assume operations, and all variables range over integers. A program is represented by a control flow automaton (CFA). A CFA $A = (L, l_0, G)$ consists of a set L of program locations, which model the program counter, an initial program location $l_0 \in L$, which models the program entry, and a set $G \subseteq L \times Ops \times L$ of control-flow edges, which model the operations that are executed when control flows from one program location to the next. The set of program variables that occur in operations from Ops is denoted by X. A *verification problem* $P = (A, l_e)$ consists of a CFA A, representing the program, and a target program location $l_e \in L$, which represents the specification, i.e., "the program must not reach location l_e".

A *concrete data state* of a program is a variable assignment $cd : X \to \mathbb{Z}$, which assigns to each program variable a value from the set $\mathbb{Z}$ of integer values. A region ϕ is a formula that represents a set of concrete data states. For a region ϕ and a CFA edge (l, op, l'), we write $\mathsf{SP}_{op}(\phi)$ to denote the strongest postcondition. Each program analysis comes with an own implementation of SP, each with possibly different expressive power. For example, a program analysis that is restricted to the theory of linear arithmetics will provide a strongest postcondition that uses formulas in the theory of linear arithmetic.

Paths, Sliced Paths, Precisions. A *path* σ is a sequence $\langle (op_1, l_1), \ldots, (op_n, l_n) \rangle$ of pairs of an operation and a location. The path σ is called *program path* if for every i with $1 \le i \le n$ there exists a CFA edge $g = (l_{i-1}, op_i, l_i)$ and l_0 is the initial program location, i.e., the path σ represents a syntactic walk through the CFA. The *semantics of a path* $\sigma = \langle (op_1, l_1), \ldots, (op_n, l_n) \rangle$ and an initial region ϕ is defined as the successive application of the strongest postcondition to each operation of the path: $\mathsf{SP}_\sigma(\phi) = \mathsf{SP}_{op_n}(\ldots \mathsf{SP}_{op_1}(\phi) \ldots)$. A path σ is *feasible* if $\mathsf{SP}_\sigma(true)$ is not contradicting. A program path $\sigma = \langle (op_1, l_1), \ldots, (op_n, l_e) \rangle$, which ends in l_e, is called *error path*, and a program is considered *safe* (the specification is satisfied) if there is no feasible error path.

A *sliced path* is a path that results from a path by omitting pairs of operations and locations from the beginning or from the end, and possibly replacing some assume operations by no-op operations. Formally, a path $\phi = \langle (op'_j, l'_j), \ldots, (op'_w, l'_w) \rangle$ is called a *sliced path* of a path $\sigma = \langle (op_1, l_1), \ldots, (op_n, l_n) \rangle$ if $j \ge 1$, $w \le n$, and for all $j \le i \le w$, $\phi.l'_i = \sigma.l_i$ and $(\phi.op'_i = \sigma.op_i$ or $(\phi.op'_i = [true]$ and $\sigma.op_i$ is an assume operation)) holds.

The definition of sliced paths is inspired by path slicing [24] and sliced prefixes [13]. To ensure that any standard interpolation-based refinement procedure can be used, the following proposition is necessary: Let σ be an infeasible path and ϕ be an infeasible sliced path of σ, then all interpolant sequences for ϕ are also interpolant sequences for σ. The proof for this proposition follows directly from the respective proof for infeasible sliced prefixes [13]. This property allows to replace a refinement procedure that uses only the original infeasible path, by a procedure that uses a set of infeasible sliced paths.

Previously, we introduced one possible approach to extract a set of infeasible sliced paths from one infeasible path: generating infeasible sliced prefixes [13]. It was only defined for a value analysis, however, it can be extended to any analysis that provides a representation of sets of concrete data states and an operator SP for computing strongest postconditions. The predicate analysis fulfills these requirements, allowing us to implement Alg. ExtractSlicedPrefixes [13] and Alg. 1 (Refine$^+$) for the predicate analysis. Other approaches for generating infeasible sliced paths from an infeasible path are equally applicable for refinement selection.

Algorithm 1. Refine$^+(\sigma)$, adopted from [13]

Input: an infeasible error path $\sigma = \langle (op_1, l_1), \ldots, (op_n, l_n) \rangle$
Output: a precision $\pi \in L \to 2^{\Pi}$
Variables: a set Σ of infeasible sliced paths of σ,
    a set τ of pairs of an infeasible sliced path and a precision
1:   $\Sigma :=$ ExtractSlicedPaths(σ)
2:   // compute precisions for each infeasible sliced path
3:   **for each** $\phi_j \in \Sigma$ **do**
4:     $\tau := \tau \cup (\phi_j, \text{Refine}(\phi_j))$ // cf. standard Alg. Refine, e. g., from [13]
5:   // select a refinement based on original path, infeasible sliced paths, and resp. precisions
6:   **return** SelectRefinement(σ, τ)

A *precision* is a function $\pi : L \to 2^{\Pi}$, where Π depends on the abstract domain used by the analysis. It assigns to each program location some analysis-dependent information that defines the level of abstraction. For example, if using predicate abstraction, the set Π is a set of predicates over program variables.

Counterexample-Guided Abstraction Refinement. CEGAR [17] is a technique used for automatic, iterative refinement of an abstract model and aims at automatically finding a suitable level of abstraction that is precise enough to prove the specification while being as abstract as possible to enable an efficient analysis. It is based on the following components: a *state-space exploration algorithm*, which computes the abstract model, a *precision*, which determines the current level of abstraction, a *feasibility check*, which decides if an error path is feasible, and a *refinement* procedure to refine the precision of the abstract model.

The *state-space exploration algorithm* computes the abstract state space that is reachable according to the current *precision*, which initially is coarse or even empty. If all program states have been exhaustively checked, and no error was found, then the CEGAR algorithm terminates and reports the verdict TRUE, i.e., the program is correct. Otherwise, i.e., if an error path was found in the abstract state space, this error path is passed to the *feasibility check*, and if the path is feasible, then this error path represents an actual violation of the specification and the CEGAR algorithm terminates with verdict FALSE. If, however, the error path is infeasible, i.e., does not correspond to a concrete program execution, then the precision was too coarse and needs to be refined. The *refinement* procedure takes as input the infeasible error path and returns a new precision that is strong enough that the state-space exploration algorithm will not explore that infeasible error path again in the next CEGAR iterations. The refinement procedure is often based on interpolation [18], which was first applied to the predicate domain [22], and later to the value-analysis domain [11].

Extracting good precisions from the infeasible error paths is key to the CEGAR technique. Experiments have shown that the heuristic for refinement selection influences significantly the quality of the precision, and thus, the effectiveness of the analysis [13]. Here, we are interested in studying such heuristics.

3   Refinement Selection Using Heuristics

CEGAR needs a module Refine that takes as input an infeasible program path and yields as output a precision that is used for refinement of the abstract model. Instead of using an infeasible program path directly for a standard interpolation-based refinement, and being stuck with the arbitrary and potentially "bad" interpolants that the internal heuristics of an interpolation engine produce, we use a new module Refine$^+$. Algorithm 1 can be substituted for the refinement procedure of CEGAR-based analyses. This new module first extracts a set of infeasible sliced paths by calling method ExtractSlicedPaths, which are more abstract than the original program path. (ExtractSlicedPrefixes [13] is one possible implementation of method ExtractSlicedPaths.) Second, Alg. Refine$^+$ calculates the precision for each infeasible sliced path (using a regular refinement procedure) and stores the pairs in set τ. Third, the algorithm selects the precision that is the most promising from τ, i.e., which will hopefully prevent the analysis from diverging. The selection is implemented in a method SelectRefinement and uses details from the precisions, e.g., which variables are referenced in the precision. Each implementation of SelectRefinement, i.e., each heuristic, receives as input the original infeasible path as well as the set of all pairs of infeasible sliced paths and respective precisions. The remainder of this section presents some possible heuristics that can be used to implement SelectRefinement.

Selection by Domain-Type Score of Precision. Our first heuristic inspects the types of variables in the resulting precisions and prefers refinements with simpler or smaller types. In C, the type of a variable is quite coarse and distinguishing variables on a more fine-grained level can be beneficial for verification. For example, the C type int is typically used even for variables with a boolean character. For this purpose, domain types [2] have been proposed, which refine the type system of a programming language and allow to classify program variables according to their actual range or usage in a program. With domain types, one can distinguish between variables that are used as booleans, variables that are used in equality relations only, in arithmetic expressions, or in bit-level operations, and variables that share characteristics of a loop counter [19,28,29].

Loop counters are a class of variables that a program analysis should ideally omit in many cases from the abstract model of a program. Because loop-counter variables occur in assume operations at the loop exit, they often relate to a reason of infeasibility of a given infeasible error path. Thus, those variables are often included in the interpolant sequence that a standard interpolation engine might produce, forcing the program analysis to track them. Therefore, a promising heuristic is to avoid precisions that contain loop counters, and prefer precisions with only variables of "simpler" (e.g., boolean) types. The rationale behind this heuristic is that variables with only a small number of different valuations have less values to grow the state-space, and therefore are to be preferred. If, however, reasoning about the specification demands unrolling a loop, then the termination of the verification process may be delayed by first refining towards other, irrelevant properties of the program.

In order to compute the domain-type score for a precision $\pi : L \mapsto 2^{\Pi}$, we first define a function $\delta : X \mapsto \mathbb{N} \setminus \{0\}$ that assigns to each program variable its domain-type score. The domain type for all program variables can be inferred by an efficient data-flow analysis [2], and we use low score values for variables with small ranges (e.g., boolean variables), and a specifically high value for loop counters. Thus, we define the domain-type score of a precision as the product of the domain-type scores of every variable that is referenced in the precision:

$$\mathsf{DomainTypeScoreOfPrecision}(\pi, \delta) = \prod_{x \text{ referenced in } \pi} \delta(x).$$

This function, as well as the design of function δ, are mere proposals for assessing the quality of a precision. However, we experimented with several different implementations for both functions, and come to the conclusion that the most important requirement to be fulfilled is that precisions with only boolean variables should be associated with a low score, and precisions referencing loop-counter variables should be penalized with a high score.

Selection by Depth of Pivot Location of Precision. The structure of a refinement, i.e., which parts of the path and the state space are affected, can also be used for refinement selection. For example, refining close to the error location may have a different effect than refining close to the program entry. We define the *pivot location* of an infeasible error path σ as the first location in σ where the precision is not empty. If using lazy abstraction [23], this is typically the location from which on the reached state space is pruned and re-explored after the refinement. The depth of this pivot location can be used for comparing possible refinements and selecting one of them. Formally, for a precision π for a path $\sigma = \langle (op_1, l_1), \ldots, (op_n, l_n) \rangle$, the depth of the pivot location is defined as $\mathsf{PivotDepthOfPrecision}(\pi, \sigma) = \min \{i \mid \pi(l_i) \neq \emptyset\}$. (The minimum always exists because there is always at least one location with a non-empty precision.)

Selecting a refinement with a deep pivot location (close to the end of the path) is similar to counterexample minimization [1]. It has the advantage that (if using lazy abstraction) less parts of the state space have to be pruned and re-explored, which can be more efficient. Furthermore, the precision will specify to track preferably information local to the error location and thus avoid unfolding the state space in other parts of the program. However, preferring a deep pivot location may have negative effects if some information close to the program entry is necessary for proving program safety (e.g., initialization of global variables). Refining at the beginning of an error path might also help to rule out a large number of similar error paths with the same precision, which might otherwise be discovered and refined individually.

Selection by Width of Precision. Another heuristic that is based on the structure of a refinement is to use the number of locations in the infeasible error path for which the precision is not empty, which we define as the *width* of a precision. This corresponds to how long on a path the analysis has to track additional information during the state-space exploration, and thus correlates to how long the precision contributes to the state-space unfolding. Similarly to the depth of the pivot location, this heuristic also deals with some form of "locality", but instead of using the locality in relation to the depth, it uses the locality in relation to the width. Formally, for a precision π produced for a path $\sigma = \langle (op_1, l_1), \ldots, (op_n, l_n) \rangle$ the width of the precision is defined as $\mathsf{WidthOfPrecision}(\pi, \sigma) = 1 + \max I - \min I$, where $I = \{i \mid \pi(l_i) \neq \emptyset\}$ is the set of indices along the path with a non-empty precision.

It may seem that narrow precisions are in general preferable, because it means tracking additional information only in a small part of the state space. However, narrow precisions favor loop counters because in many loops the statements for assigning to the loop counter are close to the loop-exit edges. Thus, selecting a narrow precision often leads to loop unrollings.

Selection by Length of Infeasible Sliced Path. Selecting the shortest or longest infeasible sliced path, respectively, are two simple heuristics for refinement selection as well.

Further Heuristics. We presented and motivated several promising heuristics, but other heuristics are possible as well. For example, in the RERS challenge 2014, a heuristic specifically tailored to the characteristics of the event-condition-action systems in that competition, improved the effectiveness of CPACHECKER and allowed it to obtain good results[2]. This shows that using *domain knowledge* in the refinement step of CEGAR is a promising direction, and a specific heuristic for refinement selection is a suitable place to define this.

4   Refinement Selection for Combination of Analyses

A combination of different analyses, such as a value analysis and a predicate analysis, can be beneficial because different facts necessary to prove program correctness can be handled by the analysis that can track a fact most efficiently [8,11]. The refinement step is a natural place for choosing which of the analyses should track new information. Thus we extend the idea of refinement selection from an intra-analysis selection to an inter-analysis selection.

This concept, which can be broken down into four phases, is depicted in Figure 2, which shows an example combination of a value analysis (VA) and a predicate analysis (PA). The first phase is the standard exploration phase of CEGAR. The composite analysis performs the state-space exploration, constructing the abstract model using the initial, empty precision for all component analyses. In the figure, we refer to the precisions as π^{VA} and π^{PA} for the value analysis and the predicate analysis, respectively.

---

[2] Results available at http://www.rers-challenge.org/2014Isola/

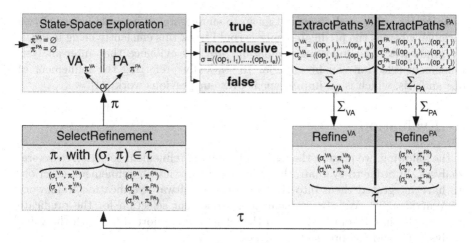

Fig. 2. Refinement selection for combination of analyses, here, consisting of a value analysis and a predicate analysis

If the outcome of the state-space exploration is the verdict TRUE (the model fulfills the specification) or the verdict FALSE (the model contains a concrete error path) then the analysis terminates. If the model contains an infeasible error path σ, then the model is inconclusive and, according to the CEGAR algorithm, a refinement is initiated.

With the refinement step, the second phase begins, which also marks the starting point of our novel approach for inter-analysis refinement selection. There, for all component analyses, we extract infeasible sliced paths stemming from the infeasible error path σ. Each program analysis provides its own strongest-postcondition SP, with each having different expressive power, and therefore, the set of infeasible sliced paths might differ for each analysis. For example, with SP^{VA} we can extract paths that are infeasible due to non-linear arithmetic, while with SP^{PA} we get paths that are infeasible due to contradicting range predicates.

In the third phase, for each infeasible sliced path from the previous phase, a precision (i.e., a possible refinement) is computed by delegating to the default refinement routine Refine of the respective analysis. At the end of the third phase, the set τ contains the available refinements (as pairs of infeasible sliced paths and precisions) for all of the component analyses.

In the fourth phase, *one* suitable precision π (in the example, either π^{VA} or π^{PA}) is selected from the set τ, which is added to the respective precision of the component analysis for state-space exploration, finishing one iteration of CEGAR. A proper strategy for refinement selection can be crucial for the effectiveness of the composite analysis, because there is no analysis superior to all other analysis for any given program, but one analysis may be a good fit for one class of programs, but less suitable for another class, while it can be the other way around for a second analysis. Suppose, for example, an infeasible error path that can only by excluded by tracking that a certain variable is within some interval.

Refining the value analysis would mean to enumerate all possible values of this variable, whereas the predicate analysis could track this efficiently using inequality predicates. The following evaluation provides evidence that inter-analysis refinement selection can be superior to statically preferring the refinement of one analysis, which is an improvement over our previous work [11].

5 Evaluation

In the following, we present the results of applying refinement selection to several analyses. In order to evaluate the presented heuristics for refinement selection, we have integrated them into the open-source software-verification framework CPACHECKER [9][3]. We also implemented refinement selection for the predicate analysis [10] in CPACHECKER , such that it is now supported for both the value analysis [11] and the predicate analysis.

Setup. For benchmarking we used machines with two Intel Xeon E5-2650v2 eight-core CPUs with 2.6 GHz and 135 GB of memory. We limited each verification run to two CPU cores, 15 min of CPU time, and 15 GB of memory. BENCHEXEC [12] was used as benchmarking framework to ensure accurate, reproducible results. We used the tag `cpachecker-1.4.6-spin15` of CPACHECKER and provide the tool, the benchmarks, and the full results on our supplementary web page[4].

Benchmarks. For evaluating the refinement-selection heuristics and our novel combination of analyses, we use a subset of the 5 803 C programs from SV-COMP'15 [6]. We select those tasks that deal with reachability properties, and exclude the categories "Arrays", "HeapManipulation", "Concurrency", and "Recursion", because they are not supported by both analyses we evaluate. Furthermore, we present here only results for those tasks where a refinement *selection* is actually possible, i. e., where at least one refinement with more than one infeasible sliced path is performed. Thus, the set of all verification tasks in our experiments contains 2 828 and 2 638 tasks for the predicate and value analysis, respectively.

Configuration. We use the approach of extracting infeasible sliced prefixes [13] for generating infeasible sliced paths during refinement (method ExtractSlicedPaths in Alg. 1). In order to properly evaluate the effect of the precisions that are chosen by the refinement-selection heuristic, we configure the analysis to interpret the precision globally, i. e., instead of a mapping from program locations to sets of precision elements, the discovered precision elements get used at all program locations. Note that this does not change the precision as seen by the refinement-selection heuristic, but only the precision that is given to the state-space exploration. For the same reason, we also restart the state-space

---

[3] Available under the Apache 2.0 License from http://cpachecker.sosy-lab.org/
[4] http://www.sosy-lab.org/~dbeyer/cpa-ref-sel/

exploration with the refined precision from the initial program location after each refinement. Otherwise, i.e., if we used lazy abstraction and re-explored only the necessary part of the state space, not only the new precision but also the amount of re-explored state space would differ depending on the selected refinement, which would have an undesired influence on the performance.

The predicate analysis is configured to use single-block encoding [10], because for larger blocks there is no single error path per refinement, but instead a sequence of blocks which encode a set of potential error paths. As we do not yet have an efficient technique to extract infeasible sliced paths from a sequence of blocks, using refinement selection is not applicable in an ABE configuration. The predicate analysis uses SMTINTERPOL [15] as SMT solver and interpolation engine.

Refinement-Selection Heuristics. We experiment with implementations of the procedure SelectRefinement in Alg. 1 based on the heuristics from Sect. 3, specifically such that it returns the precision for a (1) short or (2) long infeasible sliced path, the precision with a (3) good or (4) bad domain-type score[5], a precision that is (5) narrow or (6) wide, or a precision with a (7) shallow or (8) deep pivot location. For comparison, we report the results of using random choice as heuristic for refinement selection. We also experiment with combinations of heuristics, where at first a primary heuristic is asked, and if this does not lead to a unique selection, a secondary heuristic is used as a tie breaker to select one of those refinements that were ranked best by the primary heuristic. e heuristics "good domain-type score" and "narrow precision" for these combinations. In all configurations of refinement selection, if necessary, we use the length of the infeasible sliced path as a final tie breaker, and select from equally ranked refinements the one with the shortest infeasible sliced path[6].

In the following, we compare the potential of these selection heuristics against each other, as well as against the case where the choice of refinement is solely left to the interpolation engine, i. e., where no refinement selection is performed and the precision extraction is based on the complete, original infeasible error path.

Refinement Selection for Predicate Analysis. We evaluate the presented heuristics for refinement selection when applied to the predicate analysis. Table 1 shows the number of verification tasks that the predicate analysis could solve without refinement selection, and with refinement selection using the heuristics and combinations of heuristics listed above. The table lists the results for the full set of 2 828 verification tasks (column "All Tasks") that fit the criterion defined above, as well as for several subsets corresponding to those categories of SV-COMP'15 ("ControlFlowInteger", "DeviceDrivers64", "ECA",

---

[5] We do not expect the precision with a bad domain-type score to be actually useful, we report its results merely for comparison.

[6] Experiments showed no relevant difference between selecting the shortest or the longest infeasible sliced path in case of a tie in the primary selection heuristic.

Table 1. Number of solved verification tasks for predicate analysis without and with refinement selection using different heuristics

Tasks / Heuristic		All Tasks 2 828	ControlFlowInt. 35	DD64 679	ECA 1 140	ProductLines 597	Seq. 244
— (No Refinement Selection)		1 142	**34**	473	162	325	43
Length of Sliced Path	Short	1 278	**34**	429	261	**375**	78
	Long	1 325	18	484	322	330	73
Domain-Type Score	Good	1 291	**34**	493	247	339	76
	Bad	1 161	23	404	259	298	79
Width of Precision	Narrow	1 302	28	431	329	347	64
	Wide	1 297	27	480	309	309	76
Depth of Precision	Shallow	1 237	25	466	251	341	57
	Deep	1 260	28	421	313	352	45
Random		1 352	**34**	473	303	350	**86**
Combinations	Good&Narrow	**1 368**	30	**494**	329	338	75
	Narrow&Good	1 354	28	474	**330**	355	65

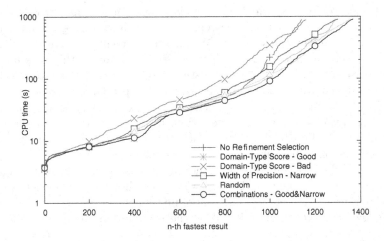

Fig. 3. Quantile plot showing the results for predicate analysis without and with refinement selection using different heuristics

"ProductLines", and "Sequentialized"), where refinement selection has a significant impact. Numbers written in bold digits highlight the best configuration(s) in each column. Figure 3 shows a plot with the quantile functions for the most interesting refinement-selection heuristics on the full set of tasks. In this figure, for each configuration the right end of the graph marks the number of tasks that the configuration could solve, and the area below the graph indicates the sum of the runtime for all solved verification tasks. Thus, in general a graph that is lower and stretches further to the right indicates a better configuration.

Refinement Selection Matters. For the full set of tasks, the analysis without refinement selection performs worse than all other refinement selection heuristics, even worse than the intentionally bad heuristic "bad domain-type score". Figure 3 shows that the analysis without refinement selection scales badly. While it is competitive for easier tasks (below 60 s of CPU time), it solves only a relatively small number of tasks with a runtime between 60 s and 900 s. Additionally, this configuration is not the best for any of the shown subsets, except for "ControlFlowInteger", where it is tied for first with others. This shows that the heuristics of the interpolation engine (with which we are stuck without diligent refinement selection) are not well-suited for verification, and that practically any deviation away from the heuristics of interpolation engine pays off, as witnessed by the relatively good results for the other heuristics.

Discussion. As Table 1 shows, none of the basic heuristics works best for all classes of programs, but instead in each subset a different heuristic is the best. In the following, we would like to highlight and explain a few interesting results for some subsets of tasks and heuristics. Note that the following discussion is based on the investigation of some program samples and our understanding of the characteristics of the programs in the SV-COMP categories, and we do not claim that our explanations are necessarily applicable to all programs.

The programs of the subset "DeviceDrivers64" contain many functions and loops, and aspects about the specification are encoded in global boolean variables that are checked right before the error location. Hence, the heuristic "good domain-type score" is effective because it successfully selects precisions with the "easy" and relevant boolean variables. The heuristics "long sliced path", "wide precision", and "shallow depth" all happen to work well, too, because those relevant variables are initialized at the beginning and read directly before the error location, meaning that corresponding infeasible sliced paths will be long, and resulting precisions containing them will be "shallow" and "wide" (starting to track information close to the program entry, and all the way to the error location). Their opposing heuristics tend to prefer precisions about less relevant local variables.

The subset "ECA" contains artificial programs that represent event-condition-action systems with up to 200 000 lines of code. Most of these programs have only a few variables, and in the majority of programs all variables have the same domain type, and thus the heuristic using the domain-type score cannot perform a meaningful selection here and degenerates to a heuristic about the number of distinct variables in the precision. Note also that relying on the interpolation heuristics of the SMT solver works particularly bad for these programs.

The programs of the subset "ProductLines" encode state machines and contain a high amount of global variables. In case they contain a specification violation, the bug is often rather shallow, although the full state space is quite complex. This explains why the heuristic "short sliced path" works especially well here, because this heuristic leads to exploring the state space as close as possible to the initial program location, driving the verification towards shallow bugs.

Combination of Refinement-Selection Heuristics. The above results show that it is worthwhile to experiment with combinations of heuristics in order to find a configuration that works well for a wide range of programs. We used the two heuristics "good domain-type score" and "narrow precision", which are not only two of the most successful basic heuristics for the predicate analysis, but are also somewhat complimentary (one has a weak spot where the other is strong, and vice versa). Indeed, regardless of the order in which the two heuristics are combined, the combination is more successful than the basic configurations if applied to the category of all tasks. The combination with "good domain-type score" as primary and "narrow precision" as secondary heuristic manages to solve 226 (20 %) more tasks than without refinement selection and is best or close to best in most subsets of tasks.

Refinement Selection for Value Analysis. We now compare the different refinement-selection heuristics if used together with a value analysis. The results are shown in Table 2, which is structured similarly to Table 1, but contains results only for the full set of 2 638 tasks and for the subsets corresponding to the SV-COMP'15 categories "DeviceDrivers64", "ECA", and "ProductLines", because for the remaining categories there is no relevant difference in the results for the value analysis. First it can be seen that the configuration without refinement selection is comparatively good for the value analysis, as opposed to the predicate analysis, where it is the worst configuration. This can be explained by the fact that the interpolation engine for the value analysis is implemented in CPACHECKER itself and is thus designed and tuned specifically for software verification, whereas the predicate analysis uses an off-the-shelf SMT solver as interpolation engine, which is not designed specifically for software verification. However, for specific subsets of tasks, refinement selection is also effective for the value analysis.

Similarly to the predicate analysis, none of the heuristics is the best for all classes of programs. Again, the basic heuristic that works best on the set of all tasks is "good domain-type score", which is especially well-suited for the subset "DeviceDrivers64" for the same reasons explained above. In fact, note that for the basic heuristics and subsets of tasks presented in Tables 1 and 2, the number of tasks solved by the value analysis often correlates closely to the number of tasks solved by the predicate analysis. One notable exception is the subset "ECA", for which the heuristic "good domain-type score" works well for the value analysis, but not for the predicate analysis. The reason for this difference is that the value analysis solves far more instances than the predicate analysis, and for some of the harder "ECA" problems, which the predicate analysis cannot solve, but the value analysis can, there exist variables with different domain-types. Hence, the heuristic "good domain-type score" is more effective.

Finally, the combination of the refinement-selection heuristics "good domain-type score" and "narrow precision" is again the most effective configuration for the set of all tasks, although the increase over the heuristic "good domain-type score" alone is not as large as for the predicate analysis.

Table 2. Number of solved verification tasks for value analysis without and with refinement selection using different heuristics

Tasks / Heuristic		All Tasks 2638	DeviceDrivers64 578	ECA 1140	ProductLines 597
— (No Refinement Selection)		1726	408	**575**	453
Length of Sliced Path	Short	1644	422	488	450
	Long	1627	484	508	361
Domain-Type Score	Good	1760	**494**	572	408
	Bad	1518	410	474	359
Width of Precision	Narrow	1685	422	507	470
	Wide	1605	483	491	355
Depth of Precision	Shallow	1658	471	518	383
	Deep	1725	414	534	**488**
Random		1622	433	527	378
Combinations	Good&Narrow	**1767**	494	569	418
	Narrow&Good	1714	492	507	428

Refinement Selection for Combination of Analyses. We now evaluate the effectiveness of using refinement selection for a combination of analyses. We compare four different analyses: (1) a sole predicate analysis without refinement selection, (2) a combination of a value analysis and a predicate analysis (both without refinement selection), where refinements are always tried first with the value analysis and the predicate analysis is refined only if the value analysis cannot eliminate an infeasible error path, (3) the same combination of a value analysis and a predicate analysis, but now with refinement selection used independently in both domains, and (4) our novel combination that is defined in Sect. 4 of a value analysis and a predicate analysis, where refinement selection is not only used within each domain but also to decide which domain to prefer in a refinement step. For all configurations with refinement selection, we use the combination of the heuristics "good domain-type score" and "narrow precision". We keep the same setup for the experiment as before, but use a new selection criteria, namely, we only consider verification tasks where an inter-analysis refinement selection is actually possible, i.e., where the analysis based on our novel combination needs to perform at least one refinement.

Results. Table 3 shows the results for this comparison. Confirming previous results [11], even a combination of value analysis and predicate analysis without refinement selection (row "VA ∥ PA") is more effective than the predicate analysis alone (row "PA"). However, this combination also has a weak spot, as it fails often in "DeviceDrivers64" due to state-space explosion where the predicate analysis alone succeeds. Row "VA$^+$ ∥ PA$^+$" shows that using refinement selection is effective not only when applied to individual analyses, but also for combinations of analyses. Finally, the fourth configuration (row "(VA$^+$ ∥ PA$^+$)$^+$") takes the idea of refinement selection to the next level. While in the other combinations the value analysis is always refined first, and the

Table 3. Number of solved verification tasks for combinations of analyses without and with refinement selection (PA: predicate analysis; VA: value analysis)

Analysis ⟍ Tasks	All Tasks 3568	DD64 1245	ECA 1139	Loops 120	ProductLines 597	Seq. 261
PA	1826	1027	161	**80**	325	42
VA ∥ PA	2288	992	495	69	**421**	115
VA$^+$ ∥ PA$^+$	2386	**1074**	517	68	404	**126**
(VA$^+$ ∥ PA$^+$)$^+$	**2389**	1068	**519**	79	404	121

predicate analysis only if the value analysis cannot eliminate an infeasible error path, our novel combination uses refinement selection to decide whether a refinement for the value or for the predicate analysis is thought to be more effective. On the full set of tasks, this approach just barely beats the previous approach, but the encouraging results in the subset "Loops" show that it works as intended. In this subset the plain predicate analysis is best (row "PA"), and a *naive* combination is less suited for such programs (rows "VA ∥ PA" and "VA$^+$ ∥ PA$^+$"). If, however, we apply *inter-analysis* refinement selection to decide which analysis to refine for a given error path, as done by our novel approach, then this does not only clearly out-perform the plain predicate analysis on "All Tasks", but it also matches the effectiveness of the predicate analysis for programs where reasoning about loops is essential.

6   Conclusion

We presented *refinement selection*, a method that guides the construction of an abstract model in a direction that is beneficial for the effectivity and efficiency of the verification process. The refinement selection works as follows: We start with a given infeasible error path as it occurs in CEGAR. Then, we extract for this infeasible error path a set of sliced paths, and, instead of computing a refinement precision for the original path only, we compute a refinement precision for each sliced path. Next, we assess all refinement precisions according to some heuristics that implement design choices of what is considered a "good" refinement precision. Finally, we select the most promising precision for the model construction.

This paper defines a variety of heuristics for utilizing the potential of refinement selection and we evaluated the ideas on a large benchmark set and two commonly-used verification methods: predicate analysis and value analysis. The experimental results demonstrate that we can improve the performance and the number of solved tasks significantly by selecting an appropriate refinement without any further changes to the analysis. Furthermore, if using a combination of a value and a predicate analysis, refinement selection can now be used to systematically select the most appropriate domain for refining the abstract model.

Refinement selection opens a fundamentally new view on verification of models with different characteristics: Instead of using portfolio checking, or trying several different abstract domains, we can, in *one* single tool, fully automatically *self-configure* the verifier, according to the property to be verified and the abstract domain that can best analyze the paths that are encountered during the analysis.

Outlook. It would be interesting to investigate heuristics that use *dynamic* information from the analysis. For example, instead of penalizing a loop-counter variable according to its domain type, we could delay the penalty until a certain threshold is reached on the number of values for this variable, similar to dynamic precision adjustment [8]. Especially for the predicate analysis, it is interesting to investigate heuristics that not only look at the domain type, but also how the variables are referenced in the precision (e.g., an equality predicate for a loop counter usually leads to loop unrolling, an inequality might avoid loop unrolling).

References

1. Alberti, F., Bruttomesso, R., Ghilardi, S., Ranise, S., Sharygina, N.: An extension of lazy abstraction with interpolation for programs with arrays. Formal Methods Syst. Des. **45**(1), 63–109 (2014)
2. Apel, S., Beyer, D., Friedberger, K., Raimondi, F., von Rhein, A.: Domain types: abstract-domain selection based on variable usage. In: Bertacco, V., Legay, A. (eds.) HVC 2013. LNCS, vol. 8244, pp. 262–278. Springer, Heidelberg (2013)
3. Ball, T., Cook, B., Levin, V., Rajamani, S.K.: SLAM and static driver verifier: technology transfer of formal methods inside microsoft. In: Boiten, E.A., Derrick, J., Smith, G.P. (eds.) IFM 2004. LNCS, vol. 2999, pp. 1–20. Springer, Heidelberg (2004)
4. Ball, T., Levin, V., Rajamani, S.K.: A decade of software model checking with SLAM. Commun. ACM **54**(7), 68–76 (2011)
5. Ball, T., Rajamani, S.K.: The SLAM project: Debugging system software via static analysis. In: Launchbury, J., Mitchell, J.C. (eds.) POPL 2002. pp. 1–3. ACM, New York (2002)
6. Beyer, D.: Software verification and verifiable witnesses. In: Baier, C., Tinelli, C. (eds.) TACAS 2015. LNCS, vol. 9035, pp. 401–416. Springer, Heidelberg (2015)
7. Beyer, D., Henzinger, T.A., Jhala, R., Majumdar, R.: The software model checker Blast. Int. J. Softw. Tools Technol. Transfer **9**(5–6), 505–525 (2007)
8. Beyer, D., Henzinger, T.A., Théoduloz, G.: Program analysis with dynamic precision adjustment. In: ASE 2008, pp. 29–38. IEEE (2008)
9. Beyer, D., Keremoglu, M.E.: CPACHECKER: a tool for configurable software verification. In: Gopalakrishnan, G., Qadeer, S. (eds.) CAV 2011. LNCS, vol. 6806, pp. 184–190. Springer, Heidelberg (2011)
10. Beyer, D., Keremoglu, M.E., Wendler, P.: Predicate abstraction with adjustable-block encoding. In: FMCAD 2010, pp. 189–197. FMCAD, IEEE (2010)
11. Beyer, D., Löwe, S.: Explicit-state software model checking based on CEGAR and interpolation. In: Cortellessa, V., Varró, D. (eds.) FASE 2013 (ETAPS 2013). LNCS, vol. 7793, pp. 146–162. Springer, Heidelberg (2013)
12. Beyer, D., Löwe, S., Wendler, P.: Benchmarking and resource measurement. In: Fischer, B., Geldenhuys, J. (eds.) SPIN 2015. LNCS, pp. 160–178. Springer, Heidelberg (2015)

13. Beyer, D., Löwe, S., Wendler, P.: Sliced path prefixes: an effective method to enable refinement selection. In: Graf, S., Viswanathan, M. (eds.) FORTE 2015. LNCS, vol. 9039, pp. 228–243. Springer, Heidelberg (2015)
14. Blanchet, B., Cousot, P., Cousot, R., Feret, J., Mauborgne, L., Miné, A., Monniaux, D., Rival, X.: A static analyzer for large safety-critical software. In: Cytron, R., Gupta, R. (eds.) PLDI 2003, pp. 196–207. ACM, New York (2003)
15. Christ, J., Hoenicke, J., Nutz, A.: SMTINTERPOL: an interpolating SMT solver. In: Donaldson, A., Parker, D. (eds.) SPIN 2012. LNCS, vol. 7385, pp. 248–254. Springer, Heidelberg (2012)
16. Cimatti, A., Griggio, A., Sebastiani, R.: A simple and flexible way of computing small unsatisfiable cores in SAT modulo theories. In: Marques-Silva, J., Sakallah, K.A. (eds.) SAT 2007. LNCS, vol. 4501, pp. 334–339. Springer, Heidelberg (2007)
17. Clarke, E.M., Grumberg, O., Jha, S., Lu, Y., Veith, H.: Counterexample-guided abstraction refinement for symbolic model checking. J. ACM **50**(5), 752–794 (2003)
18. Craig, W.: Linear reasoning. A new form of the Herbrand-Gentzen theorem. J. Symb. Log. **22**(3), 250–268 (1957)
19. Demyanova, Y., Veith, H., Zuleger, F.: On the concept of variable roles and its use in software analysis. In: FMCAD 2013, pp. 226–230. IEEE (2013)
20. D'Silva, V., Kroening, D., Purandare, M., Weissenbacher, G.: Interpolant strength. In: Barthe, G., Hermenegildo, M. (eds.) VMCAI 2010. LNCS, vol. 5944, pp. 129–145. Springer, Heidelberg (2010)
21. Graf, S., Saïdi, H.: Construction of abstract state graphs with Pvs. In: Grumberg, O. (ed.) CAV 1997. LNCS, vol. 1254, pp. 72–83. Springer, Heidelberg (1997)
22. Henzinger, T.A., Jhala, R., Majumdar, R., McMillan, K.L.: Abstractions from proofs. In: Jones, N.D., Leroy, X. (eds.) POPL 2004. pp. 232–244. ACM, New York (2004)
23. Henzinger, T.A., Jhala, R., Majumdar, R., Sutre, G.: Lazy abstraction. In: Launchbury, J., Mitchell, J.C. (eds.) POPL 2002. pp. 58–70. ACM, New York (2002)
24. Jhala, R., Majumdar, R.: Path slicing. In: Sarkar, V., Hall, M.W. (eds.) PLDI 2005. pp. 38–47. ACM, New York (2005)
25. Khoroshilov, A., Mutilin, V., Petrenko, A., Zakharov, V.: Establishing linux driver verification process. In: Pnueli, A., Virbitskaite, I., Voronkov, A. (eds.) PSI 2009. LNCS, vol. 5947, pp. 165–176. Springer, Heidelberg (2010)
26. McMillan, K.L.: Interpolation and SAT-based model checking. In: Hunt Jr, W.A., Somenzi, F. (eds.) CAV 2003. LNCS, vol. 2725, pp. 1–13. Springer, Heidelberg (2003)
27. Rümmer, P., Subotic, P.: Exploring interpolants. In: FMCAD 2013. pp. 69–76. IEEE (2013)
28. Sajaniemi, J.: An empirical analysis of roles of variables in novice-level procedural programs. In: HCC 2002. pp. 37–39. IEEE (2002)
29. van Deursen, A., Moonen, L.: Understanding COBOL systems using inferred types. In: IWPC 1999. pp. 74–81. IEEE (1999)

From HELENA Ensemble Specifications to PROMELA Verification Models

Annabelle Klarl[(✉)]

Ludwig-Maximilians-Universität München, Munich, Germany
klarl@pst.ifi.lmu.de

Abstract. With HELENA, we introduced a modeling approach for distributed systems where components dynamically collaborate in ensembles. Conceptually, components participate in a goal-oriented collaboration by adopting certain roles in the ensemble. To verify the goal-directed behavior of ensembles, we propose to systematically translate HELENA specifications to PROMELA and verify them with the model-checker Spin. In this paper, we report on tool support for an automated transition from HELENA to PROMELA. Relying on the XTEXT workbench of Eclipse, we provide a code generator from the domain-specific-language HELENA-TEXT to PROMELA. The generated PROMELA model simulates the two layers, components and their adopted roles from HELENA, and allows dynamic role creation as well as asynchronous communication of roles.

1 Introduction

Ensemble-based systems are distributed systems of components which dynamically collaborate in groups. In HELENA [5], components are thought of as a basic layer providing computing power or storage resources. Collaborations are modeled by *ensembles*, where components adopt (possibly concurrently) different *roles* to actively participate in ensembles. The concept of roles allows to focus on the particular tasks which components fulfill in collaborations and to structure implementation by realizing roles as threads executed on top of components [9].

Ensembles always collaborate for some global goal. Such goals are often temporal properties and are therefore specified in linear temporal logic (LTL) [11]. To allow verification of HELENA models for goals, we already proposed in [6] to translate HELENA to PROMELA and check satisfaction of goals with the model-checker Spin [7]. We proved the correctness of the translation for a simplified variant of HELENA which restricts ensemble specifications to their core concepts.

In this paper, we report on the extension of the translation to full HELENA and its automation based on the XTEXT workbench of Eclipse. With the extended translation, we are able to simulate the two layers of HELENA, components and their adopted roles, in PROMELA. Due to the automation of the translation, we augment HELENA ensemble specifications with immediate verification support

This work has been partially sponsored by the EU project ASCENS, 257414.

© Springer International Publishing Switzerland 2015
B. Fischer and J. Geldenhuys (Eds.): SPIN 2015, LNCS 9232, pp. 39–45, 2015.
DOI: 10.1007/978-3-319-23404-5_4

in Spin. To this end, an Eclipse plug-in is implemented which produces an executable PROMELA specification from a HELENA ensemble specification written in the domain-specific language HELENATEXT [8].

2   HELENA in a Nutshell

We introduce the concepts of the HELENA approach at a peer-2-peer network supporting the distributed storage of files which can be retrieved upon request.

Components: The foundation of HELENA ensembles [5] are *components* characterized by their type, e.g., component type Peer in Fig. 1. Such a type manages associations to other components, e.g., the association neighbor in our example. It stores basic information, that is useful in all roles the component can adopt, in attributes, e.g., the attribute hasFile. Lastly, it provides operations which can be invoked by its roles, e.g., the operation printFile (not shown).

Roles: A *role type rt* is a tuple $(rtnm, rtcomptypes, rtattrs, rtmsgs)$: $rtnm$ is the name of the role type; the set *rtcomptypes* determines the component types which can adopt the role; the set *rtattrs* allows to store data that is only relevant for performing the role; the set *rtmsgs* determines the outgoing and incoming messages supported by the role. In our example, we have three role types which can all be adopted by components of the type Peer (cf. Fig. 1): The peer adopting the role Requester wants to download the file, peers adopting the role Router forward the request through the network, and the peer adopting the role Provider provides the file. Only the role type Requester has an attribute. Outgoing and incoming messages are annotated as arrows for all role types.

Ensemble Structures: To define the structural characteristics of a collaboration, an *ensemble structure* specifies the role types whose instances form the ensemble, determines how many instances of each role type may contribute by a multiplicity, and defines the capacity of the input queue of each role type. We assume that between two role types the messages which are output on one side and input on the other side can be exchanged. For our example, instances of the three aforementioned role types collaborate (cf. Fig. 1). Thereby, an ensemble has to employ exactly one requesting peer, arbitrarily many routers, and possibly one router as determined by the multiplicities associated to each role type.

Ensemble Specifications: The *behavior* of a role is specified by a process expression built from the null process **nil**, action prefix $a.P$, guarded choice **if**$(guard_1)\{P_1\}$ **or**$(guard_2)\{P_2\}$ (branch is nondeterministically selected if several branches are executable), and process invocation [6]. Guards are predicates over component or role attributes. There are actions for creating (**create**) and retrieving (**get**) role instances, sending (!) or receiving (?) messages, and invoking operations of the owning component. These actions must fit to the declared ensemble structure, e.g., messages can be only sent by roles which declare them. Additionally, state labels are used to mark a certain progress of execution in

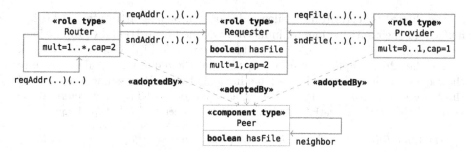

Fig. 1. Ensemble structure for the p2p example in graphical notation

the role behavior. Figure 2 shows the behavior specification of a Router. Initially, a router can receive a request for an address. Depending on whether its owner has the file, it either creates a provider role instance and sends it back to the requester in $P_{provide}$ or forwards the request to another router in P_{fwd} if possible.

> **roleBehavior** $Router$ = $?reqAddr(Requester\ rq)()$.
> > **if** (**owner**.$hasFile$) **then** $\{P_{provide}\}$
> > **or** (!**owner**.$hasFile$) **then** $\{P_{fwd}\}$
> $P_{provide}$ = $p{\leftarrow}$**create**($Provider$, **owner**) . $rq!sndAddr(p)()$. **nil**
> P_{fwd} = **if** (**plays**($Router$, **owner**.$neighbor$)) **then** $\{$**nil**$\}$
> > **or** (!**plays**($Router$, **owner**.$neighbor$)) **then** $\{P_{create}\}$
> P_{create} = $r{\leftarrow}$**create**($Router$, **owner**.$neighbor$) . $r!reqAddr(rq)()$. $Router$

Fig. 2. Role behavior of a Router for the p2p example

A complete collaboration is given by an *ensemble specification* consisting of an ensemble structure Σ and a set of role behaviors, one for each role type in Σ. The complete specification of the example can be found in [10].

Semantics: Ensemble specifications are semantically interpreted by labeled transition systems, i.e., ensemble automata [5,6]. Ensemble states capture the currently existing role instances with their data and control states. Transitions between ensemble states are triggered by role instance creation or retrieval, communication actions, and operation calls. The communication style (synchronous or asynchronous) is determined by the size of the input queues of the role types.

Goal Specifications: Goals are expressed by LTL formulae over particular HELENApropositions: A *state label proposition* is of the form $rt[n]@label$. It is satisfied if there exists a role instance n of type rt whose next performed action is the state label *label*. An *attribute proposition* must be boolean and is built from arithmetic and relational operators, data constants, and propositions of the form $rt[n]{:}attr$ (or $ct[n]{:}attr$). An attribute proposition $rt[n]{:}attr$ is satisfied if there exists a role instance n of type rt such that the value of its attribute *attr* evaluates to **true** (and analogously for component attributes). LTL formulae and their satisfaction are inductively defined from HELENA propositions, propositional operators ¬ and ∧ and LTL operators $\mathbf{X}, \Box, \Diamond, \mathbf{U}$ and $\mathbf{W}$ as usual.

For the p2p example, we want to express that the requester will always receive the requested file if the file is available in the network. We assume a network of three peers and formulate the following achieve goal in LTL which refers to the values of the attribute hasFile of component type Peer and role type Requester:

$$(Peer[1]{:}hasFile \lor Peer[2]{:}hasFile \lor Peer[3]{:}hasFile) \Rightarrow \Diamond Requester[1]{:}hasFile.$$

3   Translation from HELENA to PROMELA

To verify HELENA specifications for their intended goals, we rely on the model-checker Spin [7]. In [6], we discussed that the translation of a simplified variant of HELENA to PROMELA preserves satisfaction of $LTL_{\backslash \mathbf{X}}$, the fragment of LTL that does not contain the *next* operator $\mathbf{X}$. This translation abstracts from the underlying component-based platform and considers only role types and their interactions. In role behaviors, guarded choice and arbitrary process invocations are not allowed and any notion of data is omitted. To cope with these features, we propose to represent components and roles by two kinds of processes in PROMELA. They differ in communication abilities and behavior since components are only storage and computing resources while roles are active entities.

Communication Abilities: (1) Components only interact with roles, but not with other components. Roles advise components to adopt other roles, request references to already adopted roles from their owning components, or invoke operations on them. Thus, each PROMELA process for a component relies on a dedicated synchronous channel **self**, only used for communication between itself and its adopted roles. The roles refer to the channel under the name **owner**. (2) Roles interact by exchanging directed messages on input queues. Thus, each PROMELA process for a role relies on a dedicated (possibly asynchronous) channel **self** in addition to the aforementioned channel **owner** to model its input queue. Since channels are global in PROMELA, but input queues are local in HELENA, special care has to be taken that this channel is only available to processes which are allowed to communicate with the corresponding role in HELENA.

Behavior: (1) The PROMELA process for a component implements a **do**-loop to wait for requests from its roles on the **self** channel. Depending on the request, it runs some internal computation and sends a reply. E.g., to adopt a role, it creates a new channel and spawns a new process (representing the role) to which it hands over its own **self** channel as the role's **owner** channel and the newly created channel as the role's **self** channel. Afterwards, it sends the role's **self** channel to the role requesting the adoption such that the two roles can communicate via this channel. (2) The HELENA role behaviors must be reflected by the corresponding PROMELA process. In [6], we proposed to translate action prefix to sequential composition, nondeterministic choice to the **if**-construct, and recursive behavior invocation to a **goto** to the beginning of the role behavior. Sending and receiving messages was mapped to message exchange on the **self** channel of roles and role creation to process creation with the **run**-command. To extend this to full HELENA, guarded choice is translated to the **if**-construct with the guard as first statement. Arbitrary process invocation is realized by jumping to labels marking the beginning of processes. On the level of actions, we extend message exchange by data relying on user-defined data types in PROMELA. To cope with the component level of HELENA, a new role is created by issuing an appropriate request on the owning component and spawning the new role process from there. The introduction of components also allows us to implement role retrieval and operation calls by corresponding requests from role to component.

$LTL_{\backslash X}$ **Preservation:** Similarly to the simplified translation in [6], all HELENA constructs are directly translated to PROMELA while introducing some additional silent steps like **goto**s. These do not hamper stutter trace equivalence and thus satisfaction of $LTL_{\backslash X}$ is preserved, though not formally shown here.

4   Automation of the Translation

To automate the translation, a code generator, taking a HELENATEXT [8] ensemble specification as input, was implemented on top of the XTEXT workbench of Eclipse relying on XTEND as a template language.

Component Types: For each component type, the excerpt of the XTEND template in Fig. 3 generates a new process type in PROMELA. Most importantly, this process type implements a do-loop (line 4–10) where it can repeatedly receive requests from its adopted roles via its **self** channel. Depending on the type of the received request, i.e., req.optype, it either executes an operation (line 7), adopts a new role (line 9), or retrieves an already existing one (line 10).

```
 1 def static compileProctype(ComponentType ct, Iterable<RoleType> roleTypes) {
 2 ''' proctype «ct.name»(chan self; ...) {
 3     «FOR rt:roleTypes» chan «rt.name» = [«rt.capacity»] of { Msg }; ...
 4     do
 5     ::self?req ->
 6       if
 7     «FOR o:ct.ops» ::req.optype==«o.name» -> // execute operation ...
 8     «FOR rt:roleTypes»
 9       ::req.optype==«rt.create»-> ...run «rt.name»(self,«rt.name»);answer!«rt.name»
10       ::req.optype==«rt.get»   -> ...answer!«rt.name» ...
```

Fig. 3. Excerpt of the XTEND template for the translation of component types

Role Types: For each role type, the XTEND template in Fig. 4 generates a new process type in PROMELA. Two parameters for the **owner** and **self** channels are declared (line 2) and the role behavior is translated (line 3), e.g., action prefix is represented by sequential composition (line 4–6) and guarded choice by an **if**-construct (line 7–14). Furthermore, the generation of the reception of messages and create actions is shown in the right part of Fig. 4 since they represent two different types of communication: An incoming message is represented by a user-defined data type Msg (line 2), to cope with data parameters, and is received on the **self** channel (line 3). The role checks whether the received message was actually expected (line 4) and unpacks its parameters (line 5–7). For a create action, the component crt.comp is asked to adopt a role of type crt.roleInst.type (line 12). The component is responsible for creating the role (cf. Fig. 3) and sends back the **self** channel of the newly created role (line 13). The implementation of the generator and the HELENATEXT specification of the p2p example as well as its generated PROMELA translation can be found in [10].

```
1 def genRoleBehavior(RoleBehavior rb) {          1 def genAction(IncomingMessage m) {
2 ''' proctype «rb.name»(chan owner,self){        2 ''' Msg «m.name»;
3    «rb.genProcTerm» ...                          3    self?«m.name»;
4 def genProcTerm(ActionPrefix term) {            4    «m.name».msgtype == «m.type;
5 ''' «term.action.genAction»;                    5    «FOR p:m.rparams» chan «p.name» = ...;
6    «term.procTerm.genProcTerm» ...              6    «FOR p:m.dparams»
7 def genProcTerm(GuardedChoice term) {            7       «p.type» «p.name» = ...;
8 ''' if                                          8    ...
9 ::(«term.ifGuard.genGuard) ->                   9 def genAction(CreateAction crt) {
10   «term.ifProcTerm.genProcTerm»                 10 ''' chan «crt.roleInst.name»;
11 «FOR i : 0 ..< term.orGuards.size»              11   chan answer = [0] of { chan };
12 ::(«term.orGuards.get(i).genGuard») ->         12   «crt.comp!«crt.roleInst.type»,answer;
13   «term.orProcTerms.get(i).genProcTerm»         13   answer?«crt.roleInst.name»;
```

Fig. 4. Excerpt of the XTEND template for the translation of role types

5   Conclusion

We presented how to verify HELENA specifications for goals specified by LTL formulae with the model-checker Spin. We defined a translation of HELENA specifications and its two-layered architecture into PROMELA which was implemented on top of XTEXT. In first experiments with larger case studies, the application of Spin scales well with the size of the HELENA model since the state space only grows by a constant factor compared to HELENA. For future work, we especially want to add support for relating the Spin output back to HELENA.

Our approach is in-line with the goal-oriented requirements approach KAOS [11]. However, KAOS specifications are translated to the process algebra FSP which cannot represent directed communication and dynamic process creation. Furthermore, techniques for verifying ensemble-based systems have been proposed. In [4], ensembles are described by simplified SCEL programs and translated to PROMELA, but the translation is neither proved correct nor automated and cannot cope with dynamic creation of components. DFINDER [2] implements efficient strategies exploiting compositional verification of invariants to prove safety properties for BIP ensembles, but again does not deal with dynamic creation of components. DEECo ensembles [1] are implemented with the Java framework jDEECo and verified with Java Pathfinder [2]. Thus, they do not need any translation. However, since DEECo relies on knowledge exchange rather than message passing, they do not verify any communication behaviors.

References

1. Bures, T., Gerostathopoulos, I., Hnetynka, P., Keznikl, J., Kit, M.: DEECO: an ensemble-based component system. In: CBSE 2013, pp. 81–90. ACM (2013)
2. Combaz, J., Bensalem, S., Kofron, J.: Correctness of service components and service component ensembles. In: Wirsing, M., Hölzl, M., Koch, N., Mayer, P. (eds.) Software Engineering for Collective Autonomic Systems. LNCS, vol. 8998. Springer, Switzerland (2015)
3. De Nicola, R., et al.: The SCEL language: design, implementation, verification. In: Wirsing, M., Hölzl, M., Koch, N., Mayer, P. (eds.) Collective Autonomic Systems. LNCS, vol. 8998, pp. 3–71. Springer International Publishing, Switzerland (2015)
4. De Nicola, R., Lluch Lafuente, A., Loreti, M., Morichetta, A., Pugliese, R., Senni, V., Tiezzi, F.: Programming and Verifying Component Ensembles. In: Bensalem, S., Lakhneck, Y., Legay, A. (eds.) From Programs to Systems. LNCS, vol. 8415, pp. 69–83. Springer, Heidelberg (2014)
5. Hennicker, R., Klarl, A.: Foundations for Ensemble Modeling – The HELENA Approach. In: Iida, S., Meseguer, J., Ogata, K. (eds.) Specification, Algebra, and Software. LNCS, vol. 8373, pp. 359–381. Springer, Heidelberg (2014)
6. Hennicker, R., Klarl, A., Wirsing, M.: Model-checking helena specifications with spin. In: LRC 2015, LNCS, Springer (2015, to appear). http://goo.gl/a1dya2
7. Holzmann, G.: The Spin Model Checker. Addison-Wesley, Boston (2003)
8. Klarl, A., Cichella, L., Hennicker, R.: From Helena Ensemble Specifications to Executable Code. In: Lanese, I., Madelaine, E. (eds.) FACS 2014. LNCS, vol. 8997, pp. 183–190. Springer, Heidelberg (2015)
9. Klarl, A., Hennicker, R.: Design and implementation of dynamically evolving ensembles with the helena framework. In: ASWEC 2014, pp. 15–24. IEEE (2014)
10. Klarl, A., Hennicker, R.: The Helena Framework (2015). http://goo.gl/a1dya2
11. van Lamsweerde, A.: Requirements Engineering: From System Goals to UML Models to Software Specifications. Wiley, USA (2009)

Büchi Automata and Hashing

Fast, Dynamically-Sized Concurrent Hash Table

J. Barnat[(⊠)], P. Ročkai, V. Štill, and J. Weiser

Faculty of Informatics, Masaryk University, Brno, Czech Republic
{barnat,xrockai,xstill,xweiser1}@fi.muni.cz

Abstract. We present a new design and a C++ implementation of a high-performance, cache-efficient hash table suitable for use in implementation of parallel programs in shared memory. Among the main design criteria were the ability to efficiently use variable-length keys, dynamic table resizing to accommodate data sets of unpredictable size and fully concurrent read-write access.

We show that the design is correct with respect to data races, both through a high-level argument, as well as by using a model checker to prove crucial safety properties of the actual implementation. Finally, we provide a number of benchmarks showing the performance characteristics of the C++ implementation, in comparison with both sequential-access and concurrent-access designs.

1 Introduction

Many practical algorithms make use of hash tables as a fast, compact data structure with expected $\mathcal{O}(1)$ lookup and insertion. Moreover, in many applications, it is desirable that multiple threads can access the data structure at once, ideally without causing execution delays due to synchronisation or locking. One such application of hash tables is parallel model checking, where the hash table is a central structure, and its performance is crucial for a successful, scalable implementation of the model checking algorithm. Moreover, in this context, it is also imperative that the hash table is compact (has low memory overhead), because the model checker is often primarily constrained by available memory: therefore, a more compact hash table can directly translate into the ability to model-check larger problem instances. Another desirable property is an ability to dynamically resize (grow) the hash table, in accordance with changing needs of the model checking algorithm as it explores the state space. Finally, it is often the case that the items (state vectors) stored in the hash table by the model checker have a dynamic size, for which it is difficult to predict an upper bound. Hence, we need to be able to efficiently store variable-length keys in the hash table.

While the outlined use-case from parallel model checking was our original motivation, a data structure with the same or similar properties is useful in many other applications.

This work has been partially supported by the Czech Science Foundation grant No. 15-08772S.

P. Ročkai has been partially supported by Red Hat, Inc.

B. Fischer and J. Geldenhuys (Eds.): SPIN 2015, LNCS 9232, pp. 49–65, 2015.
DOI: 10.1007/978-3-319-23404-5_5

1.1 Related Work

As we demonstrate in Sect. 4, our design is highly competitive, improving on the state of the art in parallel data structures, as represented by the venerable Intel Threading Building Blocks library [1]. The design presented in this paper offers faster sequential access, better multi-threaded scalability and reduced memory overhead. Most of these attributes can be derived from the fact that our design is based on an open hashing scheme, in contrast to almost all existing concurrent hash tables. Often, concurrent hash table designs take advantage of the simplicity of concurrent access to linked lists (e.g. [2], but also the designs in Intel TBB [1]), leading to a closed hashing scheme. Alternatively, a concurrent, open-hashing table based on our earlier (sequential) design has been described in [3], but while providing very good performance and scalability, it was limited to statically pre-allocated hash tables (i.e. with a fixed number of slots). Our design, however, does not explicitly deal with key removal: a standard 'tombstone' approach can be used, although it may also be possible tó leverage the scheme proposed in [4], where authors focus on deletion in a concurrent (but fixed size) hash table with open addressing.

A more closely related design (without an implementation, however) was presented in [5]. In this paper, the authors present a concurrent hash table based on open hashing and arrive at solutions that are in many cases similar to ours. Especially the approach to ensuring that resize operations do not interfere with running inserts is very similar – in this particular case, we believe that the extensive and detailed correctness proofs done in [5] would transfer to our design with only minor adjustments. Our present paper, however, places more emphasis on the implementation and its practical consequences. By comparing notes with existing work on the subject, we can conclude that the design approach is sound in principle; while we did basic correctness analysis on the design, our main concern was correctness of the implementation. Unlike existing work, we make use of software model checking to ascertain that the implementation (and by extension, the design) is indeed correct.

2 Design

There are many considerations that influence the design of a data structure. Our first priorities were performance and scalability of concurrent access; in both cases, it is important to consider the hardware which will execute the code.

First, we need to realize that modern multi-core and SMP systems exhibit a deep memory hierarchy, with many levels of cache. Some of this cache is shared by multiple cores, some is private to a particular core. This translates into a complex memory layout. To further complicate matters, multi-CPU computers nowadays often use a non-uniform access architecture even for the main memory: different parts of RAM have different latency towards different cores. Most of this complexity is implicitly hidden by the architecture, but performance-wise, this abstraction is necessarily leaky.

Moreover, the gap between the first and the last rungs of the hierarchy is huge: this means that compact data structures often vastly outperform asymptotically equivalent, but sparse structures. Due to cache organisation constraints, memory cells that live close to each other are usually fetched and flushed together, as part of a single "cache line". They are also synchronised together between core-private caches. A modern data structure should therefore strive to reduce to an absolute minimum the number of cache lines it needs to access in order to perform a particular operation. On the other hand, when concurrency is involved, there is a strong preference to have threads use non-overlapping sets of cache-line-sized chunks of memory, especially in hot code paths. Cache-line awareness has also been used in design of other data structures; in the context of hash tables, papers [3, 6] discuss this topic in more detail.

2.1 Hash Functions

A hash table is represented as a vector of values in memory, associated with a function that maps *keys* to indices within this vector. The function is known as a *hash function* and should possess a number of specific properties: the distribution of key images should be uniform across the entire length of the vector, a small change in the key should produce a large change in the value, the function should be fast to compute and such a function should be available for an arbitrary index range.

In practice, to implement the last criterion, hash functions for hash tables are usually implemented over the range of all 32 (64, 128 bit) integers in such a way that the remainder of division by an arbitrary integer n (or at least a power of two) will yield a uniform distribution in $\{1, ..., n\}$. The current practice is to use a purpose-built lookup function, either providing 64 (`lookup3` [7] is a good candidate) or even 128 bits of output (the currently best available are spooky hash [8] and the city hash [9]).

2.2 Open vs Closed Hashing

Even with the best lookup function, hash collisions, and more importantly, index collisions will happen in a dynamic hash table. Hence, an important part of the hash table design is dealing with such collisions, and there are two main options: open and closed hashing (also known as open and closed *addressing*). With a closed hashing scheme, each position in the hash table is a "bucket" – capable of holding multiple values at the same time. This is implemented using an auxiliary data structure, usually a linked list. While closed hashing is easier to implement and to predict, it usually gives poor performance. An alternative is to make each position in the table only hold at most one value at a time, using alternate positions for items that cause a collision. Instead of using a single fixed position for each value, the hash table has a list of candidate indices. The most common such series are $h + ai + b$ where i is the sequence number of the index, h is the index assigned by a lookup function and a, b are arbitrary constants (a linear probing scheme). Another common choice is $h + ai^2 + bi + c$, obviously known as quadratic probing. An important property of a probing scheme is that it does not (significantly) disrupt the uniform distribution of values across indices. In case of a quadratic function and a hash table with a size that is a power of 2, a simple set of constraints can be shown to give a good distribution [10].

2.3 Cache Performance

There are many considerations when choosing a good hash table implementation for a particular application. In model checking, as well as many other use cases, the hash table often becomes very big, and as such, it usually cannot fit in the CPU cache entirely. For that reason, it is very important that all hash table operations have as much spatial and temporal locality as possible, to make best possible use of the CPU cache. The very nature of a hash table means that insert or lookup operations on different keys will access entirely different memory regions: this is unavoidable. However, with a naive implementation, even a single lookup or insert can cause many cache misses: a closed-hashing scheme, for example, will need to traverse a linked list during collision resolution, which is a notoriously cache-inefficient operation. Even if we would use a different auxiliary data structure, we would still face at least one level of indirection (pointer dereference), causing an extra cache miss. With open hashing and a linear probing function, we can expect a high degree of spatial locality in the collision resolution process: all candidate positions can be fetched in a burst read from a continuous block of memory. In fact, this is a cache-optimal solution, as it only incurs the one unavoidable initial cache miss per lookup.

However, linear probing has other problems: the property that makes it cache efficient also means that it has a strong tendency to create uneven key distribution across the hash table. The clumping of values makes the collision chains long, and even though it is cache-efficient, the linear complexity of walking the chain will dominate after reaching a certain chain length. In contrast, a quadratic scheme will scatter the collision chain across the table (consequently, the collision chains will be shorter but cause more cache misses during traversal than with a linear scheme). Hence, as a compromise, a hybrid probing function can be used: a quadratic function with a linear tail after each "jump": $h + q(\lfloor i/b \rfloor) + i \bmod b$ where q is a quadratic function and b is a small multiple of cache line size. This has the advantage of scattering keys across the table, but in small clumps that load together into cache, without seriously compromising uniformity.

2.4 Variable-Length Keys

If there is substantial variation in key size, it is inefficient to store the entire key inline in the hash table, and impossible if no upper bound on key size is known. This means that we need to store pointers in the table and the key data becomes out-of-line. Unfortunately, this has disastrous effects on cache performance: each key comparison now requires an extra memory fetch, since in order to find a key in the table, we need to compare it to each element in the collision chain.

To negate this effect, we can store the actual hash value of each key inline in the table: this way, we can first compare the hash values, without incurring a memory fetch. In the vast majority of cases, a 64-bit hash will only test as equal if the actual keys are equal – we will only pay the price of an extra memory fetch in the cases where the keys are actually equal, which is at most once per lookup, and in only a tiny fraction of cases where the keys are distinct. The main reason this optimisation works is that most collisions in the hash table are not due to identical hash values for distinct keys (as stated, those are very rare), but due to different hashes leading to the same index in the hash table, which is much smaller than 2^{64} elements.

Even though efficient, this approach doubles the memory overhead of the hash table, storing a pointer and an equal-sized hash value for each key. This is especially problematic on 64-bit machines, making the overhead 16 bytes per slot when using a 64-bit hash value. Moreover, a 64-bit hash value is needlessly big, a much smaller, 32 or even 16 bit value would provide nearly the same value in terms of avoided cache misses, as long as the part of the hash saved in the cell is distinct from the part used for computation of a cell index. On most platforms, though, this will require arranging the hash table in terms of cache lines, as 96 or 80 bit slots will cause serious mis-alignment issues. With the knowledge of a cache-line size, we can organise the hash table into "super-slots" where each super-slot fits in a cache line, and packs the pointers first and the corresponding hash values next, in the tail.

On 64-bit machines, though, there is another option, which avoids most of the layout complexity at the table level. Contemporary CPUs only actually use 48 bits out of the 64 bit pointer for addressing, the rest is unused. While it is strongly discouraged to use these 16 extra bits for storing data (and CPU vendors implement schemes to make it hard), this discouragement is more relevant at the OS level. At the expense of forward portability of the hash table implementation, we could use these 16 bits to store the hash value, reconstructing the original pointer before dereferencing it. Finally, it is also possible to use an efficient pointer indirection scheme, which explicitly uses 48-bit addressing in a portable, forward-compatible fashion [11].

2.5 Capacity and Rehashing

As we have already said, a hash table is normally implemented as a vector, whether it contains single-value slots or multi-value buckets. As such, this vector has a certain size, and as keys are added into the table, it becomes increasingly full. The ratio of slots taken to slots available is known as a load factor, and most hash table implementations perform reasonably well until load of approximately 0.75 is reached (although factors as high as 0.9 can be efficient [12]). At a certain point, though, each hash table will suffer from overlong collision chains. This problem is more pronounced with open hashing schemes: in the extreme, if there is only one free slot left, an open hashing scheme may need to iterate through the entire vector before finding it. There are three options on how to avoid this problem: the most efficient one is to approximately know the number of keys that we'll store beforehand. However, this is often impossible, so some implementations (especially in case of model checkers) resolve to allocating all available memory for the hash table. However, this does not work for the case of dynamically sized keys stored outside of the table proper, or more generally, whenever there is no good way to split memory allocation between the hash table and other components. Furthermore, such static resource allocation can be rather inappropriate on machines used by multiple users in a non-exclusive manner.

Therefore, in most cases, we need to be able to resize the table. This is usually done in the manner of a traditional dynamic array, only the values are not copied but rehashed into the newly allocated vector, which is usually twice the size of the current one.

Rehashing the entire table is at best a linear operation, but amortises over insertions down to a constant per insert. In real-time applications, gradual rehashing schemes are used to avoid the latency of full rehashing. However, in most application, latency is of no concern and monolithic rehashing is in fact more efficient. As a small bonus, rehashing the table will break up existing collision chains and give the table an optimal uniform layout.

2.6   Concurrent Access

As we have discussed, open hashing is more cache efficient, and compared to a simple closed hashing scheme is also more space efficient. However, closed hashing has an important advantage: linked lists are a data structure easily adapted for lock-free concurrent access. Hence, most concurrent hash table implementations are based on closed hashing. The situation with open hashing is considerably more complex. It is relatively straightforward to implement a fixed-size hash table (i.e. for the scenario where we know the size of the working set in advance). Since this is not the case in DIVINE [13], we have implemented a (nearly) lock-free, resizable open-hashed table, to retain the advantages of open hashing, while at the same time gaining the ability to share the closed set of the graph exploration algorithm among multiple threads.

Let us first discuss how a fixed-size open-hashed table can accommodate concurrent access. The primary data race in a non-concurrent table is between multiple inserts: it could happen that two insert operations pick the same free slot to use, and both could write their key into that slot – this way, the insert that wrote later went OK; however, the first insert apparently succeeds but the key is actually lost. To prevent this, write operations on each slot need to be serialised. The simple way to achieve this is with a lock: a spinlock over a single bit is simple and efficient on modern hardware, and since each hash table slot has its own lock, contention will be minimal. Using a lock is necessary in cases where the key cannot be written atomically, i.e. it is too long. If the key fits within a single atomic machine word, a locking bit is not required, and an atomic compare-and-swap can be used to implement writing a slot. When a lock is used, the lock is acquired first, then the value to be inserted and the locked slot are compared and possibly written. When using a compare-and-swap, in case it fails, we need to compare the keys – concurrent inserts of the same key could have occurred, and the same key must not be inserted at two different indices.

Concurrent lookups are by definition safe, however we need to investigate lookups concurrent with an insert: it is permissible that a lookup of an item that is being inserted at the same time fails, since there is no happens-before relationship between the two (this is in fact the definition of concurrency). It can be easily seen that an insert of a different key cannot disrupt a lookup of a key that is already present: all inserts happen at the end of a collision chain, never in the middle where they could affect a concurrent lookup.

In cases where variable-length keys are used based on the scheme suggested in Sect. 2.4, lock-free access is only possible for variants where the pointer and the hash (if present) are located next to each other in memory, i.e. a hash-free (pointers only) table, or the 64 bit + 64 bit variant (only on machines with atomic 128-bit compare-and-swap), or the variant with the pointer and the hash combined into a single 64 bit value.

2.7   Concurrency vs Resizing

The scheme outlined in the last section does not take the need for resizing and subsequent rehashing into account. The first problem of a concurrent resize operation is that we cannot suspend running inserts, as this would require a global lock. However, insert as a whole is not, and cannot be made, an atomic operation: only the individual probes are atomic. As a consequence, if we were to re-allocate the table at a different address and de-allocate the existing one, a concurrent insert could be still using the already freed memory. Since we cannot interrupt or cancel an insert running in a different thread, nor can we predict when will it finish, the best course of action is to defer the de-allocation. Unfortunately, even if we avoid writing into invalid memory, the same set of circumstances can cause an insert to be lost, since at the point it is written, the copying (rehashing) of the table might have progressed beyond its slot (and since the probing order is not, and cannot be made, monotonic, this cannot be prevented).

In order to clean up unused memory as soon as possible, and to solve the "lost insert" problem, we can, after each insert, verify that the currently active table is the same as the table that was active when the insert started. When they are the same, no extra work needs to be done, and the insert is successful: this case is the same as with a fixed-size table. If, however, the active table has changed, the insert has to be restarted with the new table. Additionally, we can use the opportunity to also clean up the old table if it is no longer used – if there are no further threads using the table. To reliably detect this condition, we need to associate an atomic reference counter with each table generation. The counter reflects the number of threads which consider a given generation to be the latest, and is only incremented and decremented at most once per thread.

Finally, if an insert has been restarted and succeeds, but the reference count on the old table pointer is not yet zero, the thread doing the insert can optionally help rehashing the table. This way, the resize operation can be executed safely in parallel, greatly reducing the time required: since an individual insert is already thread-safe, it is sufficient to slice the old table into sections and let each thread rehash keys from a non-overlapping subset of slices. The assignment of slices to threads can be implemented using a standard concurrent work queue.

3   Implementation

We have implemented the design laid out in the previous section[1], in order to evaluate and verify it, and also for use in the DIVINE model checker. We provide pseudocode for the most important parts of the implementation (see Algorithm 1), but for full details we refer the reader to the C++ implementation, which is unfortunately too extensive to be included here. The basic design of a sequential open-hashing hash table is very straightforward, including rehashing: the table is entirely stored in a sequential area of memory, consisting of fixed-size cells. For long or variable-length keys, the cells contain a pointer to the data itself; small fixed-size keys can be stored directly. Rehashing is realised by allocating a new, empty hash table of a larger size (usually a small multiple of the current size) and invoking the 'insert' procedure for each element present in the current table. When all elements have been rehashed this way, the old table can be de-allocated.

Our implementation follows the same scheme, but with a few provisions to deal with data races arising in concurrent use. These have been outlined in Sects. 2.6 and 2.7 – the implementation follows the design closely. We use either locked cells with 64 bits of hash, or atomic 64 bit cells which store a 48 bit pointer and 16 bits of a hash (a different part of a 128 bit hash value than used for index calculation is used in this case). Alternative cell designs can be provided using C++ templates. When resizing takes place, any thread which attempts to an insertion or a lookup will help with rehashing; chunks of the hash table to be rehashed are assigned dynamically to participating threads. To track the load of the hash table, we use a thread-local counter which is synchronized with a shared atomic counter every 1024 insertions.

To better illustrate the principles behind those provisions, we provide a schematic of the table layout in memory (Fig. 1), as well as an example course of a concurrent *insert* operation in Figs. 2 and 3 and a scheme of the concurrent resize algorithm in Figs. 4, 5 and 6.

3.1   Verification

In order to ensure that the hash table works as expected, we have used DIVINE to check some of its basic properties. The properties are expressed as small C++ programs – basically what a programmer would normally call a unit test. They are usually parametric, with the parameters governing the size and parameters of the data structure as well as the way it is used.

---

[1] The C++ source code for the hash table implementation can be found online: https://divine.fi.muni.cz/trac/browser/bricks/brick-hashset.h#L481.

```
 1  Function ReleaseMemory(index) is
 2  │   if refCount[ index ] - 1 = 0 then
 3  │   │   deallocate row at index;
 4  Function Rehash() is
 5  │   while segment is available do
 6  │   │   for cell ∈ segment do
 7  │   │   │   lock the cell;
 8  │   │   │   if cell is not empty then
 9  │   │   │   │   mark cell as invalid;
10  │   │   │   │   insert cell to the new row;
11  │   │   if was it the last segment then
12  │   │   │   ReleaseMemory(currentRow - 1);
13  │   │   │   unlock the growing lock;
14  Function Grow(newIndex) is
15  │   lock the growing lock;
16  │   if current row has changed then
17  │   │   unlock;
18  │   │   return false;
19  │   row[ newIndex ] ← array[ NextSize(oldSize) ];
20  │   refCount[ newIndex ] ← 1;
21  │   allow rehashing;
22  │   Rehash();
23  │   return true;
24  Function InsertCell(value, hash, index) is
25  │   for attempt ← 0 ... maxAttempts do
26  │   │   cell ← row[ index ][ Index(hash, attempt) ];
27  │   │   if cell is empty then
28  │   │   │   if store value and hash into cell then
29  │   │   │   │   return (Success, cell);
30  │   │   │   if index ≠ currentRow then
31  │   │   │   │   return (Growing)
32  │   │   if cell is (value, hash) then
33  │   │   │   return (Found, cell);
34  │   │   if index ≠ currentRow then
35  │   │   │   return (Growing)
36  │   return (NoSpace)
37  Function Insert(value, hash, index) is
38  │   while true do
39  │   │   res ← InsertCell(value, hash, index);
40  │   │   switch res.first do
41  │   │   │   case Success
42  │   │   │   │   return (res.second, true);
43  │   │   │   case Found
44  │   │   │   │   return (res.second, false);
45  │   │   │   case NoSpace
46  │   │   │   │   if Grow(index + 1) then
47  │   │   │   │   │   index ← index + 1;
48  │   │   │   │   │   break ;
49  │   │   │   case Growing
50  │   │   │   │   Rehash();
51  │   │   │   │   UpdateIndex();
```

Algorithm 1. Pseudocode for key procedures.

Clearly, the parameter space for various properties is infinite, and admittedly, even for fairly small values the verification problem becomes very large. Nevertheless, most bugs happen in boundary conditions, and these are identical for all parameter instantiations upwards of some structure-specific minimum.

The second limitation is that we can only currently verify the code under the assumption of sequential consistency. At first sight, this may seem like a severe limitation – on a closer look, though, it turns out that the vast majority

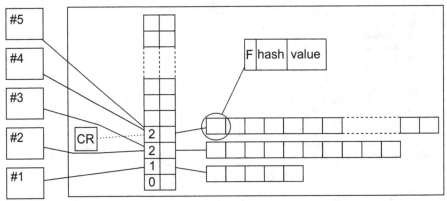

The hash table consists of two parts – global (shared) data and thread-local data. The global data are shown inside the big rectangle. All rows of the table are accessible through a row index, which is shown in the left part of the global data rectangle. There are two columns for each row – one holds a reference counter while the other stores a pointer to the row itself. The pointer CR (current row) points to a globally valid row of the hash table (this reference is not included in the reference count). Every row consists of cells, where every cell has three fields: flag, hash, and value. The flag may have four possible values: empty (e), writing (w), valid (v), and invalid (i).

The thread-local data are represented by small rectangles labeled #1 – #5, each belonging to one thread. Every thread needs to remember which row it is currently using.

Fig. 1. Overall layout of the hash table.

1. Both threads #1 and #2 are accessing the second cell; thread #3 is accessing fourth cell:

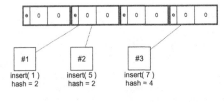

2. Thread #1 has atomically modified the flag of the cell from 'empty' to 'writing' and stored a hash of the value so that thread #2 cannot modify the content of the cell and is forced to wait until the pending writing operation finishes:

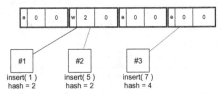

Fig. 2. Insertion algorithm, part 1.

of relevant memory accesses is already tagged as sequentially consistent using appropriate std::atomic interfaces (this translates to appropriate architecture-specific memory access instructions that guarantee sequential consistency on the value itself, as well as working as a memory fence for other nearby memory accesses). In this light, the limitation is not quite fatal, although of course it would be preferable to obtain verification results under a relaxed memory model.

3. Thread #1 stored the value, thread #2 is still waiting. Thread #3 has atomically modified the flag of the cell to 'writing':

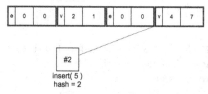

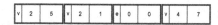

insert(1)   insert(5)   insert(7)
hash = 2   hash = 2   hash = 4

4. Thread #1 has changed the flag of the cell to 'valid' and finished the insert operation. Thread #2 found that the values are different and by using quadratic lookup, it turned to the fourth cell. Meanwhile, thread #3 has stored the value:

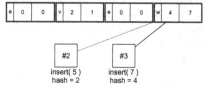

#2   #3
insert(5)   insert(7)
hash = 2   hash = 4

5. Thread #3 has finished the insert operation. Thread #2 is comparing hashes:

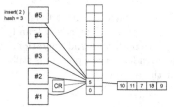

#2
insert(5)
hash = 2

6. Thread #2 found an empty cell, changed the flag and stored the hash:

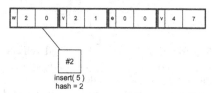

#2
insert(5)
hash = 2

7. Thread #2 has finished the insert operation:

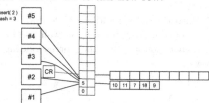

Fig. 3. Insertion algorithm, part 2.

1. The initial situation: all five threads are pointing to the second row which is also the current row. Thread #5 starts an insert operation:

2. As the current row is full, thread #5 signalized that the table needs to be grown, allocated a new row, and changed the value of CR to this new row:

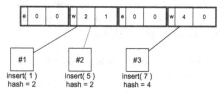

Fig. 4. Resizing the hash table, part 1.

For verification of the concurrent hashset implementation, we have opted for a property parametrised with three numbers, T – the number of threads accessing the shared data structure, N – the number of items each of those threads inserts into the data structure, and O – the number of overlapping items.

3. Thread #5 has split the original row into segments and started rehashing the first available segment. Thread #3 was about to start an insert operation, but as the table is growing, it is impossible to insert new items; thread #3 hence started rehashing the next available segment:

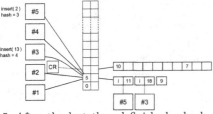

5. After the last thread finished rehashing, thread #5 unlocked the table and updated its current row index. From this moment on, the table is ready for insert and find operations (please note the reference counts for table rows: only one thread is now using the current row, so the previous row cannot be deallocated yet):

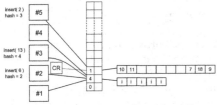

7. Both thread #2 and #3 have updated their current row indices, as well as the reference counters of the corresponding rows:

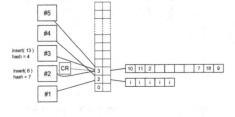

4. Thread #2 was about to start an insert operation, but it also started rehashing the next (and last, in this case) available segment. Meanwhile, thread #3 has finished rehashing and is waiting for the table to be unlocked:

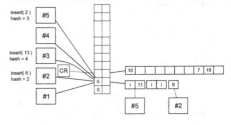

6. Thread #5 has finished its insert operation. The detail of the cell shows how an invalid state is encoded:

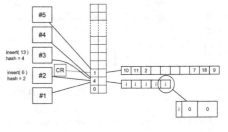

8. Both thread #2 and #3 have finished their insert operations. Threads #1 and #4 are about to perform a find operation, while their thread-local row pointer is still pointing at the old row:

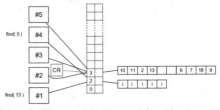

Fig. 5. Resizing the hash table, part 2.

9. Thread #4 has updated its current row index and decided that the value 5 is not present in the table:

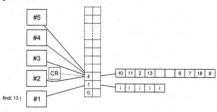

10. Finally, thread #1 has updated its current row index and deallocated the old row. It also found the value 13 present in the table:

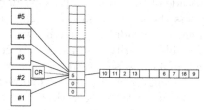

Fig. 6. Resizing the hash table, part 3.

We verified our C++ implementation directly, the only differences from the version of the hash table as used in DIVINE[2] is that when resizing new table size is 2 times old table size, whereas in DIVINE hash table would grow faster for small sizes and that initial table size is 2 slots to make table sufficiently compact for verification and allow verification of a case with 2 resizes.

The C++ program we used in our verification[3] is relatively straightforward; first, we would allocate hash table and spawn $T - 1$ worker threads, each set up to insert a specific range of items (possibly overlapping with the ranges of other threads). The last worker is then executed in the main thread to avoid unnecessary thread interleaving. After it finishes, the remaining worker threads are joined and the final state of the hash table is checked: we iterate over the underlying array and check if all the inserted values are present exactly once.

Given the C++ program described above, we used DIVINE for its verification. While DIVINE cannot directly read C++ programs, it can read and verify LLVM bitcode and uses a standard C++ compiler (`clang`) for translating C++ into LLVM. Besides the checks (assertions) in the driver program itself, the hash table implementation contains a few assertions of its own, which were checked as well.

In this particular scenario, we can observe the huge impact of the exponential state space increase. For $T = 3, N = 1$, verification of the above test-case took multiple days using 32 cores, generated over 716 million states and used about 80GiB of RAM. On the other hand, verification for $T = 2, N = 1$ finishes in less than 3 min and generates fewer than 100 000 states. Verification for $T = 2, N = 3$

---

[2] Doubts could arise when using a model checker which uses the hash table to be verified internally. An analysis of failure modes of the hash table along with the properties of the model checking algorithm indicate that this could not cause the model checker to miss a valid counterexample. Nonetheless, the entire issue is easy to side-step by using a much simpler sequential hash table and just waiting longer for the result.

[3] The code can be found online at https://divine.fi.muni.cz/trac/browser/examples/llvm/hashset.cpp.

finishes in 8 h on 32 cores and uses 14GiB of RAM, while generates roughly 120 million states.

This means that out of the desirable properties, we were able to verify that a cascade of two growths (possibly interleaved) is well-behaved when two threads access the table – using $T = 2, N = 3$ – in this scenario, a single thread can trigger a cascade of 2 growths, while other threads are inserting items. We were also able to verify that a single growth is correct (it does not lose items) in presence of 3 threads (test-case $T = 3, N = 1$), and that insertion of overlapping sets of elements from 2 threads is correct (does not lose items or cause duplicated elements – a test-case with $T = 2, N = 1, O = 1$. A scenario with 2 cascaded growths and 3 threads, however, seems to be out of our reach at this time. Nevertheless, the verification effort has given us precious insight into the behaviour of our concurrent hash table implementation.

While the hash table described in this paper was in a design and prototyping phase, we have encountered a race condition in the (prototype) implementation. The fact that there is a race condition was discovered via testing, since it happened relatively often. The problem was finding the root cause, since the observable effect of the race condition happened later, and traditional debugging tools do not offer adequate tools to re-trace the execution back in time.[4] In the end, we used DIVINE to obtain a counterexample trace, in which we were able to identify the erroneous code.

4   Benchmarks

Earlier, we have laid out the guiding principles in implementing scalable data structures for concurrent use. However, such considerations alone cannot guarantee good performance, or scalability. We need to be able to compare design variants, as well as implementation trade-offs and their impact on performance. To this end, we need a reliable way to measure performance.

The main problem with computer benchmarks is *noise*: while modern CPUs possess high-precision timers which have no impact on runtime, modern operating systems are, without exceptions, multitasking. This multitasking is a major source of measurement error. While in theory, it would be possible to create an environment with negligible noise – either by constructing a special-purpose operating system, or substantially constraining the running environment, this would be a huge investment. Moreover, we can, at best, hope to reduce the errors in our measurement, but we can hardly eliminate them entirely.

One way to counteract these problems is to choose a robust estimator, such as median, instead of the more common mean. However, since we only possess finite resources, we can only obtain limited samples – and even a robust estimator is bound to fluctuate unless the sample is very large. Ideally, we would be able to understand how good our estimate is. If our data was normally distributed

---

[4] An extension to gdb to record execution exists, but we were unable to use it successfully. Either the window in which time reversal was possible was too narrow, or the memory and time requirements too high.

(which we know is, sadly, not the case) we could simply compute the standard deviation and base a confidence interval for our estimator on that. However, since we need a computer for running the benchmarks anyway, we can turn to bootstrapping: a distribution-independent, albeit numerically intensive method for computing confidence intervals.

While bootstrapping gives us a good method to compute reliable confidence intervals on population estimators, it does not help to make those confidence intervals tighter. Given a sample with high variance, there are basically two ways to obtain a tighter confidence interval: measure more data points, or eliminate obvious outliers. While a bigger sample is always better, we are constrained by resources: each data point comes at a cost. As such, we need to strike a balance. In the measurements for this paper, we have removed outliers that fell more than 3 times the interquartile range (the distance from the 25th to the 75th percentile) of the sample from the mean, but only if the sample size was at least 50 measurements, and only if the confidence interval was otherwise more than 5 % of the mean.

To assess performance of the final design with concurrent resizing, we have created a number of synthetic benchmarks. As the baseline for benchmarking, we used implementation of `std::unordered_set` provided by `libc++` (labelled "std" in results). Additionally, we have implemented a sequential open-hashed table based on the same principles as the final design, but with no concurrency provisions (tables "scs" and "sfs") – this allowed us to measure the sequential overhead of safeguarding concurrent access.

Since `std::unordered_set` is only suitable for sequential access, as a baseline for measuring scalability, we have used a standard closed-hashing table (labelled as "cus", from `concurrent_unsorted_set`) and a similar design primarily intended for storing key-value pairs, `concurrent_hash_map` (labelled "chm"), both implementations provided in Intel Threading Building Blocks [1]. The final designs presented here are labelled "ccs" and "cfs". The middle letter indicates the size of the hash table cell c for "compact" and f for "fast": the "fast" variant uses a hash cell twice as wide as a pointer, storing a full-sized (64b) hash inside the cell. The "compact" variant uses a truncated hash that fits in the spare bits inside a 64-bit pointer. (The hash inside cells is only useful in hash tables with out-of-line keys; for integer-keyed tables, they are simply overhead).

As the common performance measure, we have chosen average time for a single operation (an insert or a lookup). For benchmarking lookup at any given load factor, we have used a constant table with no intervening inserts. Four types of lookup benchmarks were done: miss (the key was never present in the table), hit (the key was always present) and a mixture of both ($\frac{1}{2}$ hit chance, and $\frac{1}{4}$ hit chance). For insertions, we have varied the amount of duplicate keys: none, 25 %, 50 % and 75 %.

All of the insertion benchmarks have been done in a variant with a pre-sized table and with a small initial table that grew automatically as needed. Finally, all of the benchmarks outlined so far have been repeated with multiple threads

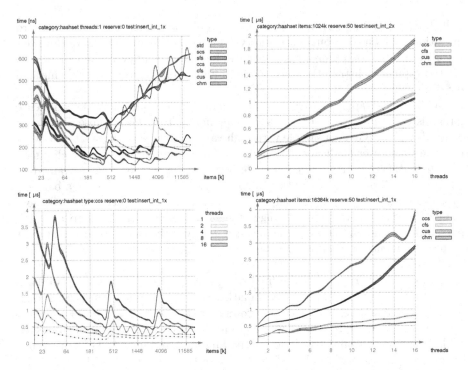

Fig. 7. Performance measurements with integer-sized keys. From top left, clockwise: (1) comparison of sequential performance of various hashtable designs (2) insertion with 50 % key duplicity rate, with 1 million items and a pre-sized hashtable with half a million cells (3) insertion with no key repeats, 16M items (4) behaviour of the final design (ccs) as a function of hash table size and a number of threads (no reserve, the hashtable is resized dynamically). The implementations are labelled as follows: std = `std::unordered_set`, scs = sequential compact set, sfs = sequential fast set, ccs = concurrent compact set, cfs = concurrent fast set, cus = `tbb::concurrent_unordered_set` and chm = `tbb::concurrent_hash_map`. Please consult the electronic version of this paper or http://divine.fi.muni.cz/benchmarks for easier-to-read plots.

performing the benchmark using a single shared table, splitting workload equivalent to the sequential benchmarks, distributed uniformly across all threads. All the benchmarks have been done on multiple different computers, with a different number of CPU cores and different CPU models, although we only report results for a single computer – a 12-core (2 sockets with 6 cores each) Intel Xeon machine.[5] We have chosen 4 plots to include in this paper; they can be seen in Fig. 7, along with descriptions.

---

[5] The full data set will be eventually published online, but is too extensive to fit in a paper. Please check http://divine.fi.muni.cz/benchmarks.

5   Conclusions

We have described, implemented and verified a hash table suitable for both small and large data sets, with fully concurrent lookup and insertion and with dynamic, concurrent resizing. The benchmarks we have done show that both the design and the implementation are highly competitive, and our experience with using the hash table as presented here in the implementation of a parallel explicit-state model checker confirms that it is well-suited for demanding applications. The C++ source code of the implementation is available online[6] under a permissive BSD-style licence. The provided code is production-ready, although for use-cases where item removal is required, it would need to be adapted using one of the approaches described in existing literature.

References

1. Intel Corporation, Threading Building Blocks (2014–06-01) (2014). http://www. threadingbuildingblocks.org
2. Shalev, O., Shavit, N.: Split-ordered lists: lock-free extensible hashtables. J. ACM **53**(3), 379–405 (2006). http://doi.acm.org/10.1145/1147954.1147958
3. Laarman, A.W., van de Pol, J.C., Weber, M.: Boosting multi-core reachability performance with shared hash tables. In: Sharygina, N., Bloem, R. (eds.) FMCAD 2010. IEEE Computer Society, Los Alamitos (2010)
4. Purcell, C., Harris, T.: Non-blocking hashtables with open addressing. In: Proceedings of the 19th International Symposium on Distributed Computing, DISC 2005, September 2005, a longer version appears as Technical report UCAM-CL-TR-639. http://research.microsoft.com/apps/pubs/default.aspx?id=67422
5. Gao, H., Groote, J.F., Hesselink, W.H.: Lock-free dynamic hash tables with open addressing. Distrib. Comput. **18**(1), 21–42 (2005)
6. Wijs, A., Bošnački, D.: Many-core on-the-fly model checking of safety properties using GPUs. Int. J. Softw. Tools Technol. Transf. 1–17 (2015) (to appear)
7. Jenkins, R.J.: A hash function for hash table lookup (2006). http://burtleburtle. net/bob/hash/doobs.html
8. Jenkins, R.J.: SpookyHash: a 128-bit Noncryptographic Hash (2012). http:// burtleburtle.net/bob/hash/spooky.html
9. Pike, G., Alakuijala, J.: Introducing CityHash (2011)
10. Batagelj, V.: The quadratic hash method when the table size is not a primenumber. Commun. ACM **18**(4), 216–217 (1975). http://doi.acm.org/ 10.1145/360715.360737
11. Ročkai, P., Šill, V., Barnat, J.: Techniques for memory-efficient model checking of C and C++ code. In: Software Engineering and Formal Methods (2015, submitted)
12. Fagin, R., Nievergelt, J., Pippenger, N., Strong, H.R.: Extendible hashing—a fast access method for dynamic files. ACM Trans. Database Syst. **4**(3), 315–344 (1979)
13. Barnat, J., et al.: DiVinE 3.0 – anexplicit-state model checker for multithreaded C & C++ programs. In: Sharygina, N., Veith, H. (eds.) CAV 2013. LNCS, vol. 8044, pp. 863–868. Springer, Heidelberg (2013)

---

[6] https://divine.fi.muni.cz/trac/browser/bricks/brick-hashset.h#L481.

On Refinement of Büchi Automata for Explicit Model Checking

František Blahoudek[1], Alexandre Duret-Lutz[2], Vojtěch Rujbr[1],
and Jan Strejček[1(✉)]

[1] Faculty of Informatics, Masaryk University, Brno, Czech Republic
{xblahoud,xrujbr,strejcek}@fi.muni.cz
[2] LRDE, EPITA, Le Kremlin-Bicêtre, France
adl@lrde.epita.fr

Abstract. In explicit model checking, systems are typically described in an implicit and compact way. Some valid information about the system can be easily derived directly from this description, for example that some atomic propositions cannot be valid at the same time. The paper shows several ways to apply this information to improve the Büchi automaton built from an LTL specification. As a result, we get smaller automata with shorter edge labels that are easier to understand and, more importantly, for which the explicit model checking process performs better.

1 Introduction

LTL model checking can be formulated as the problem of deciding whether a given system has an erroneous behavior specified by an LTL formula φ. In the automata-based approach to model checking, φ is translated into an equivalent Büchi automaton $\mathcal{A}_\varphi$ called *property automaton*. The original problem then reduces to deciding whether there exists a behavior of the system accepted by $\mathcal{A}_\varphi$. In explicit model checking, this is achieved by building a synchronous product of the system and the property automaton, and checking whether the product contains any reachable accepting cycle. This *emptiness check* can be done by several algorithms including the well-known *Nested Depth-First Search (NDFS)* [12] implemented in the model checker Spin [11]. The synchronous product is often constructed *on-the-fly*, i.e., simultaneously with the emptiness check and according to its needs. The product construction and the emptiness check form typically the most expensive part of the whole model checking process as the product to be explored is often very large. The actual difficulty of the check depends not only on the number of states in the product, but also on the number of transitions, the number and positions of accepting states, and other characteristics of the product. As the property automaton $\mathcal{A}_\varphi$ is a component of the product, the difficulty partly depends on the size and other characteristics of $\mathcal{A}_\varphi$.

For several decades, developers of algorithms and tools to translate LTL formulas into Büchi automata have aimed to produce small automata in short time. More recently, there was also a shift into producing automata that are

© Springer International Publishing Switzerland 2015
B. Fischer and J. Geldenhuys (Eds.): SPIN 2015, LNCS 9232, pp. 66–83, 2015.
DOI: 10.1007/978-3-319-23404-5_6

more deterministic, as Sebastiani and Tonetta [16] identified a relation between the performance of the model checking and the determinism of the property automata. As a result, current LTL to Büchi automata translators like Spot [6] and LTL3BA [2] produce relatively small automata that are often deterministic.

One way to create property automata that further accelerate the model checking process is to provide more information for the translation than just the LTL formula. For example, we have recently shown that the position of accepting states in the property automaton can be adjusted according to the expected result of the model checking process: if we expect that the system has no erroneous behavior specified by φ, we can move the accepting states of $\mathcal{A}_\varphi$ further from its initial state to accelerate the model checking [4]. Analogously, relocation of accepting states in the opposite direction can speed up the model checking process if the system contains an error specified by φ.

In this paper, we try to improve the property automata using partial information about the behaviors of the system. More precisely, we use information about combinations of atomic propositions (and their negations) that cannot occur in any state of the system. For example, $x = 5$ and $x > 10$ cannot hold at once. Similarly, a process cannot be in two different locations at the same time. Information about these *incompatible propositions* can often be easily obtained from an implicit description of the system, i.e., without building its state space.

We show that this *a priori knowledge* about incompatible propositions can increase the efficiency of explicit model checking of linear-time properties by *refining* the specification to be checked. In Sect. 3, we show how to perform this refinement when the specification is given either by an LTL formula (or even a PSL formula) or by a Büchi automaton (or other kind of an ω-automaton). We talk about *formula refinement* or *automaton refinement*, respectively.

By refinement, we get a property automaton that may have fewer edges or even fewer states than the initial property automaton. All these changes often have a positive effect on the rest of the model checking process, as documented by experimental evaluation in Sect. 4.

As a side effect of the specification refinement, we typically obtain automata with long edge labels. Section 5 shows that complex edge labels have a small, but measurable negative effect on the execution time of Spin. Fortunately, Sect. 5 also introduces a method that employs the information about incompatible propositions to simplify the labels.

Finally, Sect. 6 discusses some interesting cases discovered during our intensive experiments.

2 Preliminaries

Let AP be a finite set of atomic propositions. Besides atomic propositions talking about values of program variables (like $x = 5$ or $y < 10$) and their relations (like $x < y$ or $x \cdot y = z+2$), we also work with atomic propositions of the form $p@loc$ saying that process p is in location *loc*.

Let $\mathbb{B} = \{\top, \bot\}$ represent Boolean values. An assignment is a function $\ell : AP \to \mathbb{B}$ that valuates each proposition. $\mathbb{B}^{AP}$ is the set of all assignments.

We assume familiarity with Linear-time Temporal Logic (LTL) [15]. Our examples use mainly the temporal operators $F\varphi$ (meaning that φ *eventually* holds) and $G\varphi$ (saying that φ *always* holds), but the results are valid for property formulas of any linear-time logic including the linear fragment of PSL [1].

A *Büchi automaton* (BA or simply an *automaton*) is a tuple $\mathcal{A} = (Q, q_0, \delta, F)$, where Q is a finite set of states, $q_0 \in Q$ is the initial state, $\delta \subseteq Q \times \mathbb{B}^{AP} \times Q$ is a transition relation labeling each transition by an assignment, and $F \subseteq Q$ is a set of accepting states. Every triple $(r_1, \ell, r_2) \in \delta$ is called a *transition* from r_1 to r_2 under ℓ. As an implementation optimization, and to simplify illustrations, we often use *edges* labeled by Boolean formulas to group transitions with same sources and destinations: an edge $(r_1, a \vee \neg b, r_2)$ represents all transitions from r_1 to r_2 labeled with assignments ℓ such that $\ell(a) = \top$ or $\ell(b) = \bot$. To shorten the notation of edge labels, we write $\bar{a}$ instead of $\neg a$ and we omit $\wedge$ in conjunctions of atomic propositions (e.g., $a\bar{b}$ stands for $a \wedge \neg b$). An infinite sequence $\pi = (r_1, \ell_1, r_2)(r_2, \ell_2, r_3) \ldots \in \delta^\omega$ where $r_1 = q_0$ is a *run* of $\mathcal{A}$ over the word $\ell_1 \ell_2 \ldots$. The run is *accepting* if some accepting state appears infinitely often in π. A word is accepted by $\mathcal{A}$ if there is an accepting run of $\mathcal{A}$ over that word. The *language* of $\mathcal{A}$ is the set $L(\mathcal{A})$ of all words accepted by $\mathcal{A}$.

Kripke structures are a low-level formalism representing finite state systems. A Kripke structure is a tuple $\mathcal{S} = (S, s_0, R, L)$, where S is a finite set of states, $s_0 \in S$ is the initial state, $R \subseteq S \times S$ is a transition relation, $L : S \to \mathbb{B}^{AP}$ is a labeling function. A *product* of a Kripke structure $\mathcal{S} = (S, s_0, R, L)$ and an automaton $\mathcal{A} = (Q, q_0, \delta, F)$ is the automaton $\mathcal{S} \otimes \mathcal{A}$ defined as $(S \times Q, (s_0, q_0), \delta', S \times F)$, where $\delta' = \{((s_1, q_1), l, (s_2, q_2)) \mid (s_1, s_2) \in R, (q_1, l, q_2) \in \delta, L(s_1) = l\}$.

3   Specification Refinement

Assume that we have a Kripke structure $\mathcal{S}$ and an LTL formula φ that describes the infinite erroneous behaviors we do not want to see in $\mathcal{S}$. Let $AP(\varphi)$ denote the set of atomic propositions in φ. A typical explicit model checker translates φ as a Büchi automaton $\mathcal{A}_\varphi$, and then constructs a product $\mathcal{S} \otimes \mathcal{A}_\varphi$ while simultaneously checking whether the language of this product is empty or not. As the product accepts all behaviors of the system also accepted by the automaton $\mathcal{A}_\varphi$, the system contains an error if and only if $L(\mathcal{S} \otimes \mathcal{A}_\varphi) \neq \emptyset$.

In practice, the system $\mathcal{S}$ is often described in some high-level formalism, which can be a programming language or a dedicated modeling language like Promela [11, Chap. 3]. This high-level description is translated into (the relevant part of) the corresponding Kripke structure during construction of the product.

The high-level description already provides some relevant information about the system. In particular, one can detect that some combinations of propositions in $AP(\varphi)$ and their negations are never valid at the same time. For instance, $x > 10$, $y < 5$, and $x < y$ cannot hold together. This information follows directly from the atomic propositions themselves. However, a static analysis of the system can identify more impossible combinations. For instance, the analysis can find out that if a process p is in a location *loc*, then local variable $p{:}x$ has value 0, and thus atomic propositions $p@loc$ and $p{:}x > 0$ never hold together. In the following, we assume that we are given a *constraint* κ, which is a Boolean formula over $AP(\varphi)$ satisfied by all combinations of atomic propositions except the invalid combinations. For example, the constraints corresponding to the two instances mentioned above are $\neg((x > 10) \wedge (y < 5) \wedge (x < y))$ and $\neg((p@loc) \wedge (p{:}x > 0))$.

One can frequently detect sets of atomic propositions that are mutually exclusive. For example, atomic propositions saying that a process p is in various locations (e.g., $p@loc1$, $p@loc2$, and $p@loc3$) are always mutually exclusive. Similarly, atomic propositions talking about values of the same variable (e.g., $x > 10$ and $x < 5$) are often contradictory. For a set $\mathcal{E}$ of mutually exclusive propositions (also called *exclusive set*), we define the constraint as:

$$ excl(\mathcal{E}) = \bigwedge_{\substack{u,v \in \mathcal{E} \\ u \neq v}} \neg(u \wedge v) $$

While such a constraint may seems obvious to the reader, tools that translate LTL formulas into Büchi automata do not analyze the semantics of atomic propositions and thus they do not know that $x > 10$ and $x < 5$ are incompatible.

3.1   Formula Refinement

The *refinement* of an LTL formula φ with respect to a constraint κ is the formula $r_\kappa(\varphi)$ defined by

$$ r_\kappa(\varphi) = \varphi \wedge \mathsf{G}\kappa. $$

where the knowledge about the constraint is made explicit.

This extra information allows tools that translate LTL formulas into automata to produce smaller automata. For instance the Büchi automaton of Fig. 1(a) was generated by Spot [6] from the formula $\mathsf{F}(\mathsf{G}a \vee (\mathsf{GF}b \leftrightarrow \mathsf{GF}c))$. If the formula is refined with a constraint built for the exclusive set $\{a, b, c\}$, then the translator produces the smaller automaton from Fig. 1(b): the edge between states 3 and 5 labeled by bc is known to be never satisfiable, and the state 0 is found to be superfluous (its incoming edges would be labeled by $a\bar{b}\bar{c}$, so this part of the automaton is covered by state 2 already).

3.2   Automaton Refinement

Alternatively, the refinement can be performed on the property automaton $\mathcal{A}$. This allows the specification of erroneous behaviors to be supplied directly as an automaton. Given an automaton $\mathcal{A}$ and a constraint κ, we obtain the refined automaton $r_\kappa(\mathcal{A})$ by replacing any edge (r_1, ℓ, r_2) of $\mathcal{A}$ by $(r_1, \ell \wedge \kappa, r_2)$ and removing the edge whenever the new label reduces to false. Figure 1(c) shows the result of applying this to the automaton of Fig. 1(a). Note that as the edge labels are Boolean functions, they accept many representations: we display them

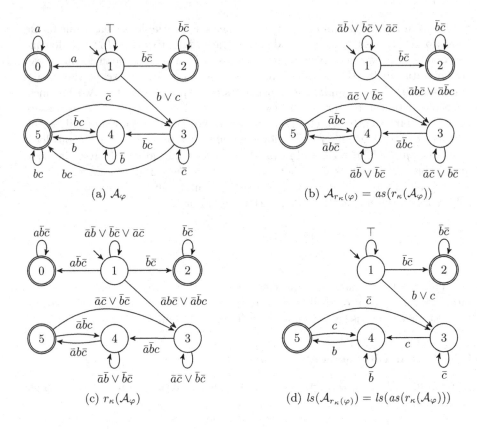

Fig. 1. Automata for $\varphi = \mathsf{F}(\mathsf{G}a \vee (\mathsf{GF}b \leftrightarrow \mathsf{GF}c))$ and $\kappa = excl(\{a, b, c\})$.

as some irredundant sums-of-products[1] by convention. In this case, state 0 is not removed, but it can be removed if we run some simplification algorithms (such as simulation-based reductions [3]), which are often employed in LTL to automata translators. The result of this simplification pass is then again in Fig. 1(b).

If $as(\mathcal{A})$ denotes the operation that simplifies an automaton $\mathcal{A}$ using the same simplification algorithms that are used by a tool translating φ into $\mathcal{A}_\varphi$, one would expect that $\mathcal{A}_{r_\kappa(\varphi)} = as(r_\kappa(\mathcal{A}_\varphi))$ always holds (as in the example of Fig. 1(b)). This is not true in practice for two reasons:

- Some translators have LTL rewriting rules that may react strangely to the refined formula, sometimes to the point of producing larger automata.
- Some translators include automata simplification algorithms (such a WDBA-minimization [5,6]) that can only be applied when the formula is known, so they cannot be run on arbitrary automata.

---

[1] A sum-of-product is irredundant if all its products are prime implicants, and no product can be removed without changing the function [13].

Table 1. Considered LTL-to-BA translators, for reference.

Translator	Version	Command
Spin [9,11]	6.3.2	`spin`
LTL2BA [10]	1.1	`ltl2ba`
LTL3BA [2]	1.1.2	`ltl3ba`
LTL3BA-det		`ltl3ba -M0`
Spot [6]	1.99b	`ltl2tgba -s`
Spot-det		`ltl2tgba -s --deterministic`

Nonetheless, both formula refinement or automaton refinement have three noticeable effects on the model checking process:

- First, the removal of unsatisfiable transitions saves the model checker from having to repeatedly evaluate the labels of these transitions during the product construction, only to finally ignore them.
- Second, the automaton constructed with formula or automaton refinement is often smaller than the original automaton (for example, removing some transitions can make two states equivalent and such states can be merged). This can have a very positive effect on the model checking process.
- Last, the longer labels produced by this refinement may take longer to evaluate depending on how the model checker is implemented. This is the only negative effect, and we fix it in Sect. 5.

4 Experimental Evaluation

First we describe the general setting of our experiments. Then we show the impact of formula refinement and automaton refinement. Finally, we compare the two refinement approaches.

Benchmark. Our benchmark is made of 3316 verification tasks (i.e., a model plus a specification) where some propositions are referring to different locations of a single process so that we can construct exclusive sets. These tasks employ 101 instances of 16 parametrized models from Beem [14]; 50 tasks use specifications from Beem, the others combine Beem models with random LTL formulas.

Tools. In our experiments, we use four LTL-to-BA translators presented in Table 1. Two of the translators, namely LTL3BA and Spot, are used with two settings: the default ones and the settings with the suffix "-det" that aim to produce more deterministic automata. All translators are restricted by 20 min timeout. For formula refinement and automata refinement, we use tools `ltlfilt` and `autfilt` from Spot 1.99.1 For emptiness checks, we use the same version of Spin with the maximum search depth set to 100 000 000, memory limit 20 GiB, option `-DNOSTUTTER` (see Sect. 6.3 for the explanation), and partial-order

Table 2. Statistics of fails and successfully solved verification tasks with and without formula refinement.

Translator	Original tasks $(\mathcal{S}, \varphi)$			Refined tasks $(\mathcal{S}, r_\kappa(\varphi))$			Both tasks solved
	Translation timeouts	Spin fails	Tasks solved	Translation timeouts	Spin fails	Tasks solved	
Spin	801	232	2283	926	201	2189	2183
LTL2BA	5	341	2970	2	302	3012	2929
LTL3BA	0	80	3236	0	55	3261	3227
LTL3BA-det	0	34	3282	0	27	3289	3279
Spot	2	27	3287	0	19	3297	3286
Spot-det	2	26	3288	0	19	3297	3287

reduction enabled for tasks with *next*-free formulas. Emptiness check is always restricted by 30 min timeout.

Hardware. All computations are performed on an HP DL980 G7 server with 8 eight-core processors Intel Xeon X7560 2.26GHz and 448 GiB DDR3 RAM. The server is shared with other users and its variable workload has led to a high dispersion of measured running times. Hence, instead of running times, we use the number of transitions visited by Spin, which is stable across multiple executions and should be proportional to the running time.

Additional data and detailed information about this benchmark are available at: http://fi.muni.cz/~xstrejc/publications/spin2015/

4.1 Impact of Formula Refinement

For each verification task $(\mathcal{S}, \varphi)$ and each translator of Table 1, we translate φ to automaton $\mathcal{A}_\varphi$ and run Spin on $\mathcal{S}$ and $\mathcal{A}_\varphi$. Then we refine the formula to $r_\kappa(\varphi)$ and repeat the process. Table 2 shows the numbers of translation timeouts, Spin fails (this number covers the cases when Spin timeouts or runs out of memory or reaches the maximum search depth), and successfully solved verification problems. The data indicates that formula refinement has a mostly positive effect on the model checking process: for all but one translator, the refinement increases the number of successfully solved tasks (we discuss the case of Spin translator in more details in Sect. 6.2). Nevertheless, the number of tasks solved both with and without formula refinement is always smaller that the number of solved original tasks, which means that the effect of formula refinement is negative in some cases. In the rest of this section, for each translator we consider only the tasks counted in the last column of the table, i.e., tasks solved both with and without formula refinement.

We now look at the effect of formula refinement on the sizes of property automata. Table 3 shows that the property automaton for a refined formula has very frequently fewer states than the automaton for the original formula. However, we cannot easily tell whether states are removed simply because they

Table 3. Effect of formula refinement on property automata. For each translator and each verification task, we compare the size of $\mathcal{A}_\varphi$ with the size of $\mathcal{A}_{r_\kappa(\varphi)}$ and report on the number of cases where the refinement resulted in additional states (+states) or fewer states (−states). In case of equality, we look at the number of edges or transitions.

Effect	Spin	LTL2BA	LTL3BA	LTL3BA-det	Spot	Spot-det
+states	514	41	15	148	13	17
−states	168	1482	1679	1723	1722	1720
=states,+edges	37	17	0	0	9	10
=states,−edges	43	337	293	326	345	344
=states,=edges,+trans.	153	211	283	173	280	280
=states,=edges,−trans.	1226	785	899	848	849	848
No size change	42	56	58	61	68	68

are inaccessible after refinement (i.e., the constraint κ removed all the transitions leading to a state) or if the refinement enabled additional simplifications as in Fig. 1. In the former case, the refinement would have a little impact on the size of the product: it is only saving useless attempts to synchronize transitions that can never be synchronized while building this product.

Finally, we turn our attention to the actual effect of formula refinement on performance of the emptiness check implemented in Spin. For each translator and each verification task, let t_1 be the number of transitions visited by Spin for the original task and t_2 be the same number for the refined task. Scatter plots of Fig. 2 show each pair (t_1, t_2) as a dot at this coordinates. The color[2] of each dot says whether the property automaton for the refined formula has more or less states than the automaton for the original formula. The data is shown separately for each translator. We also distinguish the tasks with some erroneous behavior from those without error. As many dots in the scatter plots are overlapping, we present the data also via *improvement ratios* t_2/t_1. Values of t_2/t_1 smaller than 1 correspond to cases where formula refinement actually helped Spin, while values larger than 1 correspond to cases where the refinement caused Spin to work more. Figure 3 gives an idea of the distribution of these improvement ratios in our benchmark. On this figure, all improvement ratios for a given tool are sorted from lowest to highest, and then they are plotted using their rank as x coordinate, and using a logarithmic scale for the ratio. One can immediately see on these curves that there is a large plateau around $y = 1$ corresponding to the cases where there is no substantial improvement. In the tasks without error, there are usually many cases with ratio below 0.95 (definite improvement), and very few cases above 1.05 (cases where refinement hurt more than it helped). A special class of cases that are improved are those that are found equivalent to false after refinement: those usually have a very high improvement ratio, as the exploration of the product is now limited to a

---

[2] We suggest viewing these figures in color using the electronic version of this article.

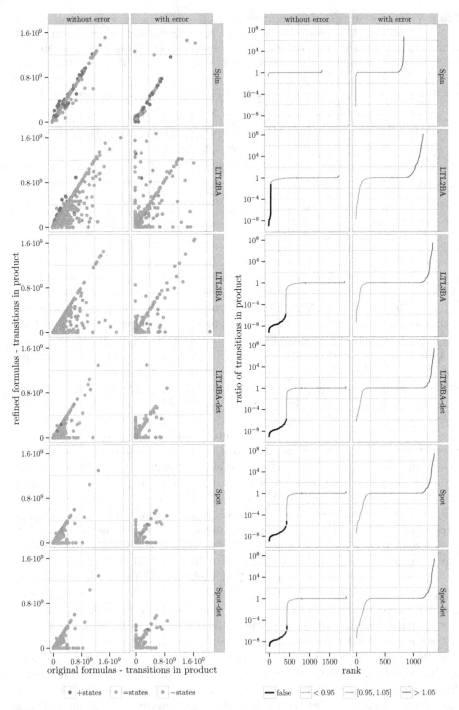

Fig. 2. Comparison of the numbers of product transitions visited by Spin on the original tasks (t_1) and their *formula-refined* versions (t_2).

Fig. 3. Distribution of the improvement ratios (t_2/t_1) using logarithmic scales. Cases that have been reduced to false are highlighted in bold.

single transition (after which Spin immediately realizes that the empty never claim cannot be satisfied). Note that in tasks with error, the refined formula cannot be equivalent to false as all states of an erroneous behavior comply with the constraint. Relatively high numbers of these "false" cases imply that the formula refinement technique is an effective sanity check detecting specifications unsatisfiable under given constraints.[3] Table 4 gives counts of improvement ratios in these classes.

Table 4. Distribution of the improvement ratios for formula refinement. The counts of false cases are not included in the <0.95 classes.

	Without error					With error			
	False	<0.95	[0.95,1.05]	>1.05	All	<0.95	[0.95,1.05]	>1.05	All
Spin	0	30	1257	50	1337	27	708	111	846
LTL2BA	61	462	1179	48	1750	288	602	289	1179
LTL3BA	374	401	1101	7	1883	194	942	208	1344
detLTL3BA	382	264	1255	12	1913	186	993	187	1366
Spot	384	300	1213	20	1917	244	902	223	1369
detSpot	385	297	1218	18	1918	248	903	218	1369

Figures 2 and 3 and Table 4 show that for tasks without error, formula refinement has negative effect only very rarely and such effect is relatively small. The positive effect is more frequent and substantial in many cases. The table implies that LTL3BA and Spot can profit more from the refinement as they identify radically more false cases and they have significantly less cases with negative effect than the other translators (some of the negative cases are discussed in Sect. 6). This observation can be explained by advanced simplification techniques implemented in LTL3BA and Spot.

In the tasks with erroneous behaviors, we observe that the number of improved cases is almost balanced by the number of degraded cases (except for Spin). This can be explained by the fact that refining an LTL formula my change the shape of the output automaton, and thus change its transition order. Therefore the model checker may have more or less luck in finding an erroneous run. When such a run is found, Spin ends the computation without exploring the rest of the product.

4.2 Impact of Automaton Refinement

As mentioned before, automaton refinement itself only cuts off some parts of the automaton that are not used in the product. It has a bigger effect only when simplification algorithms are executed after the refinement. In our experiments, we combined automaton refinement with the automata simplifications implemented in Spot.

---

[3] The high number of "false" cases is due to the use of random formulas. In real tasks, such a *false* case would likely indicate a bug in the specification.

Table 5. Statistics of fails and successfully solved verification tasks with and without automata refinement.

Original tasks $(\mathcal{S}, \mathcal{A})$		Refined tasks $(\mathcal{S}, as(r_\kappa(\mathcal{A})))$			Both tasks solved
Spin fails	Tasks solved	Simplification of $r_\kappa(\mathcal{A})$ timeouts	Spin fails	Tasks solved	
291	9061	12	99	9241	9038

Table 6. Effect of automaton refinement on property automata.

Effect	
+states	0
−states	4955
=states,+edges	0
=states,−edges	1013
=states,=edges,+trans.	0
=states,=edges,−trans.	2400
No size change	670

Table 7. Distribution of the improvement ratios for automaton refinement.

	Without error	With error
False	906	0
<0.95	853	735
$[0.95, 1.05]$	3251	2743
>1.05	5	545
All	5015	4023

To measure the effect of automaton refinement, we prepared the benchmark as follows. We took the 3316 verification tasks used before. For every task, we translated the formula with all considered translators and simplified the produced automata using Spot. The simplification is here applied to make the comparison of model checking with and without automaton refinement fair: without this step we could not really distinguish the effect of automata refinement (followed by simplification) from the effect of simplification itself. If the automaton translation and simplification successfully finishes, we get a pair of a model and a simplified automaton. In the rest of this section, we call such pairs *verification tasks*. After removing duplicates, we have 9352 verification tasks.

For each task, we run Spin with the original automaton. Then we refine and simplify the automaton and run Spin again. While automaton refinement is very cheap, its simplification can be quite expensive. So we apply a 20 min timeout. Table 5 provides numbers of Spin fails on original tasks, timeouts of refined automata simplifications, and Spin failures on refined tasks. In the following, we work only with tasks solved both with and without automaton refinement.

As in the previous section, Table 6 presents the effect of automaton refinement and simplification on the sizes of property automata. The refined and simplified automata are smaller in the vast majority of cases and never bigger.

The effect of automaton refinement and simplification on performance of emptiness check in Spin is presented in Figs. 4 and 5, and Table 7 in the same way as previously. On tasks without error, the effect is similar to formula refinement: it is often positive and almost never negative. On tasks with error, the positive effect is more frequent than the negative one.

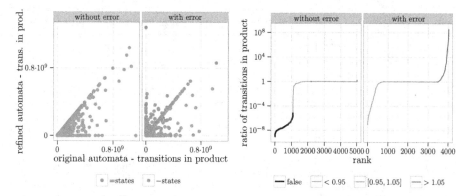

Fig. 4. Comparison of the numbers of product transitions visited by Spin on the original tasks (t_1) and their *automata*-refined versions (t_2).

Fig. 5. Distribution of the improvement ratios (t_2/t_1) using logarithmic scales. Cases that have been reduced to false are highlighted in bold.

Table 8. Statistics of fails and successfully solved verification tasks with formula refinement and automaton refinement.

Tasks with formula refinement			Tasks with automaton refinement			
Automaton construction timeouts	Spin fails	Tasks solved	Automaton construction timeouts	Spin fails	Tasks solved	Both tasks solved
0	19	3297	35	25	3256	3256

4.3 Comparison of Formula and Automaton Refinement

Here we compare the formula refinement and automaton refinement using Spot for the formula translation. For each of the 3316 considered tasks, we refine the formula, translate it by Spot, and run Spin. Then we take the task again, translate the original formula by Spot, refine and simplify the automaton, and run Spin. Table 8 provides statistics about automata construction timeouts (this comprises Spot timeouts and, in the case of automaton refinement, also simplification of refined automata timeouts), Spin timeouts, and solved tasks. Both approaches detected 380 identical cases where the refined specification reduces to false. In the following, we present the data from the $3256 - 380 = 2876$ tasks solved by both approaches and not trivially equivalent to false.

Table 9, Figs. 6 and 7, and Table 10 are analogous to the tables and figures in the previous sections (the position of original tasks in the previous sections is taken by tasks with formula refinement). Table 9 says that automaton refinement often produces property automata with more states than formula refinement. However, Fig. 6 and Table 10 show that the overall effect of automata and formula refinement on performance of Spin is fully comparable, slightly in favor of formula refinement.

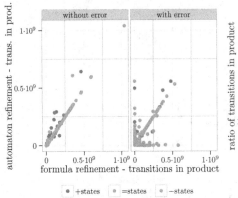
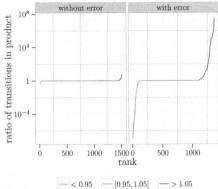

Fig. 6. Comparison of the numbers of product transitions visited by Spin in *formula*-refined tasks (t_1) and their *automata*-refined versions (t_2).

Fig. 7. Distribution of the improvement ratios (t_2/t_1) using logarithmic scales. Cases that have been reduced to false are highlighted in bold.

5   Label Simplification

As mentioned in Sect. 3, a side-effect of specification refinement is that edges get more complex labels. This is visible when comparing the automaton of Fig. 1(b) to the one of Fig. 1(a). For example the self-loop on state 3 is labeled by $\bar{a}\bar{c} \vee \bar{b}\bar{c}$ instead of the original $\bar{c}$. In our experiment, the overall average length of an edge label (counted as the number of occurrences of atomic propositions in the label) in the automata $\mathcal{A}_{r_\kappa(\varphi)}$ for refined formulas is 6.58, while the average label length in the corresponding automata $\mathcal{A}_\varphi$ for unrefined formulas is only 4.20. When executing Spin, the labels are compiled into C code to match system transitions during the construction of the synchronized product. For example, Fig. 8 depicts

Table 9. Comparison of automata produced by formula refinement and automaton refinement (+states counts tasks where $as(r_\kappa(\mathcal{A}_\varphi))$ has more states than $\mathcal{A}_{r_\kappa(\varphi)}$ and so on).

Effect	
+states	315
−states	82
=states,+edges	52
=states,−edges	51
=states,=edges,+trans.	26
=states,=edges,−trans.	428
No size change	1922

Table 10. Distribution of the improvement ratios for automaton refinement over formula refinement.

	Without error	With error
<0.95	44	133
[0.95, 1.05]	1399	970
>1.05	71	259
All	1514	1362

```
if (!((((!((((int)((P1 *)Pptr(f_pid(1)))->_p)==27))&&
        !((((int)((P1 *)Pptr(f_pid(1)))->_p)==5)))||
        (!((((int)((P1 *)Pptr(f_pid(1)))->_p)==27))&&
        !((((int)((P1 *)Pptr(f_pid(1)))->_p)==9)))))) ...
if (!( !((((int)((P1 *)Pptr(f_pid(1)))->_p)==27)))) ...
```

Fig. 8. Code listings of a `pan.m` file. The upper part resulted from the edge labeled by $a\bar{c} \vee \bar{b}\bar{c}$ and the last line is from label $\bar{c}$.

the C code corresponding to the labels $a\bar{c} \vee \bar{b}\bar{c}$ and $\bar{c}$. Clearly, longer labels can slow down the verification process without influencing any Spin statistics like visited transitions and stored states. However, the expected slowdown should be only small as checking the labels is much cheaper than computing successors for states of the system or storing the states.

To eliminate the slowdown, we simplify the labels in a step that can be though of as the converse of refinement: instead of using a given constraint to make labels more precise, we use it to make them *less* precise and shorter, but equivalent to the original labels under the given constraint. For instance, $b\bar{c}$ can be shortened as b if we know that b and c cannot be both true in the model. This simplification can be implemented by performing Boolean function simplification with *don't care* information: we do not care if the simplified label additionally covers some variable assignments that can never happen in the system. Concretely, we have implemented the simplification in Spot using the Minato-Morreale algorithm [13]. The algorithms inputs two Boolean functions $\lfloor f \rfloor$ and $\lceil f \rceil$ and produces an irredundant sum-of-product that covers at least all the assignments satisfying $\lfloor f \rfloor$, and that is not satisfiable by at least all the assignments not satisfying $\lceil f \rceil$. To simplify a label ℓ using a constraint κ, we call

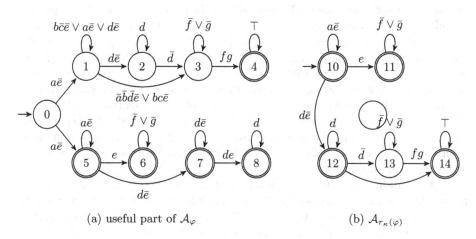

(a) useful part of $\mathcal{A}_\varphi$ (b) $\mathcal{A}_{r_\kappa(\varphi)}$

Fig. 9. An uncommon case where $\mathcal{A}_{r_\kappa(\varphi)}$ is much smaller than $\mathcal{A}_\varphi$, and yet Spin performs better with $\mathcal{A}_\varphi$.

the algorithm with $\lfloor f \rfloor = \ell \wedge \kappa$ and $\lceil f \rceil = \neg\ell \wedge \kappa$. Figure 1(d) shows the result of applying this label simplification (denoted as function ls) to Fig. 1(b).

We applied the label simplification to automata obtained by formula refinement and the average label length drops to 3.19, which is even lower that the mentioned value for automata without refinement. We selected several cases with high reduction of label length and run Spin several times with automata before and after label simplification on a weaker, but isolated machine to get reliable running times. In these tests, Spin runs up to 3.5 % slower with automata before label simplification.

6   Interesting Cases

In this section we investigate several interesting cases where using refinement caused worse performance.

6.1   The Case of Strongly Connected Components

Figure 9 shows an interesting case that we discovered among the few tasks without error where the refined formula translated by Spot degrades the performance of Spin. In this case, Spin performs better with the automaton $\mathcal{A}_\varphi$ of Fig. 9(a) than with the smaller automaton $\mathcal{A}_{r_\kappa(\varphi)}$ of Fig. 9(b). Please note that the automaton presented in Fig. 9(a) is a pruned version of the real automaton, in which we removed all transitions that do not appear in the product with the model. For instance, in this pruned automaton it is obvious that the state 7 can be merged with state 8, but the presence of other edges in the original automaton prevented this simplification.

The reason Spin works better with the larger of these two automata is related to the emptiness check used. The emptiness check procedure used in Spin by default is based on two nested depth-first searches [12]: the main DFS, which we shall call *blue*, explores the product (on-the-fly) and every time it would backtrack from an accepting state s (i.e., all successors of s have been explored by the blue DFS) it starts a second, *red* DFS from s. If the red DFS reaches any state on the blue DFS search stack, then a reachable and accepting cycle is found (since s is reachable from all states on the blue DFS search stack) and the algorithm reports it as a counterexample. Otherwise, the red DFS terminates and the blue DFS can continue. The two DFS always ignore states that have been completely explored by an instance of the red DFS, so a state is never visited more than twice.

In the automaton of Fig. 9(b), whenever the blue DFS backtracks a state of the product that is synchronized with state 12, it has to start a red DFS that will explore again states synchronized with 13 and previously explored by the blue DFS (states synchronized with 12 and 14 will be ignored as they have already been seen by a previous red DFS). This re-exploration of states synchronized with 13 is something that (i) did not happen in the original automaton because there is no accepting state above the corresponding state 3, and (ii) is useless because there is no way to get back to state 12 after moving to state 13.

The NDFS algorithm could be patched to avoid this problem by simply constraining the red DFS to explore only the states of the product whose projection on the property automaton belongs to the same strongly connected component as its starting accepting state. This optimization was already suggested by Edelkamp et al. [7,8] with the additional trick that if the current SCC is known to be weak (i.e., its states are all accepting and or all non-accepting), then running a red DFS is not needed at all, as the blue DFS is guaranteed to find any accepting cycle by itself. In the scenarios described by Figs. 9(a) and (b), all the SCCs have a single state, so the product automaton will be weak and the red DFS should not be needed. Computing the strongly connected components of the property automaton can be done in time that is linear to the size of that automaton (typically a small value) before the actual emptiness check starts, so this is a very cheap way to improve the model checking time.

6.2 Problems with LTL Simplifications

A special class of interesting cases consists of formulas where formula refinement leads to bigger automata. Such cases are surprisingly often connected with issues in the earliest phases of LTL to automata translation, namely in formula parsing or simplification. For example, LTL3BA implements several specific formula reduction rules applied after all standard formula reductions. If such a rule is applied, the reduced formula is checked again for possible application of some reduction rule, but only on its top level. Hence, some reductions are not applied when the input formula is refined with a constraint. This is considered as a bug and it will be fixed in the next release of LTL3BA.

LTL2BA has even more problems with formula simplifications as it is sensitive to superfluous parentheses. For instance, the command `ltl2ba -f '<>([]<>X p)'` generates an automaton with 2 states, while the equivalent `ltl2ba -f '<>[]<>X p'` produces an automaton with 4 states. This is because the presence of parentheses causes another pass of formula reduction to occur.

Table 3 indicates that Spin's translator benefits less than the other translators from addition of constraints. Part of the problem, it seems, is due to a change that was introduced in Spin 6 to allow LTL formulas embedding atomic propositions with arbitrary Promela conditions. As a consequence of this change, many parenthetical blocks are now considered as atomic propositions by Spin's translator, and simplifications are therefore missed. For instance, the formula $(a \mathrel{R} b) \wedge \mathsf{G}(\neg(a \wedge b))$ is translated as if $\neg(a \wedge b)$ was an independent atomic proposition. While Spin 5 translates this formula into an automaton with one state and one edge, Spin 6 outputs an automaton with two states and three edges, where the edge connecting the states has unsatisfiable label $\neg(a \wedge b) \wedge a \wedge b$.

6.3 Problem with Spin

During our experiments, we discovered a handful of cases where equivalent never claims would cause Spin to produce different results: e.g., a counterexample for automata built by some tools, and no counterexamples for (equivalent) automata built by other tools. Sometime the automata would differ only by the order in which the transitions are listed. In turned out that this bug[4] was due to a rare combination of events in the red DFS in the presence of a deadlock in the system. While it will be fixed in Spin 6.4.4, the fix came too late for us: our benchmark takes more than a week of computation. All the presented results are computed by compiling the Spin verifier with -DNOSTUTTER, which effectively means that we ignore deadlock scenario, and we are safe from this bug.

7   Conclusions

We have reported on the effect of using information about impossible combinations of propositions in the model to improve model checking. We proposed two techniques: *refinement* is the process of making this information explicit in the property automaton, while *label simplification* is the process of making this information implicit. Our experiments show that these two operations, that can be combined, have a positive effect on the model checking process. By refinement we are able to obtain automata that are usually smaller, and then by *label simplification* we shorten the labels of the automata to speedup the process of transition matching during model checking.

The refinement can also be used as a sanity check: when a refinement leads to a property automaton with no accepting state, it usually represent a bug in the specification.

In the experiments, we only considered incompatibilities between atomic propositions that denote a process being in different locations. More sources of incompatibilities could be considered, such as atomic propositions that refer to different variable values.

We could also extend the principle to more than just incompatible propositions: for instance from the model we could extract information about the validity of atomic propositions in the initial state, the order of locations in a process, or learn the fact that some variable will always be updated in a monotonous way (e.g., can only be increased). All these informations can be used to produce stricter property automata that disallow these impossible behaviors, and we think these automata should offer more opportunity for simplifications, and should also contribute to better sanity checks.

We demonstrated the usefulness of refinement to model checking, but we believe it should also be useful in other contexts like probabilistic model checking or controller synthesis.

Acknowledgments. The authors would like to thank Tomáš Babiak and Jiří Barnat for discussions and tool support. František Blahoudek and Jan Strejček have been supported by The Czech Science Foundation grant GBP202/12/G061.

---

[4] http://spinroot.com/fluxbb/viewtopic.php?pid=3316.

References

1. Accellera. Property specification language reference manual v1.1 (2004). http://www.eda.org/vfv/
2. Babiak, T., Křetínský, M., Řehák, V., Strejček, J.: LTL to büchi automata translation: fast and more deterministic. In: Flanagan, C., König, B. (eds.) TACAS 2012. LNCS, vol. 7214, pp. 95–109. Springer, Heidelberg (2012)
3. Babiak, T., Badie, T., Duret-Lutz, A., Křetínský, M., Strejček, J.: Compositional approach to suspension and other improvements to LTL translation. In: Bartocci, E., Ramakrishnan, C.R. (eds.) SPIN 2013. LNCS, vol. 7976, pp. 81–98. Springer, Heidelberg (2013)
4. Blahoudek, F., Duret-Lutz, A., Křetínský, M., Strejček, J.: Is there a best Büchi automaton for explicit model checking? In: SPIN 2014, pp. 68–76. ACM (2014)
5. Dax, C., Eisinger, J., Klaedtke, F.: Mechanizing the powerset construction for restricted classes of ω-automata. In: Namjoshi, K.S., Yoneda, T., Higashino, T., Okamura, Y. (eds.) ATVA 2007. LNCS, vol. 4762, pp. 223–236. Springer, Heidelberg (2007)
6. Duret-Lutz, A.: LTL translation improvements in Spot 1.0. Int. J. Crit. Comput. Based Syst. 5(1/2), 31–54 (2014)
7. Edelkamp, S., Lluch Lafuente, A., Leue, S.: Directed explicit model checking with HSF-SPIN. In: Dwyer, M.B. (ed.) SPIN 2001. LNCS, vol. 2057, p. 57. Springer, Heidelberg (2001)
8. Edelkamp, S., Leue, S., Lluch-Lafuente, A.: Directed explicit-state model checking in the validation of communication protocols. STTT 5(2–3), 247–267 (2004)
9. Etessami, K., Holzmann, G.J.: Optimizing büchi automata. In: Palamidessi, C. (ed.) CONCUR 2000. LNCS, vol. 1877, pp. 153–167. Springer, Heidelberg (2000)
10. Gastin, P., Oddoux, D.: Fast LTL to büchi automata translation. In: Berry, G., Comon, H., Finkel, A. (eds.) CAV 2001. LNCS, vol. 2102, pp. 53–65. Springer, Heidelberg (2001)
11. Holzmann, G.J.: The Spin Model Checker: Primer and Reference Manual. Addison-Wesley, Boston (2003)
12. Holzmann, G.J., Peled, D.A., Yannakakis, M.: On nested depth first search. In: SPIN 1996, vol. 32 of DIMACS. American Mathematical Society (1996)
13. Minato, S.: Fast generation of irredundant sum-of-products forms from binary decision diagrams. In: SASIMI 1992, pp. 64–73 (1992)
14. Pelánek, R.: BEEM: benchmarks for explicit model checkers. In: Bošnački, D., Edelkamp, S. (eds.) SPIN 2007. LNCS, vol. 4595, pp. 263–267. Springer, Heidelberg (2007)
15. Pnueli, A.: The temporal logic of programs. In: FOCS 1977, pp. 46–57. IEEE (1977)
16. Sebastiani, R., Tonetta, S.: "More Deterministic" vs. "Smaller" büchi automata for efficient LTL model checking. In: Geist, D., Tronci, E. (eds.) CHARME 2003. LNCS, vol. 2860, pp. 126–140. Springer, Heidelberg (2003)

Practical Stutter-Invariance Checks
for ω-Regular Languages

Thibaud Michaud and Alexandre Duret-Lutz[✉]

LRDE, EPITA, Le Kremlin-Bicêtre, France
{michau_n,adl}@lrde.epita.fr

Abstract. An ω-regular language is stutter-invariant if it is closed by the operation that duplicates some letter in a word or that removes some duplicate letter. Model checkers can use powerful reduction techniques when the specification is stutter-invariant.

We propose several automata-based constructions that check whether a specification is stutter-invariant. These constructions assume that a specification and its negation can be translated into Büchi automata, but aside from that, they are independent of the specification formalism. These transformations were inspired by a construction due to Holzmann and Kupferman, but that we broke down into two operations that can have different realizations, and that can be combined in different ways. As it turns out, implementing only one of these operations is needed to obtain a functional stutter-invariant check.

Finally we have implemented these techniques in a tool so that users can easily check whether an LTL or PSL formula is stutter-invariant.

1 Introduction

The notion of stutter-invariance (to be defined formally later) stems from model checkers implementing partial-order reduction techniques (e.g., [6, Chap. 10] or [4, Chap. 8]). If a model checker knows that the property to verify is stutter-invariant, it is sufficient to check that property only on a selected subset of the executions of the model, often achieving a great speedup. Such partial-order reductions are implemented by explicit model checkers such as Spin [18, Chap. 9], LTSmin [21], or DiVinE [5], to cite a few. Detecting stutter-invariant properties has also usages beyond partial-order reductions; for instance it is used to optimize the determinization construction implemented in the tool ltl2dstar [20].

To activate these optimizations, tools must decide if a property is stutter-invariant. The range of available options for this check depends on how the property is specified.

Linear-time Temporal Logic (LTL) is a common specification formalism for verification tools. It is widely known that any LTL formula that does not use the next-step operator X (a.k.a. an LTL\X formula) is stutter-invariant; this check is trivial to implement. Unfortunately there exist formulas using X that are stutter-invariant (for instance '$F(a \land X(\neg a \land b))$') and whose usage is desirable [23].

© Springer International Publishing Switzerland 2015
B. Fischer and J. Geldenhuys (Eds.): SPIN 2015, LNCS 9232, pp. 84–101, 2015.
DOI: 10.1007/978-3-319-23404-5_7

Dallien and MacCaull [8] built a tool that recognizes a stuttering LTL formula if (and only if) it matches one of the patterns of Păun and Chechik [23]. This syntactical approach is efficient, but incomplete, as not all stutter-invariant formulas follow the recognized patterns.

A more definite procedure was given by Peled and Wilke [24] as a construction that inputs an LTL formula φ with $|\varphi|$ symbols and n atomic propositions, and outputs an LTL\X formula φ' with $O(4^n|\varphi|)$ symbols, such that φ and φ' are equivalent iff they represent a stutter-invariant property. This construction, which proves that any stutter-invariant formula can be expressed without X, was later improved to $n^{O(k)}|\varphi|$ symbols, where k is the X-depth of φ, by Etessami [13]. If a disjunctive normal form is desired, Tian and Duan [29] give a variant with size $O(n2^n|\varphi|)$. To decide if an LTL formula φ is stutter-invariant, we build φ' using one of these constructions, and then check the equivalence of φ and φ'. This equivalence check can be achieved by translating these formulas into automata. This approach, based on Etessami's procedure, was implemented in our library Spot [10], but some practical performance issues prompted us to look into alternative directions.

Extending this principle to a more expressive logic is not necessarily easy. For instance, a generalization of the above procedure to the linear fragment of PSL (the Property Specification Language [1]) was proposed by Dax et al. [9], but we realized it was incorrect[1] when we recently implemented it in Spot. Still, Dax et al. [9] provide a syntactic characterization of a stutter-invariant subset of PSL (which is to PSL what LTL\X is to LTL) that can be used to quickly classify some PSL formulas as stutter-invariant.

For most practical uses these linear-time temporal formulas are eventually converted into ω-automata like Büchi automata, so one way to avoid the intricacies of the logic is to establish the stutter-invariance directly at the automaton level. This is the approach used for instance in ltl2dstar [20]. The property φ and its negation are both translated into Büchi automata A_φ and $A_{\neg\varphi}$; then the automaton A_φ is transformed (using a procedure inspired from Holzmann and Kupferman [19]) into an automaton A'_φ that accepts the smallest stutter-invariant language over-approximating the language of φ. The property φ is stutter-invariant iff A_φ and A'_φ have the same language, which can be checked by ensuring that the product $A'_\varphi \otimes A_{\neg\varphi}$ has an empty language. This procedure has the advantage of being independent of the specification formalism used (e.g., it can work with LTL or PSL, and will continue to work even if these logics are augmented with new operators).

In this paper, we present and compare several automata-based decision procedures for stutter-invariance, inspired from the one described above. We show that

---

[1] While testing our implementation we found Lemma 2 of [9] to be incorrect w.r.t. the $\cap$ operator. A counterexample is the SERE $r = a \cap (a; a)$ since $L_\sharp(r) = \emptyset$ but $L_\sharp(\kappa(r)) = \{a\}$. Also Lemma 4 is incorrect w.r.t. the $\diamondsuit\!\!\rightarrow$ operator; a counterexample is the PSL formula $a \diamondsuit\!\!\rightarrow b$ which gets rewritten as $a^+ \diamondsuit\!\!\rightarrow b$: two stutter-invariant formulas with different languages. We are in contact with the authors. (Note that these lemmas are numbered 4 and 9 in the authors' copy.)

the transformation of A_φ to A'_φ is better seen as two operations: one that allows letters to be duplicated, and another that allows duplicate letters to be skipped. These two operations can then be recombined in many ways, giving seven decision procedures. Rather surprisingly, some of the proposed checks require only one of these two operations: as a consequence, they are easier to implement than the original technique.

We first define stutter-invariant languages, and some operations on those languages in Sect. 2. The main result of Sect. 2, Theorem 1, gives several characterizations of stutter-invariant languages. In Sect. 3, we introduce automata to realize the language transformations described in Sect. 2. This gives us seven decision procedures, as captured by Theorem 2. In Sect. 4 we describe in more details the similarities between one of the proposed checks and the aforementioned construction by Holzmann and Kupferman, and we also point to some other related constructions. Finally in Sect. 5 we benchmark our implementation of these procedures.

2   The Language View

We use the following notations. Let Σ be an alphabet, and let Σ^ω denote the set of infinite words over this alphabet. Since we only consider infinite words, we will simply write *word* from now on. Given a word $w \in \Sigma^\omega$, we denote its individual letters by $w_0, w_1, w_2, \ldots$ and write $w = w_0 w_1 w_2 \ldots$ using implicit concatenation. Given some letter $\ell \in \Sigma$ and a positive integer n, we use ℓ^n as a shorthand for the concatenation $\ell\ell\ldots\ell$ of n copies of ℓ, and ℓ^ω for the concatenation of an infinite number of instances of ℓ. A *language* L over Σ is a set of words, i.e., $L \subseteq \Sigma^\omega$. Its complement language is $\overline{L} = \Sigma^\omega \setminus L$.

Definition 1 (Stutter-Invariant Language). *A language L is* stutter-invariant *iff it satisfies the following property:*

$$\forall n_0 \geq 1, \forall n_1 \geq 1, \forall n_2 \geq 1, \ldots, (w_0 w_1 w_2 \ldots \in L \iff w_0^{n_0} w_1^{n_1} w_2^{n_2} \ldots \in L)$$

In other words, in a stutter-invariant language L, duplicating any letter or removing any duplicate letter from a word of L will produce another word of L. When L is not stutter-invariant, we say that L is stutter-sensitive.

The following lemma restates the above definition for stutter-sensitive languages.

Lemma 1. *A language L is stutter-sensitive iff there exists $n_0 \geq 1, n_1 \geq 1$, $n_2 \geq 1, \ldots$ such that either*

1. *there exists a word $w_0 w_1 w_2 \ldots \in L$ such that $w_0^{n_0} w_1^{n_1} w_2^{n_2} \ldots \notin L$*
2. *or there exists a word $w_0^{n_0} w_1^{n_1} w_2^{n_2} \ldots \in L$ such that $w_0 w_1 w_2 \ldots \notin L$.*

Proposition 1. *A language L is stutter-invariant iff $\overline{L}$ is stutter-invariant.*

Proof. Assume by way of contradiction that L is stutter-invariant but $\overline{L}$ is not. Applying Lemma 1 to $\overline{L}$, there exists $n_0 \geq 1, n_1 \geq 1, \ldots$ such that either

1. there exists a word $w_0 w_1 \ldots \in \overline{L}$ such that $w_0^{n_0} w_1^{n_1} \ldots \notin \overline{L}$; but this means $w_0^{n_0} w_1^{n_1} \ldots \in L$ and because L is stutter-invariant we must have $w_0 w_1 \ldots \in L$ which contradicts the fact that this word should be in $\overline{L}$;

2. or there exists a word $w_0^{n_0} w_1^{n_1} \ldots \in \overline{L}$ such that $w_0 w_1 \ldots \notin \overline{L}$, but then $w_0 w_1 \ldots \in L$ implies that $w_0^{n_0} w_1^{n_1} \ldots$ should belong to L as well, which is also a contradiction.

The same argument can be done with L and $\overline{L}$ reversed. $\qquad\square$

Proposition 2. *If L_1 and L_2 are stutter-invariant then $L_1 \cup L_2$ and $L_1 \cap L_2$ are stutter-invariant.*

Proof. Immediate from Definition 1. $\qquad\square$

We now introduce new operations that we will combine to decide stutter-invariance.

Definition 2. *For a word* $w = w_0 w_1 w_2 \ldots$, $\mathsf{Instut}(w) = \{ w_0^{n_0} w_1^{n_1} w_2^{n_2} \ldots \mid \forall i,\, n_i \geq 1 \}$ *denotes the set of words built from w by allowing any letter of w to be duplicated (i.e., the stuttering of w can be increased).*

Conversely, $\mathsf{Destut}(w) = \{ u_0 u_1 u_2 \ldots \in \Sigma^\omega \mid$ *there exists $n_0 \geq 1, n_1 \geq 1, n_2 \geq 1, \ldots$ such that $w = u_0^{n_0} u_1^{n_1} u_2^{n_2} \ldots \}$ denotes the set of words built from w by allowing any duplicate letter to be removed (i.e., the stuttering of w can be decreased).*

We extend these two definitions to languages straightforwardly using $\mathsf{Instut}(L) = \bigcup_{w \in L} \mathsf{Instut}(w)$ *and* $\mathsf{Destut}(L) = \bigcup_{w \in L} \mathsf{Destut}(w)$.

The following lemmas are immediate from the definition:

Lemma 2. *For any two words u and v, $u \in \mathsf{Instut}(v) \iff v \in \mathsf{Destut}(u)$.*

Lemma 3. *For any language L, we have $L \subseteq \mathsf{Destut}(L) \subseteq \mathsf{Instut}(\mathsf{Destut}(L))$, $L \subseteq \mathsf{Instut}(L) \subseteq \mathsf{Destut}(\mathsf{Instut}(L))$, and $\mathsf{Instut}(\mathsf{Destut}(L)) = \mathsf{Destut}(\mathsf{Instut}(L))$.*

Lemma 4. *For any language L, we have $L \subseteq \mathsf{Instut}(L) \cap \mathsf{Destut}(L)$.*

To illustrate that Lemma 4 cannot be strengthened to $L = \mathsf{Instut}(L) \cap \mathsf{Destut}(L)$, consider the language $L = \{ a^2 b^\omega, a^4 b^\omega \}$. Then $\mathsf{Instut}(L) = \{ a^i b^\omega \mid i \geq 2 \}$, $\mathsf{Destut}(L) = \{ a^i b^\omega \mid 1 \leq i \leq 4 \}$, and $\mathsf{Instut}(L) \cap \mathsf{Destut}(L) = \{ a^i b^\omega \mid 2 \leq i \leq 4 \} \neq L$.

We now show that $L \neq \mathsf{Instut}(L) \cap \mathsf{Destut}(L)$ is only possible if L is stutter-sensitive.

Proposition 3. *L is a stutter-invariant language iff $\mathsf{Instut}(L) = L = \mathsf{Destut}(L)$.*

Proof. ($\Longrightarrow$) If L is stutter-invariant, the words added to L by $\mathsf{Instut}(L)$ or $\mathsf{Destut}(L)$ are already in L by definition. ($\Longleftarrow$) If $L = \mathsf{Instut}(L)$ and $L = \mathsf{Destut}(L)$ there is no way to find a counterexample word for Lemma 1. $\qquad\square$

Note that $\mathsf{Instut}(L) = \mathsf{Destut}(L)$ is not a sufficient condition for L to be stutter-invariant. For instance consider the stutter-sensitive language $L = \{a^i b^\omega \mid i$ is odd$\}$ for which $\mathsf{Instut}(L) = \mathsf{Destut}(L) = \{a^i b^\omega \mid i > 0\}$.

Proposition 4. *If a language L is stutter-sensitive, then either $\mathsf{Instut}(L) \cap \overline{L} \neq \emptyset$ or $\mathsf{Destut}(L) \cap \overline{L} \neq \emptyset$.*

Proof. Applying Lemma 1 to L, there exists $n_0 \geq 1, n_1 \geq 1, \ldots$ such that either

1. there exists a word $w_0 w_1 \ldots \in L$ such that $w_0^{n_0} w_1^{n_1} \ldots \notin L$, which implies that $\mathsf{Instut}(L) \cap \overline{L} \neq \emptyset$;
2. or there exists a word $w_0^{n_0} w_1^{n_1} \ldots \in L$ such that $w_0 w_1 \ldots \notin L$, which implies that $\mathsf{Destut}(L) \cap \overline{L} \neq \emptyset$.

So one of $\mathsf{Instut}(L)$ or $\mathsf{Destut}(L)$ has to intersect $\overline{L}$. $\qquad\square$

Proposition 5. *If a language L is stutter-sensitive, then $\mathsf{Instut}(L) \cap \mathsf{Instut}(\overline{L}) \neq \emptyset$.*

Proof. By Proposition 4, since L is stutter-sensitive we have either $\mathsf{Instut}(L) \cap \overline{L} \neq \emptyset$ or $\mathsf{Destut}(L) \cap \overline{L} \neq \emptyset$.

- If $\mathsf{Instut}(L) \cap \overline{L} \neq \emptyset$, then there exists a word $u \in \overline{L}$, and a word $v \in L$ such that $u \in \mathsf{Instut}(v)$. Since $u \in \overline{L}$ we have $u \in \mathsf{Instut}(\overline{L})$; however we also have $u \in \mathsf{Instut}(v) \subseteq \mathsf{Instut}(L)$. So $u \in \mathsf{Instut}(\overline{L}) \cap \mathsf{Instut}(L)$.
- If $\mathsf{Destut}(L) \cap \overline{L} \neq \emptyset$, then there exists a word $u \in \overline{L}$ and a word v in L such that $u \in \mathsf{Destut}(v)$. By Lemma 2, we have $v \in \mathsf{Instut}(u)$. Therefore we have $v \in \mathsf{Instut}(u) \subseteq \mathsf{Instut}(\overline{L})$ and $v \in L \subseteq \mathsf{Instut}(L)$, so $v \in \mathsf{Instut}(\overline{L}) \cap \mathsf{Instut}(L)$.

In both cases $\mathsf{Instut}(\overline{L}) \cap \mathsf{Instut}(L)$ is non-empty. $\qquad\square$

Proposition 6. *If a language L is stutter-sensitive, then $\mathsf{Destut}(L) \cap \mathsf{Destut}(\overline{L}) \neq \emptyset$.*

Proof. Similar to that of Proposition 5. $\qquad\square$

Theorem 1. *For any language L, the following statements are equivalent.*

(1) L is stutter-invariant
(2) $L = \mathsf{Instut}(L) = \mathsf{Destut}(L)$
(3) $\mathsf{Destut}(\mathsf{Instut}(L)) \cap \overline{L} = \emptyset$
(4) $\mathsf{Instut}(\mathsf{Destut}(L)) \cap \overline{L} = \emptyset$
(5) $\mathsf{Instut}(L) \cap \mathsf{Instut}(\overline{L}) = \emptyset$
(6) $\mathsf{Destut}(L) \cap \mathsf{Destut}(\overline{L}) = \emptyset$.

Proof. (1) $\Longleftrightarrow$ (2) is Proposition 3; (2) $\Longrightarrow$ (3) $\wedge$ (4) is immediate; (2) $\Longrightarrow$ (5) $\wedge$ (6) follows from Proposition 1 which means that the hypothesis (2) can be applied to $\overline{L}$ as well; (3) $\Longrightarrow$ (1) and (4) $\Longrightarrow$ (1) both follow from the contraposition of Proposition 4 and from Lemma 3; (5) $\Longrightarrow$ (1) and (6) $\Longrightarrow$ (1) are Propositions 5 and 6. $\qquad\square$

The most interesting part of this theorem is the last two statements: it is possible to check the stutter-invariance of a language using only Instut or only Destut. In the next section we show different implementations of these operations on automata.

3   The Automaton View

Specifications written in linear-time temporal logics like LTL or (the linear fragment of) PSL are typically converted into Büchi automata by model checkers (or specialized translators). Below we define the variant of Büchi automata we use in our tool: *Transition-based Generalized Büchi Automata* or TGBA for short.

The TGBA acronym was coined by [16], although similar automata have been used with different names before (e.g., [7,14,22]). As their name implies, these TGBAs have a generalized Büchi acceptance condition expressed in terms of transitions (instead of states). While these automata have the same expressiveness as Büchi automata (i.e., they can represent all ω-regular languages), they can be more compact; furthermore they are the natural product of many LTL-to-automata translation algorithms [2,7,11,14,16].

The transformations we define on these automata should however not be difficult to adapt to other kinds of ω-automata.

Definition 3 (TGBA [16]**).** *A Transition-based Generalized Büchi Automaton (TGBA) is a tuple $A = \langle \Sigma, Q, q_0, \mathcal{F}, \delta \rangle$ where:*

- *Σ is a finite alphabet,*
- *Q is a finite set of states,*
- *$q_0 \in Q$ is the initial state,*
- *$\delta \subseteq Q \times \Sigma \times Q$ is a transition relation labeling each transition by a letter,*
- *$\mathcal{F} = \{F_1, F_2, \ldots, F_n\}$ is a set of acceptance sets of transitions: $F_i \subseteq \delta$.*

A sequence of transitions $\rho = (s_0, w_0, d_0)(s_1, w_1, d_1) \ldots \in \delta^\omega$ is a run of A if $s_0 = q_0$ and for all $i \geq 0$ we have $d_i = s_{i+1}$. We say that ρ recognizes the word $w = w_0 w_1 \ldots \in \Sigma^\omega$.

For a run ρ, let $\mathsf{Inf}(\rho) \subseteq \delta$ denote the set of transitions occurring infinitely often in this run. The run is accepting iff $F_i \cap \mathsf{Inf}(\rho) \neq \emptyset$ for all i, i.e., if ρ visits all acceptance sets infinitely often.

Finally the language of A, denoted $\mathscr{L}(A)$, is the set of words recognized by the accepting runs of A.

Figure 1 shows some examples of TGBAs that illustrate the upcoming definitions. The membership of transitions to some acceptance sets is represented by numbered and colored circles. For instance, automaton A_1 in Fig. 1(a) has two acceptance sets F_1 and F_2 that respectively contain the transitions marked with ❶ and ❷. This automaton accepts the word $(abba)^\omega$ but rejects $(aba)^\omega$, so its language is stutter-sensitive.

We now propose some automata-based implementations of the operations from Definition 2. The next three constructions we define in the rest of this section, cl (Definition 4), sl (Definition 5), and sl_2 (Definition 6), implement respectively Destut, Instut, and again Instut.

Definition 4 (Closure). *Given a TGBA $A = \langle \Sigma, Q, q_0, \{F_1, F_2, \ldots, F_n\}, \delta \rangle$, let $\mathsf{cl}(A) = \langle \Sigma, Q, q_0, \{F'_1, F'_2, \ldots, F'_n\}, \delta' \rangle$ be the closure of A defined as follows:*

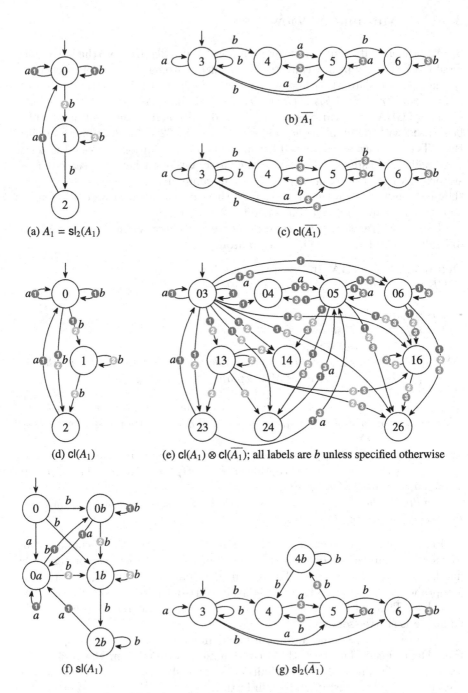

Fig. 1. An example TGBA A_1, with its closure, self-loopization, complement, closed complement, and the product between the two closures. $\mathcal{L}(A_1)$ is stutter-sensitive.

- δ' is the smallest subset of $Q \times \Sigma \times Q$ such that
  - $\delta \subseteq \delta'$,
  - if $(x, \ell, y) \in \delta'$ and $(y, \ell, z) \in \delta'$, then $(x, \ell, z) \in \delta'$.
- each F_i' is the smallest subset of δ' such that
  - $F_i \subseteq F_i'$,
  - if $(x, \ell, y) \in \delta'$, $(y, \ell, z) \in \delta'$, and either $(x, \ell, y) \in F_i$ or $(y, \ell, z) \in F_i$ then $(x, \ell, z) \in F_i'$.

Figure 1(d) illustrates this construction which can be implemented by modifying the automaton in place: for every pair of transitions of the form $\text{(x)} \xrightarrow{\ell}_1 \text{(y)} \xrightarrow{\ell}_2 \text{(z)}$, add a *shortcut* transition $\text{(x)} \xrightarrow{\ell}_{\textbf{①-②}} \text{(z)}$ that allows to skip one of the duplicated letters on a run without affecting the acceptance of this run. When the transition $\text{(x)} \xrightarrow{\ell} \text{(z)}$ already exists, we just need to update its membership to acceptance sets. So in effect, these changes let the automaton accept all shorter words that can be constructed from an accepted words by removing a duplicate letter.

In the worst case (e.g., the states of A form a ring with transitions of the form $(x, \ell, x + 1 \mod n)$ for all letters ℓ), $\mathsf{cl}(A)$ ends up with $|Q^2| \times |\Sigma|$ transitions.

Definition 5 (Self-Loopization). *Given a TGBA $A = \langle \Sigma, Q, q_0, \{F_1, F_2, \ldots, F_n\}, \delta \rangle$, let $\mathsf{sl}(A) = \langle \Sigma, Q', q_0, \{F_1', F_2', \ldots, F_n'\}, \delta' \rangle$ be the "self-loopization" of A defined by:*

- $Q' = (Q \times \Sigma) \cup \{q_0\}$,
- $\delta' = \{((x, \ell_1), \ell_2, (y, \ell_2)) \mid \ell_1 \in \Sigma, (x, \ell_2, y) \in \delta\}$
  $\cup \{((y, \ell), \ell, (y, \ell)) \mid (x, \ell, y) \in \delta\} \cup \{(q_0, \ell, (y, \ell)) \mid (x, \ell, y) \in \delta, x = q_0\}$,
- $F_i' = \{((x, \ell_1), \ell_2, (y, \ell_2)) \in \delta' \mid (x, \ell_2, y) \in F_i\}$.

Figure 1(f) illustrates this construction. For each transition, letters are "pushed" in the identifier of the destination state, ensuring that all transitions entering this state have the same letter, and then a self-loop with this letter is added if it was not already present on the original state. Note that the only self-loop that belong to acceptance sets are those that already existed in the original automaton: this ensures that the stuttering we introduce can only duplicate letters a finite amount of times.

With this construction, a state is duplicated as many times as its number of different incoming letters. In the worst case the automaton size is therefore multiplied by $|\Sigma|$.

The following definition gives another automata-transformation that implements Instut, but in such a way that is it easy to modify the automaton in place.

Definition 6 (Second Self-Loopization). *For a TGBA $A = \langle \Sigma, Q, q_0, \{F_1, F_2, \ldots, F_n\}, \delta \rangle$, let $\mathsf{sl}_2(A) = \langle \Sigma, Q', q_0, \{F_1', F_2', \ldots, F_n'\}, \delta' \rangle$ be another "self-loopization" of A with:*

Table 1. Characteristics of automata constructed from $A = \langle \Sigma, Q, q_0, \mathcal{F}, \delta \rangle$.

	Reachable states	Transitions	Language
cl(A)	$|Q|$	$O(|Q|^2 \times |\Sigma|)$	Destut($\mathcal{L}(A)$)
sl(A)	$O(|Q| \times |\Sigma|)$	$O(|\delta| \times |\Sigma|)$	Instut($\mathcal{L}(A)$)
sl$_2$(A)	$O(|Q| + \min(|Q| \times |\Sigma|, |\delta|))$	$\Theta(|\delta|)$	Instut($\mathcal{L}(A)$)

- $Q' = Q \cup (Q \times \Sigma)$,
- $\delta' = \delta \cup \displaystyle\bigcup_{\substack{(x,\ell,y)\in\delta \\ (x,\ell,x)\notin\delta \wedge (y,\ell,y)\notin\delta}} \{(x, \ell, (y, \ell)), ((y, \ell), \ell, (y, \ell)), ((y, \ell), \ell, y)\}$,
- $F_i' = F_i \cup \{(x, \ell, (y, \ell)) \in \delta' \mid (x, \ell, y) \in F_i\}$.

Figure 1(g) illustrates this construction. For each transition $(x) \xrightarrow{\ell} (y)$ such that x and y have no self-loop over ℓ, we add $(x) \xrightarrow{\ell} (y\ell) \xrightarrow{\ell} (y)$ with a self-loop ℓ, therefore allowing ℓ to appear twice or more. Note again that the added self-loop does not belong to any accepting set, so that ℓ can only be stuttered a finite amount of times.

The number of transitions of sl$_2$(A) is at most 4 times the number of transitions in A. The number of states of the form (y, ℓ) that are added is obviously bounded by $|Q| \times |\Sigma|$ but also by $|\delta|$ since we may add at most one state per original transition. This implies sl$_2$(A) has $O(|Q| + \min(|Q| \times |\Sigma|, |\delta|))$ reachable states. In automata with a lot of self-loops (which is frequent when they represent LTL formulas), it can happen that very few additions are necessary: for instance automaton A_1 from Fig. 1(a) requires no modification, while automaton $\overline{A_1}$ (Fig. 1(b) and (g)) requires only one extra state.

Table 1 summarizes the characteristics of these three constructions, that satisfy the following proposition:

Proposition 7. *For any TGBA A we have $\mathcal{L}(\text{cl}(A)) = \text{Destut}(\mathcal{L}(A))$ and $\mathcal{L}(\text{sl}(A)) = \mathcal{L}(\text{sl}_2(A)) = \text{Instut}(\mathcal{L}(A))$.*

To fully implement cases (3)–(6) of Theorem 1 we now just need to discuss the product and emptiness check of TGBAs, which are well known operations.

The product of two TGBAs is a straightforward synchronized product in which acceptance sets from both sides have to be preserved, therefore ensuring that a word in the product is accepted if and only if it was accepted by each of the operands.

Definition 7 (Product of Two TGBAs). *Let A and B be two TGBAs on the same alphabet: $A = \langle \Sigma, Q^A, q_0^A, \{F_1, F_2, \ldots, F_n\}, \delta^A \rangle$ and $B = \langle \Sigma, Q^B, q_0^B, \{G_1, G_2, \ldots, G_m\}, \delta^B \rangle$. The product of A and B, denoted $A \otimes B$, is the TGBA $\langle \Sigma, Q, \mathcal{F}, q_0, \delta \rangle$ where:*

- $Q = Q^A \times Q^B$,
- $q_0 = (q_0^A, q_0^B)$,

- $\delta = \{((x_1, x_2), \ell_1, (y_1, y_2)) \mid (x_1, \ell_1, y_1) \in \delta^A, (x_2, \ell_2, y_2) \in \delta^B, \ell_1 = \ell_2\}$,
- $\mathcal{F} = \{F'_1, F'_2, \ldots, F'_n, G'_1, G'_2, \ldots, G'_m\}$ where $F'_i = \{(x_1, x_2), \ell, (y_1, y_2) \in \delta \mid (x_1, \ell, y_1) \in F_i\}$ and $G'_i = \{(x_1, x_2), \ell, (y_1, y_2) \in \delta' \mid (x_2, \ell, y_2) \in G_i\}$.

Proposition 8. *If A and B are two TGBAs, then $\mathscr{L}(A \otimes B) = \mathscr{L}(A) \cap \mathscr{L}(B)$.*

Figure 1(e) shows an example of product.

Deciding whether a TGBA has an empty language can be done in linear time with respect to the size of the TGBA [7, 26, 28]. One way is to search for a strongly connected component that is reachable from the initial state, and whose transitions intersects all acceptance sets. The reader can verify that the product automaton from Fig. 1(e) has a non-empty language (for instance the word $a(ba)^\omega$ is accepted thanks to the cycle around ⑤ and ㉔).

We can now state our main result:

Theorem 2. *Let φ be a property expressed as a TGBA A, and assume we know how to obtain $\overline{A}$. Testing φ for stutter-invariance is equivalent to testing the emptiness of any of the following products:*

- $\mathsf{cl}(\mathsf{sl}(A)) \otimes \overline{A}$,
- $\mathsf{sl}(\mathsf{cl}(A)) \otimes \overline{A}$,
- $\mathsf{cl}(\mathsf{sl}_2(A)) \otimes \overline{A}$,
- $\mathsf{sl}_2(\mathsf{cl}(A)) \otimes \overline{A}$,
- $\mathsf{sl}(A) \otimes \mathsf{sl}(\overline{A})$,
- $\mathsf{sl}_2(A) \otimes \mathsf{sl}_2(\overline{A})$,
- $\mathsf{cl}(A) \otimes \mathsf{cl}(\overline{A})$.

Proof. Consequence of Theorem 1 (3)–(6), and Propositions 7 and 8.   □

In a typical scenario, φ is a property specified as LTL or PSL, and from that we can obtain A_φ and its negation $A_{\neg\varphi}$ by just translating φ and $\neg\varphi$ using existing algorithms.

4   Comparison with Other Automata-Based Approaches

As mentioned in the introduction, an automata-based construction described by Holzmann and Kupferman [19] was used by Klein and Baier [20] to implement a stutter-invariance check in ltl2dstar. Since our constructions have been heavily inspired by this construction, it makes sense that we discuss the similarities and differences.

Holzmann and Kupferman's construction starts from a Büchi automaton (i.e., with state-based acceptance) such as A_2 in Fig. 2(a). This automaton is first converted into a Büchi automaton with labels on states and multiple initial states, such as the automaton B_2 pictured in Fig. 2(b). From B_2, they produce the stuttering over-approximation B'_2 in Fig. 2(c). This last step essentially consists in making two copies of the automaton: one non-accepting (the left part

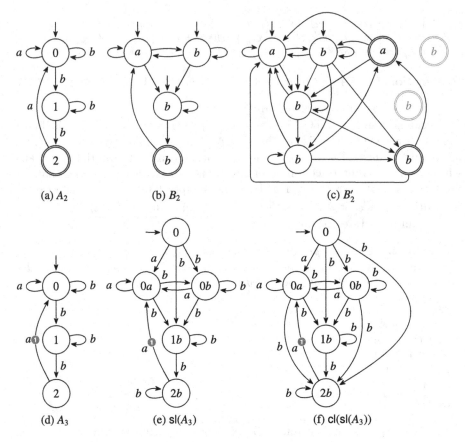

(a) A_2 (b) B_2 (c) B'_2

(d) A_3 (e) $\mathsf{sl}(A_3)$ (f) $\mathsf{cl}(\mathsf{sl}(A_3))$

Fig. 2. Illustration of the similarities between the Holzmann and Kupferman's construction (top row), and the composition of what we defined as cl and sl (bottom row).

of B'_2), and one non-accepting (the right part of B'_2, in which we grayed out some states that are not reachable in this example and need not be constructed). The non-accepting part has self-loops on all its states, and is also closed in such a way that if there exists a path of states labeled by $\ell_1 \ell_1 \ldots \ell_1 \ell_2$, there should exist a transition between the first and the last state. Additionally if this path visits an accepting state in the original automaton, there should be a transition to the accepting copy of the last state.

Now we can compare the transformation of A_2 into B'_2 and the transformation of the equivalent[2] TGBA A_3 into $\mathsf{cl}(\mathsf{sl}(A_3))$ presented at the bottom of Fig. 2. The transformation of A_2 into B_2 combined with the addition of self-loops later in B'_2 corresponds to the transformation of A_3 into $\mathsf{sl}(A_3)$. The only difference

---

[2] A_1, A_2, and A_3 are equivalent automata. The only reason we used two acceptance sets in A_1 was to demonstrate how cl deals with multiple acceptance sets.

is that we keep a single initial state. Then, the closure of B_2' corresponds to our cl operation, with two differences:

- First, using transition-based acceptance we do not have to duplicate states to keep track of paths that visit accepting states. The gain is not very important, since B_2' can have at most twice the number of states of B_2. However one should keep in mind that the duplication of states between B_2 and B_2' increases the non-determinism of the automaton, and this will be detrimental to any later product.
- Second, there is not an exact correspondence between the shortcuts added in B_2' and those added by cl due to subtle semantic differences between automata with transition-labels and automata with state-labels. For instance in Fig. 2(f), there is a transition $(0a) \xrightarrow{b} (2b)$ that is a shortcut for $(0a) \xrightarrow{b} (1b) \xrightarrow{b} (2b)$ but that has no counterpart in Fig. 2(c) because $(a) \longrightarrow (b) \longrightarrow (b)$ is not labeled by a word of the form $\ell_1\ell_1 \ldots \ell_1\ell_2$.

To conclude this informal comparison, $\mathsf{cl}(\mathsf{sl}(A))$ can be considered as an adaptation of the Holzmann and Kupferman [19] construction to TGBA. Our contribution is the rest of Theorem 2: the fact that a different implementation of sl is possible (namely, sl_2), and the fact that we can implement a stutter-invariance check using only one of the operators cl, sl, or sl_2. Furthermore, our experiments in the next section will show that running $\mathsf{sl}(\mathsf{cl}(A))$ is more efficient than $\mathsf{cl}(\mathsf{sl}(A))$ (because the intermediate automaton is smaller).

The variant of Holzmann and Kupferman's construction implemented in ltl2dstar 0.6 actually only checks stutter invariance one letter at a time. The problem addressed is therefore slightly different [20]: they want to know whether a language is invariant by repeating any occurrence of a given letter ℓ, or removing any duplicate occurrence of ℓ. In effect the automaton is cloned three times: the main copy is the original Büchi automaton, and every time a transition is labeled by ℓ, the automaton makes non-deterministic jumps into the two other copies that behaves as in Holzmann and Kupferman's construction.

Similar stuttering-checks for a single letter ℓ can be derived from any of the procedures we proposed. It suffices to modify cl, sl, or sl_2 so that they add only self-loop or shortcuts for ℓ.

Peled et al. [25, Thoerem 16] also presented an automaton-based check similar to $\mathsf{cl}(\mathsf{sl}(A))$, although in a framework that is less convenient from a developer's point of view: the transformation of an automaton into its stutter-invariant over-approximation is achieved via multi-tape Büchi automata.

Finally, there is also a related construction proposed by Etessami [12, Lemma 1] that provides a normal form for automata representing stutter-invariant properties. The construction could be implemented using $\mathsf{cl}(\mathsf{sl}(A))$ (or Holzmann and Kupferman's construction) as a base, but the result is then fixed to ensure that one cannot arrive and depart from a state using the same letter. The latter fix (which is similar to some reduction performed while constructing *testing automata* [15, 17]) is only valid if the property is known to be stutter invariant: when applied to a non-stutter invariant property, the resulting automaton is not an over-approximation of the original one, so building a stutter-invariance check on that procedure would require a complete equivalence check instead of an inclusion check.

5   Evaluation

We evaluate the procedures of Theorem 2 in the context of deciding the stutter invariance of LTL formulas. LTL formulas are defined over a set AP of Boolean propositions (called *Atomic Propositions*), and the TGBAs that encode these formulas are labeled by valuations of all these propositions. In this context we therefore have $\Sigma = 2^{AP}$.

Our motivation is very practical. Since version 1.0, Spot distributes a tool called ltlfilt with an option --stutter-invariant to extract stutter-invariant formulas from a list of LTL formulas [10]. Our original implementation was based on Etessami's rewriting function τ' [13]: if an LTL formula φ uses the X operator, we compute $\tau'(\varphi)$ and test the equivalence between φ and $\tau'(\varphi)$ by converting these formulas and their negations into TGBA and testing $\mathscr{L}(A_{\tau'(\varphi)} \otimes A_{\neg\varphi}) = \emptyset \wedge \mathscr{L}(A_{\neg\tau'(\varphi)} \otimes A_\varphi) = \emptyset$. However this equivalence[3] test proved to be quite slow due to the translation of $\tau'(\varphi)$ and its negation, which are often very large formulas.

Furthermore Spot also supports PSL formulas for which we would also like to decide stutter invariance. The checks based on automata transformations discussed in this paper therefore solve our two problems: they are faster, and they are independent on the logic used.

In this section we show to which extent ltlfilt --stutter-invariant was improved by the use of automata-based checks, and compare the various checks suggested in Theorem 2 to reveal which one we decided to use by default.

It should be noted that those benchmarks are completely implemented in Spot (See Appendix A for tool support), in which transition-based generalized Büchi acceptance is the norm, so we did not implement any technique for automata with state-based acceptance. We also know of no other publicly available tool that would offer a similar service, and to which we could compare our results.[4]

We opted to implement cl, sl, sl$_2$, and $\otimes$ as separate functions that take automata and produce new automata, the best as we could, using the TGBA data structure in the current development version of Spot. In the cases of cl and sl$_2$ our implementation modifies the input automaton in place to save time. We use Couvreur's algorithm [7] for emptiness check.

---

[3] Unlike automata-based constructions such as cl(sl(A)), the formula $\tau'(\varphi)$ is not necessarily an over-approximation of φ, so the equivalence check between φ and $\tau'(\varphi)$ cannot be replaced by a simple inclusion check.

[4] The only actual implementation of a construction similar to the one of Holzmann and Kupferman [19] that we know about is in ltl2dstar[20], but it decides only stutter-invariance for one letter at a time, is used to improve Safra's construction, and is not directly accessible to the user.

Table 2. Time to classify 500 random LTL formulas that all use the X operator and have the given number of atomic propositions.

	$|AP| = 1$	$|AP| = 2$	$|AP| = 3$
$\mathcal{L}(A_{\tau'(\varphi)} \otimes A_{\neg\varphi}) = \emptyset \wedge \mathcal{L}(A_{\neg\tau'(\varphi)} \otimes A_{\varphi}) = \emptyset$	0.32 s	40.62 s	>4801 s (OOM)
$\mathcal{L}(A_{\neg(\varphi \leftrightarrow \tau'(\varphi))}) = \emptyset$	1.18 s	3347.92 s	
$\mathcal{L}(\mathsf{cl}(\mathsf{sl}(A_{\varphi})) \otimes A_{\neg\varphi}) = \emptyset$	0.61 s	1.91 s	6.14 s
$\mathcal{L}(\mathsf{sl}(\mathsf{cl}(A_{\varphi})) \otimes A_{\neg\varphi}) = \emptyset$	0.61 s	1.91 s	6.10 s
$\mathcal{L}(\mathsf{cl}(\mathsf{sl}_2(A_{\varphi})) \otimes A_{\neg\varphi}) = \emptyset$	0.61 s	1.89 s	5.97 s
$\mathcal{L}(\mathsf{sl}_2(\mathsf{cl}(A_{\varphi})) \otimes A_{\neg\varphi}) = \emptyset$	0.61 s	1.91 s	5.97 s
$\mathcal{L}(\mathsf{sl}(A_{\varphi}) \otimes \mathsf{sl}(A_{\neg\varphi})) = \emptyset$	0.61 s	1.92 s	6.18 s
$\mathcal{L}(\mathsf{sl}_2(A_{\varphi}) \otimes \mathsf{sl}_2(A_{\neg\varphi})) = \emptyset$	0.61 s	1.90 s	5.99 s
$\mathcal{L}(\mathsf{cl}(A_{\varphi}) \otimes \mathsf{cl}(A_{\neg\varphi})) = \emptyset$	0.60 s	1.89 s	5.94 s
Number of stutter-invariant formulas found	234	162	112

Our first experiment is to compare the speed of the proposed automata-based checks to the speed achieved in our previous implementation. For Table 2 we prepared three files of 500 random formulas with a different number of atomic propositions, all using the X operator (otherwise they would be trivially stutter-invariant, and there is no point in running our algorithms), then we used our ltlfilt tool [10] with option --stutter-invariant to print only the stutter-invariant formulas of this list. The reported time is the user's experience, i.e., it accounts for the complete run of ltlfilt (including parsing of input formulas, stutter-invariance check, and output of stutter-invariant formulas) and differs only by the stutter-invariance check performed. As the first line of this table demonstrates, testing the equivalence of φ and $\tau'(\varphi)$ as we used to quickly becomes impractical: the experiment with $|AP| = 3$ aborted after 80 min with an out-of-memory error.[5]

It was recently pointed to us that Etessami [13] does not suggest to test the equivalence of φ and $\tau'(\varphi)$, but to test whether $\varphi \leftrightarrow \tau'(\varphi)$ is a tautology, i.e., whether $\neg(\varphi \leftrightarrow \tau'(\varphi))$ is satisfiable. This alternative approach is not practical in our implementation. The second line of Table 2 shows the cost of translating $\neg(\varphi \leftrightarrow \tau'(\varphi))$ into a TGBA and testing its emptiness[6]: the run-time is actually worse because in order to be translated into an automaton, the formula $\neg(\varphi \leftrightarrow \tau'(\varphi))$ has first to be put into negative normal form (i.e., rewriting the

---

[5] Measurements were done on a dedicated Intel Xeon E5-2620 2 GHz, running Debian GNU/Linux, with the memory limited to 32 GB (out of the 64 GB installed).

[6] A better implementation of this check would be to construct the automaton for $\varphi \leftrightarrow \tau'(\varphi)$ on-the-fly during its emptiness check, as done in dedicated satifiability checkers [27]. Alas, the implementation of our algorithm for translating LTL/PSL formulas into TGBA is not implemented in a way that would allow an on-the-fly construction. So this experiment should not be read as a dismissal of the idea of testing whether $\mathcal{L}(A_{\neg(\varphi \leftrightarrow \tau'(\varphi))}) = \emptyset$ but simply as a justification of why we used $\mathcal{L}(A_{\tau'(\varphi)} \otimes A_{\neg\varphi}) = \emptyset \wedge \mathcal{L}(A_{\neg\tau'(\varphi)} \otimes A_{\varphi}) = \emptyset$ in our former implementation.

Table 3. Cross-comparison of the checks of Theorem 2 on 40000 random LTL formulas with X. A value v on line (x) and column (y) indicates that there are v cases where check (x) was more than 10% slower than check (y). In other words, a line with many small numbers indicates a check that is usually faster than the others.

		(1)	(2)	(3)	(4)	(5)	(6)	(7)	Run time Total	Median
$\mathscr{L}(\mathsf{cl}(\mathsf{sl}(A_\varphi)) \otimes A_{\neg\varphi}) = \emptyset$	(1)		24615	38158	38593	1999	35200	39660	45.8 s	162 µs
$\mathscr{L}(\mathsf{sl}(\mathsf{cl}(A_\varphi)) \otimes A_{\neg\varphi}) = \emptyset$	(2)	244		38343	38832	91	34965	39813	34.9 s	135 µs
$\mathscr{L}(\mathsf{cl}(\mathsf{sl}_2(A_\varphi)) \otimes A_{\neg\varphi}) = \emptyset$	(3)	536	419		7413	67	10297	29495	11.0 s	57 µs
$\mathscr{L}(\mathsf{sl}_2(\mathsf{cl}(A_\varphi)) \otimes A_{\neg\varphi}) = \emptyset$	(4)	264	163	671		30	10223	28880	10.2 s	55 µs
$\mathscr{L}(\mathsf{sl}(A_\varphi) \otimes \mathsf{sl}(A_{\neg\varphi})) = \emptyset$	(5)	33410	39112	39746	39909		38403	39977	59.4 s	208 µs
$\mathscr{L}(\mathsf{sl}_2(A_\varphi) \otimes \mathsf{sl}_2(A_{\neg\varphi})) = \emptyset$	(6)	2689	2564	16896	18621	580		26693	11.7 s	64 µs
$\mathscr{L}(\mathsf{cl}(A_\varphi) \otimes \mathsf{cl}(A_{\neg\varphi})) = \emptyset$	(7)	16	13	3487	2993	11	2409		7.3 s	39 µs

$\leftrightarrow$ operator and pushing negation operators down to the atomic propositions), which means the the resulting formula has a size that is the sum of the sizes of each of the formulas φ, $\neg\varphi$, $\tau'(\varphi)$, and $\neg\tau'(\varphi)$ used in the first line.

On the other hand, all the tests from Theorem 2 show comparable run times in Table 2: this is because most of the time is spent in the creation of A_φ and $A_{\neg\varphi}$, and the application of cl, sl, and sl_2 only incurs a minor overhead.

We then conducted another evaluation, focused only on the checks from Theorem 2. In this evaluation, that involves 40000 unique LTL formulas (10000 formulas for each $|AP| \in \{1, 2, 3, 4\}$) using the X operator, we first translated A_φ and $A_{\neg\varphi}$, and then measured only the time spent by each of the checks (i.e., the run time of cl, sl, $\mathsf{sl2}$, the product, and the emptiness check). The resulting measurements allow to compare the 7 checks on each of the 40000 formulas, as summarized by Table 3.

The benchmark data, as well as instructions to reproduce them can be found at http://www.lrde.epita.fr/~adl/spin15/. In addition to source code, this page contains CSV files with complete measurements, and a 16-page document with more analysis than we could do here.

Based on this evaluation, we decided to use $\mathscr{L}(\mathsf{cl}(A) \otimes \mathsf{cl}(A_{\neg\varphi})) = \emptyset$, the last line in the table, as our default stutter-invariance check in ltlfilt. The operation cl seems to be more efficient than the other two because it can be performed in place without adding new states. The table also suggests that checks that involve the sl operation (i.e., the one that duplicates each state for each different incoming letter) should be avoided. sl_2 seems to be a better replacement for sl as it can be implemented in place.

Different implementations of these checks could be imagined. For instance the composed constructions like $\mathsf{sl}_2(\mathsf{cl}(A))$ or $\mathsf{cl}(\mathsf{sl}_2(A))$ could be done in such a way that the outer operator is only considering the transitions and states that were already present in A. The product and emptiness check used for $\mathsf{cl}(A) \times \mathsf{cl}(\overline{A})$ could be avoided when it is detected that neither A nor $\overline{A}$ have been altered by cl (likewise with sl_2). Also the sl and sl_2 constructions, as well at the product, could be all computed on-the-fly as needed by the emptiness check, so that only the parts of $\mathsf{sl}(A)$ and $\mathsf{sl}(\overline{A})$ that is actually needed to prove the product empty (or not) is constructed.

6   Conclusion

We have presented seven decision procedures that can be used to check whether a property (for which we know an automaton and its complement) is stutter-invariant. A typical use case is to decide whether an LTL or PSL property is stutter-invariant, and we provide tools that implement these checks. The first variant of these procedures is essentially an adaptation of a construction by Holzmann and Kupferman [19] to the context of transition-based acceptance. But we have shown that this construction can actually be broken down into two operators: cl to allow longer words and sl to allow shorter words, that can accept different realizations (e.g., sl_2), and that can be combined in different ways.

In particular, we have shown that it is possible to implement a stutter-invariance check by implementing only *one* operation among cl, sl, or sl_2. This idea is new, and it makes any implementation easier. The implementation we decided to use in our tool because it had the best performance in our benchmark uses only the cl operation.

The definition of cl, sl and sl_2 we gave trivially adapt to ω-automata with any kind of transition-based acceptance, such as those that can be expressed in the Hanoi Omega Automata format babiak.15.cav, and that our implementation fully supports. Indeed, those three operations preserve the acceptance sets seen infinitely (and finitely) often along runs that are equivalent up to stuttering, so it is not be a problem if those acceptance sets are used by pairs in a Rabin or Streett acceptance condition, for instance. The acceptance condition used is relevant only to the emptiness check used.

To implement a check in a framework using state-based acceptance, we recommend using the $\mathsf{sl}_2(A) \otimes \mathsf{sl}_2(\overline{A})$ check, because the definition of $\mathsf{sl}_2(A)$ is trivial to adapt to state-based acceptance: the acceptance sets simply do not have to be changed. As we saw in Sect. 4, the operations cl and sl are less convenient to implement using state-based acceptance since one needs to add additional states to keep track of the accepting sets visited by some path fragments. Furthermore, $\mathsf{sl}_2(A)$ has the advantage that it can be implemented by modifying A in place.

Acknowledgments. The authors are indebted to Joachim Klein and Akim Demaille for some influencing comments on the first drafts of this article, and to Etienne Renault, Souheib Baarir and the anonymous reviewers of ICALP'15 and SPIN'15 from some valuable feedback on earlier versions.

A   Tool Support

All the checks described in this article are implemented in Spot 1.99.1 which can be obtained from https://spot.lrde.epita.fr/.

Stutter-invariance of LTL or PSL formulas can be tested on-line without installing anything:

1. Load https://spot.lrde.epita.fr/trans.html.
2. Type an LTL or PSL formula.
3. Select "Desired Output: Formula" and then "property information".
4. Scan the resulting properties for "syntactic stutter invariant" (this means the formula belongs to LTL\Xor siPSL), "stutter invariant" or "stutter sensitive". In the latter two cases, the automata-based check had to be performed.

If Spot is installed, the tool `ltlfilt` can be used from the command-line to make the same decision. For instance `ltlfilt -f '$\varphi$' --stutter-invariant` will print φ back iff φ is stutter-invariant.

Similarly the tool `autfilt` can be used to apply the operations cl, sl, and sl$_2$ to any automaton (with any acceptance condition). The corresponding options are `--destut`, `--instut`, and `--instut=2` respectively.

References

1. Property specification language reference manual v1.1. Accellera (2004). http://www.eda.org/vfv/
2. Babiak, T., Křetínský, M., Řehák, V., Strejček, J.: LTL to Büchi automata translation: fast and more deterministic. In: Flanagan, C., König, B. (eds.) TACAS 2012. LNCS, vol. 7214, pp. 95–109. Springer, Heidelberg (2012)
3. Babiak, T., Blahoudek, F., Duret-Lutz, A., Klein, J., Křetínský, J., Müller, D., Parker, D., Strejček, J.: The Hanoi omega-automata format. In: Kroening, D., Păsăreanu, C.S. (eds.) CAV 2015. LNCS, vol. 9206, pp. 479–486. Springer, Heidelberg (2015)
4. Baier, C., Katoen, J.-P.: Principles of Model Checking. The MIT Press, Cambridge (2008)
5. Barnat, J., Brim, L., Ročkai, P.: Parallel partial order reduction with topological sort proviso. In: SEFM 2010, pp. 222–231. IEEE Computer Society Press (2010)
6. Clarke, E.M., Grumberg, O., Peled, D.A.: Model Checking. The MIT Press, Cambridge (2000)
7. Couvreur, J.-M.: On-the-fly verification of linear temporal logic. In: Wing, J.M., Woodcock, J. (eds.) FM 1999. LNCS, vol. 1708, pp. 253–271. Springer, Heidelberg (1999)
8. Dallien, J., MacCaull, W.: Automated recognition of stutter-invariant LTL formulas. Atlantic Electron. J. Math. 1, 56–74 (2006)
9. Dax, C., Klaedtke, F., Leue, S.: Specification languages for stutter-invariant regular properties. In: Liu, Z., Ravn, A.P. (eds.) ATVA 2009. LNCS, vol. 5799, pp. 244–254. Springer, Heidelberg (2009)
10. Duret-Lutz, A.: Manipulating LTL formulas using Spot 1.0. In: Van Hung, D., Ogawa, M. (eds.) ATVA 2013. LNCS, vol. 8172, pp. 442–445. Springer, Heidelberg (2013)

11. Duret-Lutz, A.: LTL translation improvements in Spot 1.0. Int. J. Crit. Comput.-Based Syst. **5**(1/2), 31–54 (2014)
12. Etessami, K.: Stutter-invariant languages, ω-automata, and temporal logic. In: Halbwachs, N., Peled, D.A. (eds.) CAV 1999. LNCS, vol. 1633, pp. 236–248. Springer, Heidelberg (1999)
13. Etessami, K.: A note on a question of Peled and Wilke regarding stutter-invariant LTL. Inf. Process. Lett. **75**(6), 261–263 (2000)
14. Gastin, P., Oddoux, D.: Fast LTL to Büchi automata translation. In: Berry, G., Comon, H., Finkel, A. (eds.) CAV 2001. LNCS, vol. 2102, pp. 53–65. Springer, Heidelberg (2001)
15. Geldenhuys, J., Hansen, H.: Larger automata and less work for LTL model checking. In: Valmari, A. (ed.) SPIN 2006. LNCS, vol. 3925, pp. 53–70. Springer, Heidelberg (2006)
16. Giannakopoulou, D., Lerda, F.: From states to transitions: improving translation of LTL formulæ to Büchi automata. In: Peled, D.A., Vardi, M.Y. (eds.) FORTE 2002. LNCS, vol. 2529, pp. 308–326. Springer, Heidelberg (2002)
17. Hansen, H., Penczek, W., Valmari, A.: Stuttering-insensitive automata for on-the-fly detection of livelock properties. In: FMICS 2002, vol. 66(2) of ENTCS. Elsevier (2002)
18. Holzmann, G.J.: The Spin Model Checker: Primer and Reference Manual. Addison-Wesley, Boston (2003)
19. Holzmann, G.J., Kupferman, O.: Not checking for closure under stuttering. In: SPIN 1996, pp. 17–22. American Mathematical Society (1996)
20. Klein, J., Baier, C.: On-the-fly stuttering in the construction of deterministic ω-automata. In: Holub, J., Žďárek, J. (eds.) CIAA 2007. LNCS, vol. 4783, pp. 51–61. Springer, Heidelberg (2007)
21. Laarman, A., Pater, E., van de Pol, J., Hansen, H.: Guard-based partial-order reduction. In: STTT, pp. 1–22 (2014)
22. Michel, M.: Algèbre de machines et logique temporelle. In: Fontet, M., Mehlhorn, K. (eds.) STACS 1984. LNCS, vol. 166, pp. 287–298. Springer, Heidelberg (1984)
23. Păun, D.O., Chechik, M.: On closure under stuttering. Formal Aspects Comput. **14**(4), 342–368 (2003)
24. Peled, D., Wilke, T.: Stutter-invariant temporal properties are expressible without the next-time operator. Inf. Process. Lett. **63**(5), 243–246 (1997)
25. Peled, D., Wilke, T., Wolper, P.: An algorithmic approach for checking closure properties of temporal logic specifications and ω-regular languages. Theor. Comput. Sci. **195**(2), 183–203 (1998)
26. Renault, E., Duret-Lutz, A., Kordon, F., Poitrenaud, D.: Three SCC-based emptiness checks for generalized Büchi automata. In: McMillan, K., Middeldorp, A., Voronkov, A. (eds.) LPAR-19 2013. LNCS, vol. 8312, pp. 668–682. Springer, Heidelberg (2013)
27. Schuppan, V., Darmawan, L.: Evaluating LTL satisfiability solvers. In: Bultan, T., Hsiung, P.-A. (eds.) ATVA 2011. LNCS, vol. 6996, pp. 397–413. Springer, Heidelberg (2011)
28. Tauriainen, H.: Nested emptiness search for generalized Büchi automata. In: ACSD 2004, pp. 165–174. IEEE Computer Society (2004)
29. Tian, C., Duan, Z.: A note on stutter-invariant PLTL. Inf. Process. Lett. **109**(13), 663–667 (2009)

Embedded Systems

MESS: Memory Performance Debugging on Embedded Multi-core Systems

Sudipta Chattopadhyay[✉]

Linköping University, Linköping, Sweden
sudipta.chattopadhyay@liu.se

Abstract. Multi-core processors have penetrated the modern computing platforms in several dimensions. Such systems aim to achieve high-performance via running computations in parallel. However, the performance of such systems is often limited due to the congestion in shared resources, such as shared caches and shared buses. In this paper, we propose MESS, a performance debugging framework for embedded, multi-core systems. MESS systematically discovers the order of memory-access operations that expose performance bugs due to shared caches. We leverage both on single-core performance profiling and symbolic constraint solving to reveal the interleaved memory-access-pattern that leads to a performance bug. Our baseline framework does not generate any *false positive*. Besides, its failure to find a solution highlights the absence of performance bugs due to shared caches, for a given input. Finally, we propose an approximate solution that dramatically reduces debugging time, at the cost of a reasonable amount of false positives. Our experiments with several embedded software and a real-life robot controller suggest that we can discover performance bugs in a reasonable time. The implementation of MESS and our experiments are available at https://bitbucket.org/sudiptac/mess.

1 Introduction

It is notoriously difficult to understand and discover performance bugs in software. Whereas performance bugs may appear in any application, these bugs are critical for certain class of software, such as embedded and real-time software. Embedded and real-time applications are, in general, constrained via several temporal requirements. For hard real-time applications, violation of such temporal constraints may lead to catastrophic effects, often costing human lives. Apart from hard real-time applications, the existence of performance bugs may substantially impact the quality of soft real-time applications (*e.g.* media players) as well as web applications. As the computing world is moving towards the multi-core era, it has become a critical problem to develop correct and efficient software on multi-core platforms. In this paper, broadly, we concentrate on the efficiency of applications which run on multi-core platforms.

In multi-threaded execution, software functionality might be disrupted due to the non-deterministic order in accessing shared data [11]. Similarly, the performance of multi-core systems may highly vary due to the non-deterministic

© Springer International Publishing Switzerland 2015
B. Fischer and J. Geldenhuys (Eds.): SPIN 2015, LNCS 9232, pp. 105–125, 2015.
DOI: 10.1007/978-3-319-23404-5_8

order in accessing *shared resources*, such as shared caches. Caches are managed at runtime and they store copies of memory blocks from the main memory. In current generation computing platforms, caches are several magnitudes faster than accessing the main memory. As a result, cache memory is a crucial component to bridge the performance gap between the processor and main memory, and to improve the overall performance of applications. However, since caches are managed at runtime, the order of memory-access patterns play a crucial role in deciding the content of caches. For instance, consider a shared cache which can hold only one memory block. If accesses to m_1 and m_2 are interleaved in parallel, then the ordering $(m_1 \cdot m_2)^*$ will *always* lead to cache misses. In contrast, *only the first* accesses of m_1 and m_2 will suffer cache misses, for the ordering $(m_1^* \cdot m_2^*)$. In summary, depending on the memory-access order, there might be a high variation on cache performance, which dramatically impacts the overall performance of software.

In this paper, we propose a novel approach to discover interleaving patterns that violate a given temporal constraint. For a given program input, our framework *automatically* discovers the order of memory accesses that highlights a performance bug. These bugs happen due to the cache sharing between cores and they may lead to serious performance issues at runtime. A typical usage of our framework is the reproduction of performance bugs on multi-core systems and subsequently, improve the overall performance via classic cache management techniques, such as cache locking [18]. We leverage on the recent advances in constraint solving and *satisfiability modulo theory* (SMT) to systematically explore memory-access patterns. We propose a baseline framework which does not generate *false* alarms. Moreover, if our baseline framework terminates without a solution, then we can guarantee the *validity* of given temporal constraints, for the given input. We also propose an approximation that systematically partitions the set of constraints and solve each partition in parallel. Such a strategy dramatically improves the solver performance. Our approximation guarantees *soundness*, meaning that the absence of a solution highlights the absence of performance bugs. Besides, our evaluation reveals that such an approximation exhibits reasonably low false alarms.

The generation of a performance-stressing interleaving pattern involves many technical challenges. Unlike the functionality of an application, its performance is not directly annotated in the code. Moreover, it is infeasible to execute an application for all possible interleaving patterns, due to an exponential number of possibilities. To resolve such challenges, we propose a compositional approach to discover performance bugs. Our framework broadly contains two stages. In the first stage, we monitor the performance of each core *in isolation* and compute a performance-summary for each core. In each performance-summary, the timing to access the shared cache is replaced by a symbolic variable. In the second stage, we formulate constraints that relate the order of memory accesses with the delay to access the shared-cache. In particular, we formulate constraints that *symbolically encode necessary and sufficient conditions for a memory block to be evicted from the shared-cache*. As a result, using these constraints, we could determine whether a given memory block is available in the shared-cache, when it is being accessed. In other words, we can use such constraints to bound the delay to access the shared-cache and thereby, constraining the value of symbolic variables, which were introduced in the first stage of our framework. Finally, the temporal constraint is also provided as a quantifier-free formula. All the constraints, together with the temporal constraint, is given to an SMT solver. If the solver finds a solution, the resulting solution highlights an interleaving pattern that violates the temporal constraint. Since SMT technology is continuously evolving, we believe that such a compositional approach will be appealing to discover performance bugs in multi-core systems.

To tackle the complexity of our systems, we also propose an approximate solution that significantly improves the performance of our proposed framework. For shared caches, we observed that the set of all constraints can be partitioned systematically to solve in parallel. The general intuition is to consider partitions of memory accesses which can contend in the shared-cache and solve the constraints generated for each partition independently. By increasing the size of each partition, the designer can reduce the number of *false positives* at the cost of debugging time. Therefore, our framework gives designer the flexibility to fine tune the precision, with respect to debugging time.

Contribution. In summary, we propose a performance debugging framework that exposes performance issues due to shared caches. We leverage on single-core performance profiling and symbolic-constraint solving, in order to discover the interleaving pattern that violates a given temporal constraint. Our baseline framework does not generate any *false positive* and it can also be used to prove the absence of performance bugs for a given input. Moreover, for time-critical code fragments, our baseline framework can be employed to derive the worst-case interleaving pattern (in terms of shared-cache performance), for a given input. To tackle the complexity of our constraint-based framework, we have also proposed an approximation that dramatically increases the solver performance. To show the generality of our approach, we have instantiated our framework for two different caches *(i)* caches with least-recently-used (LRU) replacement policy and *(ii)* caches with first-in-first-out (FIFO) policy. We have implemented our entire framework on top of `simplescalar` [6] – an open-source, cycle-accurate, processor simulator and `Z3` [5] – an open source, SMT solver. Our experiments with several embedded software reveals the effectiveness of our approach. For instance, our baseline framework was able to check a variety of temporal constraints for a real-life robot controller [2] within *3*min and our approximation took only *20*s on average to check the same set of constraints. This makes the idea of constraint-based formulation in performance debugging quite appealing for research in future.

2   Overview

Background on Caches. Caches are employed between the CPU and the main memory (DRAM) to bridge the performance gap between the CPU and the DRAM. A cache can be described as a three tuple $\langle \mathcal{A}, \mathcal{S}, \mathcal{L} \rangle$, where $\mathcal{A}$ is the associativity of the cache, $\mathcal{S}$ is the number of cache sets and $\mathcal{L}$ is the line size (in bytes). Each cache set can hold $\mathcal{A}$ cache lines, leading to a total cache size of $(\mathcal{A} \cdot \mathcal{S} \cdot \mathcal{L})$ bytes. When $\mathcal{A} = 1$, the respective caches are called to be *directly mapped*. Data is fetched into caches at the granularity of line size ($\mathcal{L}$). Therefore, for an arbitrary memory address x, $\mathcal{L}$ contiguous bytes are fetched into the cache starting from address $\lfloor \frac{x}{\mathcal{L}} \rfloor$ and we say that x belongs to the *memory block* $\lfloor \frac{x}{\mathcal{L}} \rfloor$. The number of cache sets ($\mathcal{S}$) decides the location where a particular memory block would be placed in the cache. For instance, a memory block, starting at address M, is always mapped to the cache set $M \bmod \mathcal{S}$. Since each cache set can hold only $\mathcal{A}$ cache lines, a cache line needs to be replaced when the number of memory blocks mapping to a cache set exceeds $\mathcal{A}$. In order to accomplish this, a replacement policy is employed when $\mathcal{A} \geq 2$. In this paper, we instantiate our framework for two widely used replacement policies – LRU and FIFO. In LRU policy, the memory block, that was not *accessed* for the longest period of time, is replaced from the cache to make room for other memory blocks. In FIFO policy, the memory block, which is *residing* in the cache for the longest period of time, is replaced to make room for other blocks. In general, the performance of a cache may greatly depend on the underlying replacement policy.

Terminologies. We use the following terminologies on caches throughout the paper.

1. *memory block:* For an arbitrary memory reference to address x, we say that it belongs to memory block $\lfloor \frac{x}{\mathcal{L}} \rfloor$ ($\mathcal{L}$ is the line size of cache, in bytes), in order to distinguish different cache lines.
2. *cache hit/miss:* For an arbitrary memory reference, we say that it is a cache hit (miss) if the referenced memory block is found (not found) in the cache.
3. *cache conflict:* Two memory blocks M_1 and M_2 conflict in the cache if they map to the same cache set. In other words, M_1 is conflicting to M_2 (and vice versa). These conflicting memory blocks might be accessed within the same core (intra-core) or across different cores (inter-core).
4. *cache-set state:* Ordered $\mathcal{A}$-tuple capturing the content of a cache set. For instance, $\langle m_1, m_2 \rangle$ captures such a tuple for caches with associativity 2. The relative position of a memory block in the tuple decides the number of unique cache conflicts required to evict the same from the cache. For instance, in $\langle m_1, m_2 \rangle$, m_1 requires two unique cache conflicts to be evicted from the cache, whereas m_2 requires only one. The generation of cache conflicts critically depends on the replacement policy and the order of memory accesses.

Motivation and Challenges. Figure 1 captures an example where two programs are executing in parallel on different processor cores and sharing a cache. For the sake of simplicity, let us assume that all the instructions in both Program x and Program y access the same shared-cache set. In Fig. 1(a), the memory block accessed by each instruction is shown within the brackets. In the following discussion, we shall capture the location i of Program x via x^i and the same of Program y via y^i.

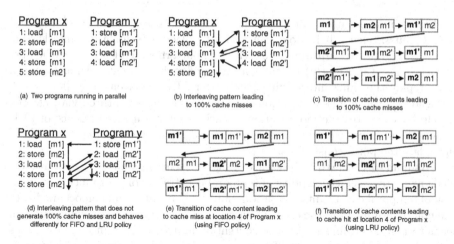

Fig. 1. An example showing the impact of interleaving pattern on shared-cache performance. The direction of an arrow captures the *happens-before* relation. Cache misses are highlighted in bold.

Let us assume a cache with associativity ($\mathcal{A}$) two and employing FIFO replacement policy. Further assume that we want to check whether *all instructions in both programs can face cache misses*. Figure 1(b) captures an interleaving pattern which leads to 100 % cache misses in both programs. The progression of the cache content for this interleaving pattern is captured via Fig. 1(c). It is worthwhile to note that many interleaving patterns will fail to generate 100 % cache misses in both programs. Figure 1(d) captures one such interleaving pattern. As a result, if the set of memory accesses (*cf.* Fig. 1(a)) appears within a loop, the memory-access delay might change dramatically depending on the interleaving pattern. The respective cache contents for the interleaving pattern in Fig. 1(d) are shown via Fig. 1(e). In general, it is infeasible to perform an exhaustive search over the set of all possible interleaving patterns, due to an exponential number of possibilities. As a result, a systematic method is required to check performance-related constraints, in the context of multi-core systems.

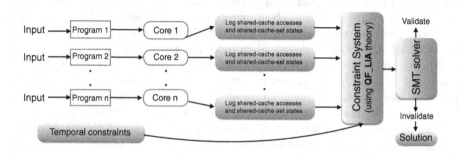

Fig. 2. Performance debugging framework for multi-core systems

Let us now assume that we want to check whether location x^4 can face a *cache miss*. Such a behaviour can also take place only for a few interleaving patterns. Figure 1(d) captures an interleaving pattern which lead to a cache miss at location x^4 (*cf.* Fig. 1(e) for the transition of cache contents). Unfortunately, if we replay the same interleaving pattern for LRU replacement policy, it will not lead to a cache miss at location x^4. This behaviour is captured via Fig. 1(f), which demonstrates the modification of cache contents in the presence of LRU policy. This shows the influence of the *cache replacement policy* to check or invalidate temporal constraints.

To summarize, due to the presence of shared caches in multi-core systems, it is challenging to check the validity of temporal constraints or reproduce any violation of temporal constraints in a production run. This phenomenon occurs due to the non-determinism in the order of interleaved memory-accesses, which, in turn leads to non-determinism in cache contention and variability in memory-access delay. In the following, we shall give an outline of our performance debugging framework.

Overall Framework. Fig. 2 outlines the overall design of MESS. For a given input to each program running in parallel, our framework is used to check the temporal constraints. We first monitor the execution on each core *in isolation*, ignoring any interference from other cores. At the end of this monitoring phase, we obtain a sequence of shared-cache accesses $\langle i^1, i^2, \ldots, i^{\mathcal{V}_i-1}, i^{\mathcal{V}_i} \rangle$ for each core i, where $\mathcal{V}_i$ is the total number of shared-cache accesses by core i. We also collect the shared-cache-set states at these access points. Using the information obtained from the monitoring phase, we build a constraint system via the theory of quantifier-free linear integer arithmetic (QF_LIA). Intuitively, this constraint system relates the order of memory accesses with the delay to access the shared cache. The size of our constraint system is *polynomial*, with respect to the number of accesses to the shared cache. Finally, the temporal constraint can be provided to the constraint system via quantifier-free predicates. The entire constraint system, along with the temporal constraints, is provided to an SMT solver. If the constraint system is *satisfiable*, then the solution returned by the SMT solver captures an interleaving pattern that *violates* certain temporal constraints. This solution can further be used for debugging performance on multi-core systems.

System Model. We assume a sequentially-consistent, multi-core system where *each core may have several levels of private caches and only the last-level cache is shared across cores.* Therefore, a shared-cache miss will lead to an access to the slow DRAM. Such a design of memory-hierarchy is typical in embedded multi-core processors [1]. In this paper, we do not address the problem of cache coherency and any cache misses resulting from the same. Such cache misses might appear due to the invalidation of cache lines that hold outdated data. In summary, we first assume that programs, running on different cores, have disjoint memory spaces. We argue that, even in the absence of cache coherency, debugging shared-cache performance is sufficiently complex. In Sect. 4, we discuss the required modifications in our framework in the presence of data sharing.

3   Methodologies

In this section, we shall introduce the formal foundation of our framework. Recall that the outcome of our framework is to compute a memory-access ordering, leading to a performance bug. This ordering is captured among all accesses to the shared cache.

Let us assume that we have a total of $\mathcal{N}$ cores, each of which might exhibit a different sequence of shared-cache accesses. We use the notation i^j to capture the j-th shared-cache access by i-th core and $\mathcal{V}_i$ to capture the total number of shared-cache accesses by core i. We also use the following notations in our framework:

- σ_i^j : The memory block accessed by the shared-cache access i^j.
- $\pi(m)$: Cache set where memory block m is mapped.
- ζ_i^j : Shared-cache-set state for cache set $\pi(\sigma_i^j)$, immediately before the access i^j.
- $\mathcal{C}_i^j$: The set of memory blocks, other than σ_i^j, mapping to the same cache set as σ_i^j in the shared cache. Therefore, for any $m' \in \mathcal{C}_i^j$, we have $m' \neq \sigma_i^j$ and $\pi(m') = \pi(\sigma_i^j)$.
- $\mathcal{O}_i^j$: The position of the shared-cache access i^j in the ordering among all accesses to the shared cache.
- δ_i^j : The delay suffered by the shared-cache access i^j.

For instance, in Fig. 1(b), $\sigma_x^1 = m1$, $\sigma_y^1 = m1'$, $\zeta_y^1 = \langle m2, m1 \rangle$ and the interleaving pattern is captured as follows: $O_x^1 < O_x^2 < O_y^1 < O_y^2 < O_x^3 < O_y^3 < O_y^4 < O_x^4 < O_x^5$. The outcome of our framework is such an interleaving pattern.

Profiling Each Core in Isolation. As outlined in the preceding section, our framework initially records the performance of each core *in isolation*. The primary purpose of this recording phase is to accurately identify accesses to the shared cache, for each core. Therefore, while profiling each core in isolation, ζ_i^j contains memory blocks accessed *only* within core i and ignores all memory blocks accessed within core $\bar{i} \neq i$.

Let us assume age_i^j denotes the relative position of σ_i^j within ζ_i^j, while profiling each core in isolation. If $\sigma_i^j \notin \zeta_i^j$ (*i.e.* i^j suffers a shared-cache miss), we assign $\mathcal{A} + 1$ to age_i^j, where $\mathcal{A}$ is the associativity of the shared-cache. Subsequently, for each core i, we encode a performance-summary α_i as a sequence of pairs. Each such pair captures a shared-cache access i^j, along with age_i^j as follows:

$$\alpha_i \equiv \langle (i^1, age_i^1), (i^2, age_i^2), \ldots, (i^{\mathcal{V}_i-1}, age_i^{\mathcal{V}_i-1}), (i^{\mathcal{V}_i}, age_i^{\mathcal{V}_i}) \rangle \qquad (1)$$

For any shared-cache access i^j, it is a shared-cache miss if and only if $\sigma_i^j \notin \zeta_i^j$, leading age_i^j being set to $\mathcal{A} + 1$. Such a cache miss can happen because of the following reasons: *(i)* σ_i^j was accessed for the first time, or *(ii)* σ_i^j was evicted from the shared-cache by some other memory block. Recall that programs running on different cores have disjoint memory spaces. As a result, while profiling each core in isolation, we can accurately identify shared-cache misses when σ_i^j

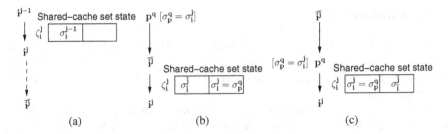

Fig. 3. The direction of arrow captures the total order between accesses to the shared cache. The left-most position in ζ_i^j captures the *most recently used* memory block. (a) $\overline{i}^{\overline{j}}$ cannot affect shared-cache set state ζ_i^j and therefore, it cannot generate cache conflict to i^j, if $\overline{i}^{\overline{j}}$ *happens after* i^j, (b) $\overline{i}^{\overline{j}}$ can affect ζ_i^j only if $\overline{i}^{\overline{j}}$ *happens before* i^j, (c) shared-cache access p^q accesses the same memory block as that of i^j (*i.e.* $\sigma_p^q = \sigma_i^j$) and therefore, access $\overline{i}^{\overline{j}}$ cannot affect the relative position of σ_i^j within ζ_i^j.

was accessed for the first time. This is because, σ_i^j was not accessed by any other core except core i. Next, we describe our constraint system (using QF_LIA theory), which formulates necessary and sufficient conditions for evicting memory blocks from the shared-cache, leading to shared-cache misses.

Program Order Constraints. These constraints are generated to capture the program order on each core. Note that $\langle i^1, i^2, \ldots, i^{\mathcal{V}_i-1}, i^{\mathcal{V}_i} \rangle$ captures the sequence of shared-cache accesses by core i. Therefore, the following constraints are generated to capture the program order semantics (note that any partial ordering between shared-cache accesses across cores, if exists, can be captured in a similar fashion).

$$\Theta_{order} \equiv \bigwedge_{i \in [1, \mathcal{N}]} \bigwedge_{j \in [2, \mathcal{V}_i]} \left(\mathcal{O}_i^j > \mathcal{O}_i^{j-1} \right) \tag{2}$$

Program-order constraints are generated irrespective of the cache replacement policy. In the following, we now instantiate the constraint formulation for LRU and FIFO policies.

3.1   Constraint System for LRU Caches

A shared-cache access i^j is a cache hit if and only if ζ_i^j contains σ_i^j. Otherwise, i^j suffers a shared-cache miss. Therefore, to accurately determine the shared-cache performance, it is crucial to track all feasible states of ζ_i^j. We accomplish this by relating the order of memory accesses with the changes in cache-set states. In order to understand the relationship between the memory-access order and cache-set states, we first define the notion of cache-conflict generation between two shared-cache accesses.

Definition 1. *(Cache Conflict Generation) Consider a shared-cache access $\overline{i}^{\overline{j}}$, which requests memory block $\overline{m}$ (i.e. $\sigma_{\overline{i}}^{\overline{j}} = \overline{m}$). A shared-cache access $\overline{i}^{\overline{j}}$ generates* (cache) conflict to i^j, only if accessing $\bar{m}$ at $\bar{i}^{\bar{j}}$ can affect the relative position of σ_i^j within ζ_i^j. For instance, in Fig. 1(d), accesses to m1′ and m2′ do not generate cache conflict to x^3, but an access to m2 does (at x^2).

We introduce a variable $\Psi_i^j(\bar{m})$ to capture whether any access to memory block $\bar{m}$ generates conflict to the shared-cache access i^j. As stated in Definition 1, the memory block $\bar{m}$ might be accessed more than once and therefore, the formulation of $\Psi_i^j(\bar{m})$ must consider all possible places where $\bar{m}$ was accessed. Consider one such place $\bar{i}^{\bar{j}}$, where $\bar{m}$ was accessed. Therefore, $\sigma_{\bar{i}}^{\bar{j}} = \bar{m}$. Figure 3 illustrates different scenarios in LRU policy, with respect to the generation of cache conflicts.

In particular, Figs. 3(a)–(b) capture the *happens-before* relationship between accesses $\bar{i}^{\bar{j}}$ and i^j. It is impossible for $\bar{i}^{\bar{j}}$ to affect the cache-set state ζ_i^j, if i^j happens before $\bar{i}^{\bar{j}}$. Moreover, if the memory block σ_i^j is accessed after $\bar{i}^{\bar{j}}$ and before i^j, then such an access will hide the cache conflict between $\bar{i}^{\bar{j}}$ and i^j. Figure 3(c) captures one such situation, where shared-cache access p^q accesses the memory block σ_i^j and prevents $\bar{i}^{\bar{j}}$ to affect the relative position of σ_i^j within cache-set state ζ_i^j.

In the following, we describe the formulation of constraints for an arbitrary shared-cache access i^j. The primary purpose of these constraints is to compute the delay δ_i^j. Considering the intuition provided in Fig. 3, we can state that a shared-cache access $\bar{i}^{\bar{j}}$ generates conflict to the shared-cache access i^j, only if the following conditions hold:

- $\psi_{cft}^{lru}\left(\bar{i}^{\bar{j}}, i^j\right)$: Shared-cache access $\bar{i}^{\bar{j}}$ happens *before* the shared-cache access i^j. Therefore, $\mathcal{O}_{\bar{i}}^{\bar{j}} < \mathcal{O}_i^j$. This is illustrated via Figs. 3(a)–(b).

- $\psi_{ref}^{lru}\left(\bar{i}^{\bar{j}}, i^j\right)$: There does not exist any shared-cache access p^q, such that p^q accesses memory block σ_i^j from the shared-cache, p^q happens *before* i^j and $\bar{i}^{\bar{j}}$ happens *before* p^q. Therefore, for any shared-cache access p^q, where $\sigma_p^q = \sigma_i^j$, conditions $\mathcal{O}_p^q < \mathcal{O}_i^j$ and $\mathcal{O}_{\bar{i}}^{\bar{j}} < \mathcal{O}_p^q$ cannot be satisfiable together. Otherwise, note that p^q will hide the cache conflict between $\bar{i}^{\bar{j}}$ and i^j, as illustrated via Fig. 3(c).

$\psi_{cft}^{lru}\left(\bar{i}^{\bar{j}}, i^j\right)$ and $\psi_{ref}^{lru}\left(\bar{i}^{\bar{j}}, i^j\right)$ can be formalized via the following constraints:

$$\psi_{cft}^{lru}\left(\bar{i}^{\bar{j}}, i^j\right) \equiv \mathcal{O}_{\bar{i}}^{\bar{j}} < \mathcal{O}_i^j \tag{3}$$

$$\psi_{ref}^{lru}\left(\bar{i}^{\bar{j}}, i^j\right) \equiv \bigwedge_{p,q:\ \sigma_p^q = \sigma_i^j} \neg\left(\mathcal{O}_{\bar{i}}^{\bar{j}} < \mathcal{O}_p^q \wedge \mathcal{O}_p^q < \mathcal{O}_i^j\right) \tag{4}$$

We combine Constraint (3) and Constraint (4) to formulate the generation of shared-cache conflict. Recall that $\mathcal{C}_i^j$ captures the set of memory blocks that map to the same shared-cache set as σ_i^j. Therefore, Constraints (3)–(4) need to be generated for each memory block in $\mathcal{C}_i^j$. Formally, for each shared-cache access

i^j, we generate the following constraints to capture cache conflicts generated across cores.

$$\Theta_1^{lru}(i,j) \equiv \bigwedge_{\bar{i}\neq i:\sigma_{\bar{i}}^{\bar{j}}\in\mathcal{C}_i^j} \left(\left(\psi_{cft}^{lru}\left(\overline{i^{\bar{j}}},i^j\right) \wedge \psi_{ref}^{lru}\left(\overline{i^{\bar{j}}},i^j\right)\right) \Rightarrow \left(\Psi_i^j\left(\sigma_{\bar{i}}^{\bar{j}}\right)=1\right)\right) \quad (5)$$

The absence of inter-core cache conflict is captured via the negation of Constraint (5). In particular, for any memory block $\bar{m} \in \mathcal{C}_i^j$, we need to consider the set of locations $\overline{i^{\bar{j}}}$ where $\bar{m}$ is accessed (*i.e.* $\sigma_{\bar{i}}^{\bar{j}} = \bar{m}$). If none of these locations satisfy either Constraints (3) or (4), we can conclude that accesses to memory block $\bar{m}$ do not generate any cache conflict to shared-cache access i^j. This behaviour can be captured via the following constraints:

$$\Theta_0^{lru}(i,j) \equiv \bigwedge_{\bar{m}\in\mathcal{C}_i^j} \left(\bigwedge_{\bar{i}\neq i:\sigma_{\bar{i}}^{\bar{j}}=\bar{m}} \left(\neg\psi_{cft}^{lru}\left(\overline{i^{\bar{j}}},i^j\right) \vee \neg\psi_{ref}^{lru}\left(\overline{i^{\bar{j}}},i^j\right)\right) \Rightarrow \left(\Psi_i^j\left(\bar{m}\right)=0\right)\right)$$
$$(6)$$

Finally, we need to link Constraints (5)–(6) to the absolute latency suffered by shared-cache access i^j (*i.e.* δ_i^j). Let us assume *HIT* and *MISS* capture the shared-cache hit latency and miss penalty, respectively. To compute the latency, we need to check whether the set of cache conflicts generated at i^j could evict the memory block σ_i^j. Therefore, we generate the following constraints to formulate the delay suffered at location i^j.

$$\Theta_{miss}^{lru}(i,j) \equiv \left(\sum_{\bar{i}\neq i:\ \sigma_{\bar{i}}^{\bar{j}}\in\mathcal{C}_i^j} \Psi_i^j(\sigma_{\bar{i}}^{\bar{j}}) \geq \mathcal{A} - age_i^j + 1\right) \Rightarrow (\delta_i^j = MISS) \quad (7)$$

$$\Theta_{hit}^{lru}(i,j) \equiv \left(\sum_{\bar{i}\neq i:\ \sigma_{\bar{i}}^{\bar{j}}\in\mathcal{C}_i^j} \Psi_i^j(\sigma_{\bar{i}}^{\bar{j}}) \leq \mathcal{A} - age_i^j\right) \Rightarrow (\delta_i^j = HIT) \quad (8)$$

age_i^j denotes the relative position of σ_i^j within ζ_i^j and $age_i^j=\mathcal{A}+1$, if $\sigma_i^j \notin \zeta_i^j$. The value age_i^j was collected while profiling each core *in isolation* (*cf.* Eq. (1)). Therefore, age_i^j already captures cache conflicts generated within core i and the quantity $\left(\mathcal{A} - age_i^j + 1\right)$ captures the minimum number of unique, inter-core cache conflicts (as formulated via Constraint (5)) to evict σ_i^j from the shared cache.

3.2 Constraint System for FIFO Caches

Unlike LRU policy, cache-set state remains unchanged for all *cache hits* in FIFO policy (*cf.* Fig. 1(e)). As a result, the necessary conditions to generate cache conflicts (*cf.* Constraints (3)–(4)) need to be modified for FIFO policy.

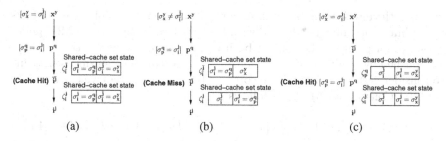

(a)   (b)   (c)

Fig. 4. The direction of arrow captures the total order between accesses to the shared cache. The left-most position in ζ_i^j captures the *most recent memory block inserted* into ζ_i^j. (a) $\bar{\imath}^{\bar{\jmath}}$ cannot affect shared-cache set state ζ_i^j as $\bar{\imath}^{\bar{\jmath}}$ is a cache hit. Therefore, $\bar{\imath}^{\bar{\jmath}}$ cannot generate cache conflict to i^j, (b) $\bar{\imath}^{\bar{\jmath}}$ can affect ζ_i^j only if $\bar{\imath}^{\bar{\jmath}}$ *happens before* i^j and it is a cache miss, (c) shared-cache access p^q accesses the same memory block as that of i^j (*i.e.* $\sigma_p^q = \sigma_i^j$), however, p^q is a cache hit. Therefore, p^q cannot hide the cache conflict generated between $\bar{\imath}^{\bar{\jmath}}$ and i^j.

To illustrate the difference between LRU and FIFO policy, let us consider the scenarios in Fig. 4. For instance, in Fig. 4(a), shared-cache access $\bar{\imath}^{\bar{\jmath}}$ *happens before* the access i^j. However, $\bar{\imath}^{\bar{\jmath}}$ cannot affect the relative position of σ_i^j within ζ_i^j and therefore, $\bar{\imath}^{\bar{\jmath}}$ cannot generate cache conflict to i^j (*cf.* Definition 1). It is worthwhile to note that, $\bar{\imath}^{\bar{\jmath}}$ would have generated conflict to i^j, in the presence of LRU policy. Figure 4(b) captures a scenario, where $\bar{\imath}^{\bar{\jmath}}$ was a cache miss, leading to the generation of cache conflict to i^j. Recall that, for LRU policy, if the memory block σ_i^j was accessed between $\bar{\imath}^{\bar{\jmath}}$ and i^j, then $\bar{\imath}^{\bar{\jmath}}$ could not generate cache conflict to i^j (*cf.* Constraint (4)). However in FIFO policy, as shown in Fig. 4(c), even though access p^q references σ_i^j and it occurs between $\bar{\imath}^{\bar{\jmath}}$ and i^j, p^q cannot hide the cache conflict between $\bar{\imath}^{\bar{\jmath}}$ and i^j. This is because p^q was a cache hit and therefore, it does not affect the relative position of σ_i^j within ζ_i^j.

In summary, a shared-cache access must be a cache miss if it affects the cache-set state ζ_i^j. In order to realize this intuition, we formulate the following constraints, which capture the necessary conditions for $\bar{\imath}^{\bar{\jmath}}$ generating cache conflict to i^j.

$$\psi_{cft}^{fifo}\left(\bar{\imath}^{\bar{\jmath}}, i^j\right) \equiv \left(\mathcal{O}_i^{\bar{\jmath}} < \mathcal{O}_i^j\right) \wedge \left(\delta_i^{\bar{\jmath}} = MISS\right) \qquad (9)$$

$$\psi_{ref}^{fifo}\left(\bar{\imath}^{\bar{\jmath}}, i^j\right) \equiv \bigwedge_{p,q:\ \sigma_p^q = \sigma_i^j} \neg\left(\left(\mathcal{O}_i^{\bar{\jmath}} < \mathcal{O}_p^q\right) \wedge \left(\mathcal{O}_p^q < \mathcal{O}_i^j\right) \wedge \left(\delta_p^q = MISS\right)\right) \qquad (10)$$

Constraint (9) ensures that $\bar{\imath}^{\bar{\jmath}}$ incurs a cache miss, in order to generate cache conflict to i^j (*cf.* Figs. 4(a)–(b)). Similarly, Constraint (10) ensures that access p^q needs to be a cache miss to hide the cache conflict between $\bar{\imath}^{\bar{\jmath}}$ and i^j (*cf.* Fig. 4(c)).

The outcome of Constraints (9)–(10) may depend on the interleaving pattern, even within a single core (*i.e.* $\bar{\imath} = i$). This is because, values of $\delta_i^{\bar{\jmath}}$ and δ_p^q may depend on the interleaving pattern. As a result, the generation of cache conflicts, even within a core, may be affected with FIFO policy. Hence, unlike LRU policy, we need to formulate cache conflict both within a core and across cores. This is accomplished by modifying Constraints (5)–(6), so that the resulting constraints also consider cache conflicts within cores. In particular, we remove the condition $\bar{i} \neq i$ from Constraints (5)–(6) as follows.

$$\Theta_1^{fifo}(i,j) \equiv \bigwedge_{\bar{i},\bar{j}:\sigma_{\bar{i}}^{\bar{j}} \in \mathcal{C}_i^j} \left(\left(\psi_{cft}^{fifo}\left(\overline{i^{\bar{j}}}, i^j\right) \wedge \psi_{ref}^{fifo}\left(\overline{i^{\bar{j}}}, i^j\right) \right) \Rightarrow \left(\Psi_i^j\left(\sigma_{\bar{i}}^{\bar{j}}\right) = 1 \right) \right)$$

(11)

$$\Theta_0^{fifo}(i,j) \equiv \bigwedge_{\bar{m} \in \mathcal{C}_i^j} \left(\bigwedge_{\bar{i},\bar{j}:\sigma_{\bar{i}}^{\bar{j}}=\bar{m}} \left(\neg\psi_{cft}^{fifo}\left(\overline{i^{\bar{j}}}, i^j\right) \vee \neg\psi_{ref}^{fifo}\left(\overline{i^{\bar{j}}}, i^j\right) \right) \Rightarrow \left(\Psi_i^j(\bar{m}) = 0 \right) \right)$$ (12)

Finally, we link Constraints (11)–(12) to compute the memory-access latency. Intuitively, we check whether the total amount of cache conflict can evict the memory block accessed by i^j. This can be formalized via the following constraints.

$$\Theta_{miss}^{fifo}(i,j) \equiv \left(\left(\sum_{\bar{m} \in \mathcal{C}_i^j} \Psi_i^j(\bar{m}) \geq \mathcal{A} \right) \vee \left(age_i^j = \mathcal{A}+1 \right) \right) \Rightarrow (\delta_i^j = MISS)$$ (13)

$$\Theta_{hit}^{fifo}(i,j) \equiv \left(\left(\sum_{\bar{m} \in \mathcal{C}_i^j} \Psi_i^j(\bar{m}) < \mathcal{A} \right) \wedge \left(age_i^j \neq \mathcal{A}+1 \right) \right) \Rightarrow (\delta_i^j = HIT)$$ (14)

$\mathcal{A}$ is the associativity of the cache. Recall that $age_i^j = \mathcal{A}+1$, if $\sigma_i^j \notin \zeta_i^j$ and age_i^j was measured while investigating each core in isolation (cf. Eq. 1). Therefore, the condition $age_i^j = \mathcal{A}+1$ guarantees to include the first-ever cache miss of σ_i^j. Once σ_i^j enters the cache, it takes at least $\mathcal{A}$ unique cache-conflicts to evict it from the cache. $\sum_{\bar{m} \in \mathcal{C}_i^j} \Psi_i^j(\bar{m})$ accounts all unique cache-conflicts faced by σ_i^j, since it enters the cache and till i^j. Therefore, Constraint (13) precisely captures all possibilities of a cache miss at i^j. The violation of Constraint (13) will result in a cache hit at i^j, as shown in Constraint (14).

Providing Temporal Constraints. For embedded software, temporal constraints can be provided in the form of an assertion. Therefore, our framework will search for an ordering on symbolic variables $\mathcal{O}_i^j$ that violates such assertions. In particular, we consider assertions that check the execution time against a threshold τ. In our framework, the non-determinism in timing behaviour appears due to the accesses to shared caches. Therefore, in our evaluation, we search for a solution that satisfy the following constraint: $\left(\sum_{i,j} \delta_i^j \geq \tau \right)$. Recall that δ_i^j symbolically captures the delay suffered by shared-cache access i^j. It is worthwhile to note that we can also check the timing behaviour of a code fragment, instead of checking the same for the entire system. In such cases, we consider only a subset of δ_i^j variables relating to the code fragment.

Putting it All Together. Our formulated constraints, along with the temporal constraint, is provided to an off-the-shelf SMT solver. As a result, any ongoing and future improvements in the solver technology will directly boost the efficiency of our approach. The SMT solver searches for a satisfying solution of the following constraints:

$$\Phi \equiv \Theta_{order} \wedge \bigwedge_{i,j} \left(\Theta_1^x(i,j) \wedge \Theta_0^x(i,j) \wedge \Theta_{miss}^x(i,j) \wedge \Theta_{hit}^x(i,j) \right) \wedge \left(\sum_{i,j} \delta_i^j \geq \tau \right)$$
$$(15)$$

where $x \in \{lru, fifo\}$, depending on the cache replacement policy. The solution of the solver captures concrete values of symbolic variables $\mathcal{O}_i^j$ that satisfy Φ. Such concrete values can be used to derive the total order among all accesses to the shared-cache.

Complexity of Constraints. The complexity of our constraints Φ (*cf.* Constraint (15)) is dominated by the number of constraints to formulate cache conflicts. For instance, in LRU policy, Constraints (5)–(6) dominate the total number of constraints. Let us assume that the total number of shared-cache accesses across all cores is $\mathcal{K}$. Therefore, the size of Constraint (2) has a complexity of $O(\mathcal{K})$. Similarly, the total size of Constraints (7)–(8), for LRU policy (respectively, the total size of Constraints (13)–(14) for FIFO policy) has a size of $O(\mathcal{K})$. Finally, during the formulation of cache conflict, each shared-cache access can be compared with all conflicting shared-cache accesses. Therefore, $\Theta_1^{lru}(i,j)$, $\Theta_0^{lru}(i,j)$, $\Theta_1^{fifo}(i,j)$ and $\Theta_0^{fifo}(i,j)$ have a worst-case size-complexity $O(\mathcal{K}^2)$. Since there exists a total of $\mathcal{K}$ shared-cache accesses, the total size of Constraints (5)–(6) has a complexity of $O(\mathcal{K}^3)$. Putting everything together, our constraint system has a worst-case size-complexity $O(\mathcal{K}^3)$. However, our evaluation reveals that the size of our constraint system is substantially lower than the worst-case complexity.

3.3   Approximate Solution

Our approximation scheme aims to reduce the pressure on the constraint solver by reducing the number of constraints to be solved together. The general intuition of our approximation is based on the design principle of caches. In particular, we leverage the fact that two different cache sets never interfere with each other, in terms of cache conflict. Therefore, we model the constraints for each cache set separately and solve them in parallel. In the following, we shall formalize the concept.

Finding a Slice of Constraints. The key idea for the approximation is to find a slice of constraints that could be solved *independently*. Recall that the symbolic variable δ_i^j captures the delay suffered by shared-cache access i^j. It is worthwhile to note that the memory block accessed at i^j (i.e. σ_i^j) can be evicted from the shared-cache only by memory blocks conflicting to σ_i^j. A memory block $\bar{m}$ conflicts to σ_i^j in the cache if and only if $\bar{m}$ and σ_i^j map to the same cache set. Therefore, we first group shared-cache accesses with respect to different cache sets and generate the respective constraints. For instance, consider that we are generating constraints with respect to cache set s. We shall use $\pi(m)$ to capture the cache set in which memory block m is mapped.

We slice out the program-order constraints by considering only the memory blocks which map to cache set s. Therefore, the set of program-order constraints, with respect to cache set s, can be defined as follows.

$$\Gamma_{order}(s) \equiv \bigwedge_{i \in [1, \mathcal{N}]} \left(\bigwedge_{j,k \in [1, \mathcal{V}_i]:\ j < k \wedge \left(\pi(\sigma_i^j) = \pi(\sigma_i^k) = s \right) \wedge (\forall m \in [j+1, k]:\ \pi(\sigma_i^j) \neq \pi(\sigma_i^m))} \mathcal{O}_i^k > \mathcal{O}_i^j \right) \tag{16}$$

Let us now consider LRU cache replacement policy. The set of constraints, with respect to cache set s, considers constraints that only influence the memory blocks mapped to cache set s. Therefore, for cache set s, we extract the constraints formulated in Eqs. (5)-(8) as follows.

$$\Gamma_1^{lru}(s) \equiv \bigwedge_{i,j:\pi(\sigma_i^j)=s} \Theta_1^{lru}(i,j); \quad \Gamma_0^{lru}(s) \equiv \bigwedge_{i,j:\pi(\sigma_i^j)=s} \Theta_0^{lru}(i,j) \tag{17}$$

$$\Gamma_{miss}^{lru}(s) \equiv \bigwedge_{i,j:\pi(\sigma_i^j)=s} \Theta_{miss}^{lru}(i,j); \quad \Gamma_{hit}^{lru}(s) \equiv \bigwedge_{i,j:\pi(\sigma_i^j)=s} \Theta_{hit}^{lru}(i,j) \tag{18}$$

Finally. we gather all constraints with respect to cache set s. Our goal is to maximize the delay faced by accessing memory blocks mapped to s. This is performed via the following constraints and objective function.

$$\Gamma(s) \equiv \Gamma_{order}(s) \wedge \Gamma_1^{lru}(s) \wedge \Gamma_0^{lru}(s) \wedge \Gamma_{miss}^{lru}(s) \wedge \Gamma_{hit}^{lru}(s) \tag{19}$$

$$\Delta(s) = maximize \sum_{i,j:\ \pi(\sigma_i^j)=s} \delta_i^j \tag{20}$$

Note that $\Gamma(s)$ includes *all* constraints that could influence $\Delta(s)$. We can use recent development in SMT solving [17] to maximize the objective function captured via Eq. 20). It is also worthwhile to mention that the preceding process can be carried out in an exactly same fashion for FIFO policy. As a result, our approximation strategy is generic, with respect to the replacement policy employed in a cache.

For each cache set s, we formulate $\Gamma(s)$ and obtain the value of $\Delta(s)$ using [17]. If $s_1, s_2, \ldots, s_q$ are all different sets in the shared cache, $\sum_{r \in [1,q]} \Delta(s_r)$ over-approximates the total delay in accessing the shared cache. More precisely, we state the crucial property of our approximation scheme as follows (see [3] for the proof).

Property 2. *Let us assume* $\{s_1, s_2, \ldots, s_q\}$ *are different sets in the shared cache. For a given temporal constraint* $\sum_{i,j} \delta_i^j < \tau$, *if our baseline constraint system* Φ *(cf. Constraint (15)) is satisfiable, then* $\sum_{r \in [1,q]} \Delta(s_r) \geq \tau$. *In other words, our approximation scheme will never miss the violation of any temporal constraint.*

However, it is worthwhile to mention that our approximation scheme may generate *false positives*. In particular, $\sum_{r \in [1,q]} \Delta(s_r)$ might over-approximate the maximum value of $\sum_{i,j} \delta_i^j$. This is due to the reason that interleaving patterns, which lead to the maximum delay for individual cache sets, may not be feasible together. In our evaluation, we empirically evaluate the amount of pessimism in our approximation scheme.

4   Extension

Applications with Shared Variables. Our framework handles interferences in the shared resources, but, not in the shared variables. As a result, we do not catch the scenario when the program control-flow changes due to updates to shared variables. However, many embedded applications are designed by a number of independent components and the communication occurs in terms of reading sensor inputs or writing to output ports. In our evaluation, we show a real-life robot controller which operates via two independent tasks – balance and navigation. Moreover, shared memory-space across cores often bypass caches, to avoid power consumption due to the coherence traffic [14]. If accessing the shared memory-space bypasses cache, our framework can be easily extended for general applications with shared variables. In order to accomplish this, we need to generate additional constraints, which encode the program control-flow observed during a failure run (*i.e.* an execution scenario violating certain temporal constraints). This can be achieved in an exactly same fashion as shown in [15].

It is slightly more involved when accessing the shared memory-space goes through caches. In particular, we need to add constraints that capture cache misses due to data coherency and false sharing. This can be accomplished by correlating writes and reads to the same memory block. Besides, we need to distinguish the *first-ever shared-cache miss* for a memory block via Constraint (21), for any cache replacement policy. Without data sharing, such cache misses can be detected during the inspection of each core in isolation.

$$\bigwedge_{i,j} \left(\bigwedge_{p,q:\ \sigma_p^q = \sigma_i^j} \left(\mathcal{O}_p^q > \mathcal{O}_i^j \right) \Rightarrow \left(\delta_i^j = MISS \right) \right) \tag{21}$$

Constraint (21) encodes the scenario of i^j being the first shared-cache access to request memory block σ_i^j. This, in turn, leads to a shared-cache miss. We are currently extending MESS to handle data sharing and cache coherency.

Performance Debugging for a Class of Inputs. With minor changes, our framework can be extended for performance debugging on a class of inputs.

The key to such extension is to collect *path conditions* [12], while monitoring the performance of each core *in isolation*. For each core, such a *path condition* captures the set of all inputs which lead to the respective execution scenario. However, depending on the value of input x, the statement $a[x]$ might access different memory blocks, for the same path condition. Therefore, we need to generate constraints for each such memory block, satisfying the respective path constraint. Let us assume that array a might access memory block m_1 if $0 \leq x \leq 2$ and it accesses memory block m_2 if $2 < x \leq 5$. Subsequently, to formulate cache conflicts generated by accesses (*i.e.* Constraints (5)–(6) for LRU policy and Constraints (11)–(12) for FIFO policy) to m_1 and m_2, we additionally constrain via conditions $(0 \leq x \leq 2)$ and $(2 < x \leq 5)$, respectively. For instance, we modify $\Theta_1^{lru}(i, j)$ to $\Theta_1^{lru}(i, j) \wedge (0 \leq x \leq 2)$ for memory block m_1 and to $\Theta_1^{lru}(i, j) \wedge (2 < x \leq 5)$ for memory block m_2. In future, we aim to build such extension to instantiate performance debugging on a set of inputs, which are captured symbolically by path conditions.

5   Evaluation

We have implemented MESS using simplescalar [6] and Z3 constraint solver [5]. In our evaluation, we configure a multi-core system with dual-core processor, where each core has a private level-one cache and all the cores share a level-two cache. This is a typical design in many embedded systems, such as devices using Exynos 5250 [4], which, in turn, contains a dual-core, ARM Cortex-A15 [1] chip. We configure 1 KB level-one caches with associativity 2 and 2 KB level-two cache with associativity 4. All caches have a line size of 32 bytes. Cache sizes are chosen in a fashion such that we obtain enough accesses to the shared cache and therefore, generate a reasonable number of constraints in our framework (see [3] for experiments with different cache configurations). To evaluate our framework, we have chosen medium to large size programs from [13], which are generally used to validate timing analyzers. We have also used a robot controller from [2], which contains two tasks — `balance` (to help the robot to keep it in upright position) and `navigation` (to drive the robot through rough terrain). These two tasks are assigned to different cores in our configured dual-core system.

Experimental Setup. For our evaluation with programs from [13], we run `jfdctint` on one core and choose different programs to run on the other core. We use such a setup in order to check the influence of the same inter-core cache conflicts on different programs. For the robot controller, we run `balance` and `navigation` on two different cores. The first two columns in Table 1 list the set of programs and the respective size of source code. We monitor the execution on each core by instrumenting memory accesses in Simplescalar. At the end of the execution, we generate a summary of memory performance for each core, which, in turn are used to generate constraints. The generated constraints are solved via Z3. All evaluations have been performed on an Intel I7 machine, having 8 GB of RAM and running ubuntu 14.04 operating systems.

Table 1. Evaluation of our baseline framework: "lines of C code" considers the sum of source code of two programs running on two different cores, "#violations" captures the number of violations within the set of 30 temporal constraints $\{\sum_{i,j} \delta_i^j < 200, \ldots, \sum_{i,j} \delta_i^j < 3100\}$.

Program	Total lines of C code	Shared-cache repl. policy	#shared-cache access	Size of constraints	#violations	Time to generate constraints (secs)	Solver time (secs) Max./Geo. Mean
cnt+ jfdctint	642	LRU	432	2111	22	1.17	25.01/1.84
		FIFO	432	6586	22	9.52	161.83/15.73
expint+ jfdctint	532	LRU	433	2166	23	1.22	10.84/2.16
		FIFO	433	6643	23	9.62	576.56/20.02
qurt+ jfdctint	541	LRU	448	2817	30	1.88	24.81/3.16
		FIFO	448	7272	30	9.38	31.77/11.59
matmult+ jfdctint	538	LRU	436	2283	28	1.31	244.39/1.91
		FIFO	436	6758	28	9.69	15495.83/ 12.82
fdct+ jfdctint	614	LRU	479	3943	30	2.99	17.49/5.01
		FIFO	479	8418	30	11.85	44.31/21.44
nsichneu+ jfdctint	4628	LRU	1679	40087	30	49.2	17120.46/ 7904.08
		FIFO	1679	44562	30	15.35	27534.20/ 15174.8
balance+ navigation	2098	LRU	772	3881	30	0.23	155.17/63.94
		FIFO	773	6770	30	0.56	389.68/184.32

Basic Results. Table 1 outlines the basic evaluation of our framework. We set the shared-cache miss-penalty (hit-latency) to be 100 (1) cycles. Recall that we aim to check the validity of temporal constraints $\sum_{i,j} \delta_i^j < \tau$. We generate a number of temporal constraints by varying τ from 200 to 3100 cycles, at a step of 100 cycles and for each such temporal constraint, we invoke our framework. Note that τ captures all possibilities between two to thirty one shared-cache misses. Besides, in $\sum_{i,j} \delta_i^j$, we only consider shared-cache accesses i^j, whose latency were unknown during the investigation of each core in isolation (*cf.* Column 4 in Table 1). Therefore, any shared-cache access i^j, which incurs the first-ever cache miss of the respective memory block σ_i^j, is not included in $\sum_{i,j} \delta_i^j$. In Table 1, we report the maximum and geometric mean over the time to check all temporal constraints. For several cases, this maximum time was recorded for a *valid* temporal constraint, meaning that the solver failed to find a violation. We can observe that, for many scenarios, the solver returns a solution in reasonable

Table 2. Efficiency and precision of our approximation. *TO* denotes timeout (>5 h). "Max. #constraints" capture the maximum number of constraints solved by Z3 over all invocations.

Program	Replacement policy of the shared-cache	Max. #con-straints		Solver time (in seconds)		Max. delay $\left(\max \sum_{i,j} \delta_i^j\right)$ (in CPU cycles)	
		baseline	approx	baseline	approx	baseline	approx
cnt+ jfdctint	LRU	2111	154	23.58	4.39	2394	3285
	FIFO	6586	513	116.49	14.35	2300≤X<2400	3285
expint+ jfdctint	LRU	2166	207	10.84	4.77	2494	3385
	FIFO	6643	526	409.39	14.58	2400≤X<2500	3385
qurt+ jfdctint	LRU	2817	305	565.91	9.2	3884	6161
	FIFO	7272	631	*TO*	29.03	≥3900	6061
matmult+ jfdctint	LRU	2283	154	244.39	5.23	2988	4473
	FIFO	6758	513	15495.83	15.98	2900≤X<3000	4473
fdct+ jfdctint	LRU	3943	304	*TO*	22.31	≥6200	10116
	FIFO	8418	599	*TO*	66.4	≥6200	10116
nsichneu+ jfdctint	LRU	40087	2862	*TO*	764.56	≥10000	31500
	FIFO	44562	3137	*TO*	926.45	≥10000	31500
balance+ navigation	LRU	3881	442	93.32	12.81	12800≤X<12900	13200
	FIFO	6770	818	182.68	25.08	12200	12200

time. However, with large number of constraints, the solver takes long time to find a solution. For instance, with program `nsichneu`, such a scenario happens due to its large size and a substantial number of accesses to the shared-cache. In general, finding a solution for FIFO policy takes longer time compared to LRU policy, due to a larger constraint-size.

Evaluation of the Approximate Solution. Table 2 compares our approximation and the baseline framework. As clearly observed, our approximation dramatically reduces the debugging time, compared to the baseline framework. This is due to the partitioning of constraints with respect to different cache sets. Such constraint partitioning drastically reduces the number of constraints to be solved together, leading to a substantial reduction of pressure to Z3. As our approximation may generate false positives, we also compare the precision of our approximation compared to the baseline framework. In order to do this, we compare the maximum delay computed by our approximation with the maximum delay computed by the baseline framework. This maximum delay captures the sum of all delays to access the shared-cache. For our baseline framework, obtaining such maximum delay may incur large overhead (we used symba [17] to compute the maximum delay). In such cases, we use the time taken by the solver to validate a temporal constraint $\sum_{i,j} \delta_i^j < \tau$. This means that the maximum delay cannot exceed $\tau - 1$. For instance, in Table 2, 2300≤X<2400 indicates that the solver found a solution for $\sum_{i,j} \delta_i^j \geq 2300$, but not for $\sum_{i,j} \delta_i^j \geq 2400$. The respective debugging-time captures the time taken by the solver for $\sum_{i,j} \delta_i^j \geq 2400$. Finally, we use a timeout of five hours for the solver. For instance, the timeout event happens for the program fdct. From Table 2, we also observe that the precision of our approximation scheme is reasonable, in the context of validating embedded software. Finally, we note that with the current state-of-the-art solutions (*e.g.* using [17]), discovering the exact worst-case ordering among memory accesses (in terms of performance), is not very efficient.

Notes on Scalability. We have implemented a *proof-of-concept* of MESS. We have also shown an approximation, which dramatically improves the solver performance, with a reasonable loss of precision. We believe that several optimizations are still possible. In particular, as shown in [15], other optimizations for parallel constraint-solving is feasible. We are exploring such techniques to further improve the efficiency of MESS.

6   Related Work

Testing and debugging of multi-threaded applications has been an active topic of research for the last few years [15,19,20,23,24]. Unlike these approaches, our work concentrates on resource sharing in parallel architectures, rather than data sharing in parallel applications. However, to consider shared data in our framework, an approach similar to [15] can be integrated easily into our constraint system. Our work is also orthogonal to efforts in program synthesis, such as the approach taken in [8]. Instead of generating correct and optimal programs from their specification [8], we aim to discover performance bugs in the original implementation of software.

Modeling shared-cache performance has been an active topic of research in the past few years [21,22]. Unlike our approach, these works do not provide strong guarantees on the presence or absence of performance bugs due to shared caches. Such guarantees are crucial for time-critical code fragments. Recent works on performance testing aim to generate performance-stressing execution in sequential [7] or parallel applications [10,16]. These works are not directly applicable to reproduce or debug performance bugs. Besides, in this paper, we provide strong guarantees on the absence of performance bugs, when a given temporal constraint is not invalidated by the solver.

Works on worst case execution time (WCET) analysis, for multi-core systems [9], predicts the maximum execution time of an application over all possible inputs and interleavings. In this paper, our goal is orthogonal and we aim to discover, for a given input, the interleaving pattern that causes the violation of temporal constraints. Therefore, our work has a significant testing and debugging flavour compared to WCET analysis.

In summary, previous works on automated debugging have mostly concentrated on functionality bugs or performance bugs on single-core systems. In this paper, we propose a systematic debugging approach that highlights performance bugs on multi-core systems, with a specific focus on shared caches.

7   Conclusion

In this paper, we have proposed MESS, a constraint-based framework to debug memory performance in multi-core systems. MESS systematically finds the interleaving pattern that causes the violation of temporal constraints. An appealing feature of our framework is its ability to provide guarantees on the absence of performance bugs, such as the validity of temporal constraints, for a given input. We have also integrated an approximation scheme, which, with a reasonable loss of precision, improves the debugging time by several magnitudes. In general, this opens up several opportunities to improve the debugging time enforced by MESS. Our evaluation with several embedded software and also with a real-life robot controller shows the effectiveness of our approach. Finally, since the performance of constraint solvers is continuously improving, we believe that MESS proposes a promising approach for performance debugging on multi-core systems. In future, we aim to build on our approach to consider shared data and other crucial shared resources in multi-core systems, such as shared buses. We also aim to use MESS to automatically synthesize fixes of performance bugs. One possible approach would be to synthesize barriers. The primary purpose of such barriers will be to satisfy a given temporal constraint, via restricting certain interleaving patterns.

Acknowledgement. We thank the anonymous reviewers for their insightful comments and feedback. This work is partially supported by the Swedish National Graduate School on Computer Science (CUGS). This support is gratefully acknowledged.

References

1. ARM Cortex-A5 processor. http://www.arm.com/products/processors/cortex-a/cortex-a5.php
2. Ballybot balancing robots. http://robotics.ee.uwa.edu.au/eyebot/doc/robots/ballybot.html
3. MESS: memory performance checker for embedded multi-core systems. http://sudiptac.bitbucket.org/papers/mess-extended.pdf
4. Samsung Exynos processor. http://www.samsung.com/global/business/semiconductor/file/product/Exynos_5_Dual_User_Manaul_Public_REV100-0.pdf
5. Z3 Constraint solver. http://z3.codeplex.com/
6. Austin, T., Larson, E., Ernst, D.: Simplescalar: an infrastructure for computer system modeling. Computer **35**(2), 59–67 (2002)
7. Banerjee, A., Chattopadhyay, S., Roychoudhury, A.: Static analysis driven cache performance testing. In: RTSS (2013)

8. Cerný, P., Chatterjee, K., Henzinger, T.A., Radhakrishna, A., Singh, R.: Quantitative synthesis for concurrent programs. In: Gopalakrishnan, G., Qadeer, S. (eds.) CAV 2011. LNCS, vol. 6806, pp. 243–259. Springer, Heidelberg (2011)
9. Chattopadhyay, S., Chong, L.K., Roychoudhury, A., Kelter, T., Marwedel, P., Falk, H.: A unified WCET analysis framework for multi-core platforms. In: TECS, vol. 13, no. 4s (2014)
10. Chattopadhyay, S., Eles, P., Peng, Z.: Automated software testing of memory performance in embedded GPUs. In: EMSOFT (2014)
11. Devietti, J., Lucia, B., Ceze, L., Oskin, M.: DMP: deterministic shared memory multiprocessing. In: ASPLOS (2009)
12. Godefroid, P., Klarlund, N., Sen, K.: DART: directed automated random testing. In: PLDI (2005)
13. Gustafsson, J., Betts, A., Ermedahl, A., Lisper, B.: The mälardalen WCET benchmarks: past, present and future. In: WCET (2010)
14. Holton, B., Bai, K., Shrivastava, A., Ramaprasad, H.: Construction of GCCFG for inter-procedural optimizations in software managed manycore (SMM) architectures. In: CASES (2014)
15. Huang, J., Zhang, C., Dolby, J.: CLAP: recording local executions to reproduce concurrency failures. In: PLDI (2013)
16. Li, G., Li, P., Sawaya, G., Gopalakrishnan, G., Ghosh, I., Rajan, S.P.: GKLEE: concolic verification and test generation for GPUs. In: PPoPP (2012). http://www.cs.utah.edu/formal_verification/GKLEE/
17. Li, Y., Albarghouthi, A., Kincaid, Z., Gurfinkel, A., Chechik, M.: Symbolic optimization with SMT solvers. In: POPL (2014)
18. Liang, Y., Mitra, T.: Instruction cache locking using temporal reuse profile. In: DAC (2010)
19. Musuvathi, M., Qadeer, S.: Iterative context bounding for systematic testing of multithreaded programs. In: PLDI (2007)
20. Nagarakatte, S., Burckhardt, S., Martin, M.M.K., Musuvathi, M.: Multicore acceleration of priority-based schedulers for concurrency bug detection. In PLDI (2012)
21. Sandberg, A., Black-Schaffer, D., Hagersten, E.: Efficient techniques for predicting cache sharing and throughput. In: PACT (2012)
22. Sandberg, A., Sembrant, A., Hagersten, E., Black-Schaffer, D.: Modeling performance variation due to cache sharing. In: HPCA (2013)
23. Sen, K.: Race directed random testing of concurrent programs. In: PLDI (2008)
24. Weeratunge, D., Zhang, X., Jagannathan, S.: Analyzing multicore dumps to facilitate concurrency bug reproduction. In: ASPLOS (2010)

DSVerifier: A Bounded Model Checking Tool for Digital Systems

Hussama I. Ismail, Iury V. Bessa$^{(\boxtimes)}$, Lucas C. Cordeiro,
Eddie B. de Lima Filho, and João E. Chaves Filho

Electronic and Information Research Center,
Federal University of Amazonas, Manaus, Brazil
iury.bessa@gmail.com

Abstract. This work presents the Digital-Systems Verifier (DSVerifier), which is a verification tool developed for digital systems. In particular, DSVerifier employs the bounded model checking technique based on satisfiability modulo theories (SMT) solvers, which allows engineers to verify the occurrence of design errors, due to the finite word-length approach employed in fixed-point digital filters and controllers. This tool consists in an additional module for the efficient SMT-based context-bounded model checker and presents command-line and graphical user interface (GUI) versions. Indeed, the GUI version is essential for reporting property violations, together with associated counterexamples. DSVerifier is implemented in C/C++ and uses JavaFX for providing GUI support.

1 Introduction

Digital filters and controllers are currently used in a wide variety of applications, due to some advantages over their analog counterparts, such as improved reliability, sensitivity, flexibility, and cost. However, errors may be introduced during the quantization process, given that such systems are typically implemented in microcomputers, microprocessors, digital signal processors, and field-programmable gate arrays. Thus, hardware choice, computational representation (e.g., direct and delta forms), and other implementation features (e.g., number of bits, fixed- or floating-point arithmetic, and sample rate) have a strong influence on precision and performance figures.

Implementations of digital systems are especially susceptible to finite word-length (FWL) effects (e.g., overflows, limit cycles, and poles and zeros sensitivity), which thus reduce their reliability and efficiency. For instance, the presence of limit cycles, in digital systems, reduces semiconductor lifespans and increases energy consumption. Besides, pole-zero positions also affect the system dynamics and fundamental requisites, such as stability.

In order to avoid performance degradation, engineers usually invest a great deal of time and effort during the design phase, aiming to solve problems caused by FWL effects. Although one finds a myriad of design tools, there is a clear lack of initiatives for validating digital systems, w.r.t. implementation aspects. In particular, software engineering techniques typically disregard the platform in which the (embedded) system software operates and restrict itself to verify software in isolation [1].

© Springer International Publishing Switzerland 2015
B. Fischer and J. Geldenhuys (Eds.): SPIN 2015, LNCS 9232, pp. 126–131, 2015.
DOI: 10.1007/978-3-319-23404-5_9

Alur et al. [2,3] introduced the earliest application of model checking for digital systems, represented by timed automata. Those influential studies inspired the development of various model checking tools for hybrid automatas and cyber-physical systems, e.g., UPPAAL [4], Open-Kronos [5], and Maellan [6]. However, such approaches are usually employed for high-level verification and have not been used for verifying resilience, i.e., system robustness related to implementation aspects. One may notice there is still a gap, regarding verification tools and methodologies to check for implementation aspects of embedded systems.

The present paper addresses this problem with the Digital-Systems Verifier (DSVerifier)[1], which is a bounded model checking (BMC) tool based on satisfiability modulo theories (SMT). DSVerifier is a powerful tool for supporting the design and verification steps of digital systems, which is more reliable and less laborious than traditional simulation tools (e.g., Matlab [7]), since it offers formal guarantees and is completely automatic.

In previous studies [8–10], an SMT-based BMC approach related to overflow, limit cycle, time constraints, stability, and minimum phase, in digital filters and controllers, was already discussed, and a novel methodology for verifying digital systems was presented. In contrast, this paper tackles implementation and usage aspects, related to a tool that provides support for the same methodology.

2   The Digital-Systems Verifier (DSVerifier)

DSVerifier is an internal module for the efficient SMT-based context-bounded model checker (ESBMC) [11], with the goal to add support for digital-system verification. The complete verification tool includes four components from ESBMC, together with DSVerifier, which are represented as dashed white boxes in Fig. 1: C parser, GOTO Program, GOTO Symex, and SMT solver.

The DSVerifier module is included before the C parser (gray box), as seen in Fig. 1. This module provides functions, which are related to quantization in fixed-point arithmetic and different digital-system realizations, and makes use of ESBMC as a verification engine, in order to check for properties related to overflow, limit cycle, time constraints, stability, and minimum phase.

In summary, DSVerifier performs three main procedures: initialization, validation, and instrumentation. When DSVerifier receives the digital-system specification, the first step is to initialize its internal parameters for quantization, that

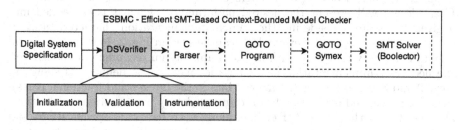

Fig. 1. An overview of the verification architecture.

---

[1] Available at http://www.dsverifier.org.

is, it computes the maximum and minimum representable numbers for the chosen FWL format. Then, during validation, DSVerifier checks whether all required parameters, for the verification procedure, were correctly provided. In the last step, DSVerifier adds explicit calls to the verification engine (for the evaluated properties), using functions available in ESBMC (e.g., _ESBMC_assume and _ESBMC_assert), in order to check for property violations.

Once the mentioned procedures are finished, an ANSI-C code file is generated, which can be verified by any C model-checker that supports bit-vector reasoning. This file is directly sent to the C parser module (see Fig. 1) and follows the normal ESBMC verification flow. In the present work, ESBMC is used, since it is the most efficient tool for reasoning about bit-vector programs, according to the last edition of the software verification competition [12]. If the verification framework finds a property violation, it produces a counterexample; otherwise, the evaluated design can be embedded into a computer-based system.

2.1 DSVerifier Features

The current version of DSVerifier supports five verification properties, regarding three direct- and delta-form implementations of digital systems, which include the cascade form. The following verifications are supported:

- **Overflow.** If a sum or product exceeds the number representation, then the resulting value will not be correctly stored. DSVerifier ensures the absence of overflows, by formally verifying every sum and product;
- **Limit Cycle.** There can be persistent oscillations in the output of a system with constant input. DSVerifier is able to check for zero-input limit cycles, for any initial condition;
- **Stability.** DSVerifier may be used for verifying digital-system stability, considering FWL effects on pole locations, i.e., on the system dynamics;
- **Minimum phase.** DSVerifier may perform a similar analysis for system zeros, in order to verify minimum phase for digital controllers;
- **Time constraints.** DSVerifier is able to investigate whether a specific computational realization respects time constraints.

2.2 DSVerifier-Aided Design Methodology

Using DSVerifier, a development engineer may verify if a digital-controller (or filter) design will present the desired performance, when it is embedded into a given hardware, considering the chosen implementation characteristics. An overview of the proposed methodology can be seen in Fig. 2. In step 1, a digital system is initially designed, with any available design technique or tool. Later, the necessary implementation characteristics have to be defined, as shown in steps 2 and 3: FWL format (number of bits in the integer and fractional parts), dynamic range, and realization form (direct or delta). The mentioned definitions are then fed to the DSVerifier engine, along with hardware specifications and other verification parameters, such as verification time (i.e., maximum time that the verification process takes) and properties to be checked. Once the configuration has been set up, in step 4, the verification process is then started, in step 5, with the chosen model checking tool (ESBMC is used as back-end).

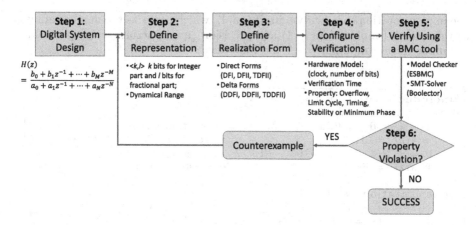

Fig. 2. Proposed methodology for digital-system verification.

DSVerifier then checks the desired properties and, in step 6, returns the verification result, which is 'successful' if there is no property violation in the proposed implementation; otherwise, it returns that the verification 'failed' and shows a counterexample, which contains inputs and states that led the system to the found property violation. With this counterexample, other implementation options (i.e., realization and representation) can be chosen, in order to avoid that failure. This process is repeated until the digital controller implementation does not present any failures, as shown in Fig. 2.

Note that this methodology has been applied to open-loop systems, where the design under verification is unwound k times, together with a property, in order to form an SMT formula, which is then passed to the SMT solver. The verification of stability and minimum-phase is complete and sound, since it does not depend on system outputs and inputs. However, the verification of other property types is typically unsound, unless some induction technique is used.

2.3 DSVerifier Usage

In order to explain the DSVerifier workflow, the following second-order controller, which can be found in a set of benchmarks available online[2], will be used:

$$H(z) = \frac{2.813z^2 - 0.0163z^1 - 1.872}{z^2 + 1.068z^1 + 0.1239}. \tag{1}$$

It was designed for an induction motor plant (extracted from an example available in Ogata [13]), with a sampling period of 0.5 s.

Command-Line Version. In this version, users must provide a description ANSI-C file, as shown in Fig. 3 for the digital controller represented by Eq. (1). This file contains the digital-system specification (ds), with numerator (ds.b = $\{2.813, -0.0163, -1.872\}$) and denominator (ds.a = $\{1.0, 1.068, 0.1239\}$), and

---

[2] http://www.dsverifier.org/benchmarks.

the implementation specification itself (impl), which contains the number of bits in the integer (impl.int_bits = 4) and precision (impl.frac_bits = 10) parts and the input range (impl.min = −5 and impl.max = 5).

```
#include<dsverifier.h>
digital_system ds = {
    .a = { 1.0, 1.068, 0.1239 },     /* denominator */
    .a_size = 3,                     /* denominator length */
    .b = { 2.813, −0.0163, −1.872 }, /* numerator */
    .b_size = 3                      /* numerator length */
};
implementation impl = {
    .int_bits = 4,       /* integer bits   */
    .frac_bits = 10,     /* precision bits */
    .min = −5.0,         /* minimum input  */
    .max = 5.0           /* maximum input  */
};
```

Fig. 3. A digital-system verification input file for DSVerifier.

In the command-line version, DSVerifier is invoked as:

dsverifier <file> --realization <i> --property <j> --x-size <k>

where $< file >$ is the digital-system specification file, $< i >$ is the chosen realization, $< j >$ is the property to be verified, and $< k >$ is the verification bound, i.e., the number of times the digital system will be unwound. Currently, 12 realizations are supported: direct form I (DFI), direct form II (DFII), transposed direct form II (TDFII), delta direct form I (DDFI), delta direct form II (DDFII), transposed delta direct form II (TDDFII), cascade direct form I (CDFI), cascade direct form II (CDFII), cascade transposed direct form II (CTDFII), cascade delta direct form I (CDDFI), cascade delta direct form II (CDDFII), and cascade transposed direct form II (CTDDFII). Furthermore, 5 different properties can be chosen: overflow, limit cycle, stability, minimum phase, and timing. Most verifications consider only FWL effects, based on the number of bits specified by the user; however, time-constraint verifications also consider hardware parameters such as processor clock, instruction count, and cycles per instruction.

Graphical User Interface (GUI). In order to facilitate the digital-system verification, a GUI was developed for DSVerifier, aiming to improve usability and, consequently, attract more digital-system engineers. The user can provide all required parameters for digital-system verifications: digital-system specification, information about the target processor, and the desired properties to be checked. Another interesting feature is the parallel execution of verification tasks, which has the potential to decrease the total verification time spent by DSVerifier. The GUI also provides graphical verification of results and counterexamples with error trace, which help adjust the verified design. It is worth noticing that users can even access documentation, benchmarks, and publications about the tool, which are also available on the DSVerifier website. In terms of software package installation, it is necessary to have at least the Java RunTime Environment Version 8.0 Update 40 (jre1.8.0_40)[3], due to the JavaFX components.

3 Conclusion

DSVerifier was presented as an SMT-based BMC tool for verifying and validating digital systems, which supports extensive verification of different properties and realization forms. With this tool, a development engineer can verify, during the design phase, if the proposed digital system will present an expected behavior, when it is embedded into a given hardware architecture.

DSVerifier can be regarded as an automated and reliable alternative, when compared with traditional simulation tools. It is freely available for download (Linux x86-64 and x86 versions), including documentation, benchmarks, experimental results presented in previous studies, publications, and source code. For future work, other properties, hardware platforms, and BMC tools will be integrated into DSVerifier, in addition to support for closed-loop systems [14].

References

1. Jackson, M.: The world and the machine. In: ICSE, pp. 283–292 (1995)
2. Alur, R., et al.: Model-checking for real-time systems. In: LICS, pp. 414–425 (1990)
3. Alur, R., et al.: Model-checking in dense real-time. IC **104**(1), 2–34 (1993)
4. Behrmann, G., David, A., Larsen, K.G.: A tutorial on UPPAAL. In: Bernardo, M., Corradini, F. (eds.) SFM-RT 2004. LNCS, vol. 3185, pp. 200–236. Springer, Heidelberg (2004)
5. Tripakis, S., et al.: Checking timed Buechi automata emptiness efficiently. FMSD **26**, 267–292 (2005)
6. Magellan, Hybrid RTL formal verification. http://www.synopsys.com/tools/verification/functionalverification/pages/magellan.aspx. Accessed 12 September 2014
7. Davis, T.A., Sigmon, K.: MATLAB Primer, 7th edn. CRC Press, Boca Raton (2005)
8. Abreu, F.N., et al.: Verifying fixed-point digital filters using SMT-based bounded model checking. SBrT (2013). doi:10.14209/sbrt.2013.57
9. Bessa, I., et al.: SMT-based bounded model checking of fixed-point digital controllers. In: IECON, pp. 295–301 (2014)
10. Bessa, I., et al.: Verification of delta form realization in fixed-point digital controllers using bounded model checking. In: SBESC, pp. 49–54 (2014)
11. Cordeiro, L., et al.: SMT-based bounded model checking for embedded ANSI-C software. TSE **38**(4), 957–974 (2012)
12. Beyer, D.: Software verification and verifiable witnesses. In: Baier, C., Tinelli, C. (eds.) TACAS 2015. LNCS, vol. 9035, pp. 401–416. Springer, Heidelberg (2015)
13. Ogata, K.: Discrete-Time Control Systems. Prentice Hall International editions, Prentice-Hall International, Upper Saddle River (1995)
14. Platzer, A.: Logic and compositional verification of hybrid systems. In: Gopalakrishnan, G., Qadeer, S. (eds.) CAV 2011. LNCS, vol. 6806, pp. 28–43. Springer, Heidelberg (2011)

---

[3] http://www.oracle.com/technetwork/java/javase/8u40-relnotes-2389089.html.

Runtime Verification of Expected Energy Consumption in Smartphones

Ana Rosario Espada, María del Mar Gallardo, Alberto Salmerón[✉],
and Pedro Merino

Dept. Lenguajes y Ciencias de la Computación, E.T.S.I. Informática,
University de Málaga, Málaga, Spain
{anarosario,gallardo,salmeron,pedro}@lcc.uma.es
http://morse.uma.es/

Abstract. Smartphones connected to Internet should work properly for days without a reset. One of the most critical non-functional properties to ensure the correct behavior is energy consumption. However, currently there is a lack of automated techniques to check whether the actual mobile consume is within the expected limits. To apply runtime verification techniques in this context, we need (a) detailed profiles of consumptions for specific actions in apps of interest (such as activate GPS, send a data packet to the network, etc.); (b) a method to automatically generate sufficiently representative use cases of the mobile behavior; (c) a language to describe the expected behavior in terms of energy consumption (energy properties); and (d) a method to monitor the mobile execution traces and analyze them against the energy properties. We aim to construct a tool chain addressing all these steps. We have already designed and implemented a model-based approach to automatically generate execution traces in mobile devices using SPIN. This paper focuses on the formalization and analysis of energy properties with a specification language inspired by the interval logic. The paper presents this logic, the implementation of runtime verification using Büchi automata, and the practical use of the whole tool chain for model-based runtime verification of energy-related properties. SPIN is a main ingredient for generating the test cases and checking the properties.

Keywords: Runtime verification · Interval logic · Energy consumption · Analysis of traces

1 Introduction

Smartphones are becoming the main devices for accessing contents on the Internet and for personal communication. The number of smartphones has surpassed the number of desktop computers and laptops and is quickly increasing and it

Work partially supported by grants P11-TIC-07659 (Regional Government of Andalusia), TIN2012-35669 (Spanish Ministry of Economy and Competitiveness), UMA-Keysight Technologies 8.06/5.47.3868-4Green and the AUIP as sponsor of the Scholarship Program Academic Mobility.

B. Fischer and J. Geldenhuys (Eds.): SPIN 2015, LNCS 9232, pp. 132–149, 2015.
DOI: 10.1007/978-3-319-23404-5_10

is expected to reach 2 billions by the end of 2015. This huge number together with user dependence on those devices makes it most important to measure and reduce their energy consumption. There is a need to contribute to the reduction of global energy consumption in the mobile networks[1], to extend the life of the device and to increase the user satisfaction. Expected energy consumption in smartphones is mainly due to the hardware, such as CPU, touch screen, GPS, WIFI and 3G/4G communication chipsets. Currently, many research efforts are oriented towards designing better batteries, but also towards optimizing mobile network protocols to reduce energy consumption. However, very often energy consumption is also due to errors in the design or the implementation of the software in the smartphone, including the operating system and the applications (or *apps*).

There are erroneous practices in mobile phone software that lead to *unexpected use of energy*. These energy bugs where studied in detail in [15], where the authors present a taxonomy of energy bugs and highlight many of their causes, including programming errors, inappropriate API usage, flaws in the design of applications or the operating system, or complicated interactions between the smartphone hardware components of smartphones. The work in [22] confirmed that energy bugs are basically the same for all smartphone operating systems.

The need to keep the smartphone working properly for days, weeks or even months without a reset makes this application domain appealing for practitioners in model checking, runtime verification and other formal automated methods for early detection of execution errors. However, the application of such techniques to analyze non-functional properties like energy consumption is still not mature.

Many works focus on some kind of monitoring to characterize the energy consumption profiles of apps [5,16,19,21]. However there is a lack of automated techniques to check that the actual consumption is within the expected limits for all the app use cases, or even for the combined execution of apps. One promising approach to verify energy consumption is the use of models to conduct test case generation and execution. For instance, a vision paper by Wilke et al. [20] introduced such ideas with the name *Model Based Energy Testing* (MBET).

Wilke et al. focused their MBET method on the use of abstract interpretation and static analysis to derive information that allows the prediction of energy consumption. They define the method for general JAVA programs and suggest that some profiling will help to implement the method for each specific computing platform.

We propose a MBET method focusing on runtime verification with real execution of test cases in the smartphones. To do that we need (a) detailed energy profiles of actions performed by the smartphone (e.g. network usage, GPS positioning); (b) an automatic method to execute the expected sequences without user intervention (test case generation and execution); (c) a language to describe the properties on the traces in terms of energy consumption (language for energy properties); and (d) a method to monitor the execution trace in the smartphone

---

[1] According to Gardner's report ICT (Information and Communications Technology) consumes 2 % of energy in the world and it is increasing 6 % every year.

and to check the energy properties (runtime verification engine). We aim to construct a tool chain addressing all these steps. Many results for step (a) are now available, which we can reuse and complement with our own measurements. Regarding step (b) we have already defined a method for model-based test case generation and execution that can be implemented using SPIN [8].

This paper contains two main novelties. The first one is the design and formalization of a new interval logic to specify energy properties (step c). The idea behind this logic is to describe properties on trace executions regarding external continuous variables such as the battery consumption. We introduce a method to define intervals of states based on propositions and then to map such intervals to time intervals where the continuous variables, like energy, are observed. The second contribution is the implementation of a runtime verification engine to check this logic on real traces of the device using SPIN (step d). The values of the continuous variable *current energy consumption* are obtained by using a physical power analyzer connected to the smartphone. We implement the runtime checking by translating the interval formula into a Büchi automata and then making the real execution trace available to the SPIN verification algorithm. The method to inject the real traces plus the external continuous variable to SPIN follows the approach used in [1]. As far as we know, this is the first completed work to apply a model based runtime verification method to check for energy consumption in smartphones, and it is also a novel combination of SPIN with a physical measurement instrument.

The rest of the paper is organized as follows. Section 2 introduces our complete framework for MBET and identifies the components previously designed and implemented and those developed in this paper. Section 3 describes the interval logic for specification of energy properties. Section 4 describes the implementation of the tool chain and its use through the use of a case study. Finally, Sects. 5 and 6 contain comparisons with related work and conclusions, respectively.

2   Model-Based Analysis Framework

The work presented in this paper is part of the process outlined in Fig. 1. This figure summarizes our approach to MBET, where we use real controlled executions on the device as the source of traces for the verification work.

The leftmost part of the figure represents the first step of the process: the generation and execution of test cases. Execution traces are generated from test cases generated using a model-based approach. We model the possible user flows within one or more apps using several independent state machines which can call one another. This loose coupling between state machines enables an easier composition of flows like the ones found on real applications, where some screens may be reached from more than one place. This model is translated into a PROMELA specification which is explored by SPIN to generate all possible test cases described in the model. Each test case corresponds to a user sequence actions that must be performed in the device in order to carry out the test, such as pressing buttons or entering text in input fields. This workflow for test case generation is described in more detail in [8].

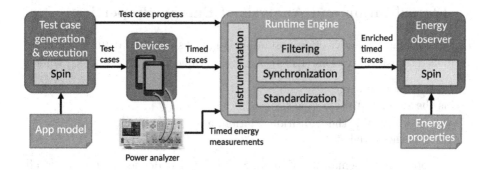

Fig. 1. Proposed architecture

The resulting test cases can be executed on real devices, where the executions are monitored by the runtime verification engine using several instrumentation techniques. These instrumentations vary in their granularity, ranging from parsing logcat traces [2] (ANDROID's standard logging facility for apps and the system), to observing individual calls to JAVA methods using the Java Debugging Interface [14] (JDI), as in [1]. The results of this monitorization are *timed traces*, i.e. sequences of states observed in a device, where each state includes an additional timestamp with the exact time in which it was produced. These states are not complete images of a device but rather a subset of information which is relevant to the apps and properties under analysis.

The runtime verification engine runs in a computer, and is connected to the smartphones via USB or WiFi. This engine can also collect additional measurements during the execution of the test cases. In this work, we connected the smartphones to a power analyzer, a N6705B DC Power Analyzer from Keysight Technologies, that can measure power consumption in real time, and which can be queried by the runtime engine. Using the timestamps of the traces, the runtime engine can combine the power consumption measurements in order to produce *enriched traces*, i.e. traces that combine information from multiple source into a single, unified sequence of states.

The resulting enriched traces are given to a set of observers [7], namely automata that check functional and nonfunctional properties (such as energy properties). To make energy properties easier to describe for users, we have defined a new interval logic to express them in a compact and user-friendly manner. The observer that evaluates these properties has been implemented with SPIN. First, properties expressed with this interval logic are translated into the Büchi automata supported by SPIN (the *never claim process*). Secondly, the enriched timed traces are provided to SPIN using a special PROMELA specification that can reconstruct execution traces from an external system as if they were generated by the PROMELA specification. This way, SPIN can check energy properties on the execution traces observed on the smartphones and other measurement devices. The following section describes this interval logic.

3   Formalization and Analysis of Energy Properties

The operational semantics of programming languages is usually defined by means of labelled transition systems (LTSs). A LTS is a tuple $P = \langle \Sigma, \longmapsto, \mathcal{L}, s_0 \rangle$ where:

- Σ is the set of states,
- $\mathcal{L}$ is the set of transition labels,
- $\longmapsto \subseteq \Sigma \times \mathcal{L} \times \Sigma$ is the transition relation, and
- $s_0 \in \Sigma$ is the initial state.

The operational semantics of an LTS P ($\mathcal{O}(P)$) is defined as the set of all possible maximal execution traces that can be constructed iteratively applying transition relation from the initial state, that is, $\mathcal{O}(P) = \{\pi | \pi = s_0 \overset{l_0}{\longmapsto} s_1 \overset{l_1}{\longmapsto} \cdots\}$. Set $\mathcal{O}(P)$ contains both infinite traces, and finite traces that correspond to executions that end successfully/erroneously. Each trace can be also described as a map $\pi : \mathbb{N} \to \Sigma$ that associates each natural number with the corresponding state in the trace, that is, $\pi(i) = s_i$. In the following, since we do not need to use transition labels, we drop them from the transition relation $\longmapsto$.

Usually, verification techniques, such as model checking, evaluate properties over traces abstracting the real time when each state occurs. This is sufficient to analyze, for instance, LTL properties. However, for some other properties, such as real time properties or memory or battery consumption properties, time is a parameter that has to be taken into account.

To formalize this, let us assume that $c : \mathbb{R}_{\geq 0} \to \mathbb{R}$ is a quantitative magnitude whose value evolves continuously with time. Thus, $c(t) \in \mathbb{R}$ represents the value of c in time instant t. We are now interested in specifying and evaluating properties on variable c related to an execution trace π. To do this, we have to synchronize the execution of π with the continuous evolution of c, as shown in the following definition.

Definition 1. *Given a trace $\pi \in \mathcal{O}(P)$, an execution e of π is given by a function $e[\pi] : \mathbb{N} \to \mathbb{R}_{\geq 0}$ that associates each state $\pi(i)$ of π with the time instant $e(\pi)(i) \in \mathbb{R}_{\geq 0}$ in which it occurs[2]. Functions $e(\pi)$ satisfy that $e[\pi](i) \leq e[\pi](j)$ iff $i < j$, that is, successive states occur at successive instants.*

Observe that each trace π may have many associated executions $e(\pi)$ that relate states to different time instants. We now explain how execution functions e may be used to synchronize traces with continuous variables that evolve in parallel with trace executions, making it possible to analyze non-functional properties on the traces.

Given a variable $c : \mathbb{R}_{\geq 0} \to \mathbb{R}$ which evolves continuously with time, and an execution, $e[\pi]$, of a trace π, we synchronize c and π by relating each state s_i to the value of c in the instant when s_i occurs $e[\pi](i)$. The diagram in Fig. 2 illustrates this synchronization. The upper row shows the states of trace $\pi = s_0 \longmapsto s_1 \longmapsto \cdots$, emphasizing in its discrete character. The middle row

---

[2] We assume that $e[\pi](i)$ represents the time instant when state s_i is created.

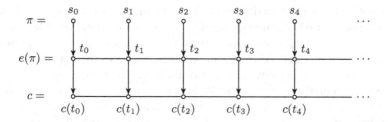

Fig. 2. Synchronization of trace π and continuous variable c using $e[\pi]$

shows the time passing, with each state s_i associated by means of $e(\pi)$ with the time instant when it occurs. Finally, the lowest row shows the evolution of a continuous variable c in time, and how it is possible to relate each state s_i to the corresponding value $c(t_i)$ that takes place at the instant t_i.

3.1   Specification of Energy Properties with Interval Logic

In this section, we introduce the specification language to be used to describe properties on trace executions regarding external continuous variables such as the battery consumption. We assume that traces π are *finite* sequences of states having an *ending state o* that repeats forever, that is, for each trace π, there exists a natural number $n > 0$ (the length of the trace denoted as $length(\pi)$) such that (1) $\pi(n-1) \neq o^3$, and (2) $\forall k \geq n.\pi(k) = o$. Finally, we also assume that if π is a finite trace of length n, execution functions $e(\pi)$ associate the ending, and successive, states of π with the time instant when the last non-ending state took place, that is, $\forall k \geq n.e(\pi)(k) = e(\pi)(n-1)$.

We make use of interval calculus to specify properties [6]. The domain of interval logic is the set of time intervals $\mathbb{Intv}$ defined as $\{[t_1, t_2] | t_1, t_2 \in \mathbb{R}, t_1 \leq t_2\}$. An *interval variable* v is defined as a function $v : \mathbb{Intv} \to \mathbb{R}$ that associates each interval with a real number. For instance, a continuous variable $c : \mathbb{R}_{\geq 0} \to \mathbb{R}$ can be used to define interval variables, such as, for instance, $diff\_c : \mathbb{Intv} \to \mathbb{R}$ given as $diff\_c([t_1, t_2]) = c(t_2) - c(t_1)$. Thus, for example, if c is the identity function, $diff\_c$ defines the *interval length function*.

We can construct *interval expressions* describing properties on intervals by using a set of interval variables, relational, boolean operators and real constants. For instance, if K is a constant, $diff\_c \leq K : \mathbb{Intv} \to \{true, false\}$ defines the property on intervals $[t_1, t_2]$ that is true iff $c(t_2) - c(t_1) \leq K$.

In the sequel, given a trace π, we use *state intervals* such as $I = [i, j]$ (with $i \leq j$) to represent the subtrace of π from state $\pi(i)$ to $\pi(j)$. Clearly, given a state interval $I = [i, j]$ of π, and an execution $e[\pi]$, we can construct $e(\pi)(I) = [e(\pi)(i), e(\pi)(j)]$ which gives us the time interval from the creation of state s_i to the creation of state s_j in execution $e(\pi)$. Thus, state intervals and executions of traces provide time intervals on which we can evaluate interval expressions such as $diff\_c \leq K$.

---

[3] To simplify the presentation, we assume that finite traces have at least one non-ending state s_0.

The rest of the section is devoted to introducing the so-called *formula intervals* which constitute the language used to specify state intervals. The idea is as follows. Assume that the continuous variable c mentioned above represents the energy consumed by device during an execution, and that we want to check that a WiFi session consumes less than a threshold K. To do this, we first need to specify the system states where the WiFi session takes place. Given a trace π, each WiFi session involves a state interval I during which WiFi is active. Once we have located the state interval I of π, using an execution function $e(\pi)$, we can evaluate the interval expression $diff\_c \leq K$ on the time interval $e(\pi)(I)$.

In the sequel, we introduce the so-called *proposition intervals* as a description language of state intervals on traces. To do this, we assume a set of state formulae *Prop*, and a satisfaction relation $\models \subseteq \Sigma \times Prop$ such that $(s,p) \in \models$ iff state s satisfies p. As usual, we write $(s,p) \in \models$ as $s \models p$. In addition, we assume that the ending state o does not satisfy any formula of *Prop*, that is, $\forall p \in Prop.o \not\models p$.

In the following, given two state formulae $p, q \in Prop$, we use *state proposition intervals*, denoted as $[p, q]$ to identify state intervals inside traces as follows.

Definition 2. *Given a trace π, we say that state interval $I = [i,j]$ of π satisfies $[p,q]$, written as $\pi \downarrow I \models [p,q]$, iff the following conditions hold:*

1. $\pi(i) \models p$
2. $\forall i < k < j.\pi(k) \not\models q$
3. $\pi(j) \models q$

that is, $[i,j]$ is a state interval of π such that $\pi(i)$ satisfies p, and $\pi(j)$ is the first state after $\pi(i)$ that satisfies q.

Now, given a finite trace π, we define $\pi \Downarrow [p, q]$ as the finite sequence of state intervals of π, written as $I_0 \cdot I_1 \cdots I_{m-1}$, that satisfy $[p, q]$ in the sense that has just been described, that is, $\forall 0 \leq i < m.\pi \downarrow I_i \models [p, q]$.

We need the following definition to formalize how $\pi \Downarrow [p, q]$ is constructed.

Definition 3. *Given $p \in Prop$, a finite trace π of length n, and $k \geq 0$, $\pi \downarrow_k p$ is the first state of π that occurs after (including) $\pi(k)$ and that satisfies p, if it exists, or symbol ∞, otherwise. We can inductively define $\pi \downarrow_k p$ as:*

1. $\pi \downarrow_k p = k$, *iff* $\pi(k) \models p$
2. $\pi \downarrow_k p = \pi \downarrow_{k+1} p$ *iff* $k < n, \pi(k) \not\models p$
3. $\pi \downarrow_k p = \infty$ *iff* $k \geq n$.

Definition 4. *Given a finite trace π, and two state formulae p, q, the sequence of state intervals determined by p, q, $\pi \Downarrow [p, q]$, is inductively defined from operator $\Downarrow_k$ with $k \geq 0$, as it is described below.*

1. $\pi \Downarrow_k [p,q] = \epsilon \iff \pi \downarrow_k p = \infty$, *or* $\pi \downarrow_k p = j \wedge \pi \downarrow_{j+1} q = \infty$[4]
2. $\pi \Downarrow_k [p,q] = [j,l] \cdot (\pi \Downarrow_{l+1} [p,q]) \iff \pi \downarrow_k p = j \wedge \pi \downarrow_{j+1} q = l$

We define $\pi \Downarrow [p, q]$ as $\pi \Downarrow_0 [p, q]$.

---

[4] ϵ represents the empty sequence.

Thus, two state formulae $p, q \in Prop$ determine a sequence of state intervals $\pi \Downarrow [p,q]$ on each trace π. Given a trace π and an execution $e(\pi)$, the following definition describes how interval expressions (such as $diff\_c \leq K$) can be specified to be checked on the time intervals determined by the state intervals of π given by $\pi \Downarrow [p,q]$. For instance, if $swifi$ and $ewifi$ are two state formulae that are satisfied by the states which switch the wifi connection on/off, respectively, $\pi \Downarrow [swifi, ewifi]$ is the sequence of state intervals of π on which the wifi is active.

The following definition states when an execution of a trace $e(\pi)$ satisfies an interval expression Φ such as $diff\_c \leq K$. We consider three types of expressions. An execution trace $e(\pi)$ satisfies formula (1) $[[\Phi]]_{[p,q]}$ iff the first state interval determined by $\pi \Downarrow [p,q]$ and $e(\pi)$ satisfies Φ, (2) $\forall[[\Phi]]_{[p,q]}$ iff all the time intervals determined of $\pi \Downarrow [p,q]$ and $e(\pi)$ satisfy Φ; $\exists[[\Phi]]_{[p,q]}$ iff it exists a state interval given the sequence $\pi \Downarrow [p,q]$ and $e(\pi)$ that satisfies Φ. Recall that if $I = [i,j]$ is a state interval of π, $e(\pi)(I)$ is the time interval $[e(\pi)(s_i), e(\pi)(s_j)]$. For instance, if $\Phi = diff\_c \leq K$, $[[\Phi]]_{[swifi,ewifi]}$ establishes that the time interval determined by the first state interval on which $[swifi, ewifi]$ holds must satisfy Φ.

Definition 5. *Let Φ and $[p,q]$ be an interval expression and a state proposition interval, respectively. Let $e(\pi)$ be an execution of a finite trace π. Then*

1. *We say that $e(\pi)$ satisfies Φ on the time intervals determined by $[p,q]$, and denote it as $e(\pi) \models [[\Phi]]_{[p,q]}$ iff $= I_1 \cdots I_n$ with $n > 0$ and $\Phi(e(\pi)(I_1))$ holds.*
2. *We say that $e(\pi)$ satisfies $\exists\Phi$ on the time intervals determined by $[p,q]$, and denote it as $e(\pi) \models \exists[[\Phi]]_{[p,q]}$ iff $[p,q] \Downarrow \pi = I_1 \cdots I_n$ with $n \geq 0$ and $\exists 1 \leq i \leq n.\Phi(e(\pi)(I_i))$ holds.*
3. *We say that $e(\pi)$ satisfies $\forall\Phi$ on the time intervals determined by $[p,q]$, and denote it as $e(\pi) \models \forall[[\Phi]]_{[p,q]}$ iff $[p,q] \Downarrow \pi = I_1 \cdots I_n$ with $n \geq 0$ and $\forall 1 \leq i \leq n.\Phi(e(\pi)(I_i))$ holds.*

3.2   From Interval Properties to LTL

In this section, we discuss how the interval properties can be practically evaluated on execution traces. Each type of interval property can be described by an LTL formula to be given to the model checker. To simplify the presentation of the formulae, we have defined proposition $\Phi(p,q)$ as:

$$\Phi(p,q) \equiv p \wedge (\neg q \, U \, (q \wedge \Phi))$$

Intuitively, $\Phi(p,q)$ is the LTL representation of property: *"p holds on the current state, q will be true in a future state and, at that moment, the time interval determined by p and q will satisfy Φ"*, as the following diagram illustrates:

For $[[\Phi]]_{[p,q]}$ properties, we use the following LTL specification:

$$[[\Phi]]_{[p,q]} \equiv (\neg p) \, U \, \Phi(p,q) \tag{1}$$

The intended meaning of this formula is as follows. We first search for the first state (s_i) on which p holds, then we search for the first state following s_i on which q holds (s_j). These two states s_i and s_j determine a time interval. If Φ is true on this interval, then formula $[[\Phi]]_{[p,q]}$ holds. Otherwise, that is, if it is not possible to find either s_i or s_j, or if the time interval does not satisfy Φ, the formula is false. The following sequence shows a trace that satisfies $[[\Phi]]_{[p,q]}$. Note that we use solid arrows to identify intervals, and dashed arrows otherwise.

$$\pi = \qquad \overset{\neg p}{\circ} \text{-} \text{-} \overset{\neg p}{\circ} \text{-} \text{-} \overset{\neg p}{\circ} \text{-} \text{-} \overset{p}{\underset{s_i}{\circ}} \longrightarrow \overset{\neg q}{\circ} \longrightarrow \overset{\neg q}{\circ} \longrightarrow \overset{q \wedge \Phi}{\underset{s_j}{\circ}} \text{-} \text{-} \text{-} \overset{}{\circ}$$

For the property $\exists\,[[\Phi]]_{[p,q]}$, we use the following LTL specification:

$$\exists\,[[\Phi]]_{[p,q]} \equiv \Phi(p,q) \vee \Diamond(\neg p \wedge \circ\, \Phi(p,q)) \tag{2}$$

that is, $\Phi(p,q)$ should be true either in the first state or in some future instant. Note that $\circ$ represents the "next" operator, which, in our case, is safe to use since we do not analyze concurrent programs, but rather linear execution traces. The use of $\circ$ is needed to assure that formula $\Phi(p,q)$ is evaluated on a maximal time interval determined by p and q, that is, the state on which p is true, if it is not the initial state, must be preceded by a state that does not satisfy p. The following sequence shows an example of a trace for which $\Phi(p,q)$ holds on the second time interval determined by p and q.

$$\pi = \quad \overset{\neg p}{\circ} \text{-} \text{-} \overset{p}{\circ} \text{-} \text{-} \overset{\neg q}{\circ} \text{-} \text{-} \overset{\neg q}{\circ} \text{-} \text{-} \overset{q \wedge \neg\Phi}{\underset{s_i}{\circ}} \text{-} \text{-} \overset{p}{\circ} \longrightarrow \overset{\neg q}{\circ} \longrightarrow \overset{\neg q}{\circ} \longrightarrow \overset{q \wedge \Phi}{\underset{s_j}{\circ}} \text{-} \text{-} \overset{}{\circ}$$

Finally, the LTL formula for $\forall\,[[\Phi]]_{[p,q]}$ is given by:

$$\forall\,[[\Phi]]_{[p,q]} \equiv p \to \Phi(p,q) \wedge \Box((\neg p \wedge \circ p) \to \circ\,\Phi(p,q)) \tag{3}$$

that is, all maximal intervals determined by $[p,q]$ properties in their ending points should satisfy Φ at the instant when the right ending point occurs. The following sequence shows a trace having two time intervals, determined by p and q, for which Φ is true. Note that last state is labelled with symbol o to indicate that the trace does not contain any state interval after $[s_{i_2}, s_{j_2}]$ satisfying $[p,q]$.

$$\pi = \quad \overset{\neg p}{\circ} \text{-} \text{-} \overset{p}{\underset{s_{i_1}}{\circ}} \longrightarrow \overset{\neg q}{\circ} \longrightarrow \overset{\neg q}{\circ} \longrightarrow \overset{q \wedge \Phi}{\underset{s_{j_1}}{\circ}} \text{-} \text{-} \overset{p}{\underset{s_{i_2}}{\circ}} \longrightarrow \overset{\neg q}{\circ} \longrightarrow \overset{\neg q}{\circ} \longrightarrow \overset{q \wedge \Phi}{\underset{s_{j_2}}{\circ}} \text{-} \text{-} \overset{}{\underset{o}{\circ}}$$

4   Tool Chain Implementation

In this section we present the implementation of the architecture for model-based energy testing we proposed in Sect. 2, and how all the pieces fit together[5]. To

---

[5] The implementation and examples are available online: http://morse.uma.es/tools/draco.

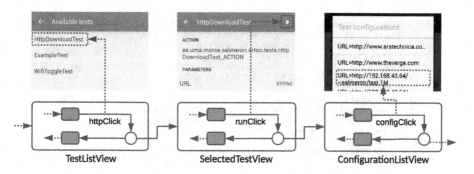

Fig. 3. Fragment of app model for test case generation

guide this description, we will use a simple case study: an ANDROID app developed internally to help characterize the energy profile of common tasks. The app contains several configurable test scenarios which can be executed and traced. We will show how our proposal can be used to check the energy consumption of a certain sequence of actions within a test case. We describe this using the following interval property, which will influence some decisions later on:

$$[energy(t_2) - energy(t1) < P]_{[[testStep=\text{START},testStep=END]]}$$

This property is of the form $[[\Phi]]_{[p,q]}$, whose translation to LTL was shown in Eq. 1, in Sect. 3.2. Recall from the previous section that t_1 and t_2 are the time instants that correspond to the start and end of an interval, respectively.

4.1 Test Case Generation

The first step is to create the test cases which will be executed and analyzed. We generate the test cases automatically from a model of the app, which describes the possible user flows of a user within our app. The app model would be created by the app developer or tester. For our case study the model is straightforward, navigating the app until one of the available test scenarios is selected and executed a number of times. The transitions of this model are associated with controls present in the app screens, such as buttons or menus, indicating which user action must be performed at each step of the test case. Figure 3 shows a fragment of the model, with several state machines connected by transitions fired when the user interacts with the corresponding control in the screenshots.

This model is automatically translated into a PROMELA specification, which is explored by SPIN in order to generate all possible test cases exhaustively. The resulting test cases are translated into JAVA classes that can be installed and executed in the smartphone to perform each test case. Listing 1.1 shows part of a test case obtained from the model in Fig. 3, in particular a user selecting the HTTP test scenario listed, and then running the selected test with one of the available configurations. More details about this workflow for model-based test case generation can be found in [8].

```
public void TestSampleApphttpClic1() throws UiObjectNotFoundException {
    UiObject control = new UiObject(new UiSelector()
        .className("android.widget.TextView").index(0)
        .textContains("HttpDownlo"));
    control.click();
    Log.v("TESTCASEGENERATOR","CONTROL-httpClick");
}
public void TestSampleApprunClic2() throws UiObjectNotFoundException {
    UiObject control = new UiObject(new UiSelector()
        .className("android.widget.TextView").index(0)
        .descriptionContains("Available tests"));
    control.click();
    Log.v("TESTCASEGENERATOR","CONTROL-runClick");
}
```

Listing 1.1. Part of automatically generated test case

4.2   Implementation of Interval Properties in SPIN

The interval properties described in Sect. 3 have been implemented in SPIN, so it can be used as one of the observers that can check for properties over the execution traces obtained from a smartphone. In particular, we use our previous work on the analysis of execution traces with SPIN [10,17] as the starting point for this implementation. In this work, instead of analyzing a regular system model, we used a PROMELA specification that communicated with an external system in order to extract and reconstruct the states of its execution trace in the SPIN's global state for its analysis. This PROMELA specification was instantiated from a template using information about the system under test, such as the variables comprising a state and the properties to analyze. Listing 1.2 shows a simplified fragment of the PROMELA specification for our case study.

The core of the PROMELA specification is a single loop, shown on lines 18 to 33 in Listing 1.2. The first branch of the loop is a c_code block (line 19) which updates the global variables (lines 1 to 4) with the values of a new state. Thus, after each iteration, the next state is available as part of SPIN's global state. This c_code block may load a new state received from the external system, but it may also fetch a previously visited state if SPIN has backtracked during the exploration. Note that execution traces are linear, but the addition of a never claim automata may produce several branches that need to be explored. See [10,17] for more details on this approach. This never claim automata is the key to evaluating interval properties. The automata, not shown in the PROMELA fragment, is obtained by negating and translating the LTL formula from Eq. 1.

Continuous variables are treated as regular variables: for each continuous variable c there is a floating point variable c in SPIN's global state, and when a new state is obtained at t_i, the values of each c variable is update with the value of $c(t_i)$. While PROMELA does not support floating point variables, we can add them to SPIN's global state using c_state declarations. Note that the usual caveats regarding floating point variables (e.g. comparing for equality) still apply and should be taken into account when writting properties. In our case study, we have one continuous variable, called **energy** (line 3).

```
c_state "short _interval" "Global"
c_state "short testStep" "Global"
c_state "double energy" "Global"
c_state "double energy_t1" "Global"

void update_interval(struct state* newState) {
    if (!(now.testStep == START) && (newState->testStep == START))
        newState->_interval = 1;
    else if (!(now.testStep == END) && (newState->testStep == END)) {
        newState->_interval = 0;
}
void update_energy_t1(struct state* newState) {
    if (!now._interval && newState->_interval)
        newState->energy_t1 = newState->energy;
}

init {
    do
    :: (running) -> c_code {
            now.currentState++;
            if (now.currentState > lastState) {
                if (!wasRunning) {
                    now.running = 0;
                } else {
                    readNewState();
                    lastState++;
                    callUpdateFunctions();
                }
            } /* else: backtracked */
            updateSpinStateFromStateStack();
        }
    :: (!running) -> break
    od
}
```

Listing 1.2. Fragment of PROMELA specification for execution trace analysis

When Φ is evaluated in an interval $[t_1, t_2]$, the initial and final values of any continuous variable c, i.e. $c(t_1)$ and $c(t_2)$, must be available. On the one hand, since Φ is evaluated at t_2, global variable c already contains the $c(t_2)$ value. On the other hand, $c(t_1)$ will be available in a new variable c_t1, which is created and updated automatically. In our case study, the corresponding variable for keeping track of $energy(t_1)$ is energy_t1 (line 4). These new variables are updated when a new interval is entered, using a so-called update function. These are C functions that are invoked (line 27) after a new state is read from the execution trace (line 25), but before it is copied over to SPIN's global state (line 30), and has access to both the previous and the new states.

In addition, another variable is automatically introduced, _interval (line 1), which is also updated using an update function. This variable is true when an interval has been entered, but not yet exited, and false otherwise. The update functions of interval variables only update their values when _interval changes from false to true, i.e. at the time instant t_1 where a new interval is entered.

The update function for _interval and energy_t1 are shown on lines 6 and 12, respectively. These functions show how _interval is updated by checking the conditions of the interval $[testStep = \text{START}, testStep = \text{END}]$, and

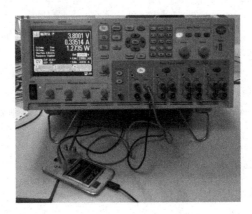

Fig. 4. Power analyzer connected to a smartphone

how `energy_t1` is updated only when entering an new interval. In these functions, `struct state* newState` is a pointer to a struct that contains all the system and interval variables, which is a subset of the contents of the `now` struct. Update functions are always called in order, so that the new value of `_interval` computed by `update_interval` is available to the following functions (`update_energy_t1`).

4.3   Monitoring and Analysis

Once we have our test cases and our energy observer implemented with SPIN, we can proceed to the next step. The generated test cases are installed on the target smartphone: a Samsung Galaxy S4. This device is connected to a computer that controls and monitors the tests, and to a N6705B DC Power Analyzer from Keysight Technologies.

The power analyzer is connected to the smartphone instead of the battery as shown in Fig. 4, and it supplies the required power. This power analyzer provides an SCPI (Standard Commands for Programmable Instruments) interface accessible over a computer network, which the runtime engine uses to extract periodic energy measurements.

In the computer, the test controller and runtime verification engine are executed as separate programs. Both programs use the Android Debug Bridge (adb) tool connected via USB to perform their tasks. As we said, the engine and observers usually only require a relevant subset of the full state present on the device. For our case study we are only interested in high level events fired when a user event is performed during a test case, in addition to the energy measurements. When one of these events is fired, a variable called `testStep` is updated, and the latest energy measurements are sent along with the new state. To perform this step, we have to implement some additional instrumentation code. This code checks the live logcat traces [2] from the smartphone, looking for a certain pattern that indicates a new test step. Since our execution trace reconstruction for SPIN does not support string variables, the string that describes the new step is transformed into a integer representation. The general observer architecture is outlined in [7].

For this case study, we are interested in the power consumption for one of app's tests scenarios, in which a file of fixed length is downloaded from a local server over WiFi. We use the interval property declared at the beginning of this section, which for our implementation would be written as:

```
[$energy - $energy_t1 < P] [[$testStep == START, $testStep == END]]
```

Note that in the property we use $ as a prefix for variables present in the execution trace. In this property, the interval is given by $testStep == START, where START is the user action performed in the test case that initiates the download test scenario, and $testStep == END, which represents the end of the test scenario. testStep is an integer variable which included in the execution trace presented to SPIN, and START and END are integer representations of the relevant logcat trace lines. The interval formula to be checked on all intervals, $energy - $energy_t1 < P, uses the continuous variable energy, which is extracted from the power analyzer. This measurement is taken at regular intervals, 1000 times per second, and is also included in the enriched execution trace.

Listing 1.3 shows part of a runtime verification log trace. First the user event selecting a test scenario from the list, and then a user event running the selected test. The log trace shows how, for each detected user event, the variables are sent to SPIN to reconstruct the next state. The messages are sent encoded using a custom communication protocol, e.g. each variable is referred by a given id instead of its name. For instance, variable testStep has been given id 2, energy has id 6, and the current Unix timestamp in milliseconds is encoded in variable 5.

The time spent in the execution and analysis of test cases can be roughly divided between the instrumentation, the analysis with SPIN, and the execution of the test cases. In our experiments we found that the impact of the model checking algorithm for the interval formulae is negligible. Since the model to be analyzed by SPIN is essentially one single sequence of with no branching (save by the branching induced by the never claim automata), the state space to be explored is significantly smaller than that of other realistic PROMELA models. Most of the time spent can be attributed to the automatic execution of the test cases on the smartphone, using the UIAUTOMATOR framework [3].

Instrumentation can also have significant influence on the global analysis time. For the case study shown here, we only needed to observe the live logcat traces from the smartphone. However, we can include additional information that is significantly slower to acquire, such as tracing each JAVA method that is entered or exited during the execution of the test cases [1]. Although this tracing can be filtered to only certain JAVA packages, we experienced serious slowdowns with real applications such as Facebook.

Other factors such as background tasks or CPU throttling mechanisms [4], e.g. changing the frequency depending on the current computational load, can also interfere with the energy measurements. To facilitate repeatable analyses

```
pLogLevel: 0 pTag: TESTCASEGENERATOR pLogMessage:
    V/TESTCASEGENERATOR(13414): CONTROL-httpClick: 01/05/2015 16:39:28
    void com.UMA.RuntimeEngine.AndroidMobile.SmartPhoneMonitoring
    .RegisterAndroidLog(String,String,String,String)
may 01, 2015 4:39:59 PM
    com.UMA.RuntimeEngine.Observer.Spin.ProtocolClientHelper sendReport
measure { id: 2, intValue: 702221648 }
measure { id: 5, longValue: 1430498399008 }
measure { id: 6, doubleValue: 6.753239800596E13 }

pLogLevel: 0 pTag: TESTCASEGENERATOR pLogMessage:
    V/TESTCASEGENERATOR(13485): CONTROL-runClick: 01/05/2015 16:39:28
    void com.UMA.RuntimeEngine.AndroidMobile.SmartPhoneMonitoring
    .RegisterAndroidLog(String,String,String,String)
may 01, 2015 4:40:05 PM
    com.UMA.RuntimeEngine.Observer.Spin.ProtocolClientHelper sendReport
measure { id: 2, intValue: 114991181 }
measure { id: 5, longValue: 1430498405000 }
measure { id: 6, doubleValue: 6.433557098917E13 }
```

Listing 1.3. Runtime verification log trace

with real devices, users are encouraged to keep a controlled environment, e.g. by removing unused apps or using a fixed CPU frequency.

5   Related Work

There are many references to previous research on estimating power consumption of mobile devices and mobile applications by using some kind of monitoring tools. Phatak et al. [15] provided one of the first classifications of energy bugs for hardware and software, and they proposed a roadmap towards developing a systematic diagnosing framework for treating these energy bugs. Later, Phatak and other authors presented the **eprof** tool [16], a fine grained energy profiler being used to gain insight of energy usage of smartphone.

Parally Yepang Liu [9] also studied characterized energy bugs (e.g., their types and manifestation) and identified common patterns. They implemented a static code analyzer, **PerfChecker**, to detect and identify bug patterns.

The **E-loupe** project [5,12] explores an alternative that mitigates the ill-effects of an energy hungry application. The framework consists in monitoring data in the mobile which is then processed in the cloud in order to detect risk of energy rain and to produce information to isolate the dangerous applications.

Memory leaks can be also a reason for energy consumption. In [21] the authors design a light memory leak detector that focuses on activity leak and a priority adjustment module to prioritize killing leaking apps. In a different way [23] built a framework to detect energy leaks using dynamic taint analysis (a form of information flow analysis).

Finally, [11,19,22] studied the energy consumed between different mobile platforms. The first one compares the energy bugs, the second compares the energy efficiency, and the last one developed a power estimation method based on battery traces.

In our runtime model based framework, we also need to monitor energy consumption, like most of the previous proposals. However we do not use this output directly, but as an input to a more sophisticated analysis. We use the interval logic to represent energy properties to drive the identification of bad behaviors of the applications running the smartphone. As result, our runtime verification technique is useful detect leak apps in a very precise way: we can provide the exact the execution sequence of one or several apps that causes the system to loos more energy than expected.

Model checking has also been applied to estimate the energy consumption in wireless sensor networks. In [18] the authors use a UPPPAAL model of the network that include aspects like time, bandwidths, and energy. Then they use model checking with different scenarios to predict the influence of a given set of parameters on energy consumption. In particular, they focus on sensors and routers. Nakajima [13] has recently introduced two new formalisms to deal with this problem, the *power consumption automaton* to represent the system under analysis and a version of LTL (Linear Time temporal Logic) with freeze quantifiers to represent expected energy consumption. The presence of time and energy in the models and formulae make this model checking problem undecidable, and the author proposes several practical subsets to run verification. Compared with these works, our approach upholds the idea of one specific logic to represent energy properties and the model checking mechanics to check this logic. However, instead of exploring a model of a system, we deal with execution traces extracted from real devices with precise energy consumption measures for each sampling period.

6   Conclusions and Future Work

The analysis of energy consumption in smartphones using formal method techniques has attracted little attention in the past. Our proposal draws from model checking and runtime verification, combining the specification power of logic with automated analysis techniques, to check real execution traces against some expected energy consumption and produce counterexamples. This work can be done using real devices and real applications. A minor effort is required to model the behavior of the applications, in order to take advantage of our model-based testing approach to generate test cases that will lead to execution traces. Our proposal addresses all these issues and produces a complete tool chain for automated model-based energy testing.

This paper has presented a novel approach to specify energy properties over real execution traces. The proposed logic, based on interval logic, does not allow the use of temporal operators, which we did not require for our case study. However, we believe the use of LTL formulae to define the intervals is feasible within our approach, and will consider such extensions in future works. Further work is planned to include additional continuous variables to the execution traces, such as network bandwidth or memory use, instead of considering just energy consumption.

References

1. Adalid, D., Salmerón, A., Gallardo, M.M., Merino, P.: Using spin for automated debugging of infinite executions of java programs. J. Syst. Softw. **90**, 61–75 (2014)
2. Android Open Source Project: logcat. http://developer.android.com/tools/help/logcat.html
3. Android Open Source Project: UIAutomatorViewer. http://developer.android.com/training/testing/ui-testing/index.html
4. Baums, A., Zaznova, N.: Power optimization of embedded real-time systems and their adaptability. Autom. Control Comput. Sci. **42**(3), 153–162 (2008). http://dx.doi.org/10.3103/S0146411608030073
5. Chandra, R., Fatemieh, O., Moinzadeh, P., Thekkath, C.A., Xie, Y.: End-to-end energy management of mobile devices. Technical report MSR-TR-2013-69, Microsoft, July 2013. http://research.microsoft.com/apps/pubs/default.aspx?id=198163
6. Chaochen, Z., Hansen, M.R.: Duration Calculus - A Formal Approach to Real-Time Systems. Monographs in Theoretical Computer Science. An EATCS Series. Springer, Heidelberg (2004). http://dx.doi.org/10.1007/978-3-662-06784-0
7. Espada, A.R., Gallardo, M.M., Salmerón, A., Merino, P.: Using model checking to generate test cases for android applications. In: Pakulin, N., Petrenko, A.K., Schlingloff, B.H. (eds.) Proceedings Tenth Workshop on Model Based Testing. Electronic Proceedings in Theoretical Computer Science, vol. 180, pp. 7–21. Open Publishing Association, Amsterdam (2015)
8. Espada, A.R., Gallardo, M.M., Adalid, D.: Dragonfly: encapsulating android for instrumentation. In: Proceedings of the XIII Jornadas de Programación y Lenguajes (PROLE 2013) (2013)
9. Liu, Y., Xu, C., Cheung, S.C.: Characterizing and detecting performance bugs for smartphone applications. In: Proceedings of the 36th International Conference on Software Engineering, ICSE 2014, pp. 1013–1024. ACM, New York (2014). http://doi.acm.org/10.1145/2568225.2568229
10. Merino, P., Salmerón, A.: Combining SPIN with ns-2 for protocol optimization. In: van de Pol, J., Weber, M. (eds.) SPIN 2010. LNCS, vol. 6349, pp. 40–57. Springer, Heidelberg (2010)
11. Metri, G., Shi, W., Brockmeyer, M.: Energy-efficiency comparison of mobile platforms and applications: a quantitative approach. In: Proceedings of the 16th International Workshop on Mobile Computing Systems and Applications, HotMobile 2015, pp. 39–44. ACM, New York (2015). http://doi.acm.org/10.1145/2699343.2699358
12. Microsoft: Eloupe project. http://research.microsoft.com/en-us/projects/eloupe/
13. Nakajima, S.: Model checking of energy consumption behavior. In: Cardin, M.A., Krob, D., Lui, P.C., Tan, Y.H., Wood, K. (eds.) Complex Systems Design & Management Asia, pp. 3–14. Springer International Publishing, Switzerland (2015). http://dx.doi.org/10.1007/978-3-319-12544-2_1
14. Oracle: Java Debug Interface. http://docs.oracle.com/javase/6/docs/jdk/api/jpda/jdi/index.html
15. Pathak, A., Hu, Y.C., Zhang, M.: Bootstrapping energy debugging on smartphones: a first look at energy bugs in mobile devices. In: Proceedings of the 10th ACM Workshop on Hot Topics in Networks, HotNets-X, pp. 5:1–5:6. ACM, New York (2011). http://doi.acm.org/10.1145/2070562.2070567

16. Pathak, A., Jindal, A., Hu, Y.C., Midkiff, S.P.: What is keeping my phone awake?: characterizing and detecting no-sleep energy bugs in smartphone apps. In: Proceedings of the 10th International Conference on Mobile Systems, Applications, and Services, MobiSys 2012, pp. 267–280. ACM, New York (2012). http://doi.acm.org/10.1145/2307636.2307661

17. Salmerón, A., Merino, P.: Integrating model checking and simulation for protocol optimization. Simulation **91**(1), 3–25 (2015). http://dx.doi.org/10.1177/0037549714557054

18. Schmitt, P.H., Werner, F.: Model checking for energy efficient scheduling in wireless sensor networks. In: Technical report (2007)

19. Wang, C., Yan, F., Guo, Y., Chen, X.: Power estimation for mobile applications with profile-driven battery traces. In: 2013 IEEE International Symposium on Low Power Electronics and Design (ISLPED), pp. 120–125, September 2013

20. Wilke, C., Götz, S., Reimann, J., Aßmann, U.: Vision paper: towards model-based energy testing. In: Whittle, J., Clark, T., Kühne, T. (eds.) MODELS 2011. LNCS, vol. 6981, pp. 480–489. Springer, Heidelberg (2011). http://dx.doi.org/10.1007/978-3-642-24485-8_35

21. Xia, M., He, W., Liu, X., Liu, J.: Why application errors drain battery easily?: a study of memory leaks in smartphone apps. In: Proceedings of the Workshop on Power-Aware Computing and Systems, HotPower 2013, pp. 2:1–2:5. ACM, New York (2013). http://doi.acm.org/10.1145/2525526.2525846

22. Zhang, J., Musa, A., Le, W.: A comparison of energy bugs for smartphoneplatforms. In: 2013 1st International Workshop on the Engineering of Mobile-Enabled Systems (MOBS), pp. 25–30, May 2013

23. Zhang, L., Gordon, M.S., Dick, R.P., Mao, Z.M., Dinda, P., Yang, L.: Adel: an automatic detector of energy leaks for smartphone applications. In: Proceedings of the Eighth IEEE/ACM/IFIP International Conference on Hardware/Software Codesign and System Synthesis, CODES+ISSS 2012, pp. 363–372. ACM, New York (2012). http://doi.acm.org/10.1145/2380445.2380503

Heuristics and Benchmarks

Directed Model Checking for PROMELA with Relaxation-Based Distance Functions

Ahmad Siyar Andisha[1], Martin Wehrle[2], and Bernd Westphal[3]($\boxtimes$)

[1] corix AG, 4562 Biberist, Switzerland
[2] University of Basel, Basel, Switzerland
[3] Albert-Ludwigs-Universität Freiburg, Freiburg im Breisgau, Germany
westphal@informatik.uni-freiburg.de

Abstract. Directed model checking uses distance functions to guide the state space exploration to efficiently find short error paths. Distance functions based on *delete-relaxation* have successfully been used for, e.g., model checking timed automata. However, such distance functions have not been investigated for formalisms with rich expression languages as provided by PROMELA. We present a generalization of delete-relaxation-based distance functions to a subclass of PROMELA. We have evaluated the resulting search behavior on a large number of models from the BEEM database within the HSF-SPIN model checker. Our experiments show significantly better guidance compared to the previously best distance function available in HSF-SPIN.

1 Introduction

A main obstacle for model checking tools is the state space explosion problem. A countermeasure is to use the memory efficient state space traversal procedure depth-first search (DFS). However, if the task is not to verify a property but to falsify it, DFS often performs badly in practice because it may unnecessarily search large error free regions of the state space first. In addition, reported error paths are often unnecessarily long, which makes it difficult for humans to understand the causes of an error. A technique to mitigate these problems is called *directed model checking* (DMC) and has been introduced by Edelkamp et al. [4]. Directed model checking applies a distance function to estimate the distance from a given state to an error state, and explores states with shortest estimated distance first. Guided by the distance function, error paths can often be found after exploring only a small fraction of the overall state space which results in time and memory savings. Furthermore, reported error paths are often shorter than those reported by so-called uninformed algorithms (like DFS) due to the guidance. Typically, there is a trade-off between the precision of the distance estimate and the cost of computing the distance function for a given state. An example for a computationally cheap distance function for PROMELA models is called h^c and is implemented in HSF-SPIN [4], a directed model checker based on version 3 of the PROMELA model checker SPIN. The h^c function estimates the distance between a given state and the end state of the model's never claim.

© Springer International Publishing Switzerland 2015
B. Fischer and J. Geldenhuys (Eds.): SPIN 2015, LNCS 9232, pp. 153–159, 2015.
DOI: 10.1007/978-3-319-23404-5_11

A class of distance functions which is successful in the area of artificial intelligence (AI) planning is based on *delete relaxation* [2]. Kupferschmid et al. [5] generalized this relaxation to simple statements over variables with arbitrary domains for a limited class of timed automata. In the latter context, the relaxation is based on collecting all values ever assigned to a variable along a path, yielding set-valued domains for variables and the current location. More formally, given a (concrete) state s, $h^+(s)$ denotes the length of the shortest path under the relaxation from s to an error state in the transition system over set-valued variables. $h^+(s)$ is often an accurate estimate of the length of a shortest path between s and an error state in the transition system over concrete states. As the computation of h^+ is NP-hard [3], Kupferschmid et al. considered approximations thereof, which showed favorable performance compared to the distance functions proposed by Edelkamp et al. [4] in the area of timed automata, and which have also found their way into timed automata model checking tools [6]. Although the idea of DMC roots in AI planning and relaxation-based distance functions have shown to be useful outside of AI planning, their potential has not yet been explored for PROMELA, i.e., for a richer expression language than considered until now.

In this work, we explore a generalization of relaxation-based distance functions to the PROMELA formalism. We have evaluated an implementation of our distance function (which generalizes the h^L function proposed by Kupferschmid et al. and is called h_P^L in the following) in HSF-SPIN on a large number of BEEM models. Our implementation supports an expressive subset of PROMELA (cf. [1]), which is sufficiently rich to cover a large range of models from the BEEM database [7]: Currently supported are basic control flow (if, goto), channel synchronisation, static processes, basic data types (no arrays, no structs), and most operators (except for modulo) in expressions. Our results show that h_P^L often provides significantly better guidance towards error states compared to HSF-SPIN's previously best-performing distance function in our experiments.

2   Relaxation for PROMELA

We start by defining *relaxed states* for PROMELA, which are the basis for the definition of our distance function h_P^L. In the PROMELA semantics, a (concrete) state assigns to each process a process location, and to each variable and channel a value. We use, e.g., $s(x)$ to denote the value assigned to variable x in state s. In contrast, a *relaxed* state s^+ assigns to each process a *set* of process locations, and to each variable and channel a *set* of values, i.e. $s^+(x)$ denotes a set of values from the domain of x. We say that relaxed state s^+ *subsumes* a state s, denoted by $s \sqsubseteq s^+$, if and only if each component of s is an element of the corresponding component of s^+, e.g., if for each variable x, $s(x) \in s^+(x)$. PROMELA expressions are *existentially* evaluated over relaxed states: Relaxed state s^+ *supports* value v for expression *expr* if there exists a state s such that $s \sqsubseteq s^+$ and *expr* evaluates to v over s. Note that a relaxed state may hence support both *true* and *false* for a Boolean expression. Statements obtain a collecting

$$a = \{0\}, b = \{0\}, c = \{\}$$
$$\downarrow \texttt{c!a}$$

c!a,c?b $\circlearrowleft$ $\{0\}, \{0\}, \{0\}$ c!a

$\downarrow$ a++ $\curvearrowright$

c?b $\circlearrowleft$ $\{0,1\}, \{0\}, \{0\}$ $\xrightarrow{\texttt{c!a}}$ $\{0,1\}, \{0\}, \{0,1\}$ $\xrightarrow{\texttt{a++}}$ $\cdots$

$\downarrow$ a++ $\downarrow$ c?b

c?b $\circlearrowleft$ $\{0,1,2\}, \{0\}, \{0\}$ $\{0,1\}, \{0,1\}, \{0,1\}$ $\circlearrowright$ c!a,c?b

a++ $\swarrow$ $\searrow$ c!a $\downarrow$ a++

$\cdots$ $\cdots$ $\cdots$

Fig. 1. Relaxed transition system of the PROMELA program shown in Listing 1.1.

semantics on relaxed states. The effect of assignment $x = expr$ on relaxed state s^+ is defined as adding all values of $expr$ supported by s^+ to the set $s^+(x)$. Note that we thereby obtain a conservative generalization of [5].

```
int a=0, b=0; chan c=[1] of {int};
active proctype S() { again: c!a; a++; goto again; }
active proctype R() { again: c?b; goto again; }
```

Listing 1.1. Two processes S and R.

The above interpretation of expressions and statements on relaxed states induces a transition system over relaxed states, called the *relaxed transition system*. It has the property that for each path π in the transition system over concrete states, there exists a path π^+ in the relaxed transition system with the same length such that the i-th relaxed state in π^+ subsumes the i-th state in π. That is, the relaxed transition system is an over-approximation of the concrete transition system: According to the idea of relaxation, the value sets in relaxed successor states grow monotonically. Thus, each statement that can be executed in a state s can also be executed in any relaxed state which subsumes s. An *error path* from relaxed state s^+ is a path which begins with s^+ and ends with a relaxed state which subsumes termination of the model's never claim. Following the literature, we denote the shortest length of an error path from *the* relaxation s^+ of state s by $h^+(s)$. We call a relaxed state s^+ the relaxation of s if and only if s^+ is the smallest relaxed state wrt. set-inclusion which subsumes s.

For an example, consider the PROMELA model in Listing 1.1. Process S repeatedly sends the value of variable a on channel c and increments a. Process R repeatedly receives a value from c and assigns it to variable b. In the relaxation, the variables and the channel become set-valued. Figure 1 shows a fragment of the computation tree of the relaxed transition system rooted at relaxed state $\{0\}, \{0\}, \{\}$. Edges are labeled with the executed statements. The relaxed state $\{0\}, \{0\}, \{\}$ is the relaxed state of the concrete initial state in which channel c is empty. Thus only the send statement c!a is executable. Executing c!a yields the relaxed state $\{0\}, \{0\}, \{0\}$. From this relaxed state on, channel c is always both empty and full, thus the synchronization in R is always enabled. So is the increment of a; executing it yields the relaxed state $\{0,1\}, \{0\}, \{0\}$, i.e. the old

---

Algorithm 1. Computation of h_P^L.

Input : Concrete state s.
Output: Distance estimate $l \in \mathbb{N}_0 \cup \{\infty\}$ to a relaxed error state.

1 $l \leftarrow 0$; $s_0^+ \leftarrow$ *process locations, variables, and channels of s*;
2 **while** *never claim not terminated in s_l^+* **do**
3     $\quad s^{+\prime} \leftarrow s_l^+$;
4     $\quad$ **for** *statement t enabled in s_l^+* **do**
5     $\quad\quad \lfloor\ s^{+\prime} \leftarrow s^{+\prime} \cup$ *effect of t on s_l^+*;
6     $\quad$ **if** $s^{+\prime} = s_l^+$ **then**
7     $\quad\quad \lfloor$ **return** ∞;
8     $\quad \lfloor\ l \leftarrow l + 1$; $s_l^+ \leftarrow s^{+\prime}$;
9 **return** l;

---

value of a is not deleted but collected. The example particularly shows that the channels' capacities become unbounded in the relaxation.

As the computation of $h^+(s)$ is NP-hard [3], we consider the distance function h_P^L, which is an approximation of h^+. The computation of h_P^L is provided in Algorithm 1. While h^+ is defined by the relaxed transition system of a PROMELA program, h_P^L is defined by an *acceleration* of the relaxed transition system: Given a relaxed state s^+, its relaxed successor state $s^{+\prime}$ is the union of the effects of executing all statements enabled in s^+ to s^+ (cf. Algorithm 1, Line 4 ff.). Note that a concrete state $s' \sqsubseteq s^{+\prime}$ is not necessarily reachable from any concrete state $s \sqsubseteq s^+$, and if s' is reachable from s then the shortest concrete path may be longer than 1. As an example, consider again Listing 1.1 with the never claim $\neg(a = 2 \wedge b = 1)$, i. e., error states have the property $a = 2$ and $b = 1$.

- Reaching the error state from s_0 takes at least 6 steps in the concrete system, e. g., witnessed by the statement sequence c!a, a++, c?b, c!a, c?b, a++.
- Shortest error paths in the delete-relaxation (i. e., in the relaxed transition graph in Fig. 1) have length 5, i. e., $h^+(s_0) = 5$, e. g., witnessed by c!a, a++, c!a, c?b, a++. Compared to the concrete, *several* values can be sent in parallel in the relaxation, hence one fewer receive step for setting the value of b is required (in the above sequence, b receives $\{0, 1\}$ via statement c?b).
- The relaxed distance function delivers an estimate of 4, i. e., $h_P^L(s_0) = 4$: After starting with c!a, all the statements c!a, c?b and a++ are repeatedly applicable in parallel in the following, yielding the sequence of relaxed states $\{0\}, \{0\}, \{\}$ (initial relaxed state), $\{0\}, \{0\}, \{0\}$ after one step, $\{0, 1\}, \{0\}, \{0\}$ after two steps, $\{0, 1, 2\}, \{0\}, \{0, 1\}$ after three steps, and finally the relaxed error state $\{0, 1, 2, 3\}, \{0, 1\}, \{0, 1, 2\}$ after four steps.
- In contrast, h^c is quite sensitive to (the model of) the never claim N. Assuming N consists of two locations and an edge between them guarded by $a = 2 \wedge b = 1$, h^c can only deliver 0 or 1, yielding an uninformed guidance.

Algorithm 1 computes $h_P^L(s)$ by taking as s_0^+ the relaxed state of s and iterating the accelerated transition relation. It always terminates because either a relaxed error state is found (Line 2) or a fixpoint is reached (Line 6). While an error need not exist, a fixpoint always exists because the state space of a PROMELA model is finite and in the relaxation, states grow monotonically.

3   Evaluation

We have implemented h_P^L in the HSF-SPIN model checker to investigate the following research questions: To which extent can h_P^L improve the guidance of the state space traversal compared to h^c, the best-performing distance function in our experiments previously available in HSF-SPIN? Does the improved guidance pay off in shorter error paths? Ultimately, does the improved guidance pay off in terms of shorter model checking runtime? The latter question addresses the issue of the increased overhead to compute h_P^L in every encountered state: Compared to h^c, the computation of h_P^L naturally becomes more expensive because of the more precise treatment of the (rather expressive) structures handled by PROMELA. In particular, this is the case for the more sophisticated handling of linear arithmetic and the resulting subsumption checks for checking the enabledness of statements and the effects supported by statements. To investigate these questions, we have applied h_P^L on faulty PROMELA models from the BEEM database [7] (12 domains, more than 80 model instances in total), using greedy best first search (GBFS). The models stem from application areas such as mutual exclusion algorithms, controller software, puzzles and communication protocols. For computational efficiency, our implementation of h_P^L additionally

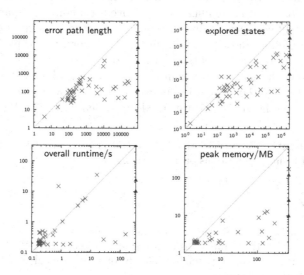

Fig. 2. $\times$: $x, y \in \mathbb{R}$, i.e., h^c and h_P^L reported a path within the time limit, $\blacktriangle$: $x \in \mathbb{R}$, y failed to find an error. (Athlon 64 2.4 GHz; mem. limit: 3 GB, time limit: 30 min.)

applies interval abstraction: If x has been assigned the values a and b with $a < b$, then we keep the whole interval $[a, b]$ instead of $\{a, b\}$ as x's relaxed value.

In order to compactly provide the results, we visualize the data by scatter plots in Fig. 2. All axes are scaled logarithmically. Each cross represents one successful run of both distance functions for one model instance, i. e., a run which neither violates our memory limit nor times out. A cross below the diagonal line indicates that h_P^L performs better (i. e., shorter path, fewer explored states, less time, less memory) than h^c on this model instance, a cross above this line indicates the opposite. A cross on the diagonal line indicates that both distance functions perform equally. We observe a significantly improved guidance of the state space traversal with h_P^L in terms of the number of explored states, which pays off in terms of a lower memory consumption, and also in reduced lengths of the error paths. In particular, we observe that the improvement is sometimes in the range of several orders of magnitude. The better guidance stems from the more accurate distance values delivered by h_P^L (e. g., in the bopdp problem instances, h_P^L's values range from 0 to 39, whereas h^c yields values between 0 and 1). More details are available online [1]. As discussed, the improved guidance naturally comes with an increased overhead to compute h_P^L. However, while the overhead does not always pay off, we also observe that there exist models where h_P^L can remarkably reduce the runtime. In addition, there are models which could be handled by h_P^L, whereas h^c failed to find an error (triangles in Fig. 2).

4   Conclusions

In this paper, we have explored a generalization of delete-relaxed distance functions for PROMELA. Our evaluation in HSF-SPIN on models from the BEEM benchmark suite show a significantly improved guidance compared to HSF-SPIN's previously best-performing distance function in our experiments. While the improved guidance mostly pays off in terms of shorter error paths and lower memory consumption, the benefits in terms of overall runtime are somewhat less significant due to the encountered computational overhead. It will be interesting to further investigate the correlation between this time overhead and the model structure, e. g., the language features used in a given PROMELA model.

Acknowledgments. The authors thank G. J. Holzmann for valuable clarifications of semantical and technical questions on PROMELA and SPIN.

References

1. http://www.informatik.uni-freiburg.de/~westphal/spin15
2. Bonet, B., Geffner, H.: Planning as heuristic search. AIJ **129**(1–2), 5–33 (2001)
3. Bylander, T.: The computational complexity of propositional STRIPS planning. AIJ **69**(1–2), 165–204 (1994)
4. Edelkamp, S., Leue, S., et al.: Directed explicit-state model checking in the validation of communication protocols. STTT **5**(2–3), 247–267 (2004)

5. Kupferschmid, S., Hoffmann, J., Dierks, H., Behrmann, G.: Adapting an AI planning heuristic for directed model checking. In: Valmari, A. (ed.) SPIN 2006. LNCS, vol. 3925, pp. 35–52. Springer, Heidelberg (2006)
6. Kupferschmid, S., Wehrle, M., Nebel, B., Podelski, A.: Faster than UPPAAL? In: Gupta, A., Malik, S. (eds.) CAV 2008. LNCS, vol. 5123, pp. 552–555. Springer, Heidelberg (2008)
7. Pelánek, R.: BEEM: benchmarks for explicit model checkers. In: Bošnački, D., Edelkamp, S. (eds.) SPIN 2007. LNCS, vol. 4595, pp. 263–267. Springer, Heidelberg (2007)

Benchmarking and Resource Measurement

Dirk Beyer, Stefan Löwe, and Philipp Wendler

University of Passau, Passau, Germany

Abstract. Proper benchmarking and resource measurement is an important topic, because benchmarking is a widely-used method for the comparative evaluation of tools and algorithms in many research areas. It is essential for researchers, tool developers, and users, as well as for competitions. We formulate a set of requirements that are indispensable for reproducible benchmarking and reliable resource measurement of automatic solvers, verifiers, and similar tools, and discuss limitations of existing methods and benchmarking tools. Fulfilling these requirements in a benchmarking framework is complex and can (on Linux) currently only be done by using the cgroups feature of the kernel. We provide BenchExec, a ready-to-use, tool-independent, and free implementation of a benchmarking framework that fulfills all presented requirements, making reproducible benchmarking and reliable resource measurement easy. Our framework is able to work with a wide range of different tools and has proven its reliability and usefulness in the International Competition on Software Verification.

1 Introduction

Performance evaluation is an effective and inexpensive method for assessing research results [13], and in some communities, like high-performance computing[1], transactional processing in databases[2], natural-language requirements processing[3], and others, performance benchmarking is standardized. Tools for automatic verification, such as solvers and verifiers, are also evaluated using performance benchmarking [3], i.e., measuring execution time, memory consumption, and other performance characteristics. Benchmarking is necessary for comparing different tools of the same domain, evaluating and comparing different features or configurations of the same tool, or for finding out how a single tool performs on different inputs or during regression testing. The ability to limit resource usage (e.g., memory consumption) of a tool during benchmarking is also a requirement for reproducible experiments. To receive reproducible results from experiments, a benchmarking infrastructure should guarantee that the data are obtained by reliable and valid measurement. Also competitions, like SAT-COMP [1], SMT-COMP [2], and SV-COMP [3], require exact measuring of resource consumption, and, in order to guarantee fairness, need to enforce the

---

[1] https://www.spec.org/
[2] http://www.tpc.org/
[3] http://nlrp.ipd.kit.edu/

© Springer International Publishing Switzerland 2015
B. Fischer and J. Geldenhuys (Eds.): SPIN 2015, LNCS 9232, pp. 160–178, 2015.
DOI: 10.1007/978-3-319-23404-5_12

agreed resource limits accurately. For example, in the International Competition on Software Verification (SV-COMP), all tools are limited to 15 min of CPU time and 15 GB of RAM [3]. Results from the tools are only counted if none of these limits exceeded.

Results are *reproducible* if it is guaranteed that the same results can be obtained later again (assuming a deterministic tool) by re-running the benchmarks on a machine with the same hardware and the same software versions. Reproducibility of experimental results requires reliable measurement. We call a measurement *reliable*, if the measurement method ensures *accuracy* (small systematic and random measurement error, i.e., no bias or "volatile" effects, resp.) and sufficient *precision* [7] (cf. also ISO 3534-2:2006). While it may appear that measuring execution time is trivial, a closer look reveals that quite the contrary is the case. In many circumstances, measuring the wall time, i.e., the elapsed time between start and end of a task, is not enough because this does not allow to compare the resource usage of multi-threaded tools, and may be inadvertently influenced by input/output operations (I/O). Measuring the CPU time is more meaningful but also more difficult, especially if child processes are involved. Furthermore, characteristics of the machine architecture such as hyper-threading or non-uniform memory access can *non-deterministically* affect results and need to be considered carefully in order to obtain reproducible results. Obtaining reliable measurement values on memory consumption is even harder, because the memory that is used by a process may increase or decrease at any point in time. Similarly, the limits on memory consumption must not be exceeded *at any point in time* during the execution of the tool. Again, child processes add further complications. Another important aspect is the potentially huge heterogeneity between different tools in a comparison: tools are written in different programming languages, require different libraries, may spawn child processes, write to storage media, or perform other I/O. All of this has to be considered in the design of a benchmarking environment, ideally in a way that does not exclude any tools from being benchmarked.

1.1 Contributions

In this work, we present the following contributions towards reproducible benchmarking for all scenarios that are described above:

- A set of necessary requirements that need to be fulfilled for reliable measurement and reproducible benchmarking are identified (Sect. 2).
- We show that some existing methods for resource measurements and limitations do not fulfill these requirements and lead to invalid experimental results in practice (Sect. 3).
- We describe how to implement a benchmarking environment on a Linux system which fulfills all mentioned requirements (Sect. 4).
- The open-source implementation BENCHEXEC is provided, a set of ready-to-use tools that fulfill the requirements for reproducible benchmarking. The tools were already used successfully in practice by competitions (Sect. 5).

1.2 Restrictions

In order to guarantee reproducible benchmarking, we need to introduce a few restrictions. However, we argue that there are important classes of tools that need to be benchmarked and for which these restrictions are acceptable, for example automatic solvers, verifiers, and similar tools. We only consider the benchmarking of tools that adhere to the following restrictions: The tool (1) is CPU-bound, i.e., if compared to CPU usage, input and output operations from and to storage media are negligible, and input and output bandwidth does not need to be limited nor measured (this assumes the tool does not make heavy use of temporary files); (2) does not perform network communication during the execution; (3) does not spread across several machines during execution, but is limited to a single machine; and (4) does not require user interaction.

These restrictions are acceptable, because (1) reading from storage media, apart from the input file, is not expected from tools in the target domains. In case a tool produces much output (e.g., by creating large log files), this would primarily have a negative impact on the performance of the tool itself, and thus does not need to be restricted by the benchmarking environment. Sometimes, I/O cannot be avoided for communicating between several processes, however, for performance this should be done without any actual storage I/O anyway (e.g., using pipes). Not supporting network communication is acceptable, because (2) we expect tools not to use any network communication. While it is in principle possible for a tool to offload work to remote servers [4], this would mean to exclude the offloaded work from benchmarking. In contrast to other ways that are shown in this paper that may allow circumventing limits imposed by the benchmarking framework, using network communication does not occur accidentally. Benchmarking a distributed tool (3) is much more complex and out of scope. However, techniques and ideas from this paper as well as our tool can be used on each individual host as part of a distributed benchmarking framework.

We do not consider security concerns. We assume the executed tool to be trusted, i.e., it will not maliciously try to interfere with measurements or other running processes. This could be addressed by running our benchmarking framework and the tool under different user accounts, but then the benchmarking framework needs additional rights (usually root access) that may not be available in every environment. We also do not consider the task of providing the necessary execution environment to the tool, i.e., the system administrator of the machines has to ensure that all necessary packages and libraries needed to run a tool are available in the correct versions. Furthermore, we assume that enough memory is installed to handle the operating system (OS), the benchmarking environment, and the benchmarked process(es) without swapping, and that no CPU-intensive tasks are running outside the control of the benchmarking environment. All I/O is assumed to be local, because network shares can have unpredictable performance.

These are well-justified requirements, needed for safe operation of our benchmarking environment, and fulfilled by setups of competitions like SV-COMP.

2   Requirements for Reliable Benchmarking

There exist two major difficulties that we need to consider for benchmarking. The first problem is that a tool may arbitrarily spawn child processes, and a benchmarking framework needs to handle this. Using child processes is common practice. For example, verifiers might start preprocessors, such as CPP, or solvers, like an SMT-backend, as child processes. Some tools start several child processes, each with a different analysis or strategy, running in parallel, while some verifiers spawn a separate child process to analyze counterexamples. In general, a significant amount of the resource usage can happen in one or many child processes that run sequentially or in parallel. Even if a tool is assumed to not start child processes, for comparability of the results with other tools it is still favorable to use a generic benchmarking framework that handles child processes correctly.[4]

The second problem occurs if the benchmarking framework should assign specific hardware resources to tool runs, especially if such runs are executed in parallel and the resources need to be divided between them. Today's machine architectures can be complex and a sub-optimal resource allocation can negatively affect the performance and lead to non-deterministic and thus non-reproducible results. Examples for differing machine architectures can be seen on the supplementary web page.[5]

In the following, we list five specific requirements that address these problems and need to be followed for reproducible benchmarking. This list should serve as a checklist not only for implementors of benchmarking frameworks, but also for assessing the quality of experimental results in research reports.

2.1   Measure and Limit Resources Accurately

Time. The CPU time of a tool must be measured and limited accurately, including the CPU time of all child processes started by the tool.

Memory. For benchmarking, we are interested in the peak resource consumption of a process, i.e., in the smallest amount of resources with which the tool could successfully be executed with the same result. Thus the memory usage of a process is defined as the peak size of all memory pages that occupy some system resources. This means, for example, that the size of the address space of a process should not be measured and limited, because it may be much larger than the actual memory usage, for example due to memory-mapped files or due to allocated but unused memory pages (which do not actually take up resources because the Linux kernel lazily allocates physical memory for a process only when a virtual memory page is first written to, not when it is allocated). The

---

[4] Our experience from competition organization shows that developers of complex tools are not always aware of how their system spawns child processes and how to properly terminate them.

[5] http://www.sosy-lab.org/~dbeyer/benchmarking

size of the heap, however, may be too low if data are stored on the stack, and the so-called resident set of a process (the memory that is currently kept in RAM) does not include pages that are in use but swapped out.

If a tool spawns several processes, these can use shared memory such that the total memory usage of a group of processes is less than the sum of their individual memory usages. Shared memory occupies system resources only once and thus needs to be counted only once by the benchmarking framework.

Setting a limit on the memory usage is important and should always be done, because otherwise the amount of memory available to the tool is the amount of free memory in the system, which varies over time and depends on lots of external factors, preventing reproducible results.

2.2   Terminate Processes Reliably

If a resource limit is violated, it is necessary to reliably terminate the tool including all of its child processes. Even if the tool terminates itself, the benchmarking environment needs to ensure that all child processes are also terminated. Otherwise a child process could keep running and occupy CPU and memory resources, which might influence later benchmarks on the same machine.

2.3   Assign Cores Deliberately

Special care is necessary for the selection of CPU cores that are assigned to one tool run. For the OS, a core is a processing unit that allows execution of one thread. This means that if the CPU supports hyper-threading (i.e., the execution of several threads at the same time in the same physical CPU core), each of the virtual cores is treated as a separate core (processing unit) by the OS, i.e., the OS does not distinguish between virtual cores and physical cores. However, because two threads on different virtual cores in the same physical CPU core can influence the performance of each other, there should never be two simultaneous tool executions on two virtual cores of one physical core (just like there should never be two simultaneous tool executions sharing one virtual core). To show that this is important, we executed benchmarks using the verifier CPACHECKER on a machine with hyper-threading, and on purpose forced two parallel executions of the verifier on the same physical core. This increased the used CPU time by 41 %. More details on this benchmark can be found in the appendix.

Another restriction that should be followed is that the cores for one run should not be split across several CPUs if the run does not need more cores than one CPU can provide, because communication between cores on the same CPU is faster than between different CPUs, and cores share certain caches.

2.4   Respect Non-uniform Memory Access

Systems with several CPUs often have an architecture with non-uniform memory access (NUMA), which also needs to be considered by a benchmarking environment. In a NUMA architecture, a single processor or a group of processors can access parts of the system memory locally, i.e., directly, while other parts of the system memory are remote, i.e., they can only be accessed indirectly via another CPU, which is slower. The effect is that once a processor has to access remote memory, this leads to a performance degradation depending on the load of the inter-CPU connection and the other CPU. Hence, a single run of a tool should be bound to memory that is local to its assigned CPU cores, in order to avoid non-deterministic delays stemming from remote memory access. To show that this is important, we executed benchmarks using the verifier CPACHECKER on a machine with two CPUs and NUMA, and on purpose assigned the cores of one CPU and the memory attached to the other CPU to each run of the tool, such that all memory accesses were indirect. This increased the used CPU time by 11 %. More details on this benchmark can be found in the appendix.

2.5 Avoid Swapping

Swapping out memory must be avoided during benchmarking, because it may degrade performance in a non-deterministic way. This is especially true for the benchmarked process(es), but even swapping of an unrelated process can negatively affect the benchmarking, if the benchmarked process has to wait for more free memory to become available. Absolutely preventing swapping can typically only be done by the system administrator by turning off all available swap space. In theory, it is not even enough to ensure that the OS, the benchmarking environment, and the benchmarked processes all fit into the available memory, because the OS can decide to start swapping even if there is still memory available, for example, if it decides to use some memory as cache for physical disks. However, for benchmarking CPU-bound tools, with high CPU and memory usage, and next to no I/O, this is unlikely to happen with modern OS. Thus, the main duty of the benchmarking environment is to ensure that there is no overbooking of memory, and that memory limits are enforced effectively. It is also helpful if the benchmarking environment monitors swap usage during benchmarking and warns the user of any swapping.

3   Limitations of Existing Methods

Some of the existing tools and methods available on Linux systems for measuring resource consumption and for enforcing resource limits of processes have several problems that make them unsuitable for benchmarking, especially if child processes are involved. Any benchmarking environment needs to be aware of these limitations and avoid using naive methods for resource measurements.

3.1   Measuring Resources May Fail

Time. Measuring wall time is simple with high precision using standard tools and methods that operating systems and most programming languages provide.

Measuring CPU time of the main process of a tool, for example using the tool `time` or a variant of the system call `wait` (which returns the CPU time after the given process terminated), does not reliably include the CPU time of child processes that were spawned by the main process. The Linux kernel only adds the CPU time used by child processes to that of the parent process *after* the child process has terminated *and* the parent process waited for the child's termination with a variant of the system call `wait`. If the child process has not yet terminated or the parent did not explicitly wait for its termination, the CPU time of the child is lost. This is a typical situation that might happen for example if a verifier starts an SMT solver as a child process and communicates with the solver via stdin and stdout. When the analysis finishes, the verifier would terminate the solver process, but usually would not bother to wait for its termination. A tool that runs different analyses in parallel in child processes would also typically terminate as soon as the first analysis returns a valid result, without waiting for the other analyses' termination.[6] In these cases, a large share of the total CPU time is spent by child processes but not included in the measurement.

Memory. Some Linux tools only provide a view on the current memory usage of individual processes, but we need to measure the peak usage of a group of processes. Calculating the peak usage by periodically sampling the memory usage and reporting the maximum is inaccurate, because it might miss peaks of memory usage. If the benchmarked process started child processes, one has to recursively iterate over all child processes and calculate the total memory usage. This contains several race conditions that can also lead to invalid measurements, for example, if a child process terminates before its memory usage could be read. In situations where several processes share memory pages (e.g., because each of them loaded the same library, or because they communicate via shared memory), we cannot sum up the memory usage of all processes. Thus, without keeping track of every memory page of each process, manually filtering out pages that do not occupy resources because of lazy allocation, and counting each remaining page exactly once, the calculated value for memory usage is invalid.

3.2 Enforcing Limits May Fail

For setting resource limits, some users apply the tool `ulimit`, which uses the system call `setrlimit`. A limit can be specified for CPU time as well as for memory, and the limited process is forcefully terminated by the kernel if one of these limits is violated. However, similar to measuring time with system call `wait`, limits imposed with this method affect only individual processes, i.e., a tool that starts n child processes could use n times more memory and CPU time than allowed. Limiting memory is especially problematic because either

---

[6] We experienced this when organizing SV-COMP'13, for a portfolio-based verifier. Initial CPU time measurements were significantly too low, which was luckily discovered by chance. The verifier had to be patched to wait for its sub-processes and the benchmarks had to be re-run.

the size of the address space or the size of the data segment (the heap) can be limited, which do not necessarily correspond to the actual memory usage of the process, as described above. Limiting the resident-set size (RSS) is no longer supported.[7] Furthermore, if such a limit is violated, the kernel terminates only the one violating process, which might not be the main process of the tool. In this case it depends on the implementation of the tool how such a situation is handled: it might terminate itself, or crash, or even continuously re-spawn the terminated child process and continue. Thus, this method is not reliable.

It is possible to use a self-implemented limit enforcement with a process that samples CPU time and memory usage of a tool with all its child processes, terminating all processes if a limit is exceeded, but this is inaccurate and prone to the same race conditions described above for memory measurement.

3.3 Terminating Processes May Fail

In order to terminate a tool and all its child processes, one could try to (transitively) enumerate all its child processes and terminate each of them. However, finding and terminating all child processes of a process may not work reliably for two reasons. First, a process might start child processes faster than the benchmarking environment is able to terminate them. While this is known as a malicious technique ("fork bomb"), it may also happen accidentally, for example due to a flawed logic for restarting crashed child processes of a tool. The benchmarking environment should guard against this, otherwise the machine might become unusable. Second, it is possible to "detach" child processes such that they are no longer recognizable as child processes of the process that started them. This is commonly used for starting long-running daemons that should not retain any connection to the user that started them, but also might happen incidentally if a parent process is terminated before the child process. In this case, an incomplete benchmarking framework could miss to terminate child processes.

The *process groups* of the POSIX standard (established with the system call setpgid) are not reliable for tracking child processes. A process is free to change its process group, and tools using child processes often use this feature.

4 State-of-the-Art Benchmarking with Cgroups

We listed aspects that are mandatory for reproducible benchmarking, and explained flaws of existing methods. In the following, we present a technology that should be used to avoid these pitfalls.

Control groups (cgroups) are a feature of the Linux kernel for managing processes and their resource usage, which is available since 2007 [11]. Differently from all other interfaces for these tasks, cgroups provide mechanisms for managing groups of processes and their resources in an atomic and race-free manner, and are not limited to single processes. All running processes of a system are

---

[7] http://linux.die.net/man/2/setrlimit

grouped in a hierarchical tree of cgroups[8], and most actions affect all processes within a specific cgroup. Cgroups can be created dynamically and processes can be moved between them. There exists a set of so-called *controllers* in the kernel, each of which affects and measures the consumption of a specific resource by the processes within each cgroup. For example, there are controllers for measuring and limiting CPU time, memory consumption, and I/O bandwidth.

The cgroups hierarchy is made accessible to programs and users as a directory tree in a virtual file system, which is typically mounted at `/sys/fs/cgroups`. Usual file-system operations can be used to read and manipulate the cgroup hierarchy and to read resource measurements and configure limits for each of the controllers (via specific files in each cgroup directory). Thus, it is easy to use cgroups from any kind of tool, including shell scripts. Alternatively, one can use a library such as `libcg`[9], which provides an API for accessing and manipulating the cgroup hierarchy. Settings for file permission and ownership can be used to fine-tune who is able to manipulate the cgroup hierarchy.

When a new process is started, it inherits the current cgroup from its parent process. The only way to change the cgroup of a process is direct access to the cgroup virtual file system, which can be prevented using basic file-system permissions. Any other action of the process, whether changing the process group, detaching from its parent, etc., will not change the cgroup. Thus, cgroups can be used to reliably track the set of (transitive) child processes of any given process by putting this process into its own cgroup. We refer to the manual for details.[10]

The following cgroup controllers are relevant for reliable benchmarking:

cpuacct measures the accumulated CPU time that is consumed by all processes in each cgroup. A time limit cannot be defined, but can be implemented in the benchmarking environment by periodically checking the accumulated time.

cpuset allows to restrict the processes in each cgroup to a subset of the available CPU cores. On systems with more than one CPU socket and NUMA, it allows to restrict the processes to specific parts of the physical memory.

freezer allows to freeze all processes of a cgroup in a single operation. This can be used for reliable termination of a group of processes by freezing them first, sending all of them the kill signal, and afterwards unfreezing ("thawing") them. This way the processes do not have the chance to start other processes because between the time the first and the last process receive the kill signal none of them can execute anything.

memory allows to restrict maximum memory usage of all processes together in each cgroup, and to measure current and peak memory consumption. If the defined memory limit is reached by the processes in a cgroup, the kernel first tries to free some internal caches that it holds for these processes (for example

---

[8] Actually, independent hierarchies are currently supported. We restrict ourselves to the single-hierarchy case because independent hierarchies are going to be deprecated.

[9] http://libcg.sourceforge.net/

[10] https://www.kernel.org/doc/Documentation/cgroups/

disk caches), and then terminates at least one process. Alternatively, instead of terminating processes, the kernel can send an event to a registered process, which the benchmarking framework can use to terminate all processes within the cgroup. The kernel counts only actually used pages towards the memory usage, and because the accounting of memory is done per memory page, shared memory is handled correctly (every page the processes use is counted exactly once).

The `memory` controller allows to define two limits for memory usage, one on the amount of physical memory that the processes can use, and one on the amount of physical memory plus swap memory. If the system has swap, both limits need to be set to the same value. If only the former limit is set to a specific value, the processes could use so much memory plus all of the available swap memory (and the kernel would automatically start swapping out the processes if the limit on physical memory is reached). Similarly, for reading the peak memory consumption, the value of physical memory plus swap memory should be used. Sometimes, the current memory consumption of a cgroup is not zero even after all processes of the cgroup have been terminated, if the kernel decided to still keep some pages of these processes in its disk cache. To avoid influencing the measurements of other runs by this, a cgroup should be used only for a single run and deleted afterwards, with a new run getting a new, fresh cgroup.[11]

The numbering system of the Linux kernel (which is also used for restricting CPU cores with the `cpuset` controller) for a system with n physical cores across all CPU sockets is as follows: The id i for $i \in [0, \dots, n-1]$ is assigned to the first virtual core (processing unit) of the i-th physical core in the system, and, in case there are physical cores with more than one virtual core, the id $i + n$ is assigned to the second virtual core of the i-th physical core, and so on. For example, consider a system with 2 CPU sockets with 8 physical cores each and 2 virtual cores per physical core. There are 16 physical cores in the system, so ids 0–15 refer to the first virtual core of each of the physical cores, and ids 16–31 refer to the other virtual cores. The ids belonging to the first CPU are 0–7 and 16–23, the ids 8–15 and 24–31 belong to the second CPU. The ids of a pair of processing units on the same physical core differ by 16 in this machine, e.g., (virtual) cores 0 and 16 belong to the same physical core and should be used together. This information can be extracted from certain files in the directories `/sys/devices/system/cpu/cpu<id>/topology/` or from `/proc/cpuinfo`.

5   BenchExec: A Framework for Reliable Benchmarking

In the following, we describe our implementation of a cgroups-based benchmarking framework that fulfills the requirements from Sect. 2 by using the techniques from Sect. 4. It is available as open source under the Apache 2.0 License on GitHub[12].

BenchExec consists of two parts, both written in Python. The first is responsible for benchmarking a single run of a given tool, including the reliable

---

[11] Or clear the caches with `drop_caches`.

[12] https://github.com/dbeyer/benchexec/

limitation and accurate measurement of resources. This part is also designed such that it is easy to use from within other benchmarking frameworks. The second part is responsible for benchmarking a whole set of runs, i.e., running one or more tools on a collection of input files by delegating each run execution to the first part, which is responsible for a single run, and then aggregating the results.

5.1   System Requirements

In order to use the cgroup-based benchmarking framework BENCHEXEC, a few requirements are necessary that may demand for assistance by the administrator of the benchmarking machine. Apart from running a Linux kernel, cgroups including the four controllers listed in the previous section must be enabled and the account for the benchmarking user needs the permissions to manipulate (a part of) the cgroup hierarchy. Any Linux kernel version of the last years is acceptable, though there have been performance improvements for the memory controller in version 3.3[13], and cgroups in general are still getting improved, thus, using a recent kernel is recommended. If the benchmarking machine has swap, swap accounting must be enabled for the `memory` controller. For enabling cgroups and giving permissions, we refer to standard Linux documentation.

After these steps, no further root access is necessary and everything can be done with a normal user account. Thus, it is possible to use machines for benchmarking that are not under own administrative control. By creating a special cgroup for benchmarking and granting rights only for this cgroup, it is also possible for the administrator to prevent the user from interfering with other processes and to restrict the total amount of resources that the benchmarking may use. For example, one can specify that a user may use only a specific subset of CPU cores and amount of memory for benchmarking, or partition the resources of shared machines among several users.

5.2   Benchmarking a Single Run

We define a *run* as a single execution of a tool, with the following input:

- the full command line, i.e., the path to the executable with all arguments, and optionally,
- the content supplied to the tool via stdin,
- the limits for CPU time, wall time, and memory, and
- the list of CPU cores and memory banks to use.

Executing a run produces the following output:

- the exit code of the main process,
- output written to stdout and stderr by the tool, and
- the CPU time, wall time, and peak memory consumption of the tool.

---

[13] http://lwn.net/Articles/484251/

The program **runexec** executes a run with the given input, provides the output, and ensures (using cgroups) adherence to the specified resource limits, reliable cleanup of processes after execution (i.e., no process survives), and accurate measurement of the resource usage. This program is runnable stand-alone, in which case the inputs are passed as command-line parameters. Alternatively, **runexec** is usable as a Python module for a more convenient integration into other Python-based benchmarking frameworks.

An example command line for executing a tool on all 16 (virtual) cores of the first CPU of a dual-CPU system, with a memory limit of 16 GB on the first memory bank and a time limit of 100 s is:

```
runexec --timelimit 100 --memlimit 16000000000
        --cores 0-7,16-23 --memoryNodes 0 -- <TOOL_CMD>
```

The output of **runexec** then looks as follows (log on stderr, result on stdout):

```
2015-01-20 10:35:35 - INFO - Starting command <TOOL_CMD>
2015-01-20 10:35:35 - INFO - Writing output to output.log
exitcode=0
returnvalue=0
walltime=1.51596093178s
cputime=2.514290687s
memory=130310144
```

In this case, the run took 1.5 s of wall time, and the tool used 2.5 s of CPU time and about 130 MB of RAM before returning successfully (exit code 0). The same could be achieved from within a Python program with three lines of code by importing **runexec** as a module as explained in the documentation[14].

5.3   Benchmarking a Collection of Runs

Benchmarking typically consists of processing tool runs on hundreds or thousands of input files, and there may be several different tools or several configurations of the same tool that run on the same input files.

The program **benchexec** executes a collection of runs. It receives as input

- a collection of input files,
- the name of the tool to use,
- command-line arguments for the tool to specify the configuration,
- any limits for CPU time, wall time, memory, and number of CPU cores, and
- the number of runs that should be executed in parallel.

These inputs are given in XML format; an example can be seen in the tool documentation[14]. Additionally, a tool-specific Python module needs to be written that contains functions for creating a command-line string for a run (including input file and user-defined command-line arguments) and for determining the

---

[14] https://github.com/dbeyer/benchexec/blob/master/doc/INDEX.md

result from the exit code and any output of the tool. Such a module typically has under 50 lines of Python code, and needs to be written only once per tool. We are often also interested in classifying the result into expected and incorrect answers. BENCHEXEC currently supports this for the domain of automatic software verification, where it gets as input a property to be verified in the format used by SV-COMP [3][15].

As an extension, benchexec and its input format also allow to specify different configuration options for subsets of the input files, as well as several different tool configurations at once, each of which will be benchmarked against all input files.

The program benchexec first tries to find a suitable allocation of the available resources (CPU cores and memory) to the number of parallel runs. It checks whether there are enough CPU cores and memory in the system to satisfy the core and memory requirements for all parallel runs. Then it assigns cores to each parallel run such that a run is not spread over different CPU sockets and different runs do not use virtual cores that belong to the same physical core, if this is possible. For memory, it ensures that enough memory is available for all runs and that every run uses only memory that is directly connected to the CPU socket(s) on which the run is executed (to avoid measurement problems due to NUMA). Thus, benchexec automatically guarantees valid resource allocations.

Afterwards, benchexec uses runexec to execute the benchmarked tool on each input file with the appropriate command line, resource limits, etc. It also interprets the output of the tool and determines whether the result was correct. The result of benchexec is a table (in XML format) that contains all information from the executed runs: returned result, exit code, CPU time, wall time, and memory usage. The output of the tool for each run is available in separate files. Additional information such as current date and time, the host and its system information (CPU and RAM), and the effective resource limits are also recorded.

The program table-generator allows to produce tables from the results of one or more executions of benchexec. If several result sets are given, they are combined and presented one per column group in the table, allowing to easily compare the results, for example, across different configurations or revisions of a tool, or across different tools. Each line of the generated table contains the result for one input file. There are columns for the output of the tool, the CPU time, the wall time, the memory usage, etc. These tables are written in two formats. A CSV-based format allows further processing, such as with gnuplot or R for producing plots and statistical evaluations, a spreadsheet program, or LaTeX for producing a paper by using a package for CSV import. The second format is HTML, which allows the user to view the tables conveniently with nothing more than a browser. The HTML table is interactive and generates scatter and quantile plots for selected columns, allows columns and rows to be filtered, and provides access to the text output of the tool for each individual run. Examples of such tables can be seen on the supplementary webpage.[16]

---

[15] Tools that do not support this specification format can also be benchmarked. In this case, the specification is used by BENCHEXEC only to determine the expected result.

[16] http://www.sosy-lab.org/~dbeyer/benchmarking#tables

If a tool outputs more interesting data (e.g., time statistics for individual parts of the analysis, number of created abstract states, or SMT queries), those data can also be added to the generated tables if a function is added to the tool-specific Python module which extracts such data values from the output of the tool. All features of the table (such as generating plots) are immediately available for the columns with such data values as well.

5.4 Discussion

We would like to discuss a few of the design decisions and goals of BENCHEXEC.

BENCHEXEC aims at not impacting the external validity of benchmarks by avoiding to use an overly artificial environment (such as a virtual machine) or influencing the benchmarked process in any way (except for the specified resource limits). Resource limitations and measurements are done using the respective kernel features that are present and active on a standard machine anyway.

We designed BENCHEXEC with extensibility and flexibility in mind. Support for other tools and result classifications can be added with a few lines of Python code. The program runexec, which does the actual benchmark execution and resource measurement, can be used separately as a stand-alone tool or a Python module, for example within other benchmarking frameworks. Result data are present as CSV tables, which allows processing with standard software.[17]

We choose not to base BENCHEXEC on a container solution such as LXC or Docker because, while these provide resource limitation and isolation, they typically do not focus on benchmarking. With containers, a fine-grained controlling of resource allocation as well as measuring of resource consumption may be difficult or impossible. Furthermore, requiring a container solution to be installed would significantly limit the amount of machines on which BENCHEXEC can be used, for example, because on many machines (especially in bigger HPC clusters) the Linux kernel is too old, or such an installation is not possible due to administrative restrictions. Using cgroups directly minimizes the necessary version requirements, the installation effort, and the necessary access rights.[18]

We use XML as input and output format because it is a structured format that is readable and writable by both humans and tools, and it is self-documenting. Users can also use comments in the input file. We can store not only customized result data, but also additional meta data in the result file. This allows to document information about the benchmarking environment, which is important in scientific work because it increases the reproducibility and trust of the results.

Python was chosen as programming language because it is expected to be available on every relevant Linux machine, and it is easy to write the tool-specific module even for people that do not have much experience in programming.

---

[17] For example, BENCHEXEC is used to automatically check for regressions in the integration test-suite of CPACHECKER.

[18] We successfully use BENCHEXEC on four different clusters, each under different administrative control and with software as old as SuSE Enterprise 11 and Linux 3.0, and on the machines of the student computer pool of our department.

6   Related Work

Besides the issues that we discussed, there are more sources of non-deterministic effects that may influence performance measurement, such as size of environment variables and order of objects during linking [9].

For computer networking, the MININET HI-FI project [6] also advocates reproducible experiments in their community. In order to achieve resource isolation of processes that belong to different virtual hosts, the project relies on cgroups.

In the verification community, there exist several benchmarking tools that have the same intent and features as our benchmarking framework. However, as of April 2015, no tool we investigated fulfills all requirements for reliable benchmarking, which are presented in Sect. 2. In the following, we discuss several existing benchmarking tools in their latest versions as of April 2015. Our selection is not exhaustive, because there exist many such tools.

The tool RUNLIM[19], in version 1.7, allows to benchmark another executable and limits both CPU time and memory. It does so by sampling time and memory consumption recursively for a process hierarchy, and thus cannot guarantee accurate measurements and limit enforcement. The tool cannot terminate a process hierarchy reliably, because it only terminates the main process with `kill`. The tool PYRUNLIM[20], a port of RUNLIM to the Python programming language, has a few more features, such as setting the CPU affinity of a process, and aims at killing process hierarchies more reliably. However, in the latest version 2.11, it does not use cgroups and also takes sample measurements recursively over process hierarchies, which —like all sampling-based methods— is not accurate.

The Satisfiability Modulo Theories Execution Service (SMT-Exec)[21] was a solver execution service provided by the SMT-LIB initiative. For enforcing resource limits, SMT-Exec used the tool TREELIMITEDRUN[22]. It uses the system calls `wait` and `setrlimit`, and thus, is prone to the restrictions argued in Sect. 3.

StarExec [12], a web-based service developed at the Universities of Iowa and Miami, is the successor of SMT-Exec. The main goal of StarExec is to facilitate the execution of logic solvers. The Oracle Grid Engine takes care of queuing and scheduling runs. For measuring CPU time and memory consumption, as well as enforcing resource limits, StarExec delegates to RUNSOLVER[23] [10], available in version 3.3.5, that also is prone to the limitations (Sect. 3).

The CProver Benchmarking Toolkit (CPBM)[24], available in version 0.5, ships helpers for verification-task patch management and result evaluation, and also supports benchmarking. However, the limits for CPU time and memory are enforced by `ulimit`[25], and thus, the benchmarking is not accurate.

---

[19] http://fmv.jku.at/runlim/

[20] http://alviano.net/2014/02/26/

[21] http://smt-exec.org

[22] http://smtexec.cs.uiowa.edu/TreeLimitedRun.c

[23] http://www.cril.univ-artois.fr/~roussel/runsolver/

[24] http://www.cprover.org/software/benchmarks/

[25] c.f. `verify.sh` in the CPBM package

The Versioning Competition Workflow Compiler (VCWC) [5] is an effort to create a fault-tolerant competition platform that supports competition maintainers in order to minimize their amount of manual work. This project, in the latest development version[26], defines its own benchmarking container, also relying on ulimit to enforce time limits. If the administrator of the benchmarking machine manually designed and created a cgroup hierarchy that enforces an appropriate partitioning of CPU cores and memory nodes, and defined a memory limit, the scripts of VCWC can execute runs within these existing cgroups, but they cannot automatically create the appropriate cgroups like BenchExec. Furthermore, measurement of CPU time and memory, as well as termination of processes, is not implemented with cgroups, and hence, may fail.

The tool BenchKit [8], available in version $\beta 2$, is also used for competitions, where participants submit a virtual-machine (VM) image with their tool and all necessary software. BenchKit executes the tool within an instance of this VM and measures the resource usage of the tool and the OS in the VM together. Our framework executes all tools natively on the host system and allows precise measurement of the resource consumption of the tool in isolation, without influence from factors such as the VM's OS. BenchKit measures CPU time and memory consumption of the VM using sampling with the performance monitoring tool sysstat[27]. BenchKit does not ensure that the CPU cores and the memory for a run are assigned such that hyper-threading and NUMA are respected. For each single run with BenchKit, i.e., each pair of tool and input file, a new VM has to be booted, which on average takes 40 s to complete [8]. Execution of a tool inside a VM can also be slower than directly on the host machine. Our approach based on cgroups has a similar effect of isolating the resource usage of individual runs but comes at practically zero overhead. Our tool implementation was successfully used in SV-COMP'15, in which 54 000 runs were executed, consuming a total of 120 CPU days [3]. Using BenchKit in this competition would have imposed an overhead of 25 CPU days for the 54 000 runs. When also counting runs that were executed by the competition organizers during the testing phase, the total increases to 170 000 runs and a prohibitive overhead.

7   Conclusion

The goal of this work is to establish a technological foundation for performance evaluation of tools that is based on modern technology and makes it possible to reliably measure and control resources in a reproducible way in order to obtain scientifically valid experimental data. First, we established reasons why there is a need for such a benchmarking technology in the area of automatic verification. Tool developers, as well as competitions, need reliable performance measurements to evaluate their research results. Second, we motivated and discussed several requirements that are indispensable for reproducible benchmarking and resource measurement, and also identified limitations and restrictions of existing

---

[26] git revision 9d58031 from 2013-09-13, c.f. https://github.com/tkren/vcwc/

[27] http://sebastien.godard.pagesperso-orange.fr/

methods. We demonstrate, using rather simple experiments on a large set of tool runs, the high risk of invalidating measurements if certain technical constraints are not taken care of. Such problems have been detected in practice, and nobody knows how often they went unnoticed, and how many wrong conclusions were drawn from flawed benchmarks. In order to overcome the existing deficits and establish a scientifically valid method, we presented our lightweight implementation BENCHEXEC, which is built on the concept of Linux cgroups. The implementation fulfills all requirements for reproducible benchmarking, since it avoids the pitfalls that existing tools are prone to. This is a qualitative improvement over the state-of-the-art, because existing approaches may produce arbitrarily large (systematic and random) measurement errors, e.g., if sub-processes or NUMA are involved.

BENCHEXEC is not just a prototypical implementation. The development of BENCHEXEC was driven by the demand for reproducible scientific experiments in our research projects (for the CPACHECKER project, we execute about 2 million tool runs per month in our research lab) and during the repeated organization of the International Competition on Software Verification (SV-COMP). Especially in the experiments of SV-COMP, we learned how difficult it can be to accurately measure resource consumption for a considerable zoo of tools that were developed using different technologies and strategies. BENCHEXEC makes it easy to tame the wildest beast, and was successfully used to benchmark 22 tools in SV-COMP'15[28], with all results approved by the 77 authors of these tools.

Acknowledgement. We thank Hubert Garavel, Jiri Slaby, and Aaron Stump for their helpful comments regarding BENCHKIT, cgroups, and StarExec, respectively.

Appendix: Impact of Hyper-threading and NUMA

To show that hyper-threading and non-uniform memory access (NUMA) can have a negative influence on benchmarking if not handled appropriately, we executed benchmarks using the predicate analysis of the verifier CPACHECKER[29] in revision 15 307 from the project repository[30]. We used 4011 C programs from SV-COMP'15 [3] (excluding categories not supported by CPACHECKER) and a CPU-time limit of 900 s. Tables with the full results and the raw data are available on our supplementary webpage.[31]

Note that the actual performance impact will differ according to the resource-usage characteristics of the benchmarked tool. For example, a tool that uses only very little memory but fully utilizes its CPU core(s) will be influenced more by hyper-threading than by non-local memory, whereas for a tool that relies more on memory accesses it might be the other way around. In particular, the results for CPACHECKER that are shown here are not generalizable and show only that

---

[28] List on http://sv-comp.sosy-lab.org/2015/participants.php

[29] http://cpachecker.sosy-lab.org

[30] https://svn.sosy-lab.org/software/cpachecker/trunk

[31] http://www.sosy-lab.org/~dbeyer/benchmarking#benchmarks

there is such an impact. Because the quantitative amount of the impact is not predictable and might be non-deterministic, it is important to rule out these factors for reproducible benchmarking in any case.

Impact of Hyper-threading. To show the impact of hyper-threading, we executed benchmarks on a machine with a single Intel Core i7-4770 3.4 GHz CPU socket (with four physical cores and hyper-threading) and 33 GB of memory. We executed the verifier twice in parallel and assigned one virtual core and 4.0 GB of memory to each run. In one instance of the benchmark, we assigned each of the two parallel runs a virtual core from separate physical cores. In a second instance of the benchmark, we assigned each of the two parallel runs one virtual core from the same physical core, such that both runs had to share the hardware resources of one physical core. A scatter plot with the results is shown in Fig. 1. For the 2 472 programs from the benchmark set that CPACHECKER could solve on

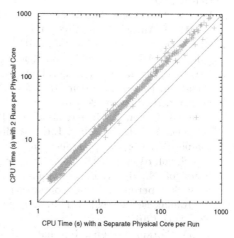

Fig. 1. Scatter plot showing the influence of hyper-threading for 2 472 runs of CPACHECKER: the data points above the diagonal show a performance decrease due to an inappropriate assignment of CPU cores during benchmarking

this machine, 13 h of CPU time were necessary using two separate physical cores and 19 h of CPU time were necessary using the same physical core, an increase of 41 % caused by the inappropriate core assignment.

Impact of NUMA. To show the impact of non-uniform memory access, we executed benchmarks on a NUMA machine with two Intel Xeon E5-2690 v2 2.6 GHz CPUs with 63 GB of local memory each. We executed the verifier twice in parallel, assigning all cores of one CPU socket and 60 GB of memory to each of the two runs. In one instance of the benchmark, we assigned memory to each run that was local to the CPU the run was executed on. In a second instance of the benchmark, we deliberately forced each of the two runs to use only memory from the *other* CPU socket, such that all memory accesses were indirect. For the 2 483 programs from the benchmark set that CPACHECKER could solve on this machine, 19 h of CPU time were necessary using local memory and 21 h of CPU time were necessary using remote memory, an increase of 11 % caused by the inappropriate memory assignment. The wall time also increased by 9.5 %.

References

1. Balint, A., Belov, A., Heule, M., Järvisalo, M.: Proceedings of SAT competition 2013: Solver and benchmark descriptions. Technical report B-2013-1, University of Helsinki (2013)
2. Barrett, C., Deters, M., de Moura, L., Oliveras, A., Stump, A.: 6 years of SMT-COMP. J. Autom. Reasoning 50(3), 243–277 (2012)
3. Beyer, D.: Software verification and verifiable witnesses. In: Baier, C., Tinelli, C. (eds.) TACAS 2015. LNCS, vol. 9035, pp. 401–416. Springer, Heidelberg (2015)
4. Beyer, D., Dresler, G., Wendler, P.: Software verification in the Google App-Engine Cloud. In: Biere, A., Bloem, R. (eds.) CAV 2014. LNCS, vol. 8559, pp. 327–333. Springer, Heidelberg (2014)
5. Charwat, G., Ianni, G., Krennwallner, T., Kronegger, M., Pfandler, A., Redl, C., Schwengerer, M., Spendier, L.K., Wallner, J.P., Xiao, G.: VCWC: a versioning competition workflow compiler. In: Cabalar, P., Son, T.C. (eds.) LPNMR 2013. LNCS, vol. 8148, pp. 233–238. Springer, Heidelberg (2013)
6. Handigol, N., Heller, B., Jeyakumar, V., Lantz, B., McKeown, N.: Reproducible network experiments using container-based emulation. In: Barakat, C., Teixeira, R., Ramakrishnan, K.K., Thiran, P. (eds.) CoNEXT 2012. pp. 253–264. ACM, New York (2012)
7. JCGM Working Group 2. International vocabulary of metrology - basic and general concepts and associated terms (VIM), 3rd edn. Technical report JCGM 200:2012, BIPM (2012)
8. Kordon, F., Hulin-Hubard, F.: BenchKit, a tool for massive concurrent benchmarking. In: ACSD 2014. pp. 159–165. IEEE (2014)
9. Mytkowicz, T., Diwan, A., Hauswirth, M., Sweeney, P.F.: Producing wrong data without doing anything obviously wrong! In: Soffa, M.L., Irwin, M.J. (eds.) ASPLOS. pp. 265–276. ACM, New York (2009)
10. Roussel, O.: Controlling a solver execution with the runsolver tool. J. Satisfiability, Boolean Model. Comput. 7, 139–144 (2011)
11. Singh, B., Srinivasan, V.: Containers: challenges with the memory resource controller and its performance. In: Ottawa Linux Symposium (OLS), p. 209. (2007)
12. Stump, A., Sutcliffe, G., Tinelli, C.: StarExec: a cross-community infrastructure for logic solving. In: Demri, S., Kapur, D., Weidenbach, C. (eds.) IJCAR 2014. LNCS, vol. 8562, pp. 367–373. Springer, Heidelberg (2014)
13. Tichy, W.F.: Should computer scientists experiment more? IEEE Comput. 31(5), 32–40 (1998)

PICKLOCK: A Deadlock Prediction Approach under Nested Locking

Francesco Sorrentino[(✉)]

Cloudera Inc., Palo Alto, USA
francesco@cloudera.com

Abstract. We study the problem of determining whether from a run of a concurrent program, we can predict alternate deadlocking executions of it. We show that if a concurrent program adopts *nested locking*, the problem of predicting deadlocks is efficiently solvable without exploring all interleavings.

In this work we present a fundamentally new predictive approach to detect deadlocks in concurrent programs, not based on cycle detection in lock-graphs [1]. The idea is to monitor an arbitrary run of a concurrent program, use it to predict alternate runs that could be deadlocking, and reschedule them accurately. We implement our prediction algorithm in a tool called PICKLOCK, which is a modular extension of the PENELOPE framework [32].

We show experimentally that PICKLOCK scales well and is effective in predicting deadlocks. In particular, we evaluate it over 13 benchmark concurrent programs and find about 11 deadlocks by using only a single test run as the prediction seed for each benchmark.

1 Introduction

A common cause for unreactiveness in concurrent programs is deadlocked configurations. Deadlocks in a shared-memory concurrent program are unintended conditions that can be mainly classified into two types: *resource-deadlocks* and *communication deadlocks*. A set of threads is resource-deadlocked if each thread deadlocked is waiting for a resource, like a lock, held by another thread in the set, which forms a cycle of lock requests. In communication deadlocks some threads wait for messages that do not get sent because the sender threads are blocked or they have already sent the messages before receiving threads start to wait. In [23] the authors illustrate that it could be really hard to precisely detect all kinds of deadlocks by the same techniques. In this study we focused only on resource deadlocks, from now on referred to as deadlocks.

Deadlocks are very common in concurrent programs— Lu et al. [27] showed that a relevant number of errors (about 30 %) found in a characteristic study of concurrency bugs on a collection of software systems can be attributed to deadlocks. Moreover, avoiding other concurrency problems like races and atomicity-violations often involves introducing new synchronizations, which in turn can introduce new deadlocks [27,28].

© Springer International Publishing Switzerland 2015
B. Fischer and J. Geldenhuys (Eds.): SPIN 2015, LNCS 9232, pp. 179–199, 2015.
DOI: 10.1007/978-3-319-23404-5_13

Deadlocks often occur under subtle interleaving patterns that the programmer has not taken into consideration. There are too many interleavings to test for, even for a single concurrent program on a single input, making concurrency testing a difficult problem. With the rise of multicore hardware platforms, finding solutions to this problem is very important, as testing is still the most effective way of finding bugs today. Current testing technologies such as stress testing are inadequate in exposing such subtle interleavings.

In this study, we focus on *prediction techniques for discovering deadlocks*—we observe an arbitrary execution of a concurrent program and from it predict alternate interleavings that can deadlock. We show that if a concurrent program adopts *nested locking* policies (i.e., locks are released by threads in the reverse order in which they were acquired), the problem of predicting potential deadlocks involving any number of threads is efficiently solvable without exploring all interleavings. Nested locking is guaranteed on *Java* (using *synchronized* blocks or methods) and *C#*.

Deadlocks can be detected using dynamic analysis [10,14,15,24,28], model checking [18,22], runtime monitoring [36], static analysis [19,29,31,37] or a combination thereof. Analysis based on lock order graphs [1] or a combination of them with happen-before relation has been already explored [15]. Static analysis and model checking are both typically complete (no false negatives), and model checking in addition is typically sound (no false positives). However, model checking is computationally expensive making the entire state space exploration impractical (resulting in false negative). In order to reduce the state space abstractions are performed introducing false positive. Precision is gained using dynamic techniques, even if may still yield false positives, as well as false negatives, and requires code instrumentation that results in a slow down of the analyzed program. Dynamic confirmation techniques work well in confirming if a potential deadlock is a real one. Recent deadlock detection techniques [24,28] use lock-set based strategies to predict potential deadlocks. Unfortunately, the re-execution phase they provide is weak, largely because such re-execution phases are based on time triggered approaches.

The solution we propose for predicting potential deadlocks and for confirming them is not based on the simple cycle lock requests detection like most of the deadlocks detection work available in the literature [1,13,14,19,25,34,35,37]. It instead involves taking a concurrent program and a test harness, executing the program under test to get an arbitrarily interleaved execution, and then *predicting* alternate executions leading to deadlocks. Finally, in order to check if a real deadlock has been found, the program being tested is re-executed precisely under these predicted deadlocking schedules.

The main contribution of this paper is the prediction algorithm, which reasons at an abstract level in order to efficiently and accurately predict deadlocking schedules. The algorithm is based on *lock-sets* and *acquisition histories* (the latter are a kind of hierarchical lock-set information), which only ensure that the predicted run respects *lock* acquisitions and releases in the run. In other words, the predicted runs are certainly not guaranteed to be feasible in the original program— if the original program had threads that communicated through shared variables in a way that orchestrated the control flow, the predicted runs may simply not be feasible. However, in the absence of such communication, the predicted runs do respect the locking semantics and hence assure feasibility at that level of abstraction. To realize a more precise prediction we could have used a more sophisticated mechanism, such as the one that uses constraint solvers we proposed in [20]. However, we decided to pursue scalability and use a more lightweight solution here. The crucial observation is that acquisition histories give not only enough traction to detect alternate deadlocking interleavings (which entirely eliminates false positives), but also provide an effective mechanism to *re-schedule* the precise interleaving under which deadlock will occur.

We have implemented this methodology in a tool, PickLock, that monitors and reschedules interleavings for Java programs. The infrastructure of the tool is partially built on the Penelope framework, presented in [32]. We have applied PickLock to a suite of multi-threaded Java programs and showed that it is efficient and effective in predicting deadlocking schedules. The methodology we present is language-independent and can be applied to other contexts as long as nested locking policies are used.

2   Related Work

Prior work on deadlock detection in concurrent programs have exploited different techniques: dynamic (including postmortem) analysis, model checking and static analysis.

Static approaches attempt to detect possible deadlocks directly on the source code and do not require the execution of the application being tested [12,19,29, 31,37]. Even if this approach exhaustively explores all potential deadlocks, it suffers from high false positives, aggravating the user. For example, Williams et al. in [37] report that on 100,000 potential deadlocks only 7 were real deadlocks. In order to reduce the number of false positives numerous directions have been explored. Williams et al. [37] have used heuristics to try to remove some of the false positives but these have the potential of removing some real deadlocks. von Praun [34] uses a context-sensitive lock-set and a lock graph in his approach. To reduce false positives they suppress certain deadlocks based on lock alias set information, again potentially removing real deadlocks. RacerX [19] is a static data race and deadlock detection tool for concurrent programs written in C. Additional programmer's annotations are used to inject the programmer's intent and consequently suppress false positives and improve the RacerX's accuracy. More recently, Naik et al. [29] combine a suite of static analysis techniques to cut the false positive rates. Unfortunately, scalability and problems related to conditional statements still remain a drawback of static analysis.

Several researchers have explored a model-checking approach to detect deadlocks in concurrent programs using model checker such as SPIN and Java Pathfinder [18,22,33,39]. Joshi et al. [23] monitor the annotated conditional variables as well as lock synchronization and threading operations in a program to generate a trace program containing not only thread and lock operations but also the value of conditionals. Then they apply `Java Pathfinder` to check all abstracted and inferred execution paths of the trace program to detect deadlocks. However, the technique proposed requires manual effort to design and add annotations, which can be error-prone, and suffers from the scalability issue to handle largescale programs. Dynamic analysis techniques have been extensively explored as well [10,14,15]. With this approach the execution of one or more runs of a concurrent program are monitored to determine if a deadlock may occur in another execution of the program. Bensalem et al. [14,15] find potential deadlocks in Java programs by finding cycles in the lock graph generated during program execution. All cycles in the lock graph are considered to be potential deadlocks, generating false positives (as well as false negative). They use the happen-before relation to improve the precision of cycle detection and use a guided scheduler to confirm a deadlock. Farchi et al. [10] proposed an approach where they generate a lock graph across multiple runs of the code. Deadlocks prediction is done searching cycles in this graph; unfortunately, this approach may also produce false alarms. `MulticoreSDK` [28] and `DeadlockFuzzer` [24] use lock-set based strategies to predict potential deadlocks. Once a potential deadlock has been found, deadlock confirmation, avoidance, or healing strategies can be applied. Neither approaches are capable of completing large executions, moreover the rescheduling phase is not robust enough to guarantee that the right time to trigger a deadlock is used.

`MagicFuzzer` [16] is a dynamic resource deadlock detection technique based on locks dependencies. It locates potential deadlock cycle from an execution, it iteratively prunes lock dependencies that have no incoming or outgoing relations with other lock dependencies. Similarly to our approach it has a trace recording phase, a potential deadlock detection phase and a deadlock confirmation phase — which avoids false positives. However, like most of the techniques based on cycle detection, the detection phase is not precise, even assuming that the communication between threads occurs only through locks, overloading the confirmation phase. `ConLock` [38] is the most recent work that implements predictive detection techniques following our same motivations. `ConLock` analyzes a given cycle and the execution trace that produce the cycle. It generates a set of constraints and a set of nearest scheduling points. Then, it schedules a confirmation run with the aim to not violate a reduced set of constraints from the chosen nearest scheduling points. `ConLock` is able to detect false positives, however the confirmation phase still lacks of robustness (deadlocks are hit with a probability $> 71\%$).

3   Motivating Example

It is very common to incur a deadlock when programs misuse APIs offered by third-party libraries [25,37]. Even if the program does not contain logic bugs per se, the interaction of methods defined in synchronized classes may still result

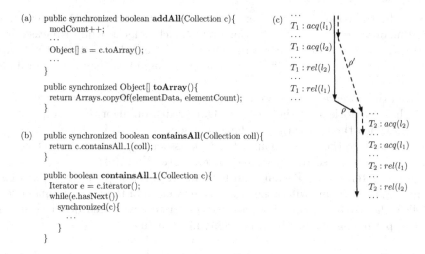

(a) public synchronized boolean **addAll**(Collection c){
       modCount++;
       ...
       Object[] a = c.toArray();
       ...
     }

     public synchronized Object[] **toArray**(){
       return Arrays.copyOf(elementData, elementCount);
     }

(b) public synchronized boolean **containsAll**(Collection coll){
       return c.containsAll_1(coll);
     }

     public boolean **containsAll_1**(Collection c){
       Iterator e = c.iterator();
       while(e.hasNext())
         synchronized(c){
           ...
         }
     }

(c) ...
     $T_1 : acq(l_1)$
     ...
     $T_1 : acq(l_2)$
     ...
     $T_1 : rel(l_2)$
     ...
     $T_1 : rel(l_1)$
     ...

     ρ'
     ρ

     ...
     $T_2 : acq(l_2)$
     ...
     $T_2 : acq(l_1)$
     ...
     $T_2 : rel(l_1)$
     ...
     $T_2 : rel(l_2)$
     ...

Fig. 1. (a) – Simplified code for *addAll* and *toArray* of the *Vector* library of Java 1.4. (b) – Simplified code for *containsAll* and *containsAll_1* of the *Collections* library of Java 1.4. (c) – Observed execution ρ of the program under test (dotted arrows indicate the predicted run ρ' generated from ρ).

in deadlocks. This is a general problem for all synchronized Collection classes in the JDK, including the `Vector` library. Since `Vector` is a synchronized class, programmers could easily assume that concurrent accesses to vectors are not a concern. However, potential deadlocks could still be present and hidden from the calling application.

In Fig. 1(a), we show a simplified version of the methods *addAll* and *toArray* as defined in the JDK library. *addAll* appends all of the elements in the specified collection c to the end of *this* Vector. Internally it calls the method *toArray*, which returns an array containing all the elements in *this* Vector in the correct order. As the *addAll* needs to be multi-thread safe, it follows that locks for the vector being added to and the parameter need to be acquired. Specifically, the method acquires the lock associated with the vector being added to first, and then it acquires the lock associated with the parameter. Similarly, in Fig. 1(b), we report a simplified version of the methods *containsAll* and *containsAll_1* (in AbstractCollection.java) as defined in the JDK. *containsAll* acquires the lock associated with *this* vector first, then from inside the method *containsAll_1* it acquires the lock associated with the specified collection c.

Let us assume that in the program under test there are two threads that execute concurrently and use two vectors V_1 and V_2. T_1 wants to add all elements of V_2 to V_1, calling the method $V_1.addAll(V_2)$, while T_2 concurrently invokes the method $V_2.containsAll(V_1)$, in order to check if the vector V_2 contains all the elements of V_1.

In Fig. 1(c), we report a possible observed run ρ (focus on the solid arrows) of the program under test. We are assuming that the code of T_1 is entirely executed followed by the code of T_2 (this execution does not deadlock). Our prediction algorithm observes the synchronization events (such as locks acquire/release) but suppresses the semantics of computations entirely and does not observe them. They have been replaced by "..." symbols in the figure as they play no role in our analysis.

Given the observed run ρ, we ask whether there exists an alternative run ρ' in which a deadlock potentially occurs. Our prediction algorithm will predict a run ρ' in which the acquisition of the lock associated with V_1 (let us say l_1) by T_1 is followed by the acquisition of the lock associated with V_2 (let us say l_2) done by T_2 (illustrated by the dotted arrows in the Fig. 1(c)).

Once a potential deadlocking run is found, in the last phase of PICKLOCK, our re-execution engine will orchestrate the execution of the program under test to follow the predicted run. The program under test will then deadlock inside the JDK, producing a concrete deadlocking interleaving.

4   Preliminaries

In this Section we introduce some notations that will be used in the rest of the paper. Then, we elaborate on some observations that motivate our various design choices.

4.1   Prediction Model

We assume a countably infinite set of thread identifiers $\mathcal{T} = \{T_1, T_2, \ldots\}$ and a countably infinite set of global locks $\mathcal{L} = \{l_1, l_2, \ldots\}$, used in a nested fashion (i.e. threads release locks in the reverse order in which they were acquired).

PickLock observes three kinds of actions for a given thread T_i, defined as:

$$\Sigma_{T_i} = \{T_i\colon acq(l),\ T_i\colon rel(l)|\ l \in \mathcal{L}\} \cup \{T_i\colon tc\ T_j\ |\ T_j \in \mathcal{T}\}$$

Action $T_i\colon acq(l)$ represents acquiring the lock l and the action $T_i\colon rel(l)$ represents releasing of the lock l, by thread T_i. The action $T_i\colon tc\ T_j$ denotes the thread T_i creating the thread T_j. We define $\Sigma = \bigcup_{T_i \in \mathcal{T}} \Sigma_{T_i}$ as the set of actions of all threads. A word w in Σ^*, in order to represent a run, must satisfy several syntactic restrictions, represented by the following definitions. ($\sigma|_A$ denotes the word σ projected to the letters in A).

Definition 1 (Lock-Validity). *A run $\rho \in \Sigma^*$ is lock-valid if it respects the semantics of the locking mechanism. Formally, let $\Sigma_l = \{T_i\colon acq(l), T_i\colon rel(l)\ |\ T_i \in \mathcal{T}\}$ denote the set of locking actions on lock l. Then ρ is lock-valid if for every $l \in \mathcal{L}$, $\rho|_{\Sigma_l}$ is a prefix of*

$$\left[\bigcup_{T_i \in \mathcal{T}} (T_i\colon acq(l)\ T_i\colon rel(l))\right]^*$$

This definition specify a semantic property on locks that the predicted run should respect, the nested nature is automatically forced from the initial assumption (i.e. the original run uses locks in a nested fashion) and from the program order constraint.

Definition 2 (Creation-Validity). *A run $\rho \in \Sigma^*$ over a set of threads $\mathcal{T}$ is creation-valid if every thread is created at most once and its events happen after this creation, i.e., for every $T_i \in \mathcal{T}$, there is at most one occurrence of the form T_j: tc T_i in w, and, if there is such an occurrence, then all occurrences of letters of Σ_{T_i} happen after this occurrence.*

Let ρ be a global execution, let $\{\rho_T\}_{T \in \mathcal{T}}$ be its set of local executions and $e = (T, i)$ be an event in ρ_T. Then we say that the j'th action $(1 \leq j \leq |\rho|)$ in ρ *is the event* e (or, $Event(\rho[j]) = e = (T, i)$), if $\rho[j] = T{:}a$ (for some action a) and $\rho_T[1, i] = \rho[1, j]|_T$. In other words, the event $e = (T, i)$ appears at the position j in ρ in the particular interleaving of the threads that constitutes ρ. Reversely, for any event e in $\{\rho_T\}_{T \in \mathcal{T}}$, let $Occur(e, \rho)$ denote the (unique) j $(1 \leq j \leq |\rho|)$ such that the j'th action in ρ is the event e, i.e. $Event(\rho[j]) = e$. Therefore, we have $Event(\rho[Occur(e, \rho)]) = e$, and $Occur(Event(\rho[j])) = j$. Finally, let $Tid(e, \rho)$ denote the thread $T \in \mathcal{T}$ executing the event e in ρ.

While the run ρ defines a total order on the set of events in it $(E, \leq)$, there is an induced total order between the events of each thread. We formally define this as $\sqsubseteq_i$ for each thread T_i, as follows: for any $e_m, e_n \in E$, if e_m and e_n belong to thread T_i and $m \leq n$ then $e_m \sqsubseteq_i e_n$. The partial order that is the union of all the program orders is $\sqsubseteq = \cup_{T_i \in \mathcal{T}} \sqsubseteq_i$.

Given an execution ρ over a set of locks $\mathcal{L}$ and threads $\mathcal{T}$, we would like to *infer* alternative executions ρ' from ρ that deadlock. Our prediction model respect *lock-validity, creation-validity* and the program-order of the original run.

Definition 3 (Prediction Model [32]). *Let ρ be a run over a set of threads $\mathcal{T}$ and locks $\mathcal{L}$. A run ρ' is inferred from ρ if (i) for each $T_i \in \mathcal{T}$, $\rho'|_{T_i}$ is a prefix of $\rho|_{T_i}$, (ii) ρ' is lock-valid, (iii) creation-valid. We will refer to the set of executions inferred from ρ with $Infer(\rho)$.*

Notice that our prediction model is an *abstraction* of the problem of finding alternate executions that are deadlocking in the concrete program. Not all the executions in $Infer(\rho)$ may be valid/feasible in the original program (this could happen if the threads communicate using other mechanisms). In this sense we talk about *potential deadlocks*. A more precise prediction model can be obtained adding to Definition 3 the *data-validity* constraints (for more details we refer the reader to [20,30]). However, our rescheduling phase takes care of this problem, getting rid of the false positives.

4.2   Lock-Sets and Acquisition-Histories

Let ρ_T indicate the local execution of T. Consider ρ_T (for any T), the *lock-set held after ρ_T* is the set of all locks T holds: $LockSet(\rho_T) = \{l \in \mathcal{L} \mid \exists k.\rho_T[k] = T{:}acq(l)$, there is no $j, k < j \leq i$ s.t. $\rho_T[j] = T{:}rel(l)\}$. The *acquisition history* [26] of the execution of a thread has more nuanced information, and will play a crucial role in both detecting deadlocks and finding re-executions of the program that manifest the deadlocks. The acquisition history of ρ_T records,

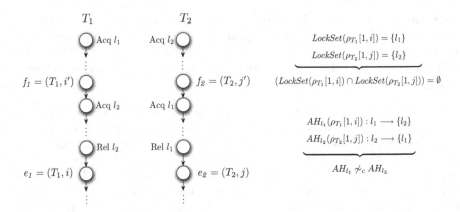

Fig. 2. Lock-sets and acquisition histories associated with a deadlocking configuration of threads T_1 and T_2.

for each lock l held by T at the end of ρ_T, the set of locks that T acquired (and possibly released) after the last acquisition of the lock l.

Formally, the acquisition history of ρ_T, $AH(\rho_T) : LockSet(\rho_T) \to 2^{\mathcal{L}}$, where $AH_l(\rho_T)$ is the set of all locks $l' \in \mathcal{L}$ such that $\exists k.\rho_T[k] = T{:}acq(l)$ and there is no $j > k$ such that $\rho_T[j] = T{:}rel(l)$ and $\exists h > k.\rho_T[h] = T{:}acq(l')$.

Two acquisition histories $AH_l(\rho_{T_1})$ and $AH_{l'}(\rho_{T_2})$ are said to be *not compatible*, denoted as $AH_l(\rho_{T_1}) \not\sim_c AH_{l'}(\rho_{T_2})$, if there exist two locks l and l' such that $l' \in AH_l(\rho_{T_1})$ and $l \in AH_{l'}(\rho_{T_2})$. They are otherwise said to be *compatible*.

4.3   Relation Between Co-reachability and Deadlock

A result by Kahlon et al. [26] argues that global reachability of two threads communicating via nested locks is effectively and precisely solvable by extracting locking information from the two threads. In particular, it states that there is an execution that ends with event e_1 in one thread and event e_2 in the other thread, if, and only if, the acquisition histories at e_1 and e_2 are compatible and the lock-sets held are disjoint.

Lemma 1 (Kahlon et al. [26]). *Let ρ be an execution of a concurrent program P and let T_1 and T_2 be two different threads. Let $e_1 = (T_1, i)$ be an event of thread T_1 and $e_2 = (T_2, j)$ be an event of thread T_2 of these local executions.*

Then the event e_1 and e_2 of T_1 and T_2 respectively are co-reachable in P if, and only if, $LockSet(\rho_{T_1}[1,i]) \cap LockSet(\rho_{T_2}[1,j]) = \emptyset$, and the acquisition history of $\rho_{T_1}[1,i]$ and the acquisition history of $\rho_{T_2}[1,j]$ are compatible.

This pairwise reachability result is the base of our approach and the following Theorem is a direct consequence of it.

Theorem 1. *There is a potential deadlocking run $\rho' \in Infer(\rho)$ involving two threads if, and only if, $\exists\ e_1 = (T_1, i)$, $e_2 = (T_2, j)$ s.t. $LockSet(\rho_{T_1}[1, i]) \cap$*

$LockSet(\rho_{T_2}, [1, j]) = \emptyset$ and the acquisition histories of $\rho_{T_1}[1, i]$ and $\rho_{T_2}[1, j]$ are not compatible.

Proof. One side of the implication follows from the Lemma 1. If there is a deadlock, involving T_1 and T_2, it means that we reached an event $f_1 = (T_1, i')$ and an event $f_2 = (T_2, j')$ in the local executions in which the two threads are not allowed to make further operations (Fig. 2). From the Lemma 1, it follows that lock-sets at f_1 and f_2 are disjoint and the acquisition histories of $\rho_{T_1}[1, i']$ and $\rho_{T_2}[1, j']$ are compatible. Moreover, because the threads T_1 and T_2 are blocked, the operation that they are trying to do is an acquire of some lock (the release is not a blocking operation).

In particular, T_1 and T_2 are trying to acquire different locks, because if they were trying to acquire the same lock at least one of the threads would have been able to move. The fact that T_1 (resp. T_2) can not make an acquire implies that it is requiring a lock, l_2 (resp. l_1) owned by T_2 (resp. T_1). It follows that at $\rho_{T_1}[1, i' + 1]$ and $\rho_{T_2}[1, j' + 1]$, the lock-sets are not disjoint. From the nested nature of the locking policies, it follows that there exists a point in ρ_{T_1} in which l_2 is released, that has the same lock-set of f_1, let us say e_1. Similarly, there exists a point in ρ_{T_2} in which l_1 is released, that has the same lock-set of f_2, let us say e_2. It follows that at e_1 and e_2 the lock-sets are disjoint (they were disjoint also in f_1 and f_2). Because T_1 held l_1 while acquired l_2 and T_2 held l_2 while acquired l_1 then l_1 and l_2 are such that the acquisition histories of $\rho_{T_1}[1, i]$ and $\rho_{T_2}[1, j]$ are not compatible, that completes this side of the proof.

It remains to prove that when $\exists e_1, e_2$ satisfying the hypothesis then there exist an event, f_1, executed by T_1 with $Occur(f_1, \rho) < Occur(e_1, \rho)$, and an event, f_2, executed by T_2 with $Occur(f_2, \rho) < Occur(e_2, \rho)$, such that T_1 and T_2 are deadlocked.

Let us pick the e_1 e_2 such that $(Occur(e_1, \rho) + Occur(e_2, \rho))$ is minimal, moreover for the sake of exposition we can assume that there is a unique pair of locks (l_1, l_2) such that the acquisition histories of $\rho_{T_1}[1, i]$ and $\rho_{T_2}[1, j]$ are not compatible. We need to prove that f_1 and f_2 respectively in T_1 and T_2 are co-reachable and deadlocking.

From the assumption it follows that in ρ_{T_1} and in ρ_{T_2}, before that the events e_1 and e_2 are respectively executed, the locks l_1 and l_2 are acquired in reverse order by T_1 and T_2. We can assume that the execution orders are those depicted in Fig. 2.

We pick as f_1 the event right before the acquisition of l_2 in ρ_{T_1} and the event right before the acquisition of l_1 in ρ_{T_2} as f_2. f_1 and f_2 are deadlocking by definition. In order to prove that they are co-reachable, from Lemma 1, we need to prove:

1. $LockSet(\rho_{T_1}[1, i']) \cap LockSet(\rho_{T_2}[1, j']) = \emptyset$.
2. acquisition histories at $\rho_{T_1}[1, i']$ and $\rho_{T_2}[1, j']$ are compatible.

Due to the nested nature of the locking policies, the event f_1 occurs after the acquisition by T_1 (resp. T_2) of l_1 (resp. l_2), belonging to $LockSet(\rho_{T_1}[1, i])$ (resp. $LockSet(\rho_{T_2}[1, j])$). It follows $LockSet(\rho_{T_1}[1, i]) \subseteq LockSet(\rho_{T_1}[1, i'])$ and $LockSet(\rho_{T_2}[1, j]) \subseteq LockSet(\rho_{T_2}[1, j'])$.

By contradiction, let us assume that $LockSet(\rho_{T_1}[1, i']) \cap LockSet(\rho_{T_2}[1, j']) \neq \emptyset$. That is, it exists a lock l_3 such that $l_3 \in LockSet(\rho_{T_1}[1, i']) \cap LockSet(\rho_{T_2}[1, j'])$. But from the inclusions stated above it follows that $l_3 \in LockSet(\rho_{T_1}[1, i]) \cap LockSet(\rho_{T_2}[1, j])$ that contradicts the hypothesis.

We can conclude that the lock-sets are disjoint when T_1 is at $\rho_{T_1}[1, i']$ and T_2 is at $\rho_{T_2}[1, j']$. It remains to prove the point 2. Let us assume by contradiction that exist l_1 and l_2 such that the acquisition histories at $\rho_{T_1}[1, i']$ and $\rho_{T_2}[1, j']$ are not compatible. We found two events satisfying the hypothesis, moreover $Occur(f_1, \rho) < Occur(e_1, \rho)$ and $Occur(f_2, \rho) < Occur(e_2, \rho)$ it follows that $(Occur(e_1, \rho) + Occur(e_2, \rho))$ was not minimal, contradicting the assumption.

4.4 The Importance of Acquisition Histories

Potential deadlocks could be detected using a multitude of approaches. The question we want to address in this Section is: *"Why use acquisition histories?"*. The ideal prediction algorithm would predict potential deadlocks that are feasible at least with respect to the synchronization mechanisms.

The majority of the approaches that have been proposed are based on cycle detection in *lock order graphs* [11,12,15]. In a lock order graph, a node represents a lock. A directed edge from node l_1 to node l_2 labeled T represents that, during the execution, the thread T acquires the lock l_2 while holding the lock l_1. For the rest of this Section we consider deadlocks involving only two threads for the sake of exposition. Let us consider a program in which two threads T_1 and T_2 run concurrently and they use four locks l_1, l_2, l_3 and l_4. Given an execution ρ of such program, in Fig. 3(a) we report the local executions ρ_{T_1} and ρ_{T_2} and the lock order graph associated with it (b). The classic technique based on cycle detection [11,12,15,16,24,28], first constructs a lock order graph. Then it detects whether there are any cycles on the graph (in Fig. 3(b) dotted lines are detected cycles). Finally, it tries to trigger the potential deadlock using active scheduling strategies.

Consider the local executions in Fig. 3(a). Two potential deadlocks are reported by the lock order graph-based algorithms as the one presented in [15]. The authors try to reduce false positives by ignoring cycles protected by a *gate lock* (i.e. lock that needs to be taken by each thread before the cycle is entered). Unfortunately, in this example there are such gate locks and it highlights the main difference between our algorithm and the others (we are able to filter out this false positive).

Another simple algorithm to detect potential deadlocks keeps the set of locks (for each event) held by the thread when an event is executed (similar to what we do), and also keeps the information about *next lock required*. A potential deadlock is found when given two events e_1 and e_2 (executed by two distinct threads), they have disjoint lock-sets and the next lock required at e_1 (resp. e_2)

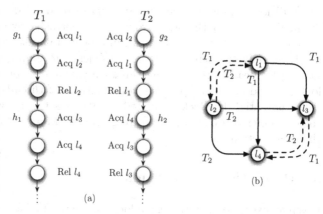

(a)

(b)

Fig. 3. (a) – A problematic scenario for the *next lock required* and the *cycle detection* approaches. (b) – Lock order graph associated with the execution on the left (dotted lines are detected cycles).

is in the lock-set associated with e_2 (resp. e_1). Even the next lock required approach will report the potential deadlock at (g_1, g_2) such as the false potential deadlock (h_1, h_2). MagicFuzzer [16] is the most recent technique based on lock order graph. With respect to its competitors, this approach is more efficient because the size of the graph built is one order of magnitude smaller. It iteratively prunes lock dependencies that each have no incoming or outgoing edge. However, even this approach will wrongly report the two potential deadlocks.

The algorithm we propose is precise and lightweight. Precise because it will report a potential deadlock configuration only when it is feasible (at least respect to the synchronization mechanisms), potentially saving significant aggravation to the user if a manual inspection of the potential deadlocks is required (or if a re-execution phase is provided). It is light-weight because it just tracks lock-sets and some small additional data, acquisition histories. Deadlock prediction algorithms would keep track of at least lock-sets in order to avoid false positive due to *gate* locks. One can develop an algorithm that executes the run till the last lock-free point, and then tries to create the deadlock. However, we still need a mechanism to generate the run with the deadlock. This is what acquisition histories helps us do.

4.5   Concise Deadlock Prediction

A set of threads is deadlocked if each thread in the set requests a lock, held by another thread in the set, forming a cycle of lock requests. A cycle with n components is a sequence, but there are n total permutations of the components to represent the same cycle. Detecting one permutation suffices to represent the cycle. In a cycle, each thread can occur only once [16]. We can then use a thread-driven approach to consider only one permutation in place of the whole set of permutations representing the same cycle.

Additionally, the algorithm we propose predicts deadlocks which have the minimal number of threads involved (as contrasted with algorithms based on cycle detection). Our algorithm is run repeatedly, it starts looking for deadlocks involving only two threads. If no deadlocks are found the algorithm proceeds looking for deadlocks involving three threads and so on until a potential deadlock is found or all the possible combinations of threads have been considered. If the potential deadlock predicted is real, this feature will be very helpful for the developer through the debugging process. More details will be discussed in the next Section.

5 Prediction Algorithms

Given an execution ρ with nested locking, we would like to *infer* other executions ρ', containing a deadlock, from ρ. Theorem 1 allows us to engineer an efficient algorithm to predict deadlocking executions. Our algorithm is based on the pairwise reachability, which is solvable compositionally by computing lock-sets and acquisition histories for each thread. In this Section we will consider first the prediction of deadlocks involving only two threads and then the more general case involving any number of threads.

5.1 Deadlocks Prediction: 2-threads

The aim of the algorithm is to find two deadlocking events, executed by two distinct threads, given an observed execution ρ. Notice that we are looking for potential deadlocks at this point. These deadlocks may not be feasible in the original program (this could happen if the threads communicate using other mechanisms; for example, if a thread writes a particular value to a global variable which another thread uses to choose an execution path).

The algorithm is divided into three phases. In the first phase, it gathers the lock-sets and acquisition histories by examining the events of each thread *individually*. In the second phase, it tests the compatibility of the lock-sets and acquisition histories of every pair of witnesses e_1 and e_2 in different threads, collected in the first phase. In the third phase from such e_1 and e_2 it rolls back to two co-reachable events, f_1 in T_1 and f_2 in T_2, such that the two threads are deadlocked.

Phase I. In the first phase, the algorithm gathers witnesses for each thread T. The algorithm gathers the witnesses by processing the local executions ρ_T in a single pass. It continuously updates the lock-set and acquisition history, adding events to the set of witnesses, making sure that there are no events with the same lock-set and acquisition history. The set of witnesses, indicated with AH_ρ^1, is a set of 3-tuples $\{((T,i), LockSet(\rho_T[1,i]), AH(\rho_T[1,i])) \mid T \in \mathcal{T}, 1 \leq i \leq |\rho_T|\}$. We use corresponding projection functions $ev(x)$, $ls(x)$ and $ah(x)$ to extract the components from $x \in AH_\rho^1$.

Note that phase I considers every event at most once, in one pass, in a streaming fashion, and hence runs in time linear in the length of the execution.

```
1 for each x, y ∈ AH¹ₚ do
2    if Tid(ev(x)) > Tid(ev(y)) then
3       if ls(x) ∩ ls(y) = ∅ ∧ ah(x) ≁c ah(y) then
4          pass the pair (ev(x), ev(y)) to the third phase;
5 end
```

Fig. 4. Phase II: prediction algorithm.

Phase II. In the second phase, the algorithm checks whether there are pairs of not compatible witnesses collected in the first phase. More precisely, it checks whether, for any pair of threads T_1 and T_2, there is an event e_1 executed by T_1 and an event e_2 executed by T_2 in AH^1_ρ that have disjoint lock-sets and not compatible acquisition histories. The existence of any such pair of events would mean (by Theorem 1) that there is a potential deadlock configuration involving the threads T_1 and T_2.

The algorithm runs the procedure in Fig. 4 for finding deadlocks. Notice that the condition > (in place of ≠) on line 2 avoids reporting redundant deadlocks, as mentioned in Sect. 4.5. This reduction is sound because the lock-sets intersection and the acquisition history's compatibility are commutative operations.

Phase III. In the third phase, the algorithm retrieves two deadlocking events f_1, f_2 from a pair of events (e_1, e_2) generated in the second phase. Acquisition histories and the lock-sets of e_1 and e_2 are used to backtrack until an appropriate deadlocking configuration (f_1, f_2) is found. The algorithm stops the backtracking process when the two events f_1 and f_2 have disjoint lock-set and compatible acquisition histories.

In particular, given a pair of events (e_1, e_2) indicating the presence of a deadlock (i.e. e_1 and e_2 have disjoint lock-set and not compatible acquisition histories) we want to retrieve a pair of deadlocking events (f_1, f_2). Let us call a *cut-point* the pair of events in the execution (f_1, f_2) such that there is an alternate schedule that can reach exactly up to f_1 and f_2 simultaneously. Any schedule that reach exactly up to f_1 and f_2 simultaneously gives a deadlock.

The algorithm to retrieve the cut-point runs the procedure in Fig. 5. Essentially T_1 and T_2 are backtracked at the events were the problematic locks were acquired (lines 2–3). Let us assume that T_1 holds l_1 when acquires l_2 at $f_1 = (T_1, i')$. Similarly, T_2 holds l_2 when acquires l_1 at $f_2 = (T_2, j')$.

If $LockSet(\rho_{T_1}[1, i']) \cap LockSet(\rho_{T_2}[1, j']) = \emptyset \wedge AH(\rho_{T_1}[1, i']) \sim_c AH(\rho_{T_2}[1, j'])$, we have found two co-reachable deadlocking point (line 6) and we return the pair (f_1, f_2) (line 7).

If the f_1 and f_2 are not co-reachable (line 4) then it can not be due to the fact that T_1 and T_2 are holding a common lock (due to the nested nature of the locks acquisition and the properties of e_1 and e_2). The only explanation is that $AH(\rho_{T_1}[1, i']) \not\sim_c AH(\rho_{T_2}[1, j'])$. Because we know that $LockSet(\rho_{T_1}[1, i']) \cap LockSet(\rho_{T_2}[1, j']) = \emptyset$ it follows that there is another deadlock involved, i.e. there is another pair of events in AH^1_ρ that will be considered in Phase II. Then we can interrupt the retrieving process (line 5).

Parameters $e_1 = (T_1, i), e_2 = (T_2, j)$
1 **for** *each* l_1, l_2 s.t. $l_2 \in AH_1(l_1)$ and $l_1 \in AH_2(l_2)$ with $AH_1 \in AH(\rho_{T_1}[1, i])$ and $AH_2 \in AH(\rho_{T_2}[1, j])$ **do**
2    $f_1 = (T_1, i')$ in ρ_{T_1} with $i' < i$ and the action performed is $T_1 : acquire(l_2)$
3    $f_2 = (T_2, j')$ in ρ_{T_2} with $j' < j$ and the action performed is $T_2 : acquire(l_1)$
4   **if** $AH(\rho_{T_1}[1, i']) \not\sim_c AH(\rho_{T_2}[1, j'])$ **then**
5   return null;
6   **else** $LockSet(\rho_{T_1}[1, i']) \cap LockSet(\rho_{T_2}[1, j']) = \emptyset \ \wedge \ AH(\rho_{T_1}[1, i']) \sim_c AH(\rho_{T_2}[1, j'])$ **then**
7   return the cut-point (f_1, f_2);
8 **end**

Fig. 5. Phase III.

5.2 Deadlocks Prediction: n-threads

Unfortunately, the lock-set/acquisition history analysis we considered is unable to catch potential deadlocks involving more than two threads. We illustrate the n-threads deadlock prediction using the classical *Dining Philosophers Problem*. Four philosophers, identifiable by a unique id $i \in \{1, 2, 3, 4\}$, sit at a table around a bowl of spaghetti. A fork is placed between each pair of adjacent philosophers. A philosopher i can only eat spaghetti when she has both left and right forks (resp. Fi and $F((i + 1) \mod 4)$). When the philosophers get hungry is not deterministic. Each fork can be held by only one philosopher and so a philosopher can use the fork only if it's not being used by another philosopher. When a philosopher i is hungry she tries to acquire her left fork first $F(i)$, and once she obtained that she tries to acquire the right fork $F((i + 1) \mod 4)$. After she finishes eating, she needs to put down both the forks so they become available to others. In particular, she puts the right fork down first and then the left fork. The code for the program is adapted from [17] and it is reported in Fig. 6.

```
class Philo {
  public static void main(String[] args) {
    Fork F1 = new Fork();
    Fork F2 = new Fork();
    Fork F3 = new Fork();
    Fork F4 = new Fork();
    new Philosopher(1, F1, F2).start();
    new Philosopher(2, F2, F3).start();
    new Philosopher(3, F3, F4).start();
    new Philosopher(4, F4, F1).start();
  }
}

class Philosopher extends Thread {
  int id;
  Fork F1, F2;
  public Philosopher(int i, Fork f1, Fork f2) {
    this.F1 = f1;
    this.F2 = f2;
    this.id = i;
  }
  public void Dine() {
    System.out.println(id);
  }
  public void run() {
    synchronized (F1) {
      synchronized (F2) {
        Dine();
      }
    }
  }
}

class Fork { public int num; }
```

Fig. 6. Dining philosophers [17].

Let us consider Fig. 7(a). All the acquisition histories associated with the events of T_1, T_2, T_3 and T_4 are pairwise compatible, and the lock-sets are pairwise disjoint. It follows that no potential deadlocks are found in this case. The problem is that the elements in AH_ρ^1 are built from single thread information, therefore

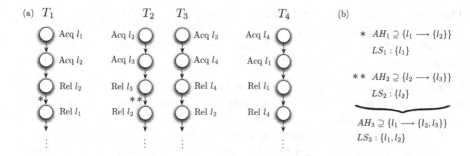

Fig. 7. (a) Local executions ρ_T for the four threads involved in the Dining Philosophers program of Fig. 6. (b) Composition of acquisition histories and locks-sets for threads T_1 (at *) and T_2 (at **).

in order to increase the power of the lock-set/acquisition history analysis, we need a set whose elements synthesize the information of multiple threads. We present in the following the algorithm for the detection of potential deadlocks involving multiple threads.

Let us consider two elements $x, y \in AH_\rho^1$ such that $T_1 = Tid(ev(x))$ and $T_2 = Tid(ev(y))$ are distinct, the intersection of the lock-sets $ls(x)$ and $ls(y)$ is empty and the acquisition histories in $ah(x)$ and $ah(y)$ are compatible.

Definition 4. *We say that x and y can be composed when the following conditions hold:*

- *$\exists l, l' \subseteq \mathcal{L}$ s.t. $l \in ls(x)$ and $l' \in ls(y)$*
- *l' is in some acquisition history defined in $ah(x)$.*

Before going through the details of the composition, we need to slightly modify the definition of the witnesses set as defined in the previous Section in order to gather composed elements. In particular, the first component of the set AH_ρ^1 was the event (T_j, i), where T_j was the thread executing the event. In place of the single thread T_j executing the event now we define a subset of T containing the thread executing the event. Notice that Theorem 1 still holds if we adapt the requirement of events executed by different threads to require that $Tid(ev(x)) \cap Tid(ev(y)) = \emptyset$.

When two elements x and $y \in AH_\rho^1$ can be composed the resulting element is $z = ((Tid(ev(x)) \cup Tid(ev(y)), (Occur(ev(x), \rho) + Occur(ev(y), \rho))), ls(x) \cup ls(y), merge(ah(x), ah(y)))$.

Figure 7(b) shows how the *merge* procedure, i.e. the composition of acquisition histories, is realized. The intuition behind this is that once we find $x, y \in AH_\rho^1$, with $Tid(ev(x)) = T_1$ and $Tid(ev(y)) = T_2$ respectively, that can be combined; we can assume that all the events executed by T_1 (up to $Occur(ev(x), \rho)$ and T_2 (up to $Occur(ev(y), \rho)$ are executed by a unique thread T'. Then, we collect events, lock-set and acquisition history of such *super thread* T'.

The new set AH_ρ^2 is defined as the union of AH_ρ^1 and all the elements obtainable by the composition of pairs of elements in AH_ρ^1.

Theorem 2. *There is a potential deadlocking run $\rho' \in Infer(\rho)$ involving 3 (or 4) threads if, and only if, $\exists x, y \in AH_\rho^2$ such that $Tid(ev(x)) \cap Tid(ev(y)) = \emptyset$, the LockSets $ls(x)$ and $ls(y)$ are disjoint and the acquisition histories in $ah(x)$ and $ah(y)$ are not compatible.*

In order to report only one permutation in place of the whole set of permutations representing the same cycle, we add some restrictions to the composition procedure. In particular, $\forall i \in Tid(ev(x))$ and $\forall j \in Tid(ev(y))$ we require $i < j$.

The result can be generalized for potential deadlocking run involving $n > 1$ threads. In particular, in order to detect potential deadlocks involving n threads where $2^{m-1} \le n \le 2^m$ for some integer $m > 1$, requires inductively constructing and analyzing the set AH_ρ^m. A deadlock involving n threads is found building $O(log(n))$ sets.

Dining Philosophers. In order to explain our algorithm for the prediction of deadlocks involving more than 2 threads we use the dining philosophers problem introduced in the previous Section. At the first round the algorithm generates the set of witnesses AH_ρ^1. No deadlocks are found in this round because $\forall x, y \in AH_\rho^1$ LockSets $ls(x)$ and $ls(y)$ are disjoint and the acquisition histories in $ah(x)$ and $ah(y)$ are compatible.

The algorithm then proceeds with the second round, generating AH_ρ^2. AH_ρ^2, contains all the elements of AH_ρ^1 and the elements obtained from the composition of T_1 and T_2, T_2 and T_3 and T_3 and T_4. Notice that the elements obtainable from the composition of T_4 and T_1 are discarded by the restriction we introduced at the end of Sect. 5.2. Moreover, no other compositions exist.

Among the elements of AH_ρ^2 there are $x = ((\{T_1, T_2\}, i), \{l_1, l_2\}, \{l_1 \rightarrow \{l_2, l_3\}, l_2 \rightarrow \{l_3\}\})$ and $y = ((\{T_3, T_4\}, j), \{l_3, l_4\}, \{l_3 \rightarrow \{l_4, l_1\}, l_4 \rightarrow \{l_1\}\})$. x and y satisfy the Theorem 2, so a potential deadlock is found.

At the moment PICKLOCK does not implement the phases II and III for the case when $n > 2$. PICKLOCK is fully implemented for the two threads deadlock case, and all experiments in Table 1 were conducted using this full implementation of the deadlock prediction algorithms involving exactly 2 threads. We did not implement the $n > 2$ case as we have not found practical examples where this was necessary. We did apply prediction algorithms for deadlocks involving $n > 2$ threads (i.e. only phase I), but did not detect any potential deadlocks in these benchmarks.

6   Implementation

In this Section, we present an overview of the structure of PICKLOCK. Many of the components are developed upon our previous work, PENELOPE [32]. Here, we will briefly review the monitoring and rescheduling phases as they largely derive from [32]. We then focus on the schedule generation phase that provides the main core of this work and includes the algorithms presented in the Sect. 5.

Monitoring: We implemented our monitoring instrumenter using the Bytecode Engineering Library (BCEL) [3]. Every class file in bytecode is (automatically) transformed so a *call* to a global monitor is made after each *relevant* action is performed. These relevant actions include thread creations, entry/exit to synchronized blocks, and methods. Thread creation events are used to capture the hard causality constraint of thread creation. Specifically, if a predicted run is not feasible with respect to the thread creation it will be filtered out from the set of predicted runs.

Rescheduling Predicted Schedules: The scheduler is implemented using BCEL [3]; we instrument the scheduling algorithm into the Java classes using bytecode transformations so that the events that were monitored interact with the scheduler. At each point according to the predicted run, the scheduler orchestrates the appropriate thread to perform an exact sequence of events. Each thread stops at the first relevant event and waits for a signal from the scheduler to proceed. Only then does the thread execute the number of events it was asked to execute. The thread then notifies the scheduler, releases the processor, and waits for further instructions.

Once the execution reaches the potential deadlocking points, the scheduler releases all threads to execute as they please. There is a timeout mechanism after which the status of the threads is checked and, if a real deadlock is found, PICKLOCK will report it to the user.

Schedule Generation: After finding a pair of deadlocking events (f_1, f_2) (Sect. 5), PICKLOCK generates alternate schedules that reach these events concurrently and hopefully expose deadlocks. Schedules that reach the deadlocking events concurrently are theoretically possible (indeed the Theorem 1 relies on the existence of such a schedule [21,26]). Our scheduling algorithm guarantees that the predicted deadlock is reproduced if in the original program the threads do not use mechanisms other than locks to communicate. However, note that the rescheduling phase controls only the interleaving of the program's statements, by instrumenting a controller of threads and rewriting the program. External nondeterminism caused by the OS, *events*, etc. is not controlled, and it is not controlled by this current PICKLOCK release. Our algorithm synthesizes a schedule that also (heuristically) ensures maximum conformance to the original observed execution. Building schedules that adhere as much as possible to the causal order of the original observed execution is crucial to building feasible schedules— the program under test may have many causal orderings such as communications that need to be respected to ensure feasibility. Experiments in this paper and earlier papers on PENELOPE [20,21,32] show that most predicted runs are indeed feasible and validate our choices and algorithms.

In order to achieve such results we use a pruning technique for the runs that removes a large prefix of them while maintaining the property that any run predicted from the suffix will still be feasible. Consider an execution ρ and a pair of deadlocking events $\alpha = (f_1, f_2)$. The idea behind pruning is to first construct the causal partial order of events of ρ and then remove two sets of events from it. The first set consists of events that are *causally after* f_1 and f_2. The second

Table 1. Experimental results for deadlocks prediction using PICKLOCK.

Application(LOC)	Base time	Number of threds	Number of syncs events	Number of observed events	Time to monitor	Number of predicted runs	Number of schedulable predictions	Total time	Deadlocks found
Elevator (566)	7.3 s	3	6.6 K	14 K	7.4 s	0	-	7.6 s	0
	7.3 s	5	22 K	30 K	7.4 s	0	-	7.5 s	0
	19.2 s	5	138 K	150 K	19.4 s	0	-	19.9 s	0
RayTracer (1.5 K)	5.0 s	10	20	648	5.0 s	0	-	5.2 s	0
	3.6 s	20	40	1.7 K	4.4 s	0	-	4.1 s	0
	42.4 s	10	20	648	42.5 s	0	-	43.1 s	0
DBCP 1.2.1 (168 K)	1.6 s	4	216	1.5 K	1.8 s	2	1	4.1 s	1
Vector (1.3 K)	<1 s	4	108	525	<1 s	1	1	1.0 s	1
	<1 s	4	12	63	<1 s	1	1	1.1 s	1
Stack(1.4 K)	<1 s	4	112	527	<1 s	1	1	1.1 s	1
	<1 s	4	14	69	<1 s	1	1	1.3 s	1
StringBuffer(1.4 K)	<1 s	3	18	82	<1 s	1	1	1.2 s	1
	<1 s	4	16	75	<1 s	1	1	1.1 s	1
ArrayList (1.6 K)	< 1 s	4	60	783	< 1 s	1	1	1.2 s	1
PrintWriter (1.2 K)	< 1 s	4	14	80	< 1 s	1	1	1.2 s	1
HashMap (1.3 K)	< 1 s	4	28	138	< 1 s	1	1	1.3 s	1
Java Logging (43 K)	<1 s	5	228	1.4 K	< 1 s	2	2	2.3 s	1
Apache FtpServer(22 K)	60 s	4	20	582	1 m 1 s	0	-	1 m 2 s	0
Hedc (30 K)	1.71 s	7	198	774	1.74 s	0	-	1.73 s	0
Weblech v.0.0.3 (35 K)	4.91 s	3	114	1.6 K	4.92 s	0	-	4.95 s	0

set is a causally prefix-closed set of events (a configuration) that are *causally before* f_1 and f_2, and in which all the locks are free at the end of execution of this configuration. The intuition behind this is that such a configuration can be replayed in the newly predicted execution precisely as it occurred in the original run, and then stitched to a run predicted from the suffix, since the suffix will start executing in a state in which no locks are held.

Let f_1' and f_2' be the *last* events in T_1 and T_2, respectively, that are before f_1 and f_2, in the local executions, with lock-sets empty. The crux of the scheduling phase is then to schedule from f_1' and f_2' through f_1 and f_2.

The algorithm, borrowed from [32], works by building a graph of *causal edges* between events. For every lock l in the lock-set of f_2, if l occurs in the acquisition history of f_1 with respect to some lock l', then we know that after the last acquisition of l' by T_1 there was an acquisition (followed by a release) of the lock l. Hence we know that we must schedule the last release of lock l' in T_1 (say event f_1'') *before* the last acquisition of l in T_2 (say f_2''). We capture this by adding a causal edge from f_1'' to f_2''. Similarly, we examine the lock-set of f_1 and the acquisition history of f_2 and throw in causal edges.

It turns out that since the acquisition histories are compatible, this graph will by *acyclic*, and hence there is a schedule that respects these orderings. The algorithm simply topologically sorts this graph to obtain a schedule (in the implementation, the topological sorting gives preference to the ordering in the original execution— if f_1'' and f_2'' have no causal ordering, we pick f_1'' first if f_2'' occurred before f_1'' in the original schedule).

7 Evaluation

We ran PickLock on a benchmark suite of 13 concurrent programs against several test cases and input parameters. Experiments were performed on an Apple MacBook with 2.4 Ghz Intel Core i5 processors and 4 GB of memory, running OS × 10.7.3 and Sun's Java HotSpot 32-bit Client VM 1.5.0.

The benchmarks are all concurrent Java programs that use synchronized blocks and methods as means of synchronization. They include Elevator from ETH [35], RayTracer from the Java Grande MT benchmarks [8], Vector, Stack, StringBuffer, ArrayList, PrintWriter and Hashmap from Java Collections Framework, Logging from Java Library, DBCP from the Apache Commons Project [2], Apache FtpServer from [7], Hedc from [5] and Weblech from [9].

The concurrent program Elevator simulates multiple lifts in a building; RayTracer renders a frame of an arrangement of spheres from a given view point; DBCP is the Database Connection Pool in the Apache Commons suite; Apache FtpServer is a FTP server by Apache; and Vector, Stack, StringBuffer, Logging, ArrayList, PrintWriter and Hashmap are Java libraries; Hedc is a Web crawler application and Weblech is a websites download tool.

Our tool was also applied to other programs. For example, Colt [6] and Pool from the Apache Common Project [4] in three different releases 1.2, 1.3, 1.5. However, no deadlocks were found and to the best of our knowledge no resource deadlocks have been reported for these programs. Because no additional insights were given by these programs we did not report them in the Table 1.

Table 1 provides information about the benchmarks for *deadlocks* as well as information about all three phases: monitoring, run prediction, and scheduling. For the monitoring phase, the number of threads, the number of synchronization events, and the total number of observed events are reported, as well as the monitoring time. For the prediction phase, we report the number of potential deadlocks found. In the scheduling part, we report the total number of schedulable predictions. Finally, we present the total time for the test and the number of deadlocks found.

PickLock found all previously known deadlocks in the benchmarks analyzed. More details about the test harnesses used and the deadlocks found are available at http://web.engr.illinois.edu/~sorrent1/papers/SPIN15.html. We ran the programs under the test harness several times, and found none of the reported bugs in any of these benchmarks by merely running tests randomly. PickLock predicts about 11 deadlocking executions, a successful attempt at finding deadlocks on these benchmarks. The runtime overhead for the testing is minimal, around 10 % of the base run time. This is in contrast to similar tools (e.g. Jade [29]) analyzing the same benchmarks. PickLock does not produce false positives. If a deadlock is reported by PickLock, it is a real deadlock.

References

1. http://jlint.sourceforge.net/
2. http://commons.apache.org/dbcp
3. http://jakarta.apache.org/bcel
4. http://commons.apache.org
5. http://www.hedc.ethz.ch
6. http://acs.lbl.gov/hoschek/colt
7. http://mina.apache.org/ftpserver
8. http://www.javagrande.org/
9. http://weblech.sourceforge.net
10. Agarwal, R., Bensalem, S., Farchi, E., Havelund, K., Nir-Buchbinder, Y., Stoller, S.D., Ur, S., Wang, L.: Detection of deadlock potentials in multi-threaded programs. IBM J. Res. Dev. **54**(5), 520–534 (2010)
11. Agarwal, R., Stoller, S.D.: Run-time detection of potential deadlocks for programs with locks, semaphores, and condition variables. In: PADTAD, pp. 51–60 (2006)
12. Agarwal, R., Wang, L., Stoller, S.D.: Detecting potential deadlocks with static analysis and runtime monitoring. In: PADTAD, pp. 191–207 (2005)
13. Artho, C., Biere, A.: Applying static analysis to large-scale, multi-threaded java programs. In: Australian Software Engineering Conference, pp. 68–75 (2001)
14. Bensalem, S., Fernandez, J.C., Havelund, K., Mounier, L.: Confirmation of deadlock potentials detected by runtime analysis. In: PADTAD, pp. 41–50 (2006)
15. Bensalem, S., Havelund, K.: Dynamic deadlock analysis of multi-threaded programs. In: Ur, S., Bin, E., Wolfsthal, Y. (eds.) HVC 2005. LNCS, vol. 3875, pp. 208–223. Springer, Heidelberg (2006)
16. Cai, Y., Chan, W.K.: MagicFuzzer: Scalable deadlock detection for large-scale applications. In: ICSE, pp. 606–616 (2012)
17. Chen, F., Farzan, A., Meseguer, J., Rosu, G.: Formal analysis of java programs in javafan. In: CAV, pp. 501–505 (2004)
18. Demartini, C., Iosif, R., Sisto, R.: A deadlock detection tool for concurrent java programs. Softw. Pract. Exper. **29**(7), 577–603 (1999)
19. Engler, D., Ashcraft, K.: Racerx: effective, static detection of race conditions and deadlocks. SIGOPS Oper. Syst. Rev. **37**, 237–252 (2003)
20. Farzan, A., Madhusudan, P., Razavi, N., Sorrentino, F.: Predicting null-pointer dereferences in concurrent programs. In: SIGSOFT FSE, pp. 47–58 (2012)
21. Farzan, A., Madhusudan, P., Sorrentino, F.: Meta-analysis for atomicity violations under nested locking. In: Bouajjani, A., Maler, O. (eds.) CAV 2009. LNCS, vol. 5643, pp. 248–262. Springer, Heidelberg (2009)
22. Havelund, K., Pressburger, T.: Model checking java programs using java pathfinder. STTT **2**(4), 366–381 (2000)
23. Joshi, P., Naik, M., Sen, K., Gay, D.: An effective dynamic analysis for detecting generalized deadlocks. In SIGSOFT FSE, pp. 327–336 (2010)
24. Joshi, P., Park, C.S., Sen, K., Naik, M.: A randomized dynamic program analysis technique for detecting real deadlocks. In: PLDI, pp. 110–120 (2009)
25. Jula, H., Tralamazza, D.M., Zamfir, C., Candea, G.: Deadlock Immunity: enabling systems to defend against deadlocks. In OSDI, pp. 295–308 (2008)
26. Kahlon, V., Ivančić, F., Gupta, A.: Reasoning about threads communicating via locks. In: Etessami, K., Rajamani, S.K. (eds.) CAV 2005. LNCS, vol. 3576, pp. 505–518. Springer, Heidelberg (2005)

27. Lu, S., Park, S., Seo, E., Zhou, Y.: Learning from mistakes: a comprehensive study on real world concurrency bug characteristics. In: ASPLOS, pp. 329–339 (2008)
28. Luo, Z.D., Das, R., Qi, Y.: Multicore SDK: A practical and efficient deadlock detector for real-world applications. In: ICST, pp. 309–318 (2011)
29. Naik, M., Park, C.S., Sen, K., Gay, D.: Effective static deadlock detection. In: ICSE, pp. 386–396 (2009)
30. Şerbănuţă, T.F., Chen, F., Roşu, G.: Maximal causal models for sequentially consistent systems. Technical report, University of Illinois at Urbana-Champaign, October 2011
31. Shanbhag, V.K.: Deadlock-detection in java-library using static-analysis. In: APSEC, pp. 361–368 (2008)
32. Sorrentino, F., Farzan, A., Madhusudan, P.: PENELOPE: weaving threads to expose atomicity violations. In: SIGSOFT FSE, pp. 37–46 (2010)
33. Visser, W., Havelund, K., Brat, G.P., Park, S., Lerda, F.: Model checking programs. Autom. Softw. Eng. 10(2), 203–232 (2003)
34. von Praun, C.: Detecting synchronization defects in multi-threaded object-oriented programs. In Ph.D. thesis, Swiss Federal Institute of Technology, Zurich (2004)
35. von Praun, C., Gross, T.R.: Object race detection. In: OOPSLA, pp. 70–82 (2001)
36. Wang, Y., Kelly, T., Kudlur, M., Lafortune, S., Mahlke, S.A.: Gadara: Dynamic deadlock avoidance for multithreaded programs. In OSDI, pp. 281–294 (2008)
37. Williams, A., Thies, W., Awasthi, P.: Static deadlock detection for java libraries. In: Gao, X.-X. (ed.) ECOOP 2005. LNCS, vol. 3586, pp. 602–629. Springer, Heidelberg (2005)
38. Cai, Y., Wu, S., Chan, W.K.: ConLock: a constraint-based approach to dynamic checking on deadlocks in multithreaded programs. In: ICSE, pp. 491–502 (2014)
39. Havelund, K.: Using runtime analysis to guide model checking of java programs. In: Havelund, K., Penix, J., Visser, W. (eds.) SPIN 2000. LNCS, vol. 1885. Springer, Heidelberg (2000)

SAT/SMT-Based Approaches

Symbolic Causality Checking Using Bounded Model Checking

Adrian Beer[1], Stephan Heidinger[1], Uwe Kühne[2], Florian Leitner-Fischer[1], and Stefan Leue[1(✉)]

[1] University of Konstanz, Konstanz, Germany
Stefan.Leue@uni-konstanz.de
[2] Airbus Defence and Space, Bremen, Germany

Abstract. In precursory work we have developed *causality checking*, a fault localization method for concurrent system models relying on the Halpern and Pearl counterfactual model of causation that identifies ordered occurrences of system events as being causal for the violation of non-reachability properties. Our first implementation of causality checking relies on explicit-state model checking. In this paper we propose a symbolic implementation of causality checking based on bounded model checking (BMC) and SAT solving. We show that this BMC-based implementation is efficient for large and complex system models. The technique is evaluated on industrial size models and experimentally compared to the existing explicit state causality checking implementation. BMC-based causality checking turns out to be superior to the explicit state variant in terms of runtime and memory consumption for very large system models.

1 Introduction

In precursory work we have defined a fault localization and debugging technique for concurrent system models called *causality checking* [16,18]. Causality checking relies on *counterfactual reasoning* à la Lewis [21], i.e., an event is considered a cause for some effect in case (a) whenever the event presumed to be a cause occurs, the effect occurs as well, and (b) when the presumed cause does not occur, the effect will not occur either (counterfactual argument). This simple form of counterfactual reasoning is inadequate to represent logically complex causal structures. In their seminal work [12], Halpern and Pearl have defined a model for causation, based on counterfactual reasoning, that encompasses logically complex relationships amongst events. In our precursory work we have adopted their model and (a) related it to models of concurrent computation, in particular transition systems and traces, (b) extended it to accommodate the order of events occurring as a causal factor, and (c) included the non-occurrence of events as a potential causal factor. The key ingredients of our causality checking algorithm are a complete enumeration of all traces leading to a property violating state, as well as an enumeration of all traces not leading to such a state, in order to establish the counterfactual argument.

© Springer International Publishing Switzerland 2015
B. Fischer and J. Geldenhuys (Eds.): SPIN 2015, LNCS 9232, pp. 203–221, 2015.
DOI: 10.1007/978-3-319-23404-5_14

An application of causality checking is fault localization within system models. While a model checker will return a simple counterexample for a (non-) reachability property, causality checking will return a temporal logic formula representing the events that are considered to be causal, as well as their order of occurrence in case the order is determined to be causal. The causalities computed by causality checking are much more succinct than counterexamples produced by model checkers and contain more precise error location information than single counterexamples.

We have implemented causality checking up to the work described in this paper most efficiently in the SpinCause tool [20] that relies on explicit state model checking and is based on SpinJa [14], a Java re-implementation of the explicit state model checker SPIN [13]. We have embedded causality checking in our QuantUM tool as the core analysis engine. QuantUM reads system architecture models given in UML or SysML directly out of industrial design tools, such as IBM Rational Rhapsody, performs a reachability analysis for undesired system states using the causality checking components, and outputs the computed causalities as temporal logic fomulae and fault trees [17]. An application of QuantUM is the support of safety cases in the analysis of safety-critical system and software architectures [4,16].

We have applied SpinCause inside the QuantUM context to various industrial sized case studies. At the upper end of the size scale of those case studies the memory consumption of SpinCause starts to be a limiting factor. It is the objective of this paper to propose an implementation of causality checking using an alternative model checking technology, in particular one that relies on bounded model checking (BMC) [6], a symbolic representation of the state space and SAT-solving as a verification engine, in order to evaluate whether this gives us a causality checking implementation which is superior to the explicit state variant in terms of memory consumption.

To this end we define an iterative BMC-based causality checking algorithm. As argued above, in the explicit state causality checking implementation all traces through a system need to be generated. The BMC-based causality checking algorithm presented in this paper uses the underlying SAT-solver invoked by the bounded model checker in order to generate the causal event combinations in an iterative manner. In the course of an iteration only those error traces are generated that contain new information regarding the cause to be computed whereas traces that do not provide new information are automatically excluded from further consideration by constraining the SAT-solver with what is already known about the causal relationships amongst events. With this approach a large number of error traces that would otherwise need to be considered and stored in the explicit state approach can remain unconsidered, which contributes to the memory efficiency of this BMC-based causality checking implementation. We have implemented our algorithm as an addition to the NuSMV2 model checker [9], which encompasses a BMC component, and evaluate its performance using various case studies from various domains and of different sizes. It turns out that for the largest models analyzed the BMC-based implementation requires up to two orders of magnitude less memory than the explicit state implementation. As a consequence, causality checking now scales to a class of significantly more complex models that could previously not be analyzed.

Structure of the Paper. In Sect. 2 we will present the technical foundations of our work. In Sect. 3 we describe the proposed iterative BMC-based approach to causality checking. In Sect. 4 we experimentally evaluate the BMC-based causality checking approach by comparing its performance to the explicit-state causality checking implementation. Related work will be discussed in Sect. 5 before we conclude in Sect. 6.

2 Preliminaries

2.1 Running Example

We will illustrate the formal framework that we present in this paper using the running example of a simple railroad crossing system. In this system, a train can approach the crossing (Ta), enter the crossing (Tc), and finally leave the crossing (Tl). Whenever a train is approaching, the gate shall close (Gc) and will open again when the train has left the crossing (Go). It might also be the case that the gate fails (Gf). The car approaches the crossing (Ca) and crosses the crossing if the gate is open (Cc) and finally leaves the crossing (Cl). We are interested in finding those events that are causal for the hazard that the car and the train are in the crossing at the same time.

2.2 System Model

The model of concurrent computation that we use in this paper is that of a transition system:

Definition 1 (Transition System [2]). *A transition system M is a tuple $(S, A, \rightarrow, I, AP, L)$ where S is a finite set of states, A is a finite set of actions/events, $\rightarrow \subseteq S \times A \times S$ is a transition relation, $I \subseteq S$ is the set of initial states, AP is the set of atomic propositions, and $L{:}S \rightarrow 2^{AP}$ is a labeling function.*

We use the notation $s \xrightarrow{\alpha} s'$ to denote $(s, \alpha, s') \in \rightarrow$.

Definition 2 (Execution Trace [2]). *An execution trace π in transition system M is defined as an alternating sequence of states $s \in S$ and actions $a \in A$ ending with a state. $\pi = s_0 \ \alpha_1 \ s_1 \ \alpha_2 \ s_2 \ ... \ \alpha_n \ s_n$, s.t. $s_i \xrightarrow{\alpha_{i+1}} s_{i+1}$ for all $0 \leq i < n$.*

An execution sequence which ends in a property violation is called an error trace or a counterexample. In the railroad crossing example, $s_0 \xrightarrow{\text{Ta}} s_1 \xrightarrow{\text{Gf}} s_2 \xrightarrow{\text{Tc}} s_3 \xrightarrow{\text{Ca}} s_4 \xrightarrow{\text{Cc}} s_5$ is a counterexample, because the train and the car are inside the crossing at the same time.

2.3 Linear Temporal Logic

Linear Temporal Logic (LTL) [22] is a propositional modal logic based on a linear system execution model. An LTL formula can be used to express properties of infinite paths in a given system model.

Definition 3 (Syntax of Linear Temporal Logic). *An LTL formula φ over a set of atomic propositions* AP *is defined according to the following grammar:*

$$\varphi ::= \text{TRUE} \mid a \mid \varphi_1 \wedge \varphi_2 \mid \varphi_1 \vee \varphi_2 \mid \neg \varphi \mid \bigcirc \varphi \mid \square \varphi$$
$$\mid \Diamond \varphi \mid \varphi_1 \ U \ \varphi_2$$

where $a \in$ AP.

The operators $\bigcirc$, $\square$, $\Diamond$ and U are used to express temporal behavior, such as *"in the next state sth. happens"*($\bigcirc$), *"eventually sth. happens"*($\Diamond$) and *"sth. is always true"*($\square$). The U-operator denotes the case that *"φ_1 has to be true until φ_2 holds"*. We use $M \vDash_l \varphi$ to express that an LTL formula φ holds on a system model M and $\pi \vDash_l \varphi$ for a execution trace in M.

The properties that are expressible in LTL can be separated into two classes, safety and liveness properties. Safety properties can be violated by a finite prefix of an infinite path, while liveness properties can only be violated by an infinite path. For now, causality checking has only been defined for safety properties, namely the non-reachability of an undesired state, which can be characterized using an LTL formula. For instance, the non-reachability property that we want to express in the railroad crossing example is that the train and the car shall never be in the crossing at the same time: $\square\neg(\text{Tc} \wedge \text{Cc})$.

2.4 Event Order Logic

Event Order Logic (EOL) is a linear time temporal logic that is used in causality checking to specify the ordered event occurrences that are computed to be causal. Every EOL formula can be translated into an equivalent standard LTL formula [3].

Definition 4 (Syntax of the Event Order Logic). *Simple event order logic formulae are defined over the set A of event variables:*

$$\phi ::= a \mid \phi_1 \wedge \phi_1 \mid \phi_1 \vee \phi_2 \mid \neg\phi$$

where $a \in A$ and ϕ, ϕ_1 and ϕ_2 are simple EOL formulae. Complex EOL formulae are formed according to the following grammar:

$$\psi ::= \phi \mid \psi_1 \wedge \psi_1 \mid \quad \psi_1 \vee \psi_2 \quad \mid \psi_1 \wedge \psi_2 \mid \psi_1 \wedge_{[} \phi$$
$$\mid \psi_1 \wedge_{]} \phi \mid \psi_1 \wedge_< \phi \wedge_> \psi_2$$

where ϕ is a simple EOL formula and ψ, ψ_1 and ψ_2 are complex EOL formulae.

We define that a transition system M satisfies the EOL formula ψ, written as $M \vDash_e \psi$, iff $\exists \pi \in M.\ \pi \vDash_e \psi$. The informal semantics of the operators can be given as follows.

- $\psi_1 \wedge \psi_2$: ψ_1 has to happen before ψ_2.
- $\psi_1 \wedge_[\phi$: ψ_1 has to happen at some point and afterwards ϕ holds forever.
- $\phi \wedge_] \psi_1$: ϕ has to hold until ψ_1 holds.
- $\psi_1 \wedge_< \phi \wedge_> \psi_2$: ψ_1 has to happen before ψ_2, and ϕ has to hold all the time between ψ_1 and ψ_2.

For example, the formula Gc $\wedge$ Tc states that the gate has to close before the train enters the crossing. The full formal semantics definition for EOL is given in [19].

2.5 Event Order Normal Form

In order to enable the processing of EOL formulas and counterexamples in the BMC-based causality checking algorithm it is necessary to define a normal form for EOL formulas that we refer to as the event order normal form (EONF) [3,16]. EONF permits the unordered *and-* ($\wedge$) and *or*-operator ($\vee$) only to appear in a formula if they are not sub formulas in any ordered operator or if they are sub formulas of the between operators $\wedge_<$ and $\wedge_>$.

Definition 5. *Event Order Normal Form (EONF) [3,16] The set of EOL formulas over a set $\mathcal{A}$ of event variables in event order normal form (EONF) is given by:*

$$\phi ::= a \mid \neg\phi \qquad \phi_\wedge ::= \phi \mid \neg\phi_\wedge \mid \phi_{\wedge_1} \wedge \phi_{\wedge_2}$$

$$\psi ::= \phi \mid \phi_1 \wedge \phi_2 \mid \phi_1 \wedge_[\phi_2 \mid \phi_1 \wedge_] \phi_2 \mid \phi_1 \wedge_< \phi_2 \wedge_> \phi_3$$

$$\psi_\wedge ::= \psi \mid \phi_\wedge \mid \psi_{\wedge_1} \wedge \psi_{\wedge_2} \mid \psi_{\wedge_1} \vee \psi_{\wedge_2}$$

where $a \in \mathcal{A}$ and ϕ are simple EOL formulas only containing single events and $\phi_\wedge$, $\phi_{\wedge_1}$, $\phi_{\wedge_2}$ and $\phi_{\wedge_3}$ are EOL formulas only containing the $\wedge$-operator, ψ is a EOL formula containing the ordered operator, and $\psi_\wedge$, $\psi_{\wedge_1}$ and $\psi_{\wedge_2}$ are EOL formulas containing the $\wedge$-operator and/or the $\vee$-operator which can be combined with formulas in EONF containing ordered operators.

Every EOL formula can be transformed into an equivalent EOL formula in EONF by rewriting using the equivalence rules defined in [3,16]. For instance, the EOL formula Ta $\wedge$ Gc $\wedge$ Tc can be expressed in EONF as $\psi_{EONF} = (\text{Ta} \wedge \text{Gc}) \wedge (\text{Gc} \wedge \text{Tc}) \wedge (\text{Ta} \wedge \text{Tc})$.

2.6 Causality Reasoning

Our goal is to identify events that cause a system to reach a property violating state. We hence need to define the notion of causality that we will base our approach on. The notion of causality that we use, as proposed in [15], is based on *counterfactual reasoning* and the notion of *actual cause* defined by Halpern and Pearl in [12]. It not only considers the occurrence of events to potentially be causal, but also the order in which they occur as well as their non-occurrence. For example, an event a may always occur before an event b for an error to happen, but if b occurs first and a afterwards there is no error. In this case, a occurring before b is considered to be causal for the error to happen. Work described in [19] defines when, according to this extended causality notion, an EOL formula ψ describes a causal process for the violation of a non-reachability property, specified using an LTL formula. The causal process [12] consists of the events causing the violation and all events mediating between the causal events and the property violation. Notice that in case there are multiple instances of event occurrences belonging to the same event type in the model, the multiple instances are discriminated. For instance, if along a trace to events of type Gc can be observed, we refer to them as Gc_1 and Gc_2. Otherwise it would not be possible to distinguish between two separate occurrences of the same type of event using standard LTL semantics, which EOL is based on.

Definition 6 (Cause for a Property Violation [12,18]). *Let π, π' and π'' be paths in a transition system M. The set of event variables is partitioned into sets Z and W. The variables in Z are involved in the causal event chain for a property violation while the variables in W are not. The valuations of the variables along a path π are represented by $val_z(\pi)$ and $val_w(\pi)$, respectively. $\psi_\wedge$ denotes the rewriting of an EOL formula ψ where the ordering operator $\wedge$ is replaced by the normal EOL operator $\wedge$, all other EOL operators are left unchanged. An EOL formula ψ consisting of event variables $X \subseteq Z$ is considered to be a cause for an effect represented by the violation of an LTL property φ, if the following conditions hold:*

- *AC 1: There exists an execution π for which both $\pi \vDash_e \psi$ and $\pi \nvDash_l \varphi$*
- *AC 2.1: $\exists \pi'$ s.t. $\pi' \nvDash_e \psi \wedge (val_x(\pi) \neq val_x(\pi') \vee val_w(\pi) \neq val_w(\pi'))$ and $\pi' \vDash_l \varphi$. In other words, there exists an execution π' where the order and occurrence of events is different from execution π and φ is not violated on π'.*
- *AC 2.2: $\forall \pi''$ with $\pi'' \vDash_e \psi \wedge (val_x(\pi) = val_x(\pi'') \wedge val_w(\pi) \neq val_w(\pi''))$ it holds that $\pi'' \nvDash_l \varphi$ for all subsets of W. In words, for all executions where the events in X have the value defined by $val_x(\pi)$ and the order defined by ψ, the value and order of an arbitrary subset of events on W has no effect on the violation of φ.*
- *AC 3: The set of variables $X \subseteq Z$ is minimal: no subset of X satisfies conditions AC 1 and AC 2.*
- *OC 1: The order of events $X \subseteq Z$ represented by the EOL formula ψ is not causal if the following holds: $\pi \vDash_e \psi$ and $\pi' \nvDash_e \psi$ and $\pi' \nvDash_e \psi_\wedge$.*

The EOL formula $Gf \wedge ((Ta \wedge (Ca \wedge Cc)) \wedge_< \neg Cl \wedge_> Tc)$ is a cause for the occurrence of the hazard in the railroad crossing example since it fulfills all of the above defined conditions (AC 1-3, OC 1) for the corresponding system model that we defined.

2.7 Bounded Model Checking

The basic idea of Bounded Model Checking (BMC) [6] is to find error traces, also called counterexamples, in executions of a given system model where the length of the traces that are analyzed are bounded by some integer k. If no counterexample is found for traces of some length $l \leq k$, then l is increased until either a counterexample is found, or $l = k$. The BMC problem is translated into a propositional satisfiability problem and can be solved using propositional SAT solvers. Modern SAT solvers can handle satisfiability problems in the order of 10^6 variables.

Given a transition system M, an LTL formula f and a bound k, the propositional formula of the system is represented by $[[M, f]]_k$. Let $s_0, ..., s_k$ be a finite sequence of states on a path π. Each s_i represents a state at time step i and consists of an assignment of truth values to the set of state variables. The formula $[[M, f]]_k$ encodes a constraint on $s_0, ..., s_k$ such that $[[M, f]]_k$ is satisfiable iff π is a witness for f. The propositional formula $[[M, f]]_k$ is generated by unrolling the transition relation of the original model M and integrating the LTL property in every step s_i of the unrolling. The generated formula $[[M, f]]_k$ of the whole system is passed to a propositional SAT solver. The SAT solver tries to solve $[[M, f]]_k$. If a solution exists, this solution is considered to be a counterexample of the encoded LTL property.

3 BMC-based Causality Checking

3.1 EOL Matrix

For the BMC-based causality computation with bound k we consider sequences of event occurrences $\pi_e = e_1 e_2 e_3 \ldots e_k$ derived from paths of type $\pi = s_0 \xrightarrow{e_1} s_1 \xrightarrow{e_2} s_2 \ldots$. We use a matrix in order to represent the fact that certain events occur as well as the ordering of the event occurrences along a trace. This matrix is called EOL matrix.

Definition 7 (EOL Matrix). *Let $E = \{e_1, e_2, e_3, \ldots, e_k\}$ an event occurrence set and $\pi_e = e_1 e_2 e_3 \ldots e_k$ a trace over event occurrences. For integers $i \neq j$ a function o is then defined as follows:*

$$o(e_i, e_j) = \begin{cases} \{TRUE\} & \text{if } e_i \wedge e_j \\ \varnothing & \text{otherwise} \end{cases}$$

The EOL matrix M_E is constructed from o as follows:

$$M_E = \begin{pmatrix} \varnothing & o(e_1, e_2) & \cdots & o(e_1, e_k) \\ o(e_2, e_1) & \varnothing & \cdots & o(e_2, e_k) \\ \vdots & \vdots & \ddots & \vdots \\ o(e_k, e_1) & o(e_k, e_2) & \cdots & \varnothing \end{pmatrix}$$

where the generated entries in the matrix are either sets of event occurrences or the constant set $\{TRUE\}$. The empty set $\varnothing$ is also permitted which means no relation for the corresponding event occurrences was found.

Definition 8 (Union of EOL Matrices). *Let M_E, M_{E_1}, M_{E_2} be EOL Matrices with all identical dimensions. The EOL matrix M_E is the union of M_{E_1} and M_{E_2} according to the following rule:*

$$M_{E(i,j)} = M_{E_1(i,j)} \cup M_{E_2(i,j)} \tag{1}$$

for every entry (i,j) in the matrices.

The union of two EOL matrices represents the component-wise disjunction of two matrices. The EOL matrix M_E for an example event sequence in the railroad crossing π = Ca Cc Gf and a refinement EOL Matrix $M'_E = M_E \cup M_{E_{\pi'}}$, using the sequence π' = Gf Ca Cc is created as follows:

$$\begin{matrix} e_1 = \text{Ca} \\ e_2 = \text{Cc} \\ e_3 = \text{Gf} \end{matrix} \quad M_E = \begin{pmatrix} \varnothing & \{\text{TRUE}\} & \{\text{TRUE}\} \\ \varnothing & \varnothing & \{\text{TRUE}\} \\ \varnothing & \varnothing & \varnothing \end{pmatrix} \quad M'_E = \begin{pmatrix} \varnothing & \{\text{TRUE}\} & \{\text{TRUE}\} \\ \varnothing & \varnothing & \{\text{TRUE}\} \\ \{\text{TRUE}\} & \{\text{TRUE}\} & \varnothing \end{pmatrix}. \tag{2}$$

3.2   EOL Matrix to Propositional Logic Translation

In order to use the information stored in the EOL Matrix in the BMC-based causality checking algorithm a translation from the matrix into propositional logic is needed. First the Matrix is translated into an EOL formula in EONF and afterwards the EOL formula is translated into propositional logic.

Definition 9 (Translation from EOL Matrix to EOL Formula). *Let M_E a EOL matrix which contains the EOL formula ψ_E and the event set E. $M_{E(i,j)}$ is the set of events in the entry (i,j) in M_E and $e_{(i,j)} \in M_{E(i,j)}$. e_i and e_j denote the ordered events, respectively. Then ψ_E is defined as follows:*

$$\psi_E = \bigwedge_{i=0}^{i=k} \bigwedge_{j=0}^{j=k} \begin{cases} e_i \wedge e_j & \text{if } e_{(i,j)} = \{\textit{TRUE}\} \text{ and } e_{(j,i)} = \{\textit{TRUE}\} \text{ and } i \neq j \\ e_i \wedge e_j & \text{if } e_{(i,j)} = \{\textit{TRUE}\} \text{ and } e_{(j,i)} \neq \{\textit{TRUE}\} \text{ and } i \neq j. \end{cases}$$

Lemma 1. *An EOL formula ψ_E obtained via Definition 9 from an EOL matrix M_E is always in Event Order Normal Form (EONF).*

Proof. Sketch: A proof can easily be given using an inductive argument over the rules for the construction of the EOL matrix (Definition 7) and the construction of formula ψ_E (Definition 9).

Using this translation the EOL Matrix from Eq. 2 is translated into the following EOL formula in EONF: ψ_{EONF} = (Ca $\wedge$ Cc) $\wedge$ (Gf $\wedge$ Ca) $\wedge$ (Gf $\wedge$ Cc). The generated EOL formula can be efficiently translated into an equivalent LTL formula as it was shown in [3].

As mentioned in Sect. 2.3, only safety properties are considered for the BMC-based causality checking approach. Since safety properties can only be violated by finite prefixes of system executions, it is necessary to adapt the definition of a bounded semantics for LTL as defined in [6] for our purposes:

Definition 10 (Bounded Semantics for LTL). *Let* $k \geq 0$, *and let* π *be a prefix of an infinite path and* $\pi_e = e_0 e_1 e_2 \ldots$ *the sequence of events of* π. *Let* ψ_{LTL} *an LTL formula obtained by translating an EOL formula* ψ *into LTL.* ψ_{LTL} *is valid along* π *up to bound* k, *represented by* $\pi \models^0_k \psi_{LTL}$, *if the following holds:*

$$
\begin{aligned}
\pi \models^i_k p & \quad \textit{iff} \quad p = e_i \\
\pi \models^i_k \neg p & \quad \textit{iff} \quad p \neq e_i \\
\pi \models^i_k f \wedge g & \quad \textit{iff} \quad \pi \models^i_k f \text{ and } \pi \models^i_k g \\
\pi \models^i_k f \vee g & \quad \textit{iff} \quad \pi \models^i_k f \text{ or } \pi \models^i_k g \\
\pi \models^i_k \Box f & \quad \textit{iff} \quad \forall j, i \leq j \leq k. \; \pi \models^j_k f \\
\pi \models^i_k \Diamond f & \quad \textit{iff} \quad \exists j, i \leq j \leq k. \; \pi \models^j_k f \\
\pi \models^i_k \bigcirc f & \quad \textit{iff} \quad i < k \text{ and } \pi \models^{i+1}_k f \\
\pi \models^i_k f \, U g & \quad \textit{iff} \quad \exists j, i \leq j \leq k. \; \pi \models^j_k g \text{ and } \forall n, i \leq n \leq k. \; \pi \models^n_k f
\end{aligned}
$$

The standard translation scheme for translating LTL into propositional logic for a given bound k as described in [6] is used in order to convert the LTL formula ψ_{LTL} into a propositional logic formula.

3.3 The BMC-Based Causality Checking Algorithm

According to condition AC 1 it is necessary to know that there exists a counterexample trace which leads to the violation of the considered non-reachability property. In addition, in order to satisfy condition AC 2, however, there need to exist other traces with other events and orderings that do not lead into a violating state. As a consequence, all combinations of events have to be known. In the explicit state causality checking approach [18] all paths through a system need to be computed in order to find all causal events and orderings for a property violation. In order to avoid the explicit computation of all possible paths in the state graph we propose the use of an iterative scheme involving BMC and symbolic constraints on the underlying SAT solver. The symbolic constraint is used in order to find only those paths that contain new information on event orderings and occurrences. This new information is used to strengthen the constraints on the SAT Solver.

Figure 1 presents the informal iteration scheme of the proposed algorithm. The inputs are the model M, the property ϕ and an upper bound $k_{\max}$ for the maximum length of the considered paths. The algorithm starts at level $k = 0$:

Step 1: Generation of Traces. The model M together with the LTL property ϕ and the bound k is converted into a propositional logic formula $[[M, \neg\phi]]_k$. $[[M, \neg\phi]]_k$ is inserted into a SAT solver. The SAT solver tries to find a path that fulfills the given formula. If such a path is found, the algorithm has discovered a counterexample and continues at step 2. Otherwise, the bound k is increased until the first counterexample is found or the maximum bound $k_{\max}$ is reached.

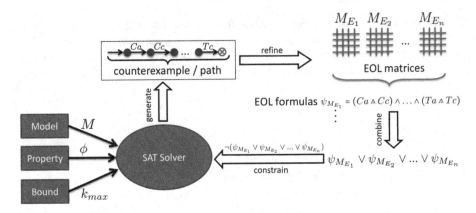

Fig. 1. The iteration schema of the BMC-based causality checking algorithm

Step 2: Matching of EOL Matrices. When a new path π is discovered the set of events E_1 occurring on this trace is compared to the already known EOL matrices, if any. If there is an EOL matrix M_{E_2} covering a set of events E_2 and if $E_1 = E_2$, then the newly discovered orderings of events in E_1 is used to refine the EOL matrix E_2 according to the operation $E_2 := E_2 \cup E_1$ as defined in Definition 8. If there is no matching matrix, a new EOL matrix is created representing a new class of causes [18] containing the ordering of events in π.

Step 3: Combination of New Constraints. All EOL matrices M_{E_i} are translated into EOL formulas $\psi_{M_{E_i}}$ according to Definition 9. The translated EOL formulas $\psi_{M_{E_i}}$ are combined disjunctively. In order to exclude the already found orderings from being found again in the next iteration, the result is negated which results in $\varphi' = \neg(\psi_{M_{E_1}} \vee \psi_{M_{E_2}} \vee \ldots \vee \psi_{M_{E_n}})$ with n the number of EOL matrices that have been computed so far.

Step 4: Constraining the SAT Solver. The formula φ' is translated into a propositional logic formula $[[\varphi']]_k$ for a given bound k. $[[\varphi']]_k$ is then used as an additional constraint for the SAT Solver (Definition 10). Afterwards, the algorithm iterates and continues with Step 1.

When the algorithm terminates, the result is stored in the EOL matrices $M_{E_i}, 0 \leq i \leq n$ where n is the number of EOL matrices found during the search.

3.4   Soundness and Completeness

We show that the results generated with the described algorithm are sound up to the pre-defined maximum bound k. Afterwards we will discuss the completeness of the BMC-based causality algorithm.

We first introduce the concept of a candidate set which is a collection of all counterexamples to the considered non-reachability property that have been

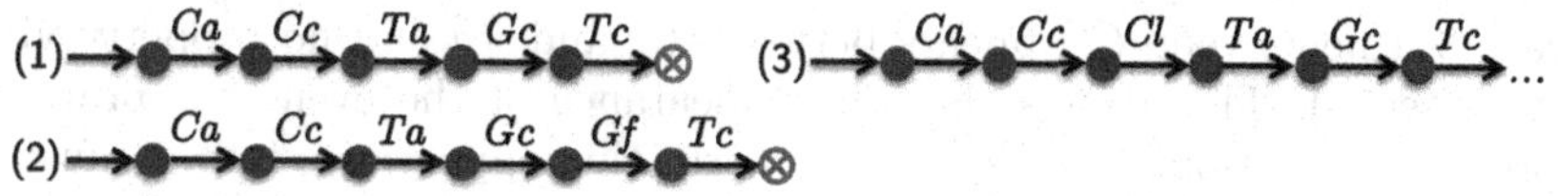

Fig. 2. Three example traces for the EOL-formula $\psi = \text{Ca} \wedge \text{Cc} \wedge \text{Ta} \wedge \text{Gc} \wedge \text{Tc}$. Trace 1 is the minimal trace. While trace 2 (non-minimal) ends in a property violation, trace 3 does not.

computed. The elements occurring along the elements of this set are candidates for being causal for the considered property violation.

Definition 11 (Candidate Set (Adapted from [19]**)).** *Let n the number of EOL matrices $M_{E_i}, 0 \leq i \leq n$ available at some point during the causality computation, $\neg\phi$ the negation of an LTL reachability property, and $\sum_C$ the set of all counterexamples to the validity of $\neg\phi$ available in the considered system model. The disjunction of all EOL formulas $\psi = \bigvee_{i=0}^{n} \psi_{M_{E_i}}$ generated from the matrices M_{E_i}, is a compact description of all computed counterexamples. The candidate set $CS(\neg\phi) = \{\pi \in \sum_C \mid \forall \pi' \in \sum_C . \pi' \subseteq \pi \Rightarrow \pi' = \pi\}$ contains the minimal set of counterexamples through the system that satisfy ψ.*

Notice that the candidate set is minimal in the sense that removing an event from some trace in the candidate set means that the resulting trace no longer is a counterexample.

Theorem 1. *The candidate set satisfies the conditions AC 1, AC 2.1, AC3 and OC specified in Definition 6.*

Proof. Soundness w.r.t. AC 1: Let $\neg\phi$ the negated LTL property and ψ the EOL formula representing the candidate set $\mathbf{CS}(\neg\phi)$. According to Definition 11, all counterexamples $\pi \in \mathbf{CS}(\neg\phi)$ are traces satisfying $\pi \models_l \neg\phi$. $\pi \models_e \psi$ holds by the definition of the creation of the EOL Matrices. Therefore AC1 holds for all $\pi \in \mathbf{CS}(\neg\phi)$.

The proofs for the conditions AC 2.1, AC 3 and OC 1 can be constructed in a similar way as shown in [19]. □

What remains to be shown is the soundness with respect to condition AC 2.2, which we shall address next.

Event Non-occurrence Detection. According to the AC 2.2 test the occurrence of events that are not considered as causal must not prevent the effect from happening. In other words, the non-occurrence of an event can be causal for a property violation. Therefore, we have to search such events and include their non-occurrence in the EOL formulas. In Fig. 2 an example is presented which explains this procedure for an EOL formula $\psi = \text{Ca} \wedge \text{Cc} \wedge \text{Ta} \wedge \text{Gc} \wedge \text{Tc}$. Trace 1 is the minimal trace ending in a property violation. Trace 2 is non-minimal and also ends in a property violation with the events Ca, Cc, Ta, Gc, Gf, Tc.

In trace 3 a new event Cl appears between Cc and Ta and no property violation is detected. This means that the appearance of the event has prevented the property violation. In order to transform this appearance into a cause for the hazard, the occurrence is negated and introduced into the EOL formula $\psi = \ldots Cc \wedge_< \neg Cl \wedge_> Ta \ldots$ The new clause states that *"if between 'the car is on the crossing' and 'the train is approaching the crossing', 'the car does NOT leave the crossing', the hazard does happen"*. In other words: The non-occurrence of Cl is causal for the property violation.

A second pass of the algorithm needs to be performed in order to find these non-occurrences. For this second pass the input parameters have to be altered compared to the first pass. The EOL Matrix definition also needs to be extended in order to account for the possible non-occurrence of events.

Definition 12 (Extended EOL Matrix). *Let $E = \{e_1, e_2, e_3, \ldots, e_k\}$ an event set and $\pi_e = e_1 e_2 e_3 \ldots e_k$ the corresponding sequence. The function o is defined for entries where $i \neq j$ and the function d is defined for entries where $i = j$:*

$$o(e_i, e_j) = \begin{cases} \{TRUE\} & \text{if } e_i \wedge e_j \\ \phi & \text{if } e_i \wedge_< \phi \wedge_> e_j \\ \varnothing & \text{otherwise} \end{cases} \qquad d(e_i) = \begin{cases} \phi & \text{if } \phi \wedge_] e_i \\ \varnothing & \text{otherwise} \end{cases}$$

The EOL matrix M_E is created as follows:

$$M_E = \begin{pmatrix} d(e_1) & o(e_1, e_2) & \cdots & o(e_1, e_k) \\ o(e_2, e_1) & d(e_2) & \cdots & o(e_2, e_k) \\ \vdots & \vdots & \ddots & \vdots \\ o(e_k, e_1) & o(e_k, e_2) & \cdots & d(e_k) \end{pmatrix}$$

where the generated entries in the matrix are sets of events or the constant set $\{TRUE\}$. The empty set $\varnothing$ indicates that no relation for the corresponding event configuration was found.

The function o returns *true* if e_1 occurs before e_2 and returns ϕ if e_1 occurs before e_2 and ϕ is true between e_1 and e_2. The function d returns ϕ if ϕ is always occurring before e_i. According to the extended EOL Matrix definition it is possible to insert EOL formulas of the form $e_i \wedge_< \phi \wedge_> e_j$ and $\phi \wedge_] e_i$ into the matrix. This can be used to insert conditions such as $\psi = Cc \wedge_< \neg Cl \wedge_> Ta$. The special case $e \wedge_[\phi$ is not considered here because this will never occur when analyzing safety properties, which is what we focus on in this paper. If a hazard state is reached no future occurrence of any event can prevent the hazard. The formula $e \wedge_[\phi$ would encode such a behavior.

Definition 13 (Extended Translation for AC 2.2). *Let M_E an EOL matrix which contains the EOL formula ψ_E and the event set E. $M_{E(i,j)}$ is the set of events in the entry (i,j) in M_E and $e_{(i,j)} \in M_{E(i,j)}$. e_i and e_j denote the ordered* *events, respectively. Then ψ_E is defined as follows:*

$$\psi_E = \bigwedge_{i=0}^{i=k} \bigwedge_{j=0}^{j=k} \bigwedge_{\substack{\forall e_{(i,j)} \\ \in M_{E(i,j)}}} \begin{cases} e_i \wedge e_j & \text{if } e_{(i,j)} = TRUE \text{ and } e_{(j,i)} = TRUE \text{ and } i \neq j \\ e_i \wedge e_j & \text{if } e_{(i,j)} = TRUE \text{ and } e_{(j,i)} \neq TRUE \text{ and } i \neq j \\ e_i \wedge_< \phi \wedge_> e_j & \text{if } \phi = e_{(i,j)} \text{ and } i \neq j \\ \phi \wedge_] e_i & \text{if } e_{(i,j)} = \phi \text{ and } i = j \end{cases}$$

The translation from EOL formulas into LTL and further into propositional logic is done according to Definition 10.

Input Parameters to the Non-occurrence Detection. In the second pass of the algorithm, the input parameters for the SAT solver have to be changed. Now the algorithm searches for paths in the system that do not end in a property violation, while fulfilling the EOL formulas that have been found so far. For instance, in Fig. 2 trace 3 also fulfills the displayed EOL formula. In order to find those paths the inputs to the SAT solver are the original LTL property ϕ, the original EOL formulas $\psi_{M_{E_i}}$, the model and the bound k. The paths obtained with this method contain the events that prevent the property violation. These events are inserted into a matching EOL matrix. Since the EOL matrices are used to search for the new paths there is always a matching matrix available to the algorithm. The matching of EOL matrices for the AC2.2 condition is defined as follows.

Definition 14 (Matching of Paths to EOL Matrix for AC2.2.). *Let π be a path discovered by the second pass, E_π the set of events occurring on π and E_i the event sets of all n EOL matrices. Then the matching EOL matrix is defined according to the following function:*

$$match(\pi) = \{M_{E_i} | \exists i, 0 \leq i \leq n. \; \forall j, 0 \leq j \leq n, \; m_i = max\left(|E_j \cap E_\pi|\right)\}$$

The *match* function returns the EOL matrix M_{E_i} whose event set E_i has the largest number of common events with the event set E_π. Note that there is always a unique maximum for this number: From the definition of the matching of EOL matrices in the first and the second pass of the algorithm two paths containing the same events are merged into one EOL matrix. This means all EOL matrices contain a unique set of events.

The refinement of the matching EOL matrix is conducted according to Definitions 8 and 12.

Theorem 2 (Soundness w.r.t. AC2.2). *For every EOL matrix M_E with the number of events $i = |E|$ the condition AC 2.2 is fulfilled for a maximum number of events x that prevent the property violation from happening and $x = k_{max} - i$.*

Proof. Sketch: Let $\pi \in \mathbf{CS}(\neg\phi)$ be a path of length i in the candidate set of the property violation and k_{max} the upper bound on the search depth. If $i = k_{max} - 1$ and there exists a single event that prevents the hazard from happening, the algorithm finds exactly those traces containing this single event and all orderings when processing level k_{max}. If $i = k_{max} - x$, the same argument applies, and up to x events are found that can prevent the error from happening. $\qquad\square$

Data: ϕ the property, S the model, k_{max} the maximum depth of the search
Result: The causal events for a property violation stored in M_{list}

```
 1  k := 0;
 2  ψ := FALSE;                                              /*EOL formula*/
 3  Mlist := empty List of EOL matrices;
 4  while k < kmax do
 5  │   π := solve(¬φ, S, ¬ψ, k);                   /* invoke SAT solver */
 6  │   while π is not empty do
 7  │   │   m := getMatchingMatrix(Mlist, π);            /*Definition 8*/
 8  │   │   refineEOLMatrix(m, π);                       /*Definition 7*/
 9  │   │   ψ := getEOLformula(Mlist);                   /*Definition 9,10*/
10  │   │   π := solve(¬φ, S, ¬ψ, k);
11  │   end
12  │   π := solve(φ, M, ψ);             /* invoke SAT solver, second pass */
13  │   while π is not empty do
14  │   │   m := getMatchingMatrixAC2_2(Mlist, π);       /*Definition 14*/
15  │   │   refineEOLMatrixAC2_2(m, π);                  /*Definition 12*/
16  │   │   ψ := getEOLformulaAC2_2(Mlist);              /*Definition 13,10*/
17  │   │   π := solve(¬φ, S, ¬ψ, k);
18  │   end
19  │   k =: k + 1;
20  end
```

Algorithm 1. BMC-based causality checking algorithm

Completeness. With BMC-based causality checking we can only find event combinations and their orderings up to a predefined bound $k_{\max}$.

Theorem 3. *All EOL matrices discovered with the BMC-based algorithm are complete in terms of conditions AC1, AC2.1, AC2.2, AC3 and OC1 up to the bound k_{max}.*

Proof. Sketch: A proof can be built via structural induction over the generation of the EOL matrices using the minimality argument of the discovered counterexamples.

The completeness of condition AC2.2 is linked to the soundness of this condition and can be proven up to a certain number of events that prevent the property violation from happening. The completeness depends on the number of events in all EOL matrices and the upper bound $k_{\max}$. For example, in Fig. 2 trace 3 is at least one step longer than the path resulting in a property violation. This means that if, for example, the maximum bound for the algorithm is set to 5, trace 1 violating the property is found, but trace 3 is not found.

The Algorithm. The pseudo code for the BMC-based causality checking algorithm is presented in Algorithm 1. The function *solve* (Line 5, 10, 12 and 17) converts the input parameters into propositional logic formulas and runs the SAT solver. The result of *solve* is a path of length k satisfying the given constraints.

4   Evaluation

In order to evaluate the proposed approach, we have implemented the BMC-based causality checking algorithm within the symbolic model checker NuSMV2 [9] which also implements BMC. Our CauSeMV extension of NuSMV2 computes the causality relationships for a given NuSMV2 model and an LTL property. The models that we analyze are the Railroad example from Sect. 2.1, an Airbag Control Unit [1], an Airport Surveillance Radar System (ASR) [4] and a automotive Electronic Control Unit (AECU) that we developed together with an industrial partner. The NuSMV models used in the experiments were automatically synthesized from higher-level design models using the QuantUM tool [17]. The ASR model consists of 3 variants. In the first variant there is only one computation channel for the radar screen (ASR1). In the second and third variant models there are two identical computation channel to raise the availability of the system. In the first two channel variant model the availability of a second channel is modeled by a counter counting component errors (ASR2a), while in the second variant the second channel is a complete copy of the first channel (ASR2b).

All experiments were performed on a PC with an Intel Xeon Processor with 8 Cores (3.60 Ghz) and 144 GBs of RAM. We compare our results with the results for the explicit state causality checking approach presented in [18], which were performed on the same computer. For all case studies, a maximum bound of $k = 20$ is chosen. For the considered case studies this value of k is sufficient to compute all relevant causalities. The explicit approach is prallelized using all 8 cores, while the BMC-based approach only uses one core.

In Table 1 the sizes of the different analyzed models are shown. Additionally we compare the number of paths that have to be stored for the explicit causality computation to the iterations needed in the BMC-based setting. For the AECU and the ASR2b the number of traces in the explicit case could not be computed, because the experiments run out of memory.

Figure 3 lists the eol formulas that were computed by the BMC-based causality checking approach. The cause for the occurrence of the considered hazard (a system state in which T_c and C_c hold) is the disjunction of cause 1 and cause 2. Cause 1 represents the case where both the car and the train are approaching the crossing, the car stays on the crossing until the gate closes, and finally the train enters the crossing. Cause 2 represents the case where the gate fails at an arbitrary point in time and the car and the train approach and enter the crossing in any possible order. Both causes are consistent with the results obtained by the explicit state causality checking implementation [18] for the same model.

Discussion. Table 2 presents a comparison of the computational resources needed to perform the explicit and the BMC-based causality checking approaches. In order to make the values comparable we limit the search depth for the explicit approach to $k_{max} = 20$ as we have done for the BMC-based approach.

The results illustrate that for the comparatively small railroad crossing model, the airbag model as well as the ASR1 model the explicit state causality checking

Table 1. Model sizes in the explicit case and iterations needed for the BMC-based approach.

	States	Transitions	Paths (explicit)	Iterations (BMC-based)
Railroad	133	237	47	6
Airbag	155,464	697,081	20,300	24
ASR1	$1 \cdot 10^6$	$7 \cdot 10^6$	$1 \cdot 10^6$	27
ASR2a	$4,6 \cdot 10^7$	$3,3 \cdot 10^8$	$1.5 \cdot 10^7$	32
AECU	$7.5 \cdot 10^7$	$8.6 \cdot 10^8$	-	70
ASR2b	$1 \cdot 10^{12}$	$1 \cdot 10^{13}$	-	208

Cause 1:
$(Ca \wedge Cc) \wedge (Ca \wedge Ta) \wedge$
$(Ca \wedge_< \neg Tl \wedge_> Ta) \wedge (Ca \wedge Gc) \wedge$
$(Ca \wedge Tc) \wedge (Cc \wedge Ta) \wedge$
$(Cc \wedge_< \neg Cl \wedge_> Gc) \wedge (Cc \wedge Gc) \wedge$
$(Ta \wedge Tc) \wedge (Gc \wedge Tc) \wedge$
$(Gc \wedge_< \neg Cl \wedge_> Tc) \wedge (Cc \wedge Tc) \wedge$
$(Tc \wedge_< \neg Tl \wedge_> Ca) \wedge (Ta \wedge Gc)$

Cause 2:
$(Ca \wedge Gf) \wedge (Ca \wedge Ta) \wedge$
$(Ca \wedge_< \neg Tl \wedge_> Cc) \wedge$
$(Ca \wedge Tc) \wedge (Ca \wedge Cc) \wedge$
$(Gf \wedge Ta) \wedge (Gf \wedge Tc) \wedge$
$(Gf \wedge Cc) \wedge (Ta \wedge Tc) \wedge$
$(Tc \wedge_< \neg Tl \wedge_> Ca) \wedge$
$(Tc \wedge Cc) \wedge (Cc \wedge_< \neg Tl \wedge_> tc)$

Fig. 3. Causalities computed for the Railroad Crossing case study.

outperforms the BMC-based approach both in terms of time and memory. For the ASR2 and the AECU models the BMC-based approach uses less memory and finishes the computation faster than in the explicit case. These results reflect a frequently encountered observation when comparing explicit state and symbolic BMC techniques: For small models explicit state model checking is faster and uses less memory since the bounded model checker faces a lot of memory overhead due to the translation of the system into propositional logic. On the other hand, for large models such as ASR2 and AECU the explicit techniques need a lot of memory in order to explicitly store all paths needed to compute the causality classes while the SAT/BMC-based symbolic approach represents whole sets of paths symbolically using propositional logic formulas.

Table 2. Experimental results comparing the explicit state approach to the BMC-based approach for $k_{max} = 20$. OOM: experiment ran out of available memory.

		RT (sec.)	Mem. (MB)			RT (sec.)	Mem. (MB)
Railroad	explicit	0.73	17.9	ASR2a	explicit	91.22	826.73
	BMC-b.	17.16	121.55		BMC-b.	186.48	300.54
Airbag	explicit	1.61	18.53	AECU	explicit	238.13	10,900.00
	BMC-b.	34.55	192.36		BMC-b.	63.0	183.7
ASR1	explicit	9.24	50.97	ASR2b	explicit	OOM	OOM
	BMC-b.	50.97	303.34		BMC-b.	2,924.74	1,452.45

Threats to Validity. The current prototypical tool implementation of the BMC-based causality checking approach, which was used to carry out the experiments described above, is in a somewhat preliminary state. As we argued earlier in the paper, we need to discriminate repeated occurrences of some event type. This requires modifications to the code of the NuSMV, in particular to routines that accomplish the unrolling of the transition relation. The NuSMV code is not designed to be easily modifiable, which is why the proper unrolling accounting for discernible event occurrences of the same type has not yet been fully implemented. As a consequence, the current implementation computes incorrect results for those models for which there are execution paths with repeated occurrences of some event type. However, we believe that this qualitative problem has no significant impact on the quantitative results regarding memory consumption, which are our main concern in this paper. In any event, out of the considered case studies, only the AECU case study contains such events, in all other models this does not happen and the computed causalities are hence correct.

5   Related Work

In [5,10,11] a notion of causality was used to explain the violations of properties in different scenarios. While [5,11] use symbolic techniques for the counterexample computation, they focus on explaining the causal relationships for a single counterexample and thus only give partial information on the causes for a property violation. All of the aforementioned techniques rely on the generation of the counterexamples prior to the causality analysis while our approach computes the necessary counterexamples on-the-fly. Also, our approach is the first and, as far as we know, currently only one that relates the Halpern and Pearl model of causation to the model of transition system and which considers the ordering of events to be potentially causal. In [7,8], a symbolic approach to generate Fault Trees [23] is presented. In this approach all single component failures have to be known in advance while in our approach these failures are computed as a result of the algorithm. They do not use an explicitly defined notion of causality, contrary to what we do. The ordering and the non-occurrence of events can not be detected in this approach as being causal for a property violation.

6   Conclusion and Future Work

We have discussed how causal relationships in a system according to the causality checking approach that we previously developed can be established using symbolic system and cause representations together with bounded model checking. The BMC-based causality checking approach presented in this paper was evaluated on six case studies, four of them industrially sized, and compared to the explicit state causality checking approach. It was observed that BMC-based causality checking outperforms explicit state causality checking on large models both in terms of computation time and memory consumption.

In future work the influence of different SAT solving strategies on the speed of discovering new event orderings in the system have to be evaluated. Furthermore, we plan to transform the EOL formulas in EONF into a compact representation in order to enable an automatic Fault Tree generation.

Acknowledgements. We wish to acknowledge early discussions with John Rushby and Alessandro Cimatti on solving causality checking using bounded model checking.

References

1. Aljazzar, H., Fischer, M., Grunske, L., Kuntz, M., Leitner-Fischer, F., Leue, S.: Safety analysis of an airbag system using probabilistic FMEA and probabilistic counterexamples. In: Proceedings of the QEST 2009, Sixth International Conference on the Quantitative Evaluation of Systems. IEEE Computer Society (2009)
2. Baier, C., Katoen, J.P.: Principles of Model Checking. The MIT Press, New York (2008)
3. Beer, A., Leitner-Fischer, F., Leue, S.: On the relationship of event order logic and linear temporal logic. Technical report soft-14-01, Univ. of Konstanz, Germany, January 2014. http://www.inf.uni-konstanz.de/soft/research/publications/pdf/soft-14-01.pdf, available from: http://www.inf.uni-konstanz.de/soft/research/publications/pdf/soft-14-01.pdf
4. Beer, A., Kühne, U., Leitner-Fischer, F., Leue, S., Prem, R.: Analysis of an Airport Surveillance Radar using the QuantUM approach. Technical report soft-12-01, Chair for Software Engineering, University of Konstanz (2012). http://www.inf.uni-konstanz.de/soft/research/publications/pdf/soft-12-01.pdf
5. Beer, I., Ben-David, S., Chockler, H., Orni, A., Trefler, R.: Explaining counterexamples using causality. In: Bouajjani, A., Maler, O. (eds.) CAV 2009. LNCS, vol. 5643, pp. 94–108. Springer, Heidelberg (2009)
6. Biere, A., Cimatti, A., Clarke, E., Zhu, Y.: Symbolic model checking without BDDs. In: Cleaveland, W.R. (ed.) TACAS 1999. LNCS, vol. 1579, pp. 193–207. Springer, Heidelberg (1999)
7. Bozzano, M., Cimatti, A., Tapparo, F.: Symbolic fault tree analysis for reactive systems. In: Namjoshi, K.S., Yoneda, T., Higashino, T., Okamura, Y. (eds.) ATVA 2007. LNCS, vol. 4762, pp. 162–176. Springer, Heidelberg (2007)
8. Bozzano, M., Villafiorita, A.: Improving system reliability via model checking: The FSAP/NuSMV-SA safety analysis platform. In: Anderson, S., Felici, M., Littlewood, B. (eds.) SAFECOMP 2003. LNCS, vol. 2788, pp. 49–62. Springer, Heidelberg (2003)
9. Cimatti, A., Clarke, E., Giunchiglia, E., Giunchiglia, F., Pistore, M., Roveri, M., Sebastiani, R., Tacchella, A.: NuSMV 2: an opensource tool for symbolic model checking. In: Brinksma, E., Larsen, K.G. (eds.) CAV 2002. LNCS, vol. 2404, p. 359. Springer, Heidelberg (2002)
10. Gössler, G., Le Métayer, D., Raclet, J.-B.: Causality analysis in contract violation. In: Barringer, H., Falcone, Y., Finkbeiner, B., Havelund, K., Lee, I., Pace, G., Roşu, G., Sokolsky, O., Tillmann, N. (eds.) RV 2010. LNCS, vol. 6418, pp. 270–284. Springer, Heidelberg (2010)
11. Groce, A., Chaki, S., Kroening, D., Strichman, O.: Error explanation with distance metrics. Int. J. Softw. Tools Technol. Transfer (STTT) 8(3), 229–247 (2006)

12. Halpern, J., Pearl, J.: Causes and explanations: A structural-model approach. Causes. Br. J. Philos. Sci., Part I **56**, 843–887 (2005)
13. Holzmann, G.J.: The SPIN Model Checker: Primer and Reference Manual. Addision-Wesley, Reading (2003)
14. de Jonge, M., Ruys, T.C.: The SPINJA model checker. In: van de Pol, J., Weber, M. (eds.) SPIN 2010. LNCS, vol. 6349, pp. 124–128. Springer, Heidelberg (2010)
15. Kuntz, M., Leitner-Fischer, F., Leue, S.: From probabilistic counterexamples via causality to fault trees. In: Flammini, F., Bologna, S., Vittorini, V. (eds.) SAFE-COMP 2011. LNCS, vol. 6894, pp. 71–84. Springer, Heidelberg (2011)
16. Leitner-Fischer, F.: Causality Checking of Safety-Critical Software and Systems. Ph.D. thesis, Universitét Konstanz, Konstanz (2015). http://kops.uni-konstanz.de/handle/123456789/30778?locale-attribute=en
17. Leitner-Fischer, F., Leue, S.: QuantUM: Quantitative safety analysis of UML models. In: Proceedings Ninth Workshop on Quantitative Aspects of Programming Languages (QAPL 2011). EPTCS, vol. 57, pp. 16–30 (2011)
18. Leitner-Fischer, F., Leue, S.: Causality checking for complex system models. In: Giacobazzi, R., Berdine, J., Mastroeni, I. (eds.) VMCAI 2013. LNCS, vol. 7737, pp. 248–267. Springer, Heidelberg (2013)
19. Leitner-Fischer, F., Leue, S.: Probabilistic fault tree synthesis using causality computation. Int. J. Critical Comput.-Based Syst. **4**, 119–143 (2013)
20. Leitner-Fischer, F., Leue, S.: Spincause: A tool for causality checking. In: Proceedings of the International SPIN Symposium on Model Checking of Software (SPIN 2014). ACM, San Jose (2014)
21. Lewis, D.: Counterfactuals. Blackwell Publishers, Oxford (1973)
22. Pnueli, A.: The temporal logic of programs. In: 18th Annual Symposium on Foundations of Computer Science, pp. 46–57. IEEE (1977)
23. Vesely, W.E., Goldberg, F.F., Roberts, N.H., Haasl, D.F.: Fault Tree Handbook. Tech. rep., Defense Technical Information Center OAI-PMH Repository [http://stinet.dtic.mil/oai/oai] (United States) (2002). http://handle.dtic.mil/100.2/ADA354973

Model Counting for Complex Data Structures

Antonio Filieri[1]([✉]), Marcelo F. Frias[2], Corina S. Păsăreanu[3],
and Willem Visser[4]

[1] University of Stuttgart, Stuttgart, Germany
antonio.filieri@gmail.com
[2] Instituto Tecnológico de Buenos Aires and CONICET, Buenos Aires, Argentina
[3] Carnegie Mellon Silicon Valley, NASA Ames,
Moffet Field, Mountain View, CA, USA
[4] Stellenbosch University, Stellenbosch, South Africa

Abstract. We extend recent approaches for calculating the probability of program behaviors, to allow model counting for complex data structures with numeric fields. We use symbolic execution with lazy initialization to compute the input structures leading to the occurrence of a target event, while keeping a symbolic representation of the constraints on the numeric data. Off-the-shelf model counting tools are used to count the solutions for numerical constraints and field bounds encoding data structure invariants are used to reduce the search space. The technique is implemented in the Symbolic PathFinder tool and evaluated on several complex data structures. Results show that the technique is much faster than an enumeration-based method that uses the Korat tool and also highlight the benefits of using the field bounds to speed up the analysis.

Keywords: Model counting · Probabilistic software analysis · Symbolic execution

1 Introduction

Model counting is the problem of computing the number of solutions (models) that satisfy a set of constraints. Model counting has found applications in worst case execution time estimation [27], increasing parallelism [38], quantitative information flow analysis [34], and many others.

We focus here on another important application, namely Probabilistic Software Analysis (PSA) [7,15,21,36]. PSA is an emerging technique to quantify the probability of reaching program events of interest assuming that program inputs follow given probabilistic distributions [15]. The input distributions allow data from real world observations to be incorporated in the analysis of programs that interact with their environment, as well as to encode uncertainty in design assumptions about the usage profile of a program, including the interactions with third-party components and systems. PSA is useful in many domains including debugging, cryptographic protocols, cyber-physical systems, biology, and reliability analysis [21].

© Springer International Publishing Switzerland 2015
B. Fischer and J. Geldenhuys (Eds.): SPIN 2015, LNCS 9232, pp. 222–241, 2015.
DOI: 10.1007/978-3-319-23404-5_15

Recent PSA techniques [15,16,18,28] use symbolic execution of the program to collect symbolic constraints on the inputs that lead to the occurrence of target program events. The number of satisfying assignments for these constraints are then calculated using *model counting procedures*. This gives a measure of how likely it is for an input distributed according to a given probabilistic distribution to satisfy the constraints.

Most work on probabilistic symbolic execution has focused on integers and used off-the-shelf model counting tools for computing the number of integer values within the volume of a convex polytope, e.g. LattE [2], to compute probabilities [15,16,18,28]. Recent techniques have been introduced to estimate the (approximate) number of solutions for floating point constraints [7]. However these techniques can not directly be applied to complex data structures, such as lists and trees. Analysis of programs that manipulate complex data is well studied with many approaches available, see e.g. shape analysis [40], specification-based testing [9] and constraint solving [24], among others. However model counting for data structures has not been addressed so far.

In this paper we propose a model counting procedure for a combination of heap and numeric constraints collected along a symbolic execution of a program. A simple approach is to enumerate all the possible data structures up to a given size and then to check their validity against the given constraints. However this becomes quickly intractable for large solution sets. We instead propose an approach based on symbolic execution and *lazy initialization* [25] to generate and thus count data structures that satisfy mixed heap and numeric constraints; we further use off-the-shelf model counting procedures [2] for the numeric constraints.

Lazy initialization extends symbolic execution with the ability of handling input data structures: it constructs the heap as the program paths are explored, and defers concretization of symbolic heap objects as much as possible. It produces symbolic heaps that are pairwise non-isomorphic while guaranteeing that no relevant states are missed. It can thus be used as a powerful procedure for generating and *counting* all the structures (up to a given bound). We further use relational field bounds [35] to reduce the search space for the solutions. Intuitively, field bounds restrict the number of choices that lazy initialization needs to consider when it concretizes a part of the heap.

We have implemented the model counting procedure in the Symbolic PathFinder tool-set [32] and have evaluated it on several complex data structure subjects from the literature. The experiments show that our proposed approach scales much better than an optimized enumeration-based method that uses the Korat tool [9]. The experiments also show the benefits of relational bounds on the overall cost of model counting.

2 Background

2.1 Symbolic Execution

Symbolic Execution [12,26] is a program analysis technique that executes programs on unspecified inputs, by using symbolic inputs instead of concrete data.

The state of a symbolically executed program is defined by the (symbolic) values of the program variables, a *path condition* (*PC*), and a program counter. The path condition is a (quantifier-free) boolean formula over the symbolic inputs; it accumulates constraints on the inputs to follow that path. The program counter defines the next statement to be executed.

A *symbolic execution tree* characterizes the execution paths followed during symbolic execution. The tree nodes represent program states and the arcs the transitions between states due to the execution of program instructions. Typical applications of symbolic execution include test case generation and error detection, with many tools available [10,20,32,37]. Symbolic execution of looping programs may result in an infinite symbolic execution tree. For this reason, symbolic execution is typically run with a (user-specified) bound on the search depth. Our work on probabilistic software analysis uses the symbolic execution tool Symbolic PathFinder (SPF) [32].

Lazy Initialization. SPF uses lazy initialization [25] to handle dynamic input data structures (e.g., lists and trees). The components of the program inputs are initialized on an "as-needed" basis. The intuition is as follows. To symbolically execute method m of class C, SPF creates a new object o of class C, leaving all its fields uninitialized. When a reference field f of type T is accessed in m for the first time, SPF non-deterministically sets f to null, to a new object of type T with uninitialized fields, or to an alias to a previously initialized object of type T. This enables the systematic exploration of different heap configurations during symbolic execution. Here we will also consider an optimized form of lazy initialization called Bounded Lazy Initialization (BLISS) [35] that uses relational bounds and SAT solving to reduce the number of possible structures to consider. BLISS reduces the time and memory requirements over lazy initialization and therefore makes the techniques for counting discussed here tractable.

2.2   Probabilistic Software Analysis

We build on our previous work from [7,15,18], that uses symbolic execution for PSA. The goal of the analysis is: (1) to identify the symbolic constraints characterizing the inputs that make the execution satisfy a given property, and then (2) to quantify the probability of satisfying the constraints. For simplicity, we assume the satisfaction of the target property to be characterized by the occurrence of a target event (e.g. successful termination or failure), but our work extends to bounded LTL [41] as well.

The analysis works with a limited budget of symbolic paths, obtained with a bounded symbolic execution of the program. Some of these paths lead to failure and some of them to success (termination without failure). These path conditions are classified in two disjoint sets: $PC^s = \{PC_1^s, PC_2^s, \ldots, PC_m^s\}$ and $PC^f = \{PC_1^f, PC_2^f, \ldots, PC_p^f\}$. The path conditions may not cover the full input domain due to inherent incompleteness in the analysis, e.g. due to non-terminating loops or non-exhaustive path exploration. These remaining paths are called *grey* paths and are used in [15] to quantify the confidence one can put in the bounded symbolic analysis.

Probabilistic Usage Profiles. The constraints generated with symbolic execution are analyzed to quantify the likelihood of an input to satisfy them, where the inputs are distributed according to given *usage profiles* [15]. A usage profile is a probabilistic characterization of the software interactions with the external world, e.g. the users or the physical execution environment. It assigns to each valid combination of inputs its probability to occur during execution. Usage profiles can be specified based on physical phenomena, known sensor parameters or other domain specific knowledge about the program and its deployment context. They can also be built automatically based on observed data from past usages of the program [5, 19].

In [15], we assumed that all the input variables range over finite discrete domains, whose joining is generically indicated as D. We relaxed this assumption in more recent work [7]. We profile the expected usage for the program through a profile UP, which is a set of pairs $\langle c_i, p_i \rangle$ where c_i is a *usage scenario* defined as a (constraint representing a) subset of D and p_i ($p_i \geq 0$) is the probability that a user input belongs to c_i. We further require, for simplicity, $\{c_i\}$ to be a complete partition of D, and thus $\sum_i p_i = 1$. Intuitively, UP is the distribution over the input space. Notice that c_i could contain even a single element of D, allowing for the finest grained specifications of UP.

Given the output of symbolic execution, the probability of success can be defined as the probability of executing the program (P) with an input satisfying any of the successful path conditions, given the profile UP. This definition can be formalized as $Pr^s(P) = \sum_i Pr(PC_i^s \mid UP)$. An analogous definition is provided for the probability of failure, $Pr^f(P)$. The probability of grey paths is $1 - (Pr^s(P) + Pr^f(P))$ and it quantifies the ratio of elements of the input domain for which neither success nor failure have been revealed for the current analysis. This information is a measure of the confidence we can put on the probability estimation, under the current exploration bound.

Computing Probabilities with Model Counting. To compute the probabilities of path conditions, we use a quantification procedure for the generated constraints. In [15] we used model counting techniques, i.e. LattE [14], to calculate the exact number of points of a bounded (possibly very large) discrete domain that satisfy linear constraints. Recently [7], we developed quantification procedures for the analysis of programs that have mixed integer and floating point constraints of arbitrary complexity.

To compute the probability of a path (described by PC) we use the fact that UP defines a partition of the input domain and then, from the law of total probability [33]:

$$Pr(PC \mid UP) = \sum_i Pr(PC \mid c_i) \cdot p_i$$

Furthermore, from the definition of conditional probability [33]: $Pr(PC \mid c_i) = Pr(PC \wedge c_i)/Pr(c_i)$.

To use model-counting techniques for the computation of the conditional probabilities, let us define for a constraint c the function $\#(c)$ that returns the number of elements of D satisfying c. $\sharp(\cdot)$ is always a finite non negative integer because we assumed D finite and countable. Under this same assumption, $Pr(c)$ is, by definition [33], $\sharp(c)/\sharp(D)$ (where $\sharp(D)$ is the size of the non-empty input domain). Thus, one can express the probability of success as:

$$Pr^s(P) = \sum_i Pr(PC_i^s \mid UP) = \sum_i \sum_j Pr(PC_i^s \mid c_j) \cdot p_j = \sum_i \sum_j \frac{\sharp(PC_i^s \wedge c_j)}{\sharp(c_j)} \cdot p_j.$$

3   Approach

We describe here how the probabilistic software analysis is extended to handle programs that take as input structured data types, e.g. lists or trees.

3.1   Usage Profiles

Usage profiles (UP) for data structures are defined with the help of Java predicates (i.e., boolean methods) that define data structure properties that *partition* the input state space. To each element of this partition a probability value is assigned, with the sum of those values being equal to 1. For example, for a program with an input list, the UP may specify that the input list is non-null 90 % of the time (and null 10 %). Alternatively, the UP may specify that the list is acyclic say 95 % (and cyclic 5 %), or that the list is "small" (number of nodes less than 10) most of the time (90 %) and "large" (number of nodes greater than 10) rest of the time (10 %) etc.

As before, we restrict ourselves to finite input domains, which for data structures also lead to a limited number of possible heap nodes for the input. It is the responsibility of the user to ensure that the predicates in the UP define a partition of the input domain (i.e. a division of the domain as the union of non-overlapping non-empty subdomains).

3.2   Symbolic Constraints

SPF can analyze programs with unbounded data structures as inputs, using lazy initialization [25]. The result of symbolic execution is a set of paths, each characterized by a path condition that encodes both numeric and heap constraints.

The numeric constraints are generated whenever a branching condition on primitive (numeric) fields is evaluated. The heap constraints are generated during the lazy initialization of instructions that perform a first access to an uninitialized field (i.e., bytecodes `aload`, `getfield`, and `getstatic`).

The heap constraints can have the following forms:

- $ref = null$. Reference ref points to $null$.
- $ref \neq null$. Reference ref is non $null$.
- $ref_1 = ref_2$. References ref_1 and ref_2 are aliased (point to the same object).
- $ref_1 \neq ref_2$. References ref_1 and ref_2 are not aliased.

PC_1: $in.next = null \wedge in \neq null$
PC_2: $in.next = in \wedge in \neq null$
PC_3: $in.next \neq in \wedge in.next \neq null \wedge in \neq null \wedge in.elem \leq in.next.elem$
PC_4: $in.next.next = null \wedge in.next \neq in \wedge in.next \neq null \wedge in \neq null \wedge in.elem > in.next.elem$
PC_5: $in.next.next = in \wedge in.next \neq in \wedge in.next \neq null \wedge in \neq null \wedge in.elem > in.next.elem$
PC_6: $in.next.next = in.next \wedge in.next \neq in \wedge in.next \neq null \wedge in \neq null \wedge in.elem > in.next.elem$
PC_7: $in.next.next \neq in \wedge in.next.next \neq in.next \wedge in.next.next$
      $\neq null \wedge in.next \neq in \wedge in.next \neq null \wedge in \neq null \wedge in.elem > in.next.elem$

Fig. 1. Symbolic paths from method `swapNode`.

Example. Consider the Java code in Listing 1.1 [25] that declares a class `Node` for a linked lists. Fields `elem` and `next` represent the node's integer value and a reference to the next node in the list, respectively. Method `swapNode` destructively updates its input list, referenced by the implicit parameter `this`, according to a numeric condition on the first two nodes.

Listing 1.1. List example.

```java
1 class Node {
2    int elem;
3    Node next;
4
5    Node swapNode() {
6       if(elem > next.elem) {
7          Node t = next;
8          next = t.next;
9          t.next = this;
10         return t;
11      }
12      return this;
13   }
14 }
```

Symbolic execution with lazy initialization results in seven symbolic paths (see Fig. 1), due to the `if` condition and the different aliasing possibilities in the input

These symbolic execution paths together represent all possible actual executions of `swapNode`. The PCs represent an isomorphism partition of the input space, e.g., PC_7 describes all (cyclic or acyclic) input lists with at least three nodes such that the first element is greater than the second element. The analysis reports a *failure* for PC_1 – the method raises an unhandled `NullPointer Exception`. There are no grey paths (since there are no loops).

As an illustration of lazy initialization consider the symbolic execution of `next = t.next;` for the symbolic heap configuration depicted in the root of the tree in Fig. 2. In the figure a "blob" indicates field `next` pointing to it is uninitialized (it has not been accessed yet by the symbolic execution along this path). "E0" and "E1" represent some fresh symbolic values for the numeric field `elem`; a "?" means that a field of numeric (or other primitive) type has not been initialized yet. Dashed arrows depict a branching of nondeterministic choices, describing all the possible instantiations of the symbolic structure. Since `t.next` is uninitialized, SPF uses "lazy initialization" to assign it either `null`, a new symbolic object with uninitialized fields, or an object created during a previous initialization (resulting for our example in two instances of circular lists).

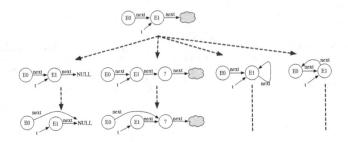

Fig. 2. Lazy initialization.

Intuitively, this means that SPF makes four different assumptions about the shape of the input list according to different aliasing possibilities and it explores all of them systematically. The PCs are updated according to these choices. Once t.next has been initialized the execution proceeds according to the Java semantics.

3.3 Model Counting for Data Structures

Though the counting-based probabilistic analysis method from Sect. 2 can be applied on any finite input domain, we need an efficient procedure for counting data structures. In the worst case a complete (and expensive) enumeration of all the possible input instances (up to a pre-specified bound) might be performed. A less expensive alternative, that we proposed in [15] is to use Korat [9] for the data structure enumeration. Korat is a tool that performs constraint-based generation of structurally complex test inputs for Java programs. Korat's goal is to systematically generate all complex test data structures (within prescribed bounds) for the purpose of testing. Although Korat was not designed for model counting we can use it to compute all input data structures that satisfy a complex predicate within pre-defined bounds. The predicate is written as a boolean method often called repOk, whose body can embed any arbitrarily complex computation. The *finitization* of the input domain is accomplished by specific Korat methods to specify bounds on the size of input data structures as well as on the domain of primitive fields.

Thus we can encode the constraints provided by symbolic execution together with the constraints from the usage profile as a repOK predicate and run Korat to count the data structures that satisfy the constraints for the given finitization. Experiments with this approach (see Sect. 4) show that it often scales poorly when the path constraints contain a combination of heap and numeric constraints, and the numeric domains are very large. This is due to the enumeration of the valid values for integer fields performed by Korat. In the next section we propose an efficient alternative method.

3.4   Model Counting Using Lazy Initialization

We propose to use symbolic execution with lazy initialization to efficiently generate and count the data structures that satisfy given constraints. The core insight is to use lazy initialization to enumerate the structures, but to keep the constraints on the numeric fields of the structures *symbolic*; the valid assignments for these symbolic fields can then be counted with an off-the-shelf model counting procedure, such as LattE [2]. LattE implements Barvinok's algorithm [4], which constructs a generating function suitable for determining the number of points within a convex polytope without enumeration.

To count the number of solutions to a set of mixed heap and numeric constraints, we apply symbolic execution with lazy initialization to a boolean method encoding the constraints (similar to the repOk method in Korat). The model counting procedure requires thus two inputs:

Method repOk: Java boolean method encoding the constraints; returns true if the structure satisfies the constraints (e.g. the list is acyclic).

Finitization: Domain bounds for both reference and numeric data (e.g., a list may have up to 5 nodes, whose elements are between 1 and 10).

For example, if we want to count all the acyclic lists having at most 6 nodes, whose elements are between 1 and 10, we would use the code reported in Listing 1.2.

Listing 1.2. Counting acyclic lists.

```
 1 class List{
 2     Node head;
 3     boolean repOkacyclic(){
 4         Set<Node> nodes = new HashSet<Node>();
 5         Node iterator = head;
 6         while(iterator!=null){
 7             // check acyclic
 8             if(!nodes.add(iterator))
 9                 return false;
10             //check bounds
11             if(iterator.elem<1||iterator.elem>10)
12                 return false;
13             if(nodes.size>6)
14                 return false;
15
16             iterator=iterator.next;
17         }
18         return true;
19     }
20
21     public static void main(String[] args){
22         List L0 = new List();
23         L0=(List) Debug.makeSymbolicRef(''L0'',L0);
24         if(L0!=null)
25             assert (L0.repOkacyclic());
26     }
27 }
```

The symbolic execution of the program in Listing 1.2 collects as successful path conditions (i.e. not leading to an exception) all the symbolic structures representing an acyclic list with at most 6 nodes, whose elements are integers between 1 and 10.

The main method summarizes the steps required for counting these structures:

1. Create a symbolic instance of the structure. In SPF syntax, see lines 22 and 23.
2. Execute the method repOkacyclic. This step drives the execution toward exploring all the valid structures, expanding and concretizing all of them, i.e. leaving only symbolic numeric variables to be analyzed.
3. Preempt the execution from exploring structure outside the valid domain or not satisfying the constraints. For brevity, we just assert the repOkacyclic predicate.

The total number of acyclic lists can thus be obtained applying established model counting solutions on the success path conditions, which now predicate only on the numeric fields. The result in this case would be 6,543,210 acyclic lists out of 7,654,321 lists with up to 6 nodes (and elements between 1 and 10).

Note that encoding the repOk is subtle, as it not only encodes the given constraints but it also includes code to enumerate all the structures up to bounds given in the finitization. Similar to Korat, the structure of the repOk is crucial to the efficiency of the method. If repOk would first enumerate all structures and only then determine if they are valid (according to the given constraints) our approach would not benefit from lazy initialization (but it would still benefit from solving the numeric constraints separately).

In our implementation we provide a code skeleton for enumerating all data structures (to which users can add their constraints). Input bounds are provided in a configuration file. Internally SPF backtracks when the bounds on heap nodes are reached. Bounds on numeric fields are fed directly to the constraint solvers.

3.5   Probabilistic Software Analysis

Counting the instances of a data structure satisfying a given predicate enables us to compute the probability of target program events to occur, given a specific usage profile.

As an example let us compute the probability of failure (in this case, throwing a NullPointerException) when executing the swapNode method of Listing 1.1. Assume a usage profile that specifies that the input list is acyclic with probability 0.9 and it is cyclic with remaining probability 0.1. There is only one failure symbolic path (revealed by a null pointer exception in the evaluation of the if condition). The path condition for the failure path, as revealed by SPF, is

$$input \neq null \wedge input.next = null$$

Since this path condition is only satisfiable for acyclic lists, we get the probability of failure $Pr^f(P)$:

$$0.9 \cdot \frac{\sharp(input \neq null \wedge input.next = null \wedge acyclic(input))}{\sharp(acyclic(input))}$$

The results of model counting are $\sharp(input \neq null \wedge input.next = null \wedge acyclic(input)) = 10$ and $\sharp(acyclic(input)) = 1,111,111$, for lists with up to 6 nodes and elem ranging over 1..10, giving probability of failure $8.1 \cdot 10^{-6}$.

One can argue that we should simply correct the error in method swapNode (for example adding a null check). However imagine a scenario where this method is part of a large code base and that usage (calling context) of the method indicates that the probability of the list being null is very small. In such cases PSA becomes very useful, for example, to "rank" the errors according to the likelihood of occurrence, allowing developers to focus on high probability errors first. More example applications of PSA will be discussed in Sect. 4.

Embedded Usage Profiles. In the computation above we have followed the approach in [15] and computed the effects of the UP after the path constraints have been collected. An alternative way introduced in [28] consists in embedding the usage profile as "preconditions" (assume statements) in the code. Listing 1.3 shows an example of embedded UP for the analysis of the swapNode method. For the usage profile that states that the input list is acyclic 90 % of the time (and cyclic 10 %) We use a symbolic variable, up, uniformly distributed in the range $1 \leq up \leq 100$, for controlling the distribution of the input values.

Listing 1.3. Embedded UP for the List example.

```
1  List L0 = new List();
2  L0=(List)Debug.makeSymbolicRef("L0",L0);
3  if(up<=90){
4      Debug.assume(L0!=null && L0.repOkacyclic());
5  }else{
6      Debug.assume(L0!=null && L0.repOkcyclic());
7  }
8  L0.swapNode();
```

The assume statements are implemented using the built-in Debug.assume() method from SPF [32]. The failure probability can then be computed using model counting for the numeric constraints encoded in the path conditions for the failure paths.

Both ways for handling UPs are supported in our tool with analogous performance overhead, leaving to the developer the choice whether keeping the UP and the code separated or included in the same file.

3.6   Optimizations

In this section we describe optimizations included in our analysis that allow us to improve scalability.

BLISS (Bounded Lazy Initialization with Sat Support) [35], is an optimization specifically tailored to improve the lazy initialization of data structures during symbolic execution. Data structures usually obey strong restrictions on their structure and stored data, under the form of *class invariants*. Some typical invariants are "the items in this list are sorted", or "if a node is red, then both its children are black"(for red–black trees). BLISS exploits known class invariants to compute *tight bounds* on the data structure fields. Intuitively, a tight field bound is a relational upper bound (set of pairs) on the (relational) semantics of Java class fields. A tight field bound for a Java field f, is a binary relation between unique field identifiers that only relates pairs $\langle i_1, i_2 \rangle$ that are feasible, i.e., for which there exists a structure satisfying both the class invariant and the canonical labeling of identifiers, that includes in the memory heap objects with identifiers i_1 and i_2 such that $i_1.f = i_2$.

During lazy initialization, whenever an object o is dereferenced through a (symbolic) object field f, three possibilities have to be considered, namely [25]:

- $o.f$ is initialized as the null value,
- $o.f$ is initialized as a pre existing object o' in the memory heap, and
- $o.f$ is initialized as a new object o''.

The tight field bounds allow to reduce the choices in the first and second case (the latter being the most expensive). BLISS prunes those symbolic executions where the (partially) symbolic memory heap contains enough information to determine it can not be extended into a feasible heap. Intuitively, the concrete parts of the partially symbolic heap are translated as constraints that are conjoined with an automatically generated propositional description of the class invariant. A satisfiability checker is used to determine whether the symbolic parts of the heap can be concretized into a fully concrete memory heap satisfying the class invariant. Those partially symbolic heaps producing a negative outcome can be safely pruned from the symbolic execution process. BLISS can improve lazy initialization significantly [35] and occupies a natural place in the context of this work.

As already mentioned, in this paper we focus on integer constraints, whose models are counted with Latte [2] (to cope with floating-point numbers and nonlinear constraints, it is straightforward to use qCoral [7] in place of Latte). The complexity is in terms of the number of variables and the number of constraints. For large constraints, the procedure could be very time consuming. We address this problem by first simplifying the constraints and using a divide-and-conquer approach [15] that divides large path conditions into *independent constraints* which can then be solved independently. Intuitively two constraints are independent if the sets of variables they constrain have no intersection. The approach facilitates caching and reusing counting results.

4   Implementation and Experience

In this section we report an experimental comparison of an implementation of our approach with Korat (Sect. 4.1) and a set of case studies demonstrating its applicability for probabilistic software analysis (Sect. 4.2).

We implemented our approach on top of SPF [32] v6. The collection of path conditions followed by the probability computations are implemented by means of JPF listeners. Experiments were performed on a workstation with Intel Core i7-2600 processor with a 3.40 GHz clock speed and 8 GB DDR3 RAM, running Linux 3.2.0. 6 GB of heap memory were allocated for the Java virtual machine. All the times are in seconds. TO means the execution has been interrupted after a timeout of 5 h. OOM means the execution ran out of memory.

4.1   Comparing with Korat

We compared the result and execution time of our approach, with and without BLISS (denoted SPF and SPF+BLISS), versus Korat on counting the valid instances of four known data structures showing different complexity dimensions: linked list, red-black tree, binomial heap and AVL tree. We vary the number of nodes in each structure and the size of the domain of values that can be stored. We remark that Korat has not been designed for model counting, but its smart enumeration capabilities can be used for this goal [15] making it a good baseline for comparison. For BLISS we used the field bounds from previous studies.

The results are reported in Table 1. The columns SPF, SPF+BLISS, and Korat report the analysis time for our approach with and without BLISS and for Korat, respectively.

LinkedList. This data structure implements a doubly linked list where each node contains an integer field. Korat fails to explore the whole input domain within 5 h for all the cases where the list was composed of 10 nodes and the integer domain contained 20 or more elements. On the other hand, SPF-based analyses terminate in less than 2 s for all the considered cases. Notably, due to the simplicity of this structure, the benefit of adding BLISS does not yield any perceivable improvements.

RedBlackTree. Red-black trees are significantly more complex than linked lists, both because of the higher number of references involved and the preservation of their invariants, which requires rebalancing techniques to guarantee the red-black property [13]. The main bottleneck of Korat remains on the size of the integer domain, when the number of nodes grows. On the other hand, for smaller integer domains the increased complexity of the structure has a modest impact on the performance of Korat. The number of nodes has instead a significant impact on the performance of SPF-based tools, with SPF running out of memory already with 8 nodes. Introducing BLISS reduces significantly the execution time and memory consumption in this case, since it prevents the symbolic execution to explore unnecessary invalid structures. This allows it to cope with larger instances.

BinomialHeap. Despite being operationally simpler than red-black trees, binomial heaps can also be characterized by a set of invariants making BLISS more effective in detecting invalid structures before their complete exploration. This results in a shorter execution time of SPF+BLISS with respect to SPF. Notice how SPF and SPF+BLISS scale better than Korat even for small sizes of the integer domain.

AVLTree. AVL trees are search trees whose rebalancing is triggered by the violation of a simpler invariant than red-black trees (the heights of the subtrees of every node can differ by at most one). In this case BLISS produces a smaller improvement compared to the case of red-black trees, though still reducing the analysis time of SPF. Korat achieves a good scalability over this structure, though if does not scale for larger instances where the integer domain has 20 elements or more.

Table 1. Comparison of SPF, SPF+BLISS, and Korat (time in seconds).

	Nodes	Ints	Count	SPF	SPF + BLISS	Korat
LinkedList	5	20	168,421	0	0	0
		50	6,377,551	0	0	3
		70	24,357,971	0	0	13
		100	101,010,101	0	0	51
	10	10	1,111,111,111	1	1	986
		20	538,947,368,421	1	1	TO
		50	1,992,984,693,877,551	1	1	TO
		70	40,938,441,884,057,971	1	1	TO
		100	1,010,101,010,101,010,101	1	1	TO
	15	10	1,111,111,111	1	1	TO
		20	1,724,631,578,947,368,421	1	1	TO
		50	622,807,716,836,734,693,877,551	1	1	TO
		70	68,805,239,274,536,231,884,057,971	1	1	TO
		100	10,101,010,101,010,101,010,101,010,101	1	1	TO

	Nodes	Ints	Count	SPF	SPF + BLISS	Korat
RedBlackTree	5	10	3,197	27	8	0
		20	146,093	26	8	3
		50	17,912,981	27	8	363
		70	100,606,073	26	8	476
		100	618,318,461	26	8	2,796
	8	10	13,037	OOM	300	1
		20	10,378,733	OOM	358	238
		50	33,633,553,781	OOM	354	TO
		70	570,417,679,113	OOM	366	TO
		100	10,968,862,744,061	OOM	357	TO
	10	10	14,101	OOM	2,738	8
		20	55,795,117	OOM	2,754	2,936
		50	1,943,776,206,661	OOM	2,841	TO
		70	71,482,977,220,937	OOM	2,742	TO
		100	3,021,060,476,356,221	OOM	2,774	TO

	Nodes	Ints	Count	SPF	SPF + BLISS	Korat
BinomialHeap	5	6	2,016	2	1	0
		10	19,371	2	1	0
		20	497,616	2	1	0
		50	42,613,101	2	1	28
		70	223,543,216	2	1	152
		100	1,305,473,076	2	1	880
	10	11	276,834,504	30	13	382
		20	70,790,816,523	30	13	TO
		50	482,258,613,959,406	30	12	TO
		70	13,057,541,269,423,978	30	13	TO
		100	439,699,627,791,397,061	30	13	TO
	15	16	1,320,960,601,687,363	562	129	TO
		20	31,844,676,603,881,568	559	128	TO
		50	19,743,228,678,771,046,522,656	562	130	TO
		70	2,836,624,163,763,256,508,895,748	560	133	TO
		100	562,643,897,792,832,103,640,559,436	569	129	TO

	Nodes	Ints	Count	SPF	SPF + BLISS	Korat
AVLTree	8	4	25	47	39	0
		10	6,893	66	61	0
		20	5,617,865	66	59	92
		50	18,955,370,261	69	59	TO
		70	323,071,208,925	67	58	TO
		100	6,232,176,942,521	67	58	TO
	10	4	25	190	139	0
		10	7,393	303	249	2
		20	24,093,465	308	253	932
		50	745,531,143,261	303	253	TO
		70	26,986,817,918,525	307	255	TO
		100	1,128,548,943,898,521	304	252	TO
	13	4	25	707	423	0
		10	7,393	2,804	2,408	17
		20	95,928,665	3,318	2,983	TO
		50	194,611,435,515,261	3,362	3,000	TO
		70	24,729,749,799,273,725	3,343	2,977	TO
		100	3,588,938,338,577,002,521	3,330	2,951	TO

In summary, for SPF-based techniques varying the size of the integer domain does not produce significant variations in the analysis time, while an enumeration-based approach unable to symbolically abstract the integer fields of the structures suffers scalability issues even for relatively small integer domains (20 or 50 elements). On the other hand, the complexity of the references structure is the main bottleneck of SPF-based tools, which are required to enlarge the scope of symbolic execution, reducing the benefits of lazy initialization. The use of BLISS is particularly beneficial when rich invariants (which impose strong requirements on structures) are available, allowing to prune symbolic execution paths heading toward the exploration of invalid structures.

4.2 Probabilistic Analysis

Probabilistic software analysis can be used for answering questions like:

1. *Which program methods are worth focusing on to improve the software responsiveness perceived by the users?*
2. *How likely is a bug to show up when the program is used according to a specific profile?*
3. *What is the perceived reliability of software for different classes of usages?*

In this section we report three example applications of our probabilistic software analysis technique by casting these question on small program snippets manipulating data structures to show the applicability scope of this technique.

1. Rotations in a Red-Black Tree. Red-black trees are kept *almost balanced* after every insertion or deletion [13]. This is achieved by a potentially expensive rotation operation. Considering the insertion of an integer value within the range $0 - 20$ into a tree having from 0 to 4 nodes, *how frequently should we expect a rotation will be required to rebalance the tree?*

Though this is just an example, answering this kind of question allows one to quantify the frequency a certain method is expected to be invoked during a program execution. This would help assessing the global impact of improving the efficiency of a specific method, and support the decisions of a developer.

In this example, the problem space is given by the set of all the valid trees with up to 4 nodes and the finite subset of integers between 0 and 20. This space counts $567,882$ elements. Out of them, inserting the integer value into the tree requires at least one rotation operation in $168,112$ cases, about 29.6%.

This type of information can also be exploited to compute a complexity index for operations on data structures tailored to specific usage profiles the program is expected to handle.

2. Assessing the Criticality of an Actual Bug. Class BinomialHeap used as part of the examples in this paper was first used as part of a benchmark in [39]. In [17] it was determined that method extractMin had a subtle bug that required a binomial heap with at least 13 nodes to be exposed. An example of an input exposing this bug is given in [17, Fig. 6]. A consequence of this bug is that upon execution of `extractMin`, the resulting binomial heap no longer satisfies its required property (attribute size no longer reflects the actual number of nodes in the binomial heap).

Although there is a bug in this structure, *how likely is this bug to actually show up when the `extractMin` method is invoked?*

In order to count the number of inputs that lead to a failure state (one in which attribute size does not model the actual number of nodes in the resulting binomial heap), we analyzed the code in Listing 1.4.

Listing 1.4. Bug in BinomialHeap (BH).

```
1 public static void main(String[] args) {
2   BH B0 = new BH();
3   B0 = (BH) Debug.makeSymbolicRef("B0", B0);
4   if (B0 != null && B0.repOk()){
5     B0.extractMin();
6     assert B0.size == B0.numNodes());
7   }
8 }
```

Executing symbolically the main method allows the `repOk` to generate all valid structures. Those structures that violate the assert statement generate errors that are caught by the underlying JVM, which then stores the numeric path conditions for further counting of failing instances. Table 2 presents our results.

When 12 or less elements are inserted in the heap, the bug will never show up (confirming previous evaluations regarding this bug [23,35]). So users following this behavior will not notice the presence of the bug.

When at least 13 elements are inserted, there is the chance for the bug to show up. However, how likely this is to occur in practice heavily depends on the size of the domain allowed for the integer values. Indeed, the bug does not systematically occur for every possible set of elements. Looking at Table 2, when only integers between 0 and 13 are allowed (with each value having the same probability), more than 80 % of the executions will violate the assertion. These figures can also be used to assed the difficulty of catching such bug with naive randomized testing.

In Table 2, we report for each given numbers of nodes and integer values, the number of valid inputs in the state space, the number of inputs leading to a failure, as well as the probability of running into a faulty outcome. Running time is presented under the form $t_1 + t_2$, with t_1 the time required to compute the number of valid inputs, and t_2 the time required to compute the failing ones. Notice also in this case how times increase as the number of nodes increases, yet remain stable for a number of nodes despite the number of integer values considered.

3. Impact of Different Usage Profiles. In the following we consider the impact of different usage profiles on the running example of the *List* from Listing 1.1. We consider the case where we have at most 6 nodes and numeric values in the range 1..10.

In Sect. 3.5 we evaluate the probability of throwing an exceptions when executing the method `swapNode` on the List example. The usage profile we considered

Table 2. Number of inputs exposing the extractMin bug.

Nodes	Ints	# Valid	# Failing		Fail prob	Time (s)
12	0..12	70,401,948,540		0	0	28 + 74
	0..20	14,829,486,591,568		0	0	28 + 73
	0..30	1,269,649,449,162,048		0	0	28 + 71
13	0..13	1,921,213,899,450	1,546,032,456,492		0.804	49 + 151
	0..20	278,713,724,302,816	235,789,399,182,528		0.845	49 + 142
	0..30	36,285,348,047,086,752	31,636,080,812,285,208		0.871	48 + 147

was: 10 % cyclic lists and 90 % acyclic lists. Since we had 1,111,111 acyclic lists and for 10 cases of these the exception is thrown (see Sect. 3.5), while none of the 6,543,210 acyclic ones lead to an exception, the failure probability under this profile can be computed as:

$$Pr^f(P) = .10 \cdot 0/6543210 + .9 \cdot 10/1111111 = 8.1 \cdot 10^{-6}$$

How does this probability change if the input lists were distributed differently? Let us consider the case where we have 90 % chance of a list being not null and 10 % chance that the list is null. Obviously there is only one list that is null and the remaining 7, 654, 320 cases are not null. Therefore, we obtain the following probability for failure:

$$Pr^f(P) = .9 \cdot 10/7654320 + .1 \cdot 0/1 = 1.1758 \cdot 10^{-6}$$

The last case is where we use the length of the list in the usage profile. Let us consider there is an 80 % chance that the list length is less than 4, and a 20 % chance the list has at least 4 nodes (and no more than 6 as per the finitization). There are 4, 321 lists with up to 3 nodes and 7, 650, 000 lists of size 4 and more. Notice that none of the lists with 4 or more nodes can cause an exception. The probability for exception is thus:

$$Pr^f(P) = .8 \cdot 10/4321 + .2 \cdot 0/7650000 = 1.85 \cdot 10^{-3}$$

Concluding, the different usage profiles make a substantial difference in the probability of an exception being thrown for the analyzed null pointer dereference. This illustrates the importance of usage profiles when performing probabilistic software analysis, which is in turn able to provide quantitative results tailored for each different (probabilistic) assumption about the usage of the software.

5 Threats to Validity

We used data structures as examples. These and similar examples have been frequently used as case studies in the evaluation of SPF and come as examples with the Korat distribution, making them appropriate for the comparison.

Computing bounds and writing declarative invariants pose extra burden on the users of SPF+BLISS. This is not a part of the technique, and the user may decide not to use the BLISS optimization. Yet BLISS naturally fits in this research as one may conclude from the experiments reported in Table 1.

We did not verify the implementation. For all the subjects where at least two of the three methods completed the analysis within the time bound of 5 h, the resulting counts matched, cross validating their correctness for the cases under investigation.

6 Related Work

Several model counting tools are available but they do not support data structures directly. Birnbaum et al. [6] present an algorithm for counting (boolean) models of propositional formulas. Barvinok's algorithm uses Integer Linear Programming (ILP) to count integer models [4]. As already mentioned, LattE [14] implements (an enhanced version of) Barvinok's algorithm. RelSat solves instances of propositional SAT using constraint satisfaction problem (CSP) lookback techniques [1].

Several (dynamic) symbolic execution techniques encode data-structure constraints using a theory of select/store (e.g. KLEE [10]). In such techniques there is no need to explicitly initialize the references as they can deal with symbolic references. Note however that the counting of data-structure models can not be done simply on the symbolic formulas, using e.g. [11] for counting over SMT constraints. E.g. one can not simply count all the (cyclic and acyclic) lists up to size 100 by applying SMT-based model counting over a constraint that encodes "true". Instead, our procedure, that blends explicit enumeration with symbolic reasoning, could be used.

The SMC tool [29] addresses constraints on strings. It counts model for constraints written in a string language expressive enough to model constraints arising from JavaScript applications and UNIX C utilities. It uses a technique that leverages generating functions as a basic primitive for combinatorial counting, and it is therefore quite different than our approach, which aims at handling arbitrary data structures.

Our work is also related to probabilistic program analysis [21], probabilistic abstract interpretation [30] and probabilistic model checking [22]. We discuss this below.

Probabilistic analysis based on symbolic execution has been described in e.g., [15,18,36]. Geldenhuys et al. [18] considered uniform distributions for the inputs, linear integer arithmetic constraints, and used LattEMacchiato [14] to count solutions of path conditions produced during symbolic execution. Sankaranarayanan et al. [36] and Filieri et al. [15] proposed similar techniques to compute probabilities of violating program assertions. Both techniques remove the restriction of uniform distributions. As with [18] both approaches only consider linear constraints. Sankaranarayanan et al. developed algorithms based on Linear Programming (LP) solvers for under and over-approximations of probabilities.

Filieri et al. used the LattEtool to compute probabilities. Follow-on work provides treatment of nondeterminism [28] and describes statistical exploration of symbolic paths [16]. Another simulation-based approach for the analysis of probabilistic programs has been proposed in [31].

The technique in [7] proposed a compositional quantification of the solution space based on Monte Carlo estimation. The approach can deal with arbitrarily complex numeric constraints over floating-point domains. Bouissou *et al.* [8] and Adje *et al.* [3] handle non-linear numeric constraints with a combination of abstraction based on affine and p-box arithmetic. The approach relies on the use of noise variables to represent the uncertainty of non-linear computations.

Lazy initialization is related to materialization of summary nodes in shape analysis [40]. However its application to model counting is new.

7 Conclusions

We presented an technique for model counting over constraints on complex data structures with numeric fields. The technique uses symbolic execution with lazy initialization to compute the satisfying heap structures, while keeping the constraints on numeric data symbolic. The valid assignments for the numeric constraints are then solved with off-the-shelf model counting procedures that target numeric domain. Further field bounds and various constraint optimizations are used to speed-up the technique. Experimental results highlighted the benefits of the proposed technique.

There are many avenues for future work. First note that it is the responsibility of the user to write the complex (Java) predicates; further the user needs to make sure that the predicates in the usage profile are disjoint. To ease this burden we have defined patterns for some commonly used predicates (such as acyclic and size for linked lists) that can be used and modified easily. In the future we would like to explore established logics, such as separation logic, to simplify the specification task. We will then need to synthesize the Java predicates encoding them. We also plan to explore runtime analysis to derive profiles directly from running systems. Further we plan to apply the model counting technique in the security domain.

References

1. RelSat tool. http://code.google.com/p/relsat/
2. LattE (2013). https://www.math.ucdavis.edu/~latte/
3. Adje, A., Bouissou, O., Goubault-Larrecq, J., Goubault, E., Putot, S.: Static analysis of programs with imprecise probabilistic inputs. In: Cohen, E., Rybalchenko, A. (eds.) VSTTE 2013. LNCS, vol. 8164, pp. 22–47. Springer, Heidelberg (2014)
4. Barvinok, A.I.: A polynomial time algorithm for counting integral points in polyhedra when the dimension is fixed. Math. Oper. Res. **19**(4), 769–779 (1994)
5. Beschastnikh, I., Brun, Y., Schneider, S., Sloan, M., Ernst, M.D.: Leveraging existing instrumentation to automatically infer invariant-constrained models. In: ESEC/FSE, pp. 267–277 (2011)

6. Birnbaum, E., Lozinskii, E.L.: The good old davis-putnam procedure helps counting models. J. Artif. Intell. Res. (JAIR) **10**, 457–477 (1999)
7. Borges, M., Filieri, A., d'Amorim, M., Păsăreanu, C.S., Visser, W.: Compositional solution space quantification for probabilistic software analysis. In: PLDI, pp. 123–132. ACM (2014)
8. Bouissou, O., Goubault, E., Goubault-Larrecq, J., Putot, S.: A generalization of p-boxes to affine arithmetic. Computing **94**, 189–201 (2012)
9. Boyapati, C., Khurshid, S., Marinov, D.: Korat: automated testing based on Java predicates. In: ISSTA, pp. 123–133 (2002)
10. Cadar, C., Dunbar, D., Engler, D.R.: Klee: unassisted and automatic generation of high-coverage tests for complex systems programs. In: OSDI, pp. 209–224 (2008)
11. Chistikov, D.V., Dimitrova, R., Majumdar, R.: Approximate counting in SMT and value estimation for probabilistic programs. In: Baier, C., Tinelli, C. (eds.) TACAS 2015. LNCS, vol. 9035, pp. 320–334. Springer, Heidelberg (2015)
12. Clarke, L.A.: A system to generate test data and symbolically execute programs. IEEE Trans. Soft. Eng. **2**(3), 215–222 (1976)
13. Cormen, T.H.: Introduction to Algorithms, 3rd edn. MIT Press, Cambridge (2009)
14. De Loera, J.A., Dutra, B., Köppe, M., Moreinis, S., Pinto, G., Wu, J.: Software for exact integration of polynomials over polyhedra. ACM Commun. Comput. Algebra **45**(3/4), 169–172 (2012)
15. Filieri, A., Pasareanu, C.S., Visser, W.: Reliability analysis in symbolic pathfinder. In: ICSE, pp. 622–631 (2013)
16. Filieri, A., Pasareanu, C.S., Visser, W., Geldenhuys, J.: Statistical symbolic execution with informed sampling. In: FSE, pp. 437–448 (2014)
17. Galeotti, J.P., Rosner, N., Pombo, CGL., Frias, M.F.: Analysis of invariants for efficient bounded verification. In: ISSTA, USA, pp. 25–36 (2010)
18. Geldenhuys, J., Dwyer, M.B., Visser, W.: Probabilistic symbolic execution. In: ISSTA, pp. 166–176 (2012)
19. Ghezzi, C., Pezzè, M., Sama, M., Tamburrelli, G.: Mining behavior models from user-intensive web applications. In: ICSE, pp. 277–287 (2014)
20. Godefroid, P., Klarlund, N., Sen, K.: Dart: directed automated random testing. In: PLDI, pp. 213–223 (2005)
21. Gordon, A.D., Henzinger, T.A., Nori, A.V., Rajamani, S.K.: Probabilistic programming. In: ICSE FOSE, pp. 167–181 (2014)
22. Hinton, A., Kwiatkowska, M., Norman, G., Parker, D.: PRISM: a tool for automatic verification of probabilistic systems. In: Hermanns, H., Palsberg, J. (eds.) TACAS 2006. LNCS, vol. 3920, pp. 441–444. Springer, Heidelberg (2006)
23. Galeotti, J., Rosner, N., Lopez Pombo, C., Frias, M.F.: Taco: efficient sat-based bounded verification using symmetry breaking and tight bounds. IEEE Trans. Soft. Eng. **39**(9), 1283–1307 (2013)
24. Jackson, D.: Alloy: a lightweight object modelling notation. ACM Trans. Softw. Eng. Methodol. **11**(2), 256–290 (2002)
25. Khurshid, S., Păsăreanu, C.S., Visser, W.: Generalized symbolic execution for model checking and testing. In: Garavel, H., Hatcliff, J. (eds.) TACAS 2003. LNCS, vol. 2619, pp. 553–568. Springer, Heidelberg (2003)
26. King, J.C.: Symbolic execution and program testing. Comm. ACM **19**(7), 385–394 (1976)
27. Lisper, B.: Fully automatic, parametric worst-case execution time analysis. In: Proceedings of the 3rd International Workshop on Worst-Case Execution Time Analysis, WCET, pp. 99–102 (2003)

28. Luckow, K., Păsăreanu, C.S., Dwyer, M.B., Filieri, A., Visser, W.: Exact and approximate probabilistic symbolic execution for nondeterministic programs. In: ASE, pp. 575–586. ACM (2014)
29. Luu, L., Shinde, S., Saxena, P., Demsky, B.: A model counter for constraints over unbounded strings. In: PLDI, p. 57 (2014)
30. Monniaux, D.: An abstract Monte-Carlo method for the analysis of probabilistic programs. In: POPL, pp. 93–101 (2001)
31. Nori, A.V., Hur, C.-K., Rajamani, S.K., Samuel, S.: R2: an efficient mcmc sampler for probabilistic programs. In: AAAI Conference on Artificial Intelligence (AAAI). AAAI, July 2014
32. Pasareanu, C.S., Visser, W., Bushnell, D.H., Geldenhuys, J., Mehlitz, P.C., Rungta, N.: Symbolic pathfinder: integrating symbolic execution with model checking for Java bytecode analysis. Autom. Softw. Eng. 20(3), 391–425 (2013)
33. Pestman, W.R.: Mathematical Statistics. De Gruyter, Berlin (2009)
34. Phan, Q.-S., Malacaria, P., Păsăreanu, C.S., D'Amorim, M.: Quantifying information leaks using reliability analysis. In: SPIN, pp. 105–108. ACM (2014)
35. Rosner, N., Geldenhuys, J., Aguirre, N., Visser, W., Frias, M.F.: Bliss: improved symbolic execution by bounded lazy initialization with sat support. IEEE Trans. Soft. Eng. 99, 639–660 (2015)
36. Sankaranarayanan, S., Chakarov, A., Gulwani, S.: Static analysis for probabilistic programs: inferring whole program properties from finitely many paths. In: PLDI, pp. 447–458 (2013)
37. Tillmann, N., de Halleux, J.: Pex-white box test generation for NET. In: Beckert, B., Hähnle, R. (eds.) TAP 2008. LNCS, vol. 4966, pp. 134–153. Springer, Heidelberg (2008)
38. Turjan, A., Kienhuis, B., Deprettere, E.F.: A compile time based approach for solving out-of-order communication in Kahn process networks. In: ASAP, pp. 17–28 (2002)
39. Visser, W., Pasareanu, C.S., Pelanek, R.: Test input generation for Java containers using state matching. In: ISSTA, pp. 37–48 (2006)
40. Yorsh, G., Reps, T.W., Sagiv, M.: Symbolically computing most-precise abstract operations for shape analysis. In: Jensen, K., Podelski, A. (eds.) TACAS 2004. LNCS, vol. 2988, pp. 530–545. Springer, Heidelberg (2004)
41. Zuliani, P., Platzer, A., Clarke, E.M.: Bayesian statistical model checking with application to Simulink/Stateflow verification. In: HSCC, pp. 243–252. ACM (2010)

Parallel SAT-Based Parameterised Three-Valued Model Checking

Nils Timm[(⊠)], Stefan Gruner, and Prince Sibanda

Department of Computer Science, University of Pretoria, Pretoria, South Africa
{ntimm,sgruner}@cs.up.ac.za

Abstract. *Parameterisation* in three-valued model checking (PMC) allows to establish logical connections between unknown parts in state space models. The application of parameterisation enhances the precision of models without increasing their state space, but it leads to an exponential growth of the number of model checking instances that have to be checked consecutively. Here, we introduce a technique for PMC via parallel SAT solving which enables us to significantly reduce the time overhead of PMC by exploiting similarities among the instances. We define bounded semantics and a propositional logic encoding of PMC. Moreover, we introduce a concept for sharing clauses between the instances of parallel SAT-based PMC. Our experiments show that our new approach leads to a practically relevant speed-up of parameterised three-valued model checking.

1 Introduction

Three-valued predicate abstraction [18,22] is an established technique in software verification. It proceeds by generating a state space model of the system to be analysed over the values *true*, *false* and *unknown*, where the latter value is used to represent the loss of information due to abstraction. The evaluation of temporal logic properties on such models is known as *three-valued model checking* (3MC) [7,9,10]. In case of an *unknown* result in verification, the abstraction is iteratively and automatically refined by adding more predicates over the variables of the system until a level of abstraction is reached where the property can be either definitely proved or refuted. Refinement does, however, not guarantee that eventually a three-valued model can be constructed that is both precise enough for a definite outcome and small enough to be manageable with the available computational resources.

In [23] we introduced *parameterised three-valued model checking* (PMC) as an extension of 3MC. Predicates and transitions in PMC models can be either associated with the values *true, false, unknown*, or with expressions over *Boolean parameters*. Parameterisation is an alternative way to state that the value of certain predicates or transitions is actually not known and that the checked property has to yield the same result under each possible parameter instantiation. PMC is thus conducted via evaluating a property under all parameter instantiations and checking whether the results are consistent. Parameterisation particularly

B. Fischer and J. Geldenhuys (Eds.): SPIN 2015, LNCS 9232, pp. 242–259, 2015.
DOI: 10.1007/978-3-319-23404-5_16

allows to establish *logical connections* between unknowns in the abstract model: While unknown parts in 3MC are never related to each other, the parameterisation approach enables to represent facts like 'a certain pair of transitions has unknown but *complementary* truth values', or 'the value of a predicate is unknown but remains *unchanged* along all states of a certain path'. Such facts can be automatically derived from the system to be verified, and covering these facts in a model can be crucial for the success and the efficiency of model checking. We showed that combining classical refinement and parameterisation in abstraction-based model checking is highly suited for obtaining the necessary precision for a definite result while keeping the state space small. However, parameterisation generally leads to an *exponential* increase in time complexity, since any property of interest must be checked for each possible parameter instantiation.

Here, we introduce a technique for parameterised three-valued model checking via parallel SAT solving which enables us to considerably reduce the time overhead of PMC by effectively exploiting similarities between the occurring instances. Our approach is based on *bounded model checking* (BMC) [4]. We define bounded semantics for PMC and we introduce a parameterised propositional encoding of PMC problems. In order to obtain the overall result of an encoded PMC problem, the satisfiability of each possible parameter instantiation of the encoding is tested and it is checked whether all single results are consistent.

An integral part of modern satisfiability solving algorithms is *conflict-driven clause learning* [5]: SAT solvers search for a satisfying assignment of the input formula by successively selecting unassigned Boolean variables, assigning them to either *true* or *false*, and propagating the resulting constraints to the clauses of the formula. In case the solver decisions lead to an unsatisfied clause, a so-called conflict clause is learned and added to the formula. Then the solver tracks back by revising a former assignment decision and continuing the search from this point. Clause learning enables to quickly prune parts of the search space and is thus crucial for the performance of SAT solving. In our approach, we exploit the fact that the instances associated with a parameterised encoding exhibit considerable similarities in terms of large common subformulae. Thus, a conflict clause that was learned during the SAT test of one instance can be shared with another instance that is SAT checked at the same time, provided that the new clause was derived based on a common part of the two instances.

We implemented a parallel SAT-based model checker for PMC problems. The checks of the instances of a parameterised encoding are performed concurrently and clauses that have been learned are are shared between the instances. In experiments we show that our concept of clause sharing in parallel SAT-based PMC leads to substantial savings in verification time.

2 Background

We start with an introduction to *pure* and *parameterised* three-valued models. The key feature of these models is a third truth value $\perp$ (i.e. *unknown*) for transitions and labellings, which is used to model uncertainty. The parameterised case additionally allows *Boolean parameter expressions* for transitions and labellings, which enables to establish logical connections between unknown parts.

Definition 1 (Parameterised Three-Valued Kripke Structure). *A parameterised three-valued Kripke structure over a set of atomic predicates AP and a set of Boolean parameters $X = \{x_1, \ldots, x_m\}$ is a parameterised tuple $M(\overset{m}{x}) = (S, s_0, R(\overset{m}{x}), L(\overset{m}{x}))$ where*

- *S is a finite set of states and $s_0 \in S$ is the initial state,*
- *$R(\overset{m}{x}) : S \times S \to \{true, \bot, false\} \cup B(X)$ is a transition function with $\forall s \in S : \exists s' \in S : R(\overset{m}{x})(s, s') \in \{true, \bot\} \cup B(X)$ where $B(X)$ denotes the set of Boolean expressions over X,*
- *$L(\overset{m}{x}) : S \times AP \to \{true, \bot, false\} \cup B(X)$ is a labelling function that associates a truth value or a parameter expression with each predicate in each state.*

Note that $(\overset{m}{x})$ is an abbreviation for the parameter tuple $(x_1, \ldots, x_m)$. An *instantiation* of a parameterised three-valued Kripke structure $M(\overset{m}{x})$ is a *pure* three-valued Kripke structure $M(\overset{m}{a})$ where $(\overset{m}{a}) \in \{true, false\}^m$. Hence, all parameters are substituted by *Boolean* truth values. However, predicates and transitions that were not parameterised in $M(\overset{m}{x})$ may still hold the value *unknown* in $M(\overset{m}{a})$. A structure is also *pure* if $X = \varnothing$. If the tuple of parameters is clear from the context we will just refer to M, R, L. An example for a pure three-valued Kripke structure M and a parameterised Kripke structure $M(x_1)$ is depicted below.

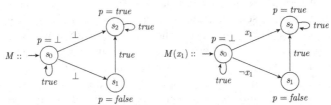

In abstraction-based model checking a parameterised three-valued Kripke structure can be obtained by refining a pure three-valued Kripke structure [23]. For instance, if the transitions (s_0, s_1) and (s_0, s_2) of our example structure M correspond to a complementary branch (e.g. *if-then-else* or *while-do*) in the modelled system, then $M(x_1)$ is a sound refinement of M.

In the following, we first introduce model checking for pure three-valued Kripke structures and then generalise it to the parameterised case. A path π of a pure three-valued Kripke structure M is an infinite sequence of states $s_0 s_1 s_2 \ldots$ with $R(s_i, s_{i+1}) \in \{true, \bot\}$. π_i denotes the i-th state of π, whereas π^i denotes the i-th suffix $\pi_i \pi_{i+1} \pi_{i+2} \ldots$ of π. By Π_M we denote the set of all paths of M starting in the initial state. We use the temporal logic LTL for specifying properties with regard to paths.

Definition 2 (Syntax of LTL). *Let AP be a set of atomic predicates and $p \in AP$. The syntax of LTL formulae ψ is given by*

$$\psi ::= p \mid \neg\psi \mid \psi \vee \psi \mid \psi \wedge \psi \mid \mathbf{X}\psi \mid \mathbf{G}\psi \mid \mathbf{F}\psi \mid \psi\mathbf{U}\psi.$$

Due to the extended domain of truth values in three-valued Kripke structures, the evaluation of LTL formulae is not based on classical two-valued logic. In three-valued model checking we operate under the three-valued Kleene logic $\mathcal{L}_3$ [12] whose semantics is given by the truth tables below.

$\wedge$	$true$	$\perp$	$false$
$true$	$true$	$\perp$	$false$
$\perp$	$\perp$	$\perp$	$false$
$false$	$false$	$false$	$false$

$\vee$	$true$	$\perp$	$false$
$true$	$true$	$true$	$true$
$\perp$	$true$	$\perp$	$\perp$
$false$	$true$	$\perp$	$false$

$\neg$	
$true$	$false$
$\perp$	$\perp$
$false$	$true$

$\mathcal{L}_3$ has a reflexive *truth ordering* $\leq_{\mathcal{L}_3}$ (in words: 'less or equally true as') with $false \leq_{\mathcal{L}_3} \perp \leq_{\mathcal{L}_3} true$. Based on $\mathcal{L}_3$, LTL formulae can be evaluated on paths of three-valued Kripke structures according to the following definition.

Definition 3 (Three-Valued Evaluation of LTL). *Let* $M = (S, s_0, R, L)$ *over AP be a pure three-valued Kripke structure. Then the evaluation of an LTL formula* ψ *on a path* $\pi \in \Pi_M$, *written* $[\pi \models \psi]$, *is defined as follows*

$$
\begin{aligned}
[\pi \models p] \quad &:= \quad L(\pi_0, p) \\
[\pi \models \neg\psi] \quad &:= \quad \neg\,[\pi \models \psi] \\
[\pi \models \psi \vee \psi'] \quad &:= \quad [\pi \models \psi] \vee [\pi \models \psi'] \\
[\pi \models \mathbf{G}\psi] \quad &:= \quad \bigwedge_{i \in \mathbb{N}} (R(\pi_i, \pi_{i+1}) \wedge [\pi^i \models \psi]) \\
[\pi \models \mathbf{F}\psi] \quad &:= \quad \bigvee_{i \in \mathbb{N}} ([\pi^i \models \psi] \wedge \bigwedge_{j=0}^{i-1} R(\pi_j, \pi_{j+1}))
\end{aligned}
$$

Due to space limitations we have omitted the definitions for the operators $\wedge$, **X** and **U**. The complete definitions can e.g. be found in [21,25]. The evaluation of LTL formulae on entire three-valued Kripke structures is what is called *three-valued model checking* (3MC) [7,9].

Definition 4 (Three-Valued LTL Model Checking). *Let* $M = (S, s_0, R, L)$ *over AP be a three-valued Kripke structure. Moreover, let* ψ *be an LTL formula over AP. The universal value of* ψ *in* M, *written* $[M \models_U \psi]$, *is defined as*

$$
[M \models_U \psi] \quad := \quad \bigwedge_{\pi \in \Pi_M} [\pi \models \psi]
$$

The existential value of ψ *in* M, *written* $[M \models_E \psi]$, *is defined as*

$$
[M \models_E \psi] \quad := \quad \bigvee_{\pi \in \Pi_M} [\pi \models \psi]
$$

Universal model checking can always be transferred into existential model checking based on the equation $[M \models_U \psi] = \neg[M \models_E \neg\psi]$.

In 3MC there exist three possible outcomes: *true*, *false* and $\perp$. For our example Kripke structure M we get $[M \models_U \mathbf{G}\neg p] = \neg[M \models_E \mathbf{F}p] = \perp$ and $[M \models_U \mathbf{GF}\neg p] = \neg[M \models_E \mathbf{FG}p] = \perp$. Hence, M is not precise enough for a definite result in these verification tasks. $\mathbf{G}\neg p$ is a temporal logic formula that is a typical example of a universal safety property, whereas $\mathbf{GF}\neg p$ is an example of a liveness property. Safety and liveness are the most vital requirements in software verification. In our approach, we therefore particularly focus on these two kinds of properties, or rather their existential counterparts $\mathbf{F}p$ and $\mathbf{FG}p$. From now on, we only consider the existential case, since it is the basis for *bounded* model checking which we later apply.

3MC reduces to two-valued model checking (2MC) if the Kripke structure M is actually two-valued, i.e. $R^{-1}(\bot) = \varnothing$ and $L^{-1}(\bot) = \varnothing$. In this case, only definite outcomes are possible. Moreover, 3MC can always be reduced to two instances of 2MC if the LTL formula is restricted to LTL^+, which is the negation-free fragment of LTL. LTL^+ formulae are evaluated on *complement-closed* Kripke structures. In these structures each $p \in AP$ has a complementary $\bar{p} \in AP$ such that $L(s,p) = \neg L(s,\bar{p})$. Every Kripke structure can be straightforwardly extended to a complement-closed one, without increasing the number of states. For the evaluation on complement-closed Kripke structures, each LTL formula can be transferred into an equivalent LTL^+ formula. Thus, the restriction to LTL^+ does not limit the expressiveness of our approach. The reduction of 3MC to two instances of 2MC is based on *completions* of complement-closed structures.

Definition 5 (Completion). *Let $M = (S, s_0, R, L)$ over AP be a three-valued Kripke structure. Then $M^p = (S, s_0, R^p, L^p)$ is the* pessimistic completion *and $M^o = (S, s_0, R^o, L^o)$ is the* optimistic completion *with $\forall s, s' \in S$ and $\forall p \in AP$:*

$$L^p(s,p) := \begin{cases} false & \text{if } L(s,p) = \bot \\ L(s,p) & else \end{cases} \quad R^p(s,s') := \begin{cases} false & \text{if } R(s,s') = \bot \\ R(s,s') & else \end{cases}$$

$$L^o(s,p) := \begin{cases} true & \text{if } L(s,p) = \bot \\ L(s,p) & else \end{cases} \quad R^o(s,s') := \begin{cases} true & \text{if } R(s,s') = \bot \\ R(s,s') & else \end{cases}$$

From [8] we now get the following theorem that allows us to reduce three-valued model checking to two-valued model checking.

Theorem 1. *Let $M = (S, s_0, R, L)$ be a complement-closed three-valued Kripke structure and ψ an LTL^+ formula. Then the following holds:*

$$[M \models_E \psi] = \begin{cases} true & \text{if } [M^p \models_E \psi] = true \\ false & \text{if } [M^o \models_E \psi] = false \\ \bot & else \end{cases}$$

Hence, if a formula holds for the pessimistic completion we can conclude that it also holds for the three-valued Kripke structure. The same applies to *false* results obtained for the optimistic completion. All definitions wrt. pure 3MC can be straightforwardly generalised to *parameterised* three-valued model checking (PMC) [23], since PMC reduces to multiple instances of pure 3MC. In PMC we consider all parameter instantiations of a parameterised Kripke structure.

Definition 6 (Parameterised Three-Valued LTL$^+$ Model Checking). *Let* $M(\overset{m}{\overrightarrow{x}}) = (S, s_0, R(\overset{m}{\overrightarrow{x}}), L(\overset{m}{\overrightarrow{x}}))$ *be a parameterised three-valued Kripke structure over* AP *and* $X = \{x_1, \ldots, x_m\}$*. Moreover, let* ψ *be an LTL$^+$ formula over* AP*. The existential value of* ψ *in* $M(\overset{m}{\overrightarrow{x}})$*, written* $[M(\overset{m}{\overrightarrow{x}}) \models_E \psi]$*, is defined as*

$$[M(\overset{m}{\overrightarrow{x}}) \models_{E,k} \psi] := \begin{cases} true & \text{if } \forall(\overset{m}{\overrightarrow{a}}) \in \{t, f\}^m \ ([M(\overset{m}{\overrightarrow{a}}) \models_{E,k} \psi] = true) \\ false & \text{if } \forall(\overset{m}{\overrightarrow{a}}) \in \{t, f\}^m \ ([M(\overset{m}{\overrightarrow{a}}) \models_{E,k} \psi] = false) \\ \bot & else \end{cases}$$

Thus, if checking a temporal logic property yields *true* for all instantiations, this result is transferred to the parameterised Kripke structure. The same holds for *false* results for all instantiations. In all other cases PMC returns *unknown*. For our example $M(x_1)$, we get $[M(x_1) \models_E \mathbf{F}p] = true$ since $\mathbf{F}p$ holds existentially for both $M(true)$ and $M(false)$. By the same argumentation we can show that $[M(x_1) \models_E \mathbf{FG}p]$ also yields *true*. In contrast to the pure three-valued M, the parameterised $M(x_1)$ captures the fact that the transition values of (s_0, s_1) and (s_0, s_2) are unknown but also *complementary*, which gives us the necessary precision for the definite verification results. In the remainder of this work we will show how PMC problems can be encoded in propositional logic and then efficiently solved via SAT solving with clause sharing. A prerequisite for the encoding is to *bound* the length of the considered paths in model checking.

3   Bounded Semantics

Bounded model checking (BMC) [3,4] via satisfiability solving requires to consider finite prefixes of paths, bounded in length by some $k \in \mathbb{N}$. Such finite prefixes $\pi_0 \ldots \pi_k$ can still represent infinite paths if the prefix has a *loop*, i.e. the last state π_k has a successor state that is also part of the prefix.

Definition 7 (k-Loop). *Let* π *be a path of a three-valued Kripke structure* M *and let* $l, k \in \mathbb{N}$ *with* $l \le k$*. Then* π *has a* (k, l)*-loop if* $R(\pi_k, \pi_l) \in \{true, \bot\}$ *and* π *is of the form* $u \cdot v^\omega$ *where* $u = \pi_0 \ldots \pi_{l-1}$ *and* $v = \pi_l \ldots \pi_k$*. Moreover,* π *has a k-loop if there exists an* $l \in \mathbb{N}$ *with* $l \le k$ *such that* π *has a* (k, l)*-loop.*

For the bounded evaluation of temporal logic formulae on paths of Kripke structures we have to distinguish between paths *with* and *without* a k-loop.

Definition 8 (Three-Valued Bounded Evaluation of LTL$^+$). *Let* $M = (S, s_0, R, L)$ *over* AP *be a complement-closed three-valued Kripke structure, let* $k \in \mathbb{N}$ *and let* π *be a path of* M *without a k-loop. Then the k-bounded evaluation of an LTL$^+$ formula* ψ *on* π*, written* $[\pi \models_k^i \psi]$ *where* $i \in \mathbb{N}$ *with* $i \le k$ *denotes the current position along the path, is inductively defined as follows*

$$\begin{aligned}
[\pi \models_k^i p] \quad &:= \ L(\pi_i, p) \\
[\pi \models_k^i \psi \vee \psi'] \quad &:= \ [\pi \models_k^i \psi] \ \vee \ [\pi \models_k^i \psi'] \\
[\pi \models_k^i \mathbf{G}\psi] \quad &:= \ false \\
[\pi \models_k^i \mathbf{F}\psi] \quad &:= \ \bigvee_{j=i}^{k}([\pi \models_k^j \psi] \wedge \bigwedge_{l=i}^{j-1} R(\pi_l, \pi_{l+1}))
\end{aligned}$$

If π has a k-loop, then $[\pi \models_k^i \psi] := [\pi^i \models \psi]$. Moreover, the existential value of ψ in M under the bounded semantics is $[M \models_{E,k} \psi] := \bigvee_{\pi \in \Pi_M} [\pi \models_k^0 \psi]$.

The bounded evaluation of LTL$^+$ approximates the unbounded evaluation wrt. the truth ordering of $\mathcal{L}_3$: $[M \models_{E,k} \psi] \leq_{\mathcal{L}_3} [M \models_E \psi]$. Hence, all *true* results in three-valued BMC can be transferred to the corresponding unbounded case, whereas *unknown* and *false* results do not allow to draw such conclusions about the unbounded case. At least, a *false* result for a bound k tells us that there is definitely no path prefix of length k for which ψ holds. Moreover, a *false* result can be transferred to the unbounded case, if k has reached a *completeness threshold*, which can be derived based on M and ψ [4]. For instance, the completeness threshold for a safety formula ψ is linear in the number of states of M. If all possible values for k are considered, then the bounded semantics is equivalent to the unbounded one: $[M \models_E \psi] = \bigvee_{k \in \mathbb{N}} [M \models_{E,k} \psi]$. The bounded semantics for 3MC can be straightforwardly extended to the parameterised case, as PMC reduces to multiple instances of pure 3MC.

Definition 9 (Bounded Parameterised Three-Valued Model Checking).
Let $M(\overset{m}{x}) = (S, s_0, R(\overset{m}{x}), L(\overset{m}{x}))$ be a parameterised three-valued Kripke structure over AP and $X = \{x_1, \ldots, x_m\}$. Moreover, let ψ be an LTL$^+$ formula over AP and $k \in \mathbb{N}$. The existential value of ψ in $M(\overset{m}{x})$ under the bounded semantics, written $[M(\overset{m}{x}) \models_{E,k} \psi]$, is defined as

$$[M(\overset{m}{x}) \models_{E,k} \psi] := \begin{cases} true & if \; \forall (\overset{m}{a}) \in \{t,f\}^m \; ([M(\overset{m}{a}) \models_{E,k} \psi] = true) \\ false & if \; \forall (\overset{m}{a}) \in \{t,f\}^m \; ([M(\overset{m}{a}) \models_{E,k} \psi] = false) \\ \bot & else \end{cases}$$

BMC is typically performed incrementally, i.e. the bound is iteratively increased until the property of interest can be either proven or the completeness threshold is reached. For our running example from the previous section, we require the following iterations in order to prove that $\mathbf{F}p$ holds existentially for $M(x_1)$.

$$[M(x_1) \models_{E,0} \mathbf{F}p] = \bot \quad [M(x_1) \models_{E,1} \mathbf{F}p] = \bot \quad [M(x_1) \models_{E,2} \mathbf{F}p] = true$$

For $k = 0$ we can only consider the state s_0 where p is $\bot$. For $k = 1$ the prefixes $(s_0 s_1)$ and $(s_0 s_2)$ are considered. Here $\mathbf{F}p$ holds for the instantiation $M(true)$ but not for $M(false)$. Thus, the overall result is still $\bot$. For $k = 2$ we get under both instantiations a prefix where finally p holds. Next, we will see how bounded PMC can be reduced to satisfiability solving.

4 Propositional Logic Encoding

Now we reduce bounded parameterised three-valued model checking to the new satisfiability problem SAT$_{X3}$. For a parameterised three-valued Kripke structure $M(\overset{m}{x}) = (S, s_0, R(\overset{m}{x}), L(\overset{m}{x}))$ over AP and X, an LTL$^+$ formula ψ and a bound $k \in \mathbb{N}$, a propositional logic formula $[M(\overset{m}{x}), \psi]_k$ is constructed such that

$$[M(\overset{m}{x}) \models_{E,k} \psi] = SAT_{X3}([M(\overset{m}{x}), \psi]_k)$$

$[\![M(\overset{m}{\vec{x}}), \psi]\!]_k$ is defined over a set of Boolean atoms, the set of Boolean parameters X, and the constants *true*, *false* and $\bot$. Hence, $[\![M(\overset{m}{\vec{x}}), \psi]\!]_k$ is parameterised wrt. X. We will show that solving SAT_{X3} reduces to solving classical SAT for each possible parameter instantiation. First, we give a step-by-step description on how $[\![M(\overset{m}{\vec{x}}), \psi]\!]_k$ is constructed for a given bounded PMC problem.

A propositional logic encoding of bounded model checking problems for Kripke structures with three-valued labelling functions was introduced in [25]. Here we generalise it to our *parameterised* three-valued Kripke structures. The construction of $[\![M(\overset{m}{\vec{x}}), \psi]\!]_k$ is divided into the translation of the Kripke structure $M(\overset{m}{\vec{x}})$ into a formula $[\![M(\overset{m}{\vec{x}})]\!]_k$ and the translation of the temporal logic property ψ into a formula $[\![\psi]\!]_k$. We start with the encoding of the Kripke structure $M(\overset{m}{\vec{x}}) = (S, s_0, R(\overset{m}{\vec{x}}), L(\overset{m}{\vec{x}}))$, which first requires to encode its states as Boolean formulae. For this, we introduce a set of Boolean atoms $\{A, B, \ldots\}$. Let L be the set of propositional logic formulae over $\{A, B, \ldots\}$ and the constants *true* and *false*. Then an encoding of the states of a Kripke structure is defined as follows.

Definition 10 (State Encoding). *Let* $M(\overset{m}{\vec{x}}) = (S, s_0, R(\overset{m}{\vec{x}}), L(\overset{m}{\vec{x}}))$ *be a parameterised Kripke structure. A Boolean encoding of its states corresponds to an injective mapping* $e : S \to L$ *where* $\forall s \in S : e(s)$ *is a conjunction of literals.*

The states s_0, s_1, and s_2 of our example structure $M(x_1)$ can be encoded over the set of atoms $\{A, B\}$ as follows: $e(s_0) = \neg A \wedge \neg B$ $e(s_1) = \neg A \wedge B$ $e(s_2) = A \wedge \neg B$.

An *assignment* is a mapping $\tau : \{A, B, \ldots\} \to \{true, false\}$. For instance, the assignment $\tau(A) = false$ and $\tau(B) = true$ characterises the state s_1, since it is the only assignment that makes the encoding $e(s_1)$ *true*. An entire Kripke structure can now be translated into the formula $[\![M(\overset{m}{\vec{x}})]\!]_k$ that characterises path prefixes of length k in $M(\overset{m}{\vec{x}})$. Since we consider states as parts of such prefixes, we have to extend the encoding of states by index values $i \in \{0, \ldots, k\}$ where i denotes the position along a path prefix. For example, $e(s_1)_i = \neg A_i \wedge B_i$ refers to s_1 as the i-th state of a certain prefix. Moreover, we get an extended set of indexed atoms $\{A_0, B_0, \ldots, A_k, B_k, \ldots\}$.

Definition 11 (Kripke Structure Encoding). *Let* $M(\overset{m}{\vec{x}}) = (S, s_0, R(\overset{m}{\vec{x}}), L(\overset{m}{\vec{x}}))$ *be a parameterised three-valued Kripke structure and* e *an encoding of its states. We define* $Init_0$ *as the predicate characterising the initial state of* $M(\overset{m}{\vec{x}})$ *with*

$$Init_0 := e(s_0)_0$$

and $T_{i,i+1}$ *as the predicate that characterises the transitions of* $M(\overset{m}{\vec{x}})$ *with*

$$T_{i,i+1} := \bigvee_{s \in S} \bigvee_{s' \in S} e(s)_i \wedge e(s')_{i+1} \wedge R(\overset{m}{\vec{x}})(s, s').$$

Then the entire encoding of $M(\overset{m}{\vec{x}})$ *for a bound* $k \in \mathbb{N}$ *is defined as*

$$[\![M(\overset{m}{\vec{x}})]\!]_k := Init_0 \wedge \bigwedge_{i=0}^{k-1} T_{i,i+1}$$

Thus, for our example $M(x_1)$ we get $Init_0 = \neg A_0 \wedge \neg B_0$ and $T_{i,i+1} = (\neg A_i \wedge \neg B_i \wedge \neg A_{i+1} \wedge \neg B_{i+1} \wedge true) \vee (\neg A_i \wedge \neg B_i \wedge \neg A_{i+1} \wedge B_{i+1} \wedge \neg x_1) \vee (\neg A_i \wedge \neg B_i \wedge A_{i+1} \wedge \neg B_{i+1} \wedge x_1) \vee (\neg A_i \wedge B_i \wedge A_{i+1} \wedge \neg B_{i+1} \wedge true) \vee (A_i \wedge \neg B_i \wedge A_{i+1} \wedge \neg B_{i+1} \wedge true)$.

As we can see, each clause of $T_{i,i+1}$ encodes a transition of the Kripke structure, where the last literal, resp. constant, of each clause encodes the value of the transition. The assignment $\tau(A_0) = false$, $\tau(B_0) = false$, $\tau(A_1) = true$ and $\tau(B_1) = false$ characterises that the first transition of a k-prefix $s_0 \ldots s_k$ is the transition (s_0, s_2) which is parameterised by x_1.

The second part of the encoding concerns the temporal logic formula ψ. Again, we need to distinguish the cases where ψ is evaluated on a path prefix *with* and *without* a loop.

Definition 12 (LTL$^+$Encoding without Loop). *Let p be an atomic predicate, ψ and ψ' LTL$^+$ formulae, and $k, i \in \mathbb{N}$ with $i \leq k$.*

$$[\![p]\!]_k^i \quad := \quad \bigvee_{s \in S} e(s)_i \wedge L(s,p) \qquad\qquad [\![\mathbf{G}\psi]\!]_k^i := \quad false$$
$$[\![\psi \vee \psi']\!]_k^i := \quad [\![\psi]\!]_k^i \vee [\![\psi']\!]_k^i \qquad\qquad [\![\mathbf{F}\psi]\!]_k^i := \quad \bigvee_{j=i}^{k} [\![\psi]\!]_k^j$$

For instance, encoding the LTL$^+$ formula $\mathbf{F}p$ for our example Kripke structure $M(x_1)$ and for bound $k = 2$ yields the following propositional logic formula

$$[\![\mathbf{F}p]\!]_2^0 = \bigvee_{i=0}^{2} ((\neg A_i \wedge \neg B_i \wedge \bot) \vee (\neg A_i \wedge B_i \wedge false) \vee (A_i \wedge \neg B_i \wedge true))$$

Encoding temporal logic formulae for the evaluation on prefixes *with* a loop additionally requires to explicitly refer to the starting position l of the loop.

Definition 13 (LTL$^+$Encoding with Loop). *Let p be an atomic predicate, ψ and ψ' LTL$^+$ formulae, and $k, i, l \in \mathbb{N}$ with $i, l \leq k$.*

$$_l[\![p]\!]_k^i \quad := \quad \bigvee_{s \in S} e(s)_i \wedge L(s,p) \qquad _l[\![\mathbf{G}\psi]\!]_k^i := \quad \bigwedge_{j=\min(i,l)}^{k} {}_l[\![\psi]\!]_k^j$$
$$_l[\![\psi \vee \psi']\!]_k^i := \quad {}_l[\![\psi]\!]_k^i \vee {}_l[\![\psi']\!]_k^i \qquad _l[\![\mathbf{F}\psi]\!]_k^i := \quad \bigvee_{j=\min(i,l)}^{k} {}_l[\![\psi]\!]_k^j$$

For our example we have that $_l[\![\mathbf{F}p]\!]_2^0 = [\![\mathbf{F}p]\!]_2^0$ for each possible l. Thus, in this particular case a distinction between loop and loop-free prefixes is not necessary. For the overall encoding we get $[\![M(x_1), \mathbf{F}p]\!]_2 := [\![M(x_1)]\!]_2 \wedge [\![\mathbf{F}p]\!]_2^0$

The general case requires to distinguish between loop and loop-free prefixes. For this, a subformula $T_{k,l}$ (similar to the transition encoding) is used that characterises all (k,l)-loops of the encoded structure. The general encoding is

$$[\![M(\vec{x}^m), \psi]\!]_k := [\![M(\vec{x}^m)]\!]_k \wedge ([\![\psi]\!]_k^0 \vee \bigvee_{l=0}^{k} (T_{k,l} \wedge {}_l[\![\psi]\!]_k^0))$$

Since $[\![M(\vec{x}^m), \psi]\!]_k$ is not only defined over atoms but also over parameters from X and the constant $\bot$, standard satisfiability testing is not straightforwardly applicable. Thus, we define our new satisfiability problem SAT$_{X3}$ for our propositional logic encoding, which reduces to multiple instances of classical SAT.

Definition 14 (SAT$_{X3}$). *Let $F = [\![M(\overset{m}{x}), \psi]\!]_k$ be a propositional logic encoding of a bounded PMC problem $[M(\overset{m}{x}) \models_{E,k} \psi]$. Then*

$$SAT_{X3}(F) := \begin{cases} true & if\ \forall(\overset{m}{a}) \in \{t, f\}^m\ (\text{SAT}([\![M(\overset{m}{x}), \psi]\!]_k^p[(\overset{m}{x})/(\overset{m}{a})]) = true) \\ false & if\ \qquad\qquad \text{SAT}([\![M(\overset{m}{x}), \psi]\!]_k^o) = false \\ \bot & else \end{cases}$$

where $[\![M(\overset{m}{x}), \psi]\!]_k^p$ is the pessimistic completion of $[\![M(\overset{m}{x}), \psi]\!]_k$, i.e. the formula obtained by substituting all occurrences of $\bot$ by false, and $[\![M(\overset{m}{x}), \psi]\!]_k^o$ is the optimistic completion obtained by substituting all occurrences of $\bot$ by true. Moreover, $[\![M(\overset{m}{x}), \psi]\!]_k^p[(\overset{m}{x})/(\overset{m}{a})]$ denotes the substitution of $(\overset{m}{x})$ in $[\![M(\overset{m}{x}), \psi]\!]_k^p$ by $(\overset{m}{a})$.

Here SAT(F) returns *true* for a propositional logic formula F if there exists an assignment that makes the formula *true*, whereas it returns *false* if there does not exist such an assignment. Note that SAT($[\![M(\overset{m}{x}), \psi]\!]_k^o) = false$ is equivalent to $\forall(\overset{m}{a}) \in \{t, f\}^m(\text{SAT}([\![M(\overset{m}{x}), \psi]\!]_k^o)[(\overset{m}{x})/(\overset{m}{a})] = false)$. Hence, checking whether SAT$_{X3}$ yields *false* requires a single SAT test only. The result of the overall SAT$_{X3}$ test is equivalent to the result of the encoded model checking problem:

Theorem 2. *Let $M(\overset{m}{x})$ be a parameterised three-valued Kripke structure over a set of atomic predicates, let ψ be an LTL$^+$ formula, and $k \in \mathbb{N}$. Then*

$$[M(\overset{m}{x}) \models_{E,k} \psi] = SAT_{X3}([\![M(\overset{m}{x}), \psi]\!]_k)$$

Proof. See http://www.cs.up.ac.za/cs/ntimm/ProofTheorem2.pdf

Thus, bounded PMC can be reduced to multiple instances of SAT. For our example encoding $[\![M(x_1), \mathbf{F}p]\!]_2$ there exists a satisfying assignment for each possible instantiation which allows us to conclude that $[M(x_1) \models_{E,2} \mathbf{F}p] = true$.

5 Solving SAT$_{X3}$ with Parallelisation and Clause Sharing

In this section we show how the SAT checks necessary to solve SAT$_{X3}$ can be simultaneously performed by a parallel composition of solvers and additionally accelerated by *clause sharing*. SAT solvers require the input formula to be in conjunctive normal form (CNF). A CNF formula F over a set Boolean variables V is a conjunction of clauses, where each clause is a disjunction of literals. The *Tseitin transformation* [24] allows to translate any propositional formula into a SAT-equivalent CNF formula which length is linear in the size of the original formula. Thus, we assume that our encoding $F = [\![M(\overset{m}{x}), \psi]\!]_k$ has been transformed into CNF, where F is defined over the indexed atoms of the encoding, the parameter set $X = \{x_1, \ldots, x_m\}$ and the constants *true*, *false* and $\bot$. Remember that checking SAT$_{X3}$ requires to test the satisfiability of the pessimistic completion under each possible parameter instantiation. Instantiating the parameters of the encoding is equivalent to adding an *assumption* for each $x \in X$. Assumptions can be implemented by an *assignment* $\tau : X \to \{true, false\}$. By $F|_\tau$ we denote the formula F under the assumption that the parameters are instantiated with regard to τ. The set of assumptions over X that we have to consider is

$$ASS = \left\{\bigcup_{i=1}^{m}\{(x_i, a_i)\} \mid a_i \in \{true, false\}\right\}$$

For our running example we get $ASS = \{\tau_1, \tau_2\}$ with $\tau_1 = \{(x_1, false)\}$ and $\tau_2 = \{(x_1, true)\}$. Checking SAT_{X3} requires to distinguish the cases where $\bot$ is assigned to $true$ resp. $false$. Only for the pessimistic case $\bot = false$ we need to consider each possible parameter instantiation. We thus extend the domain of our assumptions to $X \cup \{\bot\}$ and introduce the pessimistic set of assumptions $ASS^p := \{\tau \cup \{(\bot, false)\} \mid \tau \in ASS\}$ and the optimistic assumption $\tau^o = \{(\bot, true)\}$. The problem SAT_{X3} for F can now be reformulated as follows

$$SAT_{X3}(F) := \begin{cases} true & \text{if } \forall \tau \in ASS^p \, (SAT\,(F|_\tau) = true) \\ false & \text{if } \qquad\qquad SAT\,(F|_{\tau^o}) = false \\ \bot & \text{else.} \end{cases}$$

The number of SAT instances induced by SAT_{X3} is exponential in the number of parameters. Thus, in a sequential scenario parameterisation can lead to an exponential growth of computation time. Since all these instances are independent problems, SAT solving can be done concurrently. Provided that parallel processing is available to a sufficient extent, the runtime overhead of parameterisation can thus be significantly reduced. For our example we need three processors in order to entirely suspend the overhead induced by parameterisation:

$$T_0\left(F|_{\{(\bot, true)\}}\right)$$
$$\| \; T_1\left(F|_{\{(x_1, false),(\bot, false)\}}\right)$$
$$\| \; T_2\left(F|_{\{(x_1, true),(\bot, false)\}}\right)$$

Here T_0 to T_2 are solver threads executed concurrently that return whether the input formula is satisfiable or not. Note that it is not always necessary for all threads to terminate in order to solve SAT_{X3}. In case T_0 returns $false$ we already know that the overall result is $false$, in case T_1 and T_2 return contrary results the overall result is $\bot$, and if T_1 and T_2 both return $true$ then we also get $true$ for SAT_{X3}.

This method can be additionally accelerated by exploiting the fact that the SAT instances associated with SAT_{X3} exhibit similarity in the sense of common subformulae. Modern SAT solvers are based on the search for a satisfying assignment of the input CNF formula by incrementally selecting unassigned variables, assigning them by either $true$ or $false$, and propagating the resulting constraints to the clauses of the formula. In case the solver decisions lead to an unsatisfied clause, a so-called *conflict clause* is learned via resolution and added to the set of clauses. Moreover, the solver tracks back by revising a former assignment decision and continuing the search from this point until a satisfying assignment is found or the search space is entirely explored. Such a *conflict-driven clause learning* (CDCL) [5] can help the solver to quickly prune certain branches of the search space and is thus crucial for the performance of satisfiability solving.

Learned clauses can also be *reused* or *shared*. In *incremental SAT solving* [11] a set of similar input formulae is processed by *consecutively* executed solvers. The inputs typically have a common subformula F while the differences are expressed by adding different assumptions $\tau_1, \ldots \tau_n$ to F. These assumptions are fixed assignments which are never revoked during the solving process for an input $F|_{\tau_i}$. This guarantees that all conflict clauses learned in assumption-based incremental SAT solving inherently contain the assumptions they depend on. Hence, learned clauses can be reused without any restriction since changing from one assumption τ to another assumption τ' does not affect the clauses of F but automatically disables conflict clauses that are not compatible with τ'. In the context of *parallel* SAT solving the concept of *clause sharing* has been introduced [13,15]. In this approach multiple copies of the input formula are checked concurrently. Generated conflict clauses can be shared, which enables to prune the search space at multiple points at the same time. Clause sharing has also been considered for parallel (non-parameterised) BMC [2,26]. Here multiple solvers check the same BMC encoding but for different bounds. Similar to incremental SAT solving the differences are expressed via assumptions and learned clauses are shared via a global database or message passing.

For our *parameterised* scenario we adopt the concept of assumption-based clause sharing. We already reduced SAT_{X3} to multiple SAT instances consisting of the common formula F and different assumptions that characterise the possible parameter instantiations and the optimistic resp. pessimistic completion. Hence, all learned conflict clauses can be shared in a parallel scenario and thus used to prune the search space of multiple instances at the same time. Next, we will discuss the implementation of our approach and we will see how the runtime performance of parallel SAT-based bounded PMC can significantly profit from clause sharing.

6 Implementation and Experimental Results

We have prototypically implemented a SAT-based bounded LTL model checker for parameterised three-valued models which employs the Java-based solver library Sat4j [14]. The checker iterates over the bound k, starting with $k = 0$, until a definite result can be obtained or a predefined threshold for k is reached. In each iteration, after constructing a parameterised encoding F of a bounded PMC problem, each instance $F|_{\tau^\circ}, F|_{\tau_1}, \ldots, F|_{\tau_n}$ is processed by a solver thread. In the *basic* mode of our implementation the threads are executed in parallel whereby learned clauses are *not* shared. In the *enhanced* mode we additionally apply *clause sharing*. For this purpose, the solvers save copies of learned clauses in a global database D. The solvers provided by Sat4j inherently employ conflict-driven clause learning. Such CDCL solvers regularly *restart* while processing a SAT instance. Restarts typically happen after having learned a certain amount of clauses. For our clause sharing approach we use these restarts as the points of synchronisation with D: Every time a solver restarts, it waits for read access to D. Then, it reads the clauses that have been placed into D by other solvers since its own most recent restart. (Remember that the assumption-based approach ensures that the solver will only make use of those clauses from D for pruning its search space that were learned based on assumptions compatible to its own assumption τ.) Finally, the solver waits for exclusive read-write access to D and adds the clauses that have been learned by itself since its last restart. The shorter a conflict clause the stronger it prunes the search space. To keep the clause sharing mechanism efficient and the communication overhead caused by exclusively accessing D small, we currently only share *unit* (single-literal) clauses. In both the basic and the enhanced mode a k-bounded iteration terminates when the solver processing the optimistic completion of F returns *false*, or when all solvers processing an instance of the pessimistic completion return *true*, or as soon as the so far single results already indicate an overall *unknown* result. In the latter case, the $(k + 1)$-bounded encoding is constructed and its instances are processed in the subsequent iteration. Algorithm 1 illustrates the general procedure of a single iteration. Here the input variable *mode* indicates whether each solver thread synchronises with the initially empty shared clause database D at a restart (*enhanced*) or not (*basic*).

Data: parameterised encoding F, assumption set $ASS = \{\tau^o, \tau_1, \ldots, \tau_n\}$,
$mode \in \{basic, enhanced\}$, shared clause database $D = \varnothing$
Result: truth value of $SAT_{X3}(F)$
begin
    start new solver thread $T_0(F|_{\tau^o}, mode)$
    for $i = 1$ **to** n **do**
    | **start new** solver thread $T_i(F|_{\tau_i}, mode)$
    end
    upon event
    | T_0 returns *false* **do**
    | **return** *false*
    | T_1 to T_n return *true* **do**
    | **return** *true*
    | $\exists\, T_i, T_j$ where T_i returns *true* and T_j returns *false* **do**
    | **return** $\perp$
    end
end

Algorithm 1. *SolveSAT$_{X3}$*

In our experiments we compared the runtime performance of the basic and the enhanced mode for encodings with increasing numbers of parameters. The items of our benchmark set correspond to parameterised three-valued BMC problems with fixed bounds that we encoded with our tool according to the definitions from Sect. 4. For each item *pmc-1* to *pmc-9* we considered variants with 1 to 8 parameters, i.e. with $1 + 2^1$ to $1 + 2^8$ instances. The variants were constructed by applying different parameterisations to the Kripke structure of the underlying BMC problem. We transformed the SAT encodings into CNF. The resulting parameterised propositional logic formulae consisted of up to 40000 variables and 150000 clauses. For all possible instantiations of a parameterised three-valued encoding a solver thread was created and the satisfiability was checked concurrently. Our experiments were conducted on a 2.6 GHz quad-core Intel Core i5 with 8 GB. The results for our benchmark set are shown in the diagrams below. Note that a *logarithmic* scale is used for the runtime axis. A table containing the numerical results of our experiments can be found online[1].

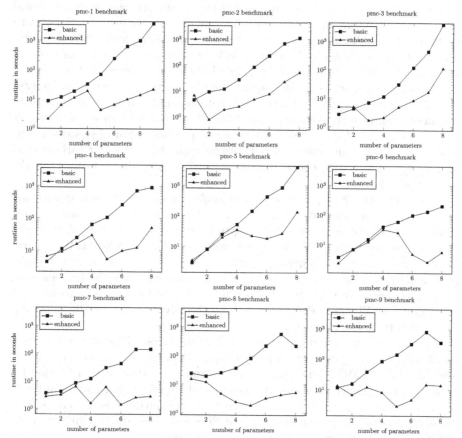

The items *pmc-1* to *pmc-3* represent PMC problems that yield *true* for each parameter variant (1 to 8). Hence, the termination of each variant necessitated that all solvers processing a parameter instance of the pessimistic completion returned *true*. Obtaining *true* results in SAT-based PMC generally involves the highest computational effort because of the high number of solvers that need to terminate. As shown by the diagrams, the runtime in the basic mode grows approximately exponentially with each additional parameter. For variants with a *small* number of parameters the runtimes of the basic and the enhanced mode are nearly on the same level. However, for variants with a *higher* number of

---

[1] http://www.cs.up.ac.za/cs/ntimm/Table.pdf.

parameters, i.e. a higher number of solvers that can share learned clauses, the enhanced mode pays off: The solving time still grows with each additional parameter but is always orders of magnitude shorter then the basic approach runtime.

The items *pmc-4* to *pmc-6* represent PMC problems that yield *unknown* for the parameter variants 1 to 7 and *true* for the variant with 8 parameters. Hence, the last parameter variant finally brought the required precision for a definite result. The termination of the variants 1 to 7 necessitated that two solvers processing a parameter instance of the pessimistic completion returned contrary results (*true* and *false*). Also here we observed an exponential growth in runtime per additional parameter in the basic mode and a significantly better performance in the enhanced mode, provided that a certain number of parameters, i.e. cooperating solvers is present. In addition, we observed that solving the variant with 8 parameters in the enhanced mode involves an exceptional increase in runtime, which complies with the fact that obtaining a *true* result (variant 8) generally requires more computational effort than obtaining an *unknown* result (variants 1 to 7). This exceptional increase in runtime is not observable in the basic mode where computational costs are generally high. Also for variant 8 the enhanced approach with clause sharing is orders of magnitude faster than the basic approach.

The items *pmc-7* to *pmc-9* represent problems that yield *unknown* for the variants 1 to 7 and *false* for variant 8. Thus, the termination of variant 8 necessitated that the solver processing the optimistic completion returned *false*. For this set of items we made the same observations as for the previous benchmark items with regard to the general performance advantage of the enhanced mode. Additionally, we observed that solving variant 8 involved no significant increase or even a decrease in runtime. This is consistent with the fact that obtaining a *false* result in SAT-based PMC only requires the solver processing the optimistic completion to terminate with *false*.

In summary, our experiments showed that, regardless of the final verification result, clause sharing can considerably improve the runtime performance of parallel SAT-based PMC. The savings in solving time are particularly significant for variants with a higher number of parameters where solver cooperation in terms of sharing clauses is possible to a large extent. This enables us to benefit from the extra precision of parameterisation in three-valued model checking, without suffering from a substantial overhead in solving time.

7   Related Work

SAT-based BMC [3,4] was originally introduced for the bounded evaluation of properties on *two-valued* models. Later, BMC has also been defined for *pure three-valued* models [17,25]. A number of approaches have been proposed to accelerate SAT solving in general and SAT-based BMC in particular. *Conflict-driven clause learning* (CDCL) [5] is a concept for using clauses that were learned during the test of a single SAT instance for pruning its search space. In *incremental SAT solving* [11] a series of similar SAT instances is solved sequentially. The differences between the instances are expressed by considering the same input formula under different assumptions. On this basis, clauses learned via CDCL can be reused when solving subsequent instances. *Parallel* SAT solving [6,16,19] is an approach to solve a single instance by dividing it into disjoint parts that are then processed by a set of solvers. In early works [6], CDCL was used by each solver for solely pruning its own search space. Later approaches [16,19] considered parallel solving with *clause sharing*: Learned clauses are ex- changed in order to increase the overall performance. In SAT-based BMC, CDCL has been applied in the sense that clauses learned for a k-bounded instance F_k are reused when solving the instance F_{k+1} [1,20]. Also here assumptions are used to express the differences between F_k and F_{k+1}. This idea has been transferred to a parallel setting where solvers concurrently operate on BMC instances with different bounds, and synchronisation with a shared clause database happens at the restarts of the solvers [2,26]. While these works deal with two-valued models, our approach considers parameterised three-valued models. Parameterisation opens another dimension for sharing clauses. We adopted assumption-based clause sharing and applied it between the *parameter instances* associated with PMC. Since these instances share large common subformulae, this enables us to accelerate the performance of SAT-based PMC.

8   Conclusion and Outlook

Parameterisation [23] is a concept for enhancing the precision of abstraction-based three-valued model checking by capturing facts in the model that can be derived from the software system to be verified. The application of parameterisation does not increase the state space but it leads to an exponential growth of the number of model checking runs. In this paper, we introduced a technique for PMC via parallel SAT solving. We defined a propositional logic encoding of bounded PMC problems and we proved that our encodings are sound in the sense that satisfiability results can be straightforwardly transferred to the encoded model checking problem. The number of SAT instances associated with an encoding is still exponential in the number of parameters. However, these instances exhibit considerable similarities in the sense of common subformulae. We showed that the concept of assumption-based clause sharing, which exploits such similarities in order to achieve a better performance in parallel SAT solving, can be transferred to our parameterised scenario. We presented a prototype tool for satisfiability-based PMC with clause sharing. In our experiments, we demonstrated that clause sharing leads to a significant acceleration of PMC. Thus, our new SAT-based approach enhances PMC as it allows us to profit from the extra precision of parametrisation in three-valued model checking, without creating a noticeable runtime overhead. Since we showed that PMC is reducible to multiple instances of classical SAT, our approach will also benefit from future improvements in SAT solver technology.

So far, we conducted our experiments on a single-processor system with multiple cores. We already achieved substantial runtime savings with our clause sharing approach by using these very limited parallel computing resources. As future work we plan more extensive experiments on a cluster for parallel computing. Moreover, we intend to extend parallelisation and clause sharing to the satisfiability checks for the different *bounds* $k = 0, 1, 2, \ldots$ in bounded PMC. We also plan to experiment with different *policies* with regard to size constraints of clauses to be shared in order to discover the best trade-off between the communication costs due to sharing and the speed-up due to additional pruning. Moreover, we intend to use *multiple copies* of each instantiation in the parallel composition of solver threads. We expect that this allows to increase the amount of clauses that can be shared and thus leads to a further acceleration of the overall solving time. Another direction for future research is to summarise the exponential number of SAT instances of the pessimistic completion to a single instance of a *quantified Boolean formula* (QBF) $F = \forall x_1 \ldots \forall x_m \exists v_1 \ldots \exists v_n \left(F|_{(\perp, false)} \right)$ and then to check F via a QBF solver. Though QBF is PSPACE-complete, whereas SAT is only NP-complete, it would be interesting to study whether the reduction to a single instance of a higher complexity class pays off in terms of solving performance for particular PMC problems.

References

1. Ábrahám, E., Becker, B., Klaedtke, F., Steffen, M.: Optimizing bounded model checking for linear hybrid systems. In: Cousot, R. (ed.) VMCAI 2005. LNCS, vol. 3385, pp. 396–412. Springer, Heidelberg (2005)
2. Ábrahám, E., Schubert, T., Becker, B., Fränzle, M., Herde, C.: Parallel SAT solving in bounded model checking. J. Logic. Comput. **21**(1), 5–21 (2011)
3. Biere, A., Cimatti, A., Clarke, E., Zhu, Y.: Symbolic model checking without BDDs. In: Cleaveland, W.R. (ed.) TACAS 1999. LNCS, vol. 1579, pp. 193–207. Springer, Heidelberg (1999)
4. Biere, A., Cimatti, A., Clarke, E.M., Strichman, O., Zhu, Y.: Bounded model checking. In: Biere, A., Heule, M., van Maaren, H., Walsh, T. (eds.) Handbook of Satisfiability, vol. 185, pp. 457–481. IOS Press, Amsterdam (2009)
5. Silva, J.P.M., Lynce, I., Malik, S.: Conflict-driven clause learning SAT solvers. In: Biere, A., Heule, M., van Maaren, H., Walsh, T. (eds.) Handbook of Satisfiability. Frontiers in Artificial Intelligence and Applications. IOS Press, Amsterdam (2009)
6. Böhm, M., Speckenmeyer, E.: A fast parallel SAT-solver - efficient workload balancing. Ann. Math. Artif. Intell. **17**(2), 381–400 (1996)
7. Bruns, G., Godefroid, P.: Model checking partial state spaces with 3-valued temporal logics. In: Halbwachs, N., Peled, D.A. (eds.) CAV 1999. LNCS, vol. 1633, pp. 274–287. Springer, Heidelberg (1999)
8. Bruns, G., Godefroid, P.: Generalized model checking: reasoning about partial state spaces. In: Palamidessi, C. (ed.) CONCUR 2000. LNCS, vol. 1877, pp. 168–182. Springer, Heidelberg (2000)
9. Chechik, M., Devereux, B., Easterbrook, S., Gurfinkel, A.: Multi-valued symbolic model-checking. ACM Trans. Softw. Eng. Methodol. (TOSEM) **12**(4), 371–408 (2003)
10. Chechik, M., Gurfinkel, A., Devereux, B.: χChek: a multi-valued model-checker. In: Brinksma, E., Larsen, K.G. (eds.) CAV 2002. LNCS, vol. 2404, pp. 505–509. Springer, Heidelberg (2002)

11. Eén, N., Sörensson, N.: Temporal induction by incremental SAT solving. Electron. Notes Theor. Comput. Sci. **89**(4), 543–560 (2003)
12. Fitting, M.: Kleene's three valued logics and their children. Fundamenta Informaticae **20**(1–3), 113–131 (1994)
13. Hamadi, Y., Jabbour, S., Sais, J.: Control-based clause sharing in parallel sat solving. In: Hamadi, Y., Monfroy, E., Saubion, F. (eds.) Autonomous Search, pp. 245–267. Springer, Berlin Heidelberg (2012)
14. Le Berre, D., Parrain, A.: The Sat4j library, release 2.2. J. Satisfiability Boolean Model. Comput. **7**, 59–64 (2010)
15. Lewis, M.D.T., Schubert, T., Becker, B.W.: Speedup techniques utilized in modern SAT solvers. In: Bacchus, F., Walsh, T. (eds.) SAT 2005. LNCS, vol. 3569, pp. 437–443. Springer, Heidelberg (2005)
16. Schubert, T., Lewis, M., Becker, B.: Pamira - a parallel SAT solver with knowledge sharing. In: Sixth International Workshop on Microprocessor Test and Verification, 2005, MTV 2005, pp. 29–36. IEEE Computer Society (2005)
17. Schuele, T., Schneider, K.: Three-valued logic in bounded model checking. In: Proceedings of the 2nd ACM/IEEE International Conference on Formal Methods and Models for Co-Design, pp. 177–186. IEEE Computer Society (2005)
18. Shoham, S., Grumberg, O.: 3-valued abstraction: more precision at less cost. Inf. Comput. **206**(11), 1313–1333 (2008)
19. Sinz, C., Blochinger, W., Küchlin, W.: PaSAT - parallel SAT-checking with lemma exchange: Implementation and applications. Electron. Notes Discrete Math. **9**, 205–216 (2001)
20. Strichman, O.: Accelerating bounded model checking of safety properties. Formal Methods Syst. Des. **24**(1), 5–24 (2004)
21. Timm, N.: Bounded model checking für partielle systeme. Masters thesis, University of Paderborn (2009)
22. Timm, N.: Three-valued abstraction and heuristic-guided refinement for verifying concurrent systems. Ph.D. thesis, University of Paderborn (2013)
23. Timm, N., Gruner, S.: Parameterisation of three-valued abstractions. In: Braga, C., Martí-Oliet, N. (eds.) SBMF 2014. LNCS, vol. 8941, pp. 162–178. Springer, Heidelberg (2015)
24. Tseitin, G.: On the complexity of derivation in propositional calculus. In: Siekmann, J., Wrightson, G. (eds.) Automation of Reasoning, pp. 466–483. Symbolic Computation, Springer, Berlin Heidelberg (1983)
25. Wehrheim, H.: Bounded model checking for partial kripke structures. In: Fitzgerald, J.S., Haxthausen, A.E., Yenigun, H. (eds.) ICTAC 2008. LNCS, vol. 5160, pp. 380–394. Springer, Heidelberg (2008)
26. Wieringa, S., Niemenmaa, M., Heljanko, K.: Tarmo: a framework for parallelized bounded model checking. In: Proceedings 8th International Workshop on Parallel and Distributed Methods in verifiCation, PDMC 2009, Eindhoven, The Netherlands, 4th November 2009, pp. 62–76 (2009)

Software Validation and Verification

Comparative Analysis of Leakage Tools on Scalable Case Studies

Fabrizio Biondi$^{(\boxtimes)}$, Axel Legay, and Jean Quilbeuf$^{(\boxtimes)}$

Inria, Rennes, France
{fabrizio.biondi,jean.quilbeuf}@inria.fr

Abstract. Quantitative security techniques have been proven effective to measure the security of systems against various types of attackers. However, such techniques are often tested against small-scale academic examples.

In this paper we analyze two scalable, real life privacy case studies: the privacy of the energy consumption data of the users of a smart grid network and the secrecy of the voters' voting preferences with different types of voting protocols.

We contribute a new trace analysis algorithm for leakage calculation in QUAIL. We analyze both case studies with three state-of-the-art information leakage computation tools: LeakWatch, Moped-QLeak, and our tool QUAIL equipped with the new algorithm. We highlight the relative advantages and drawbacks of the tools and compare their usability and effectiveness in analyzing the case studies.

1 Introduction

The protection of privacy and data security is one of the main concerns of computer science. Security often falls down to the impossibility for an attacker to obtain a given secret value. Such an impossibility can be defined by non-interference [18]. However this definition rejects any program which publishes any variable whose value depends on the secret. For instance, publishing the results of an election when each individual vote is secret breaks non-interference. Such a yes/no approach does not consider that an attacker may have a partial information about a secret.

Information-theoretical techniques have the advantage of considering the secret not as an atomic object but as a known number of secret bits, allowing the definition of measures of effectiveness of an attack based on the amount of secret bits that the attack compromises. The amount of secret bits that are compromised by an attack are known as *information leakage*. Leakage depends on the information about the secret known to the attacker before the attack, known as *prior information* and usually modeled as a *prior probability distribution* over the values of the secret. This approach dates back to Denning [16]. Different information leakage measures have been introduced, including Shannon leakage [19], min-entropy leakage [30] and the g-leakage [1], encoding different security properties of the system. All the tools we compare in this work can

© Springer International Publishing Switzerland 2015
B. Fischer and J. Geldenhuys (Eds.): SPIN 2015, LNCS 9232, pp. 263–281, 2015.
DOI: 10.1007/978-3-319-23404-5_17

compute both Shannon and min-entropy leakage with no significant difference in computation time. We compare them on the computation of Shannon leakage, but we expect no significant difference if the tools were to be compared on the computation of min-entropy leakage.

Among the results in the field, Köpf et al. studied leakage of side-channel attacks [2,21], while Boreale has defined leakage for process calculi [6] and characterized the best attack strategy of an adaptive attacker [9].

In this work we compare the three tools that compose the state of the art in Shannon leakage computation: QUAIL [5] equipped with a new trace analysis algorithm, LeakWatch [13], and Moped-QLeak [11].

QUAIL is a recent but already well established tool for precise and exact information leakage computation, and later tools by multiple authors have used it as comparison [13,25]. Nonetheless, QUAIL needs to produce a full Markov chain model of the system-attacker scenario to produce a meaningful result.

LeakWatch is the most recent of a family of tools for statistical approximation of information leakage developed by Chothia et al. [12,14]. LeakWatch analyzes Java code, requiring the programmer to annotate the code of the system with secret and observable values, then simulates the system repeatedly using the Java Virtual Machine and estimates the correlation between the secret and observable values. LeakWatch follows a different perspective than QUAIL and Moped-QLeak, since LeakWatch computes an approximated result, contrarily to QUAIL's arbitrary precision and Moped-QLeak's fixed double precision. LeakWatch's approximation can be improved at the cost of running more simulations, which is time expensive.

Moped-QLeak [11] uses the Moped tool [17] to compute a symbolic summary of the program under analysis as an Algebraic Decision Diagram (ADD), and then computes the leakage using the ADD representation. The symbolic approach is very efficient when the program can be represented in a compact way using ADDs, and in these cases Moped-QLeak is significantly faster than the other tools.

The first contribution of this paper is a new algorithm for precise information leakage computation, which is able to compute information leakage following the same Markovian semantics we introduced previously [3, Sect. 4] by performing a depth-first search analyzing the execution traces of the system. We implemented this algorithm in QUAIL, allowing it to compute leakage without having to build the full Markov chain model of the system.

As a second contribution, we provide two scalable case studies for the benchmarking of quantitative information leakage tools. Both case studies arise from real-life privacy problems. The case studies are anonymity of user data in Smart Grids and privacy comparison in voting protocols.

Smart Grids are in the family of interconnected objects and have received a growing interest over the last years. Our case study is based on a real system deployed at fortiss[1] labs [22]. In our case study, we focus on the negotiation between a set of *prosumers* and an *aggregator*. The prosumers (PROducer conSUMERS) consume, store and produce energy. To stabilize the grid, the

---

[1] http://fortiss.org.

prosumers negotiate with the aggregator how much energy they will exchange with the grid for the next period of time. This exchange might expose the consumption of one of the prosumers, and, in turn, allow a potential attacker to deduce that a house is empty or that a factory has increased its production. In that example, the difficulty is to decide not only whether the exact information can be deduced or not, but also how well an attack can approximate it. Measuring the leakage indicates how much of the secret is unveiled through the negotiation phase. We show that increasing the number of prosumers also increases security.

In the voting protocols comparison case study, we compare two different voting protocols: the *Single Preference*, where each voter expresses a single vote for his favorite candidate, and the *Preference Ranking*, where each voter ranks all candidates from his most to his least favorite. In both cases there are multiple voters and candidates, and the secret is the preference of each voter. Both protocols have a large number of possible secrets and outputs, so they become cumbersome to analyze even with a small number of voters and candidates.

We compare the tools on their computation time, precision of the answer returned, scalability and usability. Since no tool works strictly better than the others in all category, we determine the problem classes that are better suited to be analyzed by each tool.

2   Background: Information Leakage

The information leakage of a program is a measure quantifying how much information an attacker infers about the program's secret by observing the program's output. We assume that the attacker has access to the program's source code, unlimited computational power, and some prior information about the secret (e.g. the bit size of the secret). Leakage corresponds to the reduction in the attacker's uncertainty about the secret.

Let h be a random variable with values in a domain $D(h)$ representing the value of the secret and o be a random variable with values in a domain $D(o)$ modeling the value of the output. The information the attacker has on the secret is modeled by a discrete probability distribution, i.e. for a discrete random variable X a function $\pi : D(X) \rightarrow [0,1]$ such that $\sum_{x \in D(X)} \pi(x) = 1$. The information that the attacker has on the secret before the attack is modeled by the *prior distribution* $\pi(h)$ while the information the attacker has after observing the output is modeled by the *posterior distribution* $\pi(h|o)$. We consider the prior distribution as given, since it is part of the model of the attacker. Let U be an uncertainty measure defined on probability distributions, including Shannon entropy, min-entropy, and g-vulnerability. Computing leakage for the measure U reduces to computing the prior and posterior distributions and applying the formula

$$Leakage_U = U(\pi(h)) - U(\pi(h|o)) \tag{1}$$

$$= U(\pi(h)) - \sum_{\bar{o} \in D(o)} \pi(o = \bar{o}) U(\pi(h|o = \bar{o})) \tag{2}$$

In this work we want to compute Shannon leakage, and thus we use Shannon entropy as the measure of uncertainty: $U(\pi(x)) = \sum_{x \in D(X)} \pi(x) \log_2 \pi(x)$.

3   Quantitative Information Leakage Tools

We introduce the quantitative information leakage computation tools that will be tested on the case studies.

3.1   QUAIL

QUAIL [5] computes Shannon and min-entropy leakage of a program written in an imperative WHILE language. The language allows the user to program naturally with constants, arrays, and loops, which is syntactic sugar for QUAIL's if-goto Markovian semantics. Given the prior information of the attacker, QUAIL represents the program as a Markov chain, and computes the information leakage from the Markov chain with an arbitrary number of precision digits.

Syntax. We present the syntax of the QUAIL imperative language we use to model programs. We distinguish the variables in *public* and *private* variables according to their level of abstraction: public variables have precise values, while private variables have sets of possible values. The observable variable o is public, while the secret variable h is private. Let v range over names of variables and x range over reals from $[0; 1]$. Let L (resp. H) be a set of assignments of values to public variables (resp. assignments of sets of values to private variables).

Let *label*, l_0 and l_1 denote any program point and f (g) pure arithmetic (Boolean) expressions. Assume a standard set of expressions and the following statements:

$stmt ::=$ public int$n$ v $:= k \mid$ private int$n$ v $\mid$ v $:=$ f$(L) \mid$ v $:=$ rand $x \mid$
         skip $\mid$ goto *label* $\mid$ return $\mid$ if g(L, H) then goto l_a
         else goto l_b

The first statement declares a public variable v of size n bits with a given value k, while the second statement similarly declares a private variable h of size n bits with allowed values ranging from 0 to $2^n - 1$. We assume a standard type system to verify that values of n-bit variables do not exceed $2^n - 1$. The third statement assigns to a public variable the value of expression f depending on public variables; assignment to private variables or depending on the value of private variables is not allowed. The fourth statement assigns zero with probability x, and one with probability $1 - x$, to a 1-bit public variable. The return statement outputs values of all public variables and terminates. A conditional branch first evaluates an expression g dependent on private and public variables, and it jumps to label l_a if g is true and to label l_b otherwise. Since only a single variable scope exists, loops can be added in a standard way as syntactic sugar.

As a contribution, we present a method to compute information leakage of a program by analyzing the execution traces of the program. We introduce the

Markovian semantics of our language by means of a function computing the successors of each state. Then we explain how we perform a depth-first exploration of the traces of the system, obtaining a set Q of final states that represent all possible output states of the system. Finally, we show how to compute the posterior entropy from Q.

$$\frac{pc: \text{public int} n\, v\ := k}{succ(pc, L, H, p) = \{(pc + 1, L \cup \{L(v) = k\}, H, p)\}}$$

$$\frac{pc: \text{private int} n\, v}{succ(pc, L, H, p) = \{(pc + 1, L, H \cup \{H(v) = \{0, ..., 2^n - 1\}\}, p)\}}$$

$$\frac{pc: \text{skip}}{succ(pc, L, H, p) = \{(pc + 1, L, H, p)\}} \qquad \frac{pc: \text{v} := \text{f}(L)}{succ(pc, L, H, p) = \{(pc + 1, L \cup \{L(v) = \text{f}(L)\}, H, p)\}}$$

$$\frac{pc: \text{v} := \text{rand}\ x}{succ(pc, L, H, p) = \{(pc + 1, L \cup \{L(v) = 0\}, H, p \cdot x), (pc + 1, L \cup \{L(v) = 1\}, H, p \cdot (1 - x))\}}$$

$$\frac{pc: \text{goto}\ label}{succ(pc, L, H, p) = \{(label, L, H, p)\}} \qquad \frac{pc: \text{return}}{succ(pc, L, H, p) = \emptyset}$$

$$\frac{pc: \text{if}\ \text{g}(L, H)\ \text{then goto}\ l_a\ \text{else goto}\ l_b}{succ(pc, L, H, p) = \{(l_a, L, H|\text{g}(L, H), p \cdot Pr(\text{g}(L, H)|\pi(h))),}$$
$$(l_b, L, H|\neg\text{g}(L, H), p \cdot Pr(\neg\text{g}(L, H)|\pi(h)))\}$$

Fig. 1. Successor function for each state in the Markovian trace semantics.

Semantics. The Markovity of the semantics allows us to define states containing enough information to determine a probability distribution over all traces originating from any state.

Definition 1. *A state in a Markovian semantics is a tuple (pc, L, H, p) where $pc \in \mathbb{N}^0$ is the program counter, L a set of assignments of values to public variables, H an set of assignments of sets of values to private variables, and $0 \le p \le 1$ is the probability of the state.*

The *initial state* of the semantics is $(1, \emptyset, \emptyset, 1)$. The *set of successor states* of a state (pc, L, H, p) depends on the statement pointed at by the program counter pc. States pointing to a return statement have 0 successors, states pointing to a rand or if statement have up to 2 successors, and any other state has 1 successor. The successor function defining the semantics of the language is shown in Fig. 1. If a state has zero probability, e.g. when a conditional is always true, it is removed from the set of successors.

We call a state *final* if it has no successors, meaning that the program counter of the state points to a return statement. The trace analysis terminates when a final state is encountered. This means that the analysis terminates if and only if the program under analysis terminates, so non-terminating programs cannot be analyzed with this technique. Non-termination of the program under analysis raises other issues in leakage computation [4], and is not considered here.

Conditional states and random assignment states have two successors. The successors of a conditional state correspond to the guard being true or false. Since the guard can depend on the secret, both successor states may have positive probability depending on the prior distribution $\pi(h)$ on the secret, which is available at this time. The successors of a random assignment state correspond to the bit being set to 0 or 1. In both cases the probability of each successor state is computed and one of the successor states with non-zero probability is chosen to be the next step in the analysis. Successors with probability zero are dropped, pruning unreachable leaves from the trace tree.

Because of the Markovian semantics, each state contains the information to compute the probability distribution over its outgoing transitions. The probability of a trace is computed as the product of the probabilities of the transitions composing the trace. In the successor states of the conditional statement, $H|g(L,H)$ (resp. $H|\neg g(L,H)$) represents the assignment function obtained by removing from the sets of values assigned to the private variables those values that contradict (resp. respect) the guard $g(L,H)$. Similarly, $Pr(g(L,H)|\pi(h))$ (resp. $Pr(\neg g(L,H)|\pi(h))$) refers to the probability that the guard $g(L,H)$ is true (resp. false) considering the prior probability distribution $\pi(h)$ on the private variables.

When the analysis of a single trace terminates, the corresponding final state $(\bar{pc}, \bar{L}, \bar{H}, \bar{p})$ is produced, in which pc points to a return statement. The sets of allowed values assigned to the private variables in $\bar{H}$ have been appropriately reduced to account for the conditional statements visited by the trace.

Depth-First Trace Exploration. We perform a depth-first exhaustive exploration of the execution traces of the system, starting from the initial state $(1, \emptyset, \emptyset, 1)$. Each trace is explored until it gets to a final state, then the final state gets added to the multiset Q of final states. When all traces have been explored, the full multiset of final states Q of the system is produced. We then use Q to compute the posterior entropy of the system using Algorithm 1 presented below. The leakage of the system is computed as the difference between the prior and posterior entropy, as explained in Sect. 2.

Note that the exploration also depends on the prior distribution $\pi(h)$: values of the secret with a probability zero in the prior distribution are not explored. This behavior is intended, as is avoids unnecessarily exploring traces that have probability zero.

The depth-first exploration algorithm can be parallelized to take advantage of multicore architectures and is implemented in the current release of QUAIL, available at http://project.inria.fr/quail. Since this new algorithm is hundreds of times faster than the previous QUAIL implementation, we consider is as the standard QUAIL algorithm.

Posterior Uncertainty Computation. We show how to compute the posterior uncertainty $U(\pi(h|o))$ of a system with a secret h and an observable o,

---

Data: uncertainty measure U, multiset Q of final states
Result: posterior uncertainty $U(\pi(h|o))$
1 Initialize $\pi(o)$ and all $\pi(h, o = \bar{o})$ to zero;
2 **forall the** $s = (pc, L, H, p) \in Q$ **do**
3   Let $\bar{o} = L(o)$, $\{k_1, ..., k_n\} = H(h)$;
4   Set $\pi(o = \bar{o}) \leftarrow \pi(o = \bar{o}) + p$;
5   **for** $i = 1...n$ **do**
6 | Set $\pi(h = k_i, o = \bar{o}) \leftarrow \pi(h = k_i, o = \bar{o}) + p/n$;
7   **end**
8 **end**
9 For each $\bar{o} \in D(o)$ let $\pi(h|o = \bar{o}) \leftarrow \pi(h, o = \bar{o})/\pi(o = \bar{o})$;
10 Return $U(\pi(h|o)) = \sum_{\bar{o} \in D(o)} \pi(o = \bar{o})U(\pi(h|o = \bar{o}))$

Algorithm 1. Posterior uncertainty computation

given the uncertainty measure U and a multiset Q of final states of the system. Q encodes the posterior joint probability of all variables in the system and can be produced by the depth-first exploration algorithm presented above.

Let (pc, L, H, p) be a final state in Q, where L represents the assignments of given values to the public variables, H the assignments of sets of values to the private variables, and p the joint probability of such assignments. Since different traces may produce the same final assignments to variables (L, H), the joint probability of these assignments is the sum of the probabilities of all such final states. To apply the formula (2) $U(\pi(h|o)) = \sum_{\bar{o} \in D(o)} \pi(o = \bar{o})U(\pi(h|o = \bar{o}))$, we need to compute the marginal probability distribution $\pi(o)$ and for each observable output $\bar{o} \in D(o)$ s.t. $\pi(o = \bar{o}) > 0$ the corresponding conditional probability distribution on h, i.e. $\pi(h|o = \bar{o})$.

Algorithm 1 computes $\pi(o)$ and each $\pi(h|o = \bar{o})$ by analyzing a multiset of final states. For each state (pc, L, H, p) the value of the observable variable o and set of values of the secret variable h are analyzed (lines 2–8). The probability of observing the value $\bar{o}$ of the observable variable in the state is increased by p (line 4), and the probability of observing each of the n values of the secret variable conditioned on $\bar{o}$ is increased by p/n (line 6). Finally, the probability on each subdistribution $\pi(h, o = \bar{o})$ is normalized to 1 by dividing it by $\pi(o = \bar{o})$ to obtain the conditional probability $\pi(h|o = \bar{o})$ (line 9) since $P(X|Y) = P(X,Y)/P(Y)$.

Theorem 1. *Algorithm 1 terminates and outputs the posterior uncertainty $U(\pi(h|o))$ of the posterior distribution represented by Q.*

3.2   LeakWatch

LeakWatch [13] estimates the leakage of a Java program with secrets and observations by running it several times for each possible value of the secret and inferring a probability distribution on the observations for each secret. The tool automatically terminates the analysis when the precision of the estimation is deemed sufficient, but different termination conditions can be used.

For small secrets, LeakWatch gives reliably approximates the leakage of complex Java programs. For larger secret, i.e. more than 10 bits, LeakWatch takes more time to return a value. However, the user can decide an acceptable error level for the tool to reduce the computation time necessary to obtain an answer. Also, if the tool is terminated prematurely, it can still provide an answer, even if it will be potentially quite imprecise. This makes LeakWatch the only tool of the three considered that can always provide an answer in a time-limited scenario, since QUAIL and Moped-QLeak generate a leakage result only if they complete their execution.

Finally, LeakWatch provides many command-line options for tuning the analysis parameters. In particular, one of the options displays the current estimation of the leakage at regular intervals, which can be very useful when developing.

Syntax and Usage. The syntax is the same as the Java language, with the additional commands secret(name,value) to declare a secret with a given name and value, and observe(value) to declare an observation of a given value. The analysis evaluates how much information leaks from the secret to the observable values. In particular, LeakWatch can compute leakage from a point of a program to another point of the program, and not necessarily from the start to the termination of the program.

To run LeakWatch, a Java programa annotated with secret and observable statements has to be compiled linking the LeakWatch library:

```
javac -cp leakwatch-0.5.jar:. MyClass.java
```

The tool is then run passing the name of the compiled class as a parameter:

```
java -jar leakwatch-0.5.jar MyClass
```

The tool returns its leakage estimate for the Java program. Normally Leak-Watch determines automatically when it has run enough executions. We have used the -n parameter to fix the number of executions of the program when we experimented with different precisions and computation times.

3.3 Moped-QLeak

Moped-QLeak [11] uses the Moped tool [17] to compute a symbolic Algebraic Decision Diagram (ADD) representation of the *summary* of a program, which contains the relation between the inputs and outputs of the program. Moped-QLeak then computes Shannon or min-entropy leakage from this ADD representation using two algorithms introduced by the authors. To obtain the ADD representation of the program, Moped basically performs a fix-point iteration.

Moped's ability to build a symbolic representation of a program depends on the program's complexity. When such representation is computed, Moped-QLeak computes the information leakage with a small time overhead. On the other hand, some programs are not easy to reduce to a symbolic representation, and in this case Moped-QLeak's computation does not terminate within a reasonable time.

The ADD-based representation of probability distributions allows Moped-QLeak to analyze examples with large secret and observation spaces. In particular, the authors test it with 32-bit secrets and observables, whereas QUAIL's computation time tends to be exponential in the size of the observables and LeakWatch's in the size of the secret. This suggests that the ADD approach is a key improvement on the state of the art, allowing the analysis tools to analyze off-the-shelf programs using 32- and 64-bit variables.

3.4 Syntax and Usage

The tool analyzes programs written in a variant of Moped's Remopla language. We provide here a simplified version of the syntax used by Moped-QLeak.

$stmt ::=$ skip ; | $ident$ = exp; | pchoice (::$prob$->$stmt$)$^+$ choicep

   | do :: exp -> $stmt$ :: else -> $stmt$ od

   | if :: exp -> $stmt$ :: else -> $stmt$ fi

The if and do constructs from Remopla, originally non-deterministic in Moped, have been made deterministic in Moped-QLeak. The language has also been enriched with a probabilistic choice operator, pchoice which allows the programmer to probablistically define the next statement (e.g. by giving a probability $prob$ to each statement). Remopla supports loops, arrays and integers of arbitrary size. The language is normally used to encode systems for model checking against temporal logics.

The language does not provide constructs to declare secrets and observables, but assume that all global variables are at the same time secret and observable. More precisely, the initial values are considered as the input and the final values as the output. In practice, a variable is made secret by assigning it the same value in all final states.

Moped-QLeak is executed on a Remopla file MyFile.rem by calling

   mql -shannon MyFile.rem

where -shannon specifies that the tool will compute and return the Shannon leakage.

4 Case Studies

We evaluate the three tools described in the previous Section with two scalable case studies[2]. The case studies have been chosen because they model real-life systems and the results computed are representative of realistic security concerns. In order to compare them, we consider the following criteria:

Speed. Evaluating the time required by the tool to provide a result;
Accuracy. Evaluating the precision of the result returned by the tool;
Scalability. Evaluating how the tool behaves on larger instances of the case studies;
Usability. Evaluating the easiness of modeling and the usefulness of the error messages from the compiler.

---

[2] The files used for our experiments are available at https://project.inria.fr/quail/casestudies/.

4.1 Case Study A: Smart Grids

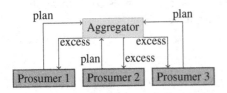

Fig. 2. Smart grid overview

A Smart grid is an energy network where every node may produce, store and consume energy. Nodes are called *prosumers* (PROducer conSUMERS). The *Living Lab* demonstrator [22] is an instance of such a prosumer, whose data can be accessed online[3]. The prosumers periodically negotiate with an aggregator in charge of balancing the consumption and production among several prosumers. Figure 2 depicts a grid with 3 prosumers. Each prosumer declares its plan, that is, how much it intends to consume or produce during the next period of time. The aggregator sends to each house the value indicating the excess of energy production or consumption. An excess of 0 indicates that the plans are feasible and terminates the negotiation. Otherwise, the prosumers adapt their plan accordingly and send the updated version. Smart grid and smart sensors raise several security and privacy concerns. The platform can ensure the information cannot flow directly between prosumers [10]. However, stability requires a feedback from the aggregator that potentially conveys information about other prosumer, where only the software can limit information leakage. In general, knowing the consumption of a particular household may reveal some sensitive information about the house (presence of people in the house, type of electrical devices ...). Therefore, the consumption of a prosumer should remain secret. The privacy of a prosumer with respect to the aggregator can be ensured in several ways [29]. However, each prosumer receives some information about the consumption of other prosumers through the excess value sent back by the aggregator.

An attacker might use the information obtained through the grid in order to decide whether a given house is occupied or not. In our scenario, we assume different types of houses with different consumptions. Each house is modeled by a private boolean value, which is true if the house is occupied. An occupied house consumes a fixed amount of energy, according to its type. An empty house does not consume anything. Table 1 presents how much a given house consumes, in two different cases that we consider.

Table 1. Consumption of houses wrt size

Size	Case A	Case B
Small	1	1
Medium	2	3
Large	3	5

For this experiment, we assume that the attacker observes the global consumption of the quarter. We consider different targets for the attack and thus different secrets. Either the attacker targets a single house of a given type (i.e. S, M or L) and only the bit corresponding to the presence in that house is secret, or the attacker wants to obtain informations about all the houses and the whole array of bits indicating the presence in each house is secret.

---

[3] livinglab.fortiss.org.

Table 2. Leakage of presence information through the global consumption

Case	Nb of houses	Single house leakage			Global leakage	Global leakage/bit
		S	M	L		
A	3	0.7500	0.7500	0.7500	2.7500	0.9166
A	6	0.0688	0.1466	0.2944	3.4210	0.5701
A	9	0.0214	0.0768	0.1771	3.7363	0.4151
A	12	0.0135	0.0544	0.1273	3.9479	0.3289
B	3	1.0000	1.0000	1.0000	3.0000	1.0000
B	6	0.1965	0.1965	0.3687	4.0243	0.6707
B	9	0.0241	0.0808	0.2062	4.3863	0.4873
B	12	0.0074	0.0510	0.1443	4.6064	0.3838

Table 3. Time to compute or approximate the leakage for a large house

Case	House Nb	Time QUAIL	Time LW	Time mql
A	3	0.1 s	0.3 s	0.02 s
A	6	0.3 s	0.3 s	0.02 s
A	9	0.6 s	0.4 s	0.02 s
A	12	1.6 s	0.4 s	0.03 s
B	3	0.2 s	0.3 s	0.02 s
B	6	0.3 s	0.5 s	0.02 s
B	9	0.6 s	0.4 s	0.02 s
B	12	1.7 s	0.4 s	0.03 s

Usability. We model the above scenario in the three tools. We consider two versions depending on the target. The program is rather simple to model, the only noticeable difference between the tools language is the declaration of unobservable variables. When targeting all the houses, the secret is an array of boolean. When targeting a single house, the secret is a single boolean. Both targets are supported by all the tools. However, the presence in the other houses is not a secret, but still an unknown and unobservable input of the program. In QUAIL, the `private` keyword allows the programmer to declare directly such variables. With LeakWatch, we chose these values randomly but do not declare them as secret. In Moped-QLeak, we choose these values randomly, as in LeakWatch.

Table 2 presents the leakage for the Smart grid case study. The first two columns indicate the case, as presented in Table 1 and the number of houses in the model. For a model with N houses, there are $N/3$ houses of each type. The columns S, M and L indicates the leakage of the variable representing the presence in a house of the corresponding type. The column "Global leakage" contains the leakage of the whole array of presence information bits and the column "Global leakage/bit" indicates the average leak per bit of secret.

In Case B with only 3 houses, the presence information can be deduced from the global consumption information, which is indicated by a leakage of 1 for each presence bit. Otherwise, the average leakage per bit from a global attack

Table 4. Average relative error and computation time over 100 runs for computing the leakage of the presence in a large house within 12 houses in Case B.

Tool	mql	QUAIL	LeakWatch						
Nb. of Simulations	-	-	Default	1000	2000	5000	10000	20000	50000
Error	0 %	0 %	14.0 %	10.4 %	6.4 %	4.8 %	2.8 %	2.1 %	1.4 %
Time	0.031 s	1.7 s	0.4 s	0.7 s	1.0 s	2.1 s	3.7 s	6.9 s	16.6 s

is more important that the information obtained by focusing on a single house. This means than obtaining information about the whole array, for instance the number of occupied houses, is easier than obtaining information about a single bit, i.e. presence information of a single house. In both cases, the leakage, and thus the loss of anonymity of prosumers, diminishes when the number of houses increases.

Speed. In Table 3 we show the time needed by QUAIL, LeakWatch and Moped-QLeak for computing the leakage of the presence information in a house of size L. Moped-QLeak takes around 20 ms to compute this value, LeakWatch takes between 300 and 500 ms and QUAIL takes between 100 and 1700 ms, depending on the size of the model. Furthermore, Moped-QLeak and QUAIL compute the exact leakage value, whereas LeakWatch computes an approximation. For a more precise comparison, we need to take precision into account.

Accuracy. We compare QUAIL, LeakWatch and Moped-QLeak on computing the leakage of the presence information of a single large house, in Case B. QUAIL takes 1.7 s to compute the exact leakage. With the default parameters, Leak-Watch takes 0.4 s to compute an approximation with a relative error of 14 % (average on 100 runs). It requires 500 to 700 simulations.

To compare execution times with respect to errors, we did an additional experiment, where we requested LeakWatch to run more simulations. For each requested number of simulations we provide in Table 4 the average relative error (over 100 runs) and the time needed for the computation. We see that for an equivalent amount of time, LeakWatch provides a result with a relative error of 4 to 6 %, whereas QUAIL returns the exact result. Moped-QLeak is the fastest and most precise.

Scalability. Finally, we evaluate the scalability of the tools by increasing the number of houses until the analysis time reaches 1 h. For this experiment, we evaluate the leakage of the presence information, in Case B, for a single house of size L (1 bit secret), or for all the houses simultaneously (N bits of secret). The results are shown in Table 5.

We see that LeakWatch can handle a very large number of houses when computing the leakage from a small secret, but is not much more scalable than QUAIL with a large secret. Recall that LeakWatch provide an approximation of the leakage, whereas QUAIL and Moped-QLeak provide the exact value. Moped-QLeak scales relatively well with both a small and a large secret to analyze.

Table 5. Maximal size analyzable in one hour

Target	LW	QUAIL	mql
L-size house	150000	27	234
All houses	15	12	150

4.2   Case Study B: Voting Protocols

In an election, each voter is called to express his preference for the competing candidates. The *voting system* defines the way the voters express their preference: either on paper in a traditional election, or electronically in e-voting. After the votes have been cast, the *results* of the vote are published, usually in an aggregated form to protect the anonymity of the voters. Finally, the winning candidate or candidates is chosen according to a given *electoral formula*.

In this section we present two typologies of voting, representing two ways in which the voters can express their preference: in the *Single Preference* protocol the voters declare their preference for exactly one of the candidates, while in the *Preference Ranking* protocol each voter ranks the candidate from his most favorite to his least favorite.

Single Preference. This protocol typology models all electoral formulae in which each of the N voters expresses one vote for one of the C candidates, including plurality and majority voting systems and single non-transferable vote [24]. The votes for each candidate are summed up and only the results are published, thus hiding information about which voter voted for which candidate. The candidate or candidates to be elected are decided according to the electoral formula used.

The secret is an array of integers with a value for each of the N voters. Each value is a number from 0 to $C-1$, representing a vote for one of the C candidates. The observable is an array of integers with the votes obtained by each of the C candidates.

The protocol is simple, and its information leakage can be computed formally, as shown by the following lemma:

Lemma 1. *The information leakage for the Single Preference protocol with n voters and c candidates corresponds to*

$$- \sum_{k_1+k_2+\ldots+k_c=n} \frac{n!}{c^n k_1! k_2! \ldots k_c!} \log_2 \left(\frac{n!}{c^n k_1! k_2! \ldots k_c!} \right)$$

While the lemma provides a formula to "manually" compute the leakage, it is very hard to find such a formula for an arbitrary process. Therefore automated tools should be employed.

Preference Ranking. This protocol typology models all electoral formulae in which each of the n voters expresses an order of preference of the c candidates, including the alternative vote and single transferable vote systems [24]. In the Preferential Voting protocol the voter does not express a single vote, but rather a ranking of the candidates; thus if the candidates are A, B, C and D the voter could express the fact that he prefers B, then D, then C and finally A. Then each candidate gets c points for each time he appears as first choice, $c-1$ points for each time he appears as second choice, and so on. The points of each candidate are summed up and the results are published.

The secret is an array of integers with a value for each of the N voters. Each value is a number from 0 to $C!-1$, representing one of the possible $C!$ rankings of the C candidates. The observable is an array of integers with the points obtained by each of the C candidates.

Table 6. Voting protocols: percent of secret leaked by Single Preference (on the left) and Preference Ranking (on the right) computed with the QUAIL tool. Timeout is set at 1 h.

SP	Candidates					PR	Candidates		
Voters	**2**	**3**	**4**	**5**	**6**	Voters	**2**	**3**	**4**
3	60.4 %	65.7 %	69.0 %	71.3 %	73.0 %	**3**	60.4 %	61.9 %	62.0 %
4	50.8 %	56.5 %	60.2 %	62.9 %	64.9 %	**4**	50.8 %	51.0 %	timeout
5	44.0 %	49.6 %	53.5 %	56.4 %	58.6 %	**5**	44.0 %	43.4 %	timeout
6	38.9 %	44.4 %	48.3 %	51.2 %	53.5 %	**6**	38.9 %	37.9 %	timeout

Experimental Results

Usability. We model the two voting systems, where the secret is the votes, and the observable the results. In single preference voting, the secret is an array of integer that represent individual votes. The range of this integer corresponds to the number of candidates. In QUAIL, it is possible to declare the range of a secret integer. In LeakWatch, each vote is drawn uniformly in the range and then declared secret. In Moped-QLeak, this case requires more work. The range of a secret integer depends on the chosen size bits. A special variable, out_of_domain, is set to true if one of the votes is not in the valid range and the corresponding input is not considered. Furthermore, when using this variable, it's not possible to use local variables, which is indicated by the error message "The first computed value is not a constant.". The impossibility to use local variables and the imprecision of the error message increased considerably the modelling time.

For the Preferential Voting, we were not able to produce a Moped-QLeak program that terminates. We suspect that Moped is unable to compute a symbolic representation of the Preferential Voting protocol due to its inherent complexity. Indeed, this program decodes an integer between 0 and the factorial of the number of candidates into a sorted list of the candidates, to assign the corresponding points to the candidates.

Accuracy. Table 6 shows the percentage of the secret leaked by the Single Preference and Preference Ranking protocols for different numbers of voters and candidates. The results for 2 candidates are identical, since in this case in both protocols the voters can vote in only 2 different ways. The results obtained for Single Preference are correct with respect to the formula stated in Lemma 1. The table shows that the Single Preference protocol leaks a larger part of its secret than the Preference Ranking protocol.

Table 7 shows the percent error of the leakage value obtained with Leak-Watch. Indeed, LeakWatch computes an approximation of the leakage based on simulation, whereas QUAIL and Moped-QLeak compute the exact value. Furthermore, the leakage computed by LeakWatch for a given program may change

Table 7. Percent error of the leakage obtained by LeakWatch relatively to the exact value for Single Preference (on the left) and Preference Ranking (on the right). Timeout is set to 1 h.

SP	Candidates					PR	Candidates		
	2	3	4	5	6		2	3	4
Voters 3	-3.8 %	-3.7 %	-3.2 %	-2.8 %	-2.2 %	**Voters** 3	-3.8 %	-2.6 %	timeout
4	-5.1 %	-3.7 %	-2.6 %	-2.3 %	-2.1 %	4	-5.1 %	-2.6 %	timeout
5	-5.0 %	-3.2 %	-2.6 %	-2.2 %	-1.9 %	5	-5.0 %	-2.2 %	timeout
6	-5.1 %	-3.2 %	-2.4 %	timeout	timeout	6	-5.1 %	timeout	timeout

Table 8. Time in seconds needed to compute the leakage for Single Preference with QUAIL (left), LeakWatch (middle) and Moped-QLeak (right). Timeout is set to 1 h.

SP QUAIL	Candidates					SP LW	Candidates					SP mql	Candidates				
	2	3	4	5	6		2	3	4	5	6		2	3	4	5	6
Voters 3	0.2	0.3	0.4	0.5	0.8	**Voters** 3	0.4	0.8	2.5	6.9	19.1	**Voters** 3	0.8	0.8	0.9	1.0	1.1
4	0.3	0.5	1.0	1.6	2.7	4	0.5	2.4	14.1	64.6	232.3	4	0.9	0.5	0.9	1.2	1.6
5	0.3	0.9	2.5	6.8	13.3	5	0.7	8.1	81.6	549.4	2688.3	5	1.0	1.1	1.2	6.8	2.7
6	0.5	2.8	13.3	56.7	214.4	6	1.1	29.0	481.6	to	to	6	1.1	1.2	1.6	2.5	4.6

at each invocation of the tool, because LeakWatch samples random executions. Here, LeakWatch slightly underestimates the leakage, by 2 to 5 %.

Speed. We compare the execution time of the three tools in Table 8 for Single Preference and in Table 9 for Preference Ranking. These execution times have been obtained on a laptop with a i7 quad-core running at 3.3 GHz and 16 GB of RAM. The results show that QUAIL is significantly faster than LeakWatch on these examples. This shows that QUAIL performs better than LeakWatch with large secrets, in line with previous results [5]. For single preference, Moped-QLeak clearly outperforms QUAIL on large examples. The results for Moped-QLeak in the preferential voting case studies are missing from Table 9 because the tool did not terminate in this case study, even with the smallest instance of 2 voters and 2 candidates.

Scalability. Concerning the Scalability, we see that QUAIL and Moped-Qleak are more scalable than LeakWatch, since the latter times out in Tables 8 and 9. For Single Preference, QUAIL stops at 7 voters and 6 candidates, due to an error. Moped-QLeak finished with 12 voters and 6 candidates but returned -inf as leakage value, instead of 11. With 9 voters and 6 candidates, the result has approximately 1 bit of errors. Therefore, we conjecture that the -inf value is

Table 9. Time in seconds needed to compute the leakage for Preference Ranking with QUAIL (on the left) and LeakWatch (on the right). Timeout is set to one hour.

PR	Candidates				PR	Candidates		
QUAIL	2	3	4		LW	2	3	4
Voters 3	0.3	2.0	89.4		**Voters** 3	0.4	13.7	timeout
4	0.4	9.0	timeout		4	0.5	121.0	timeout
5	0.7	76.7	timeout		5	0.8	1267.3	timeout
6	1.1	2987.8	timeout		6	1.2	timeout	timeout

a precision error. On these examples, no tool seems to be much more scalable than the others, due to various reasons.

5 Conclusions

In this paper, we provided two scalable case studies for the leakage computation and used them for comparing the existing tools able to perform such an approximation. We have compared the state of the art in information leakage tools – LeakWatch, QUAIL and Moped-QLeak – on their speed, accuracy, scalability and usability in addressing the case studies. We summarize here our observations and experience with the tools.

Speed. Concerning the execution time, Moped-QLeak is usually the fastest tool in providing an exact result. However, in the preferential voting example Moped-QLeak was unable to terminate its analysis in less than one hour even for the smallest instances of the problem. We can note that LeakWatch is faster than QUAIL on small secrets (e.g. 1 bit) but QUAIL outperforms LeakWatch on larger secrets. Finally, LeakWatch is very fast on small secrets, but its result and evaluation of the system (presence or absence of leakage) tends to change between different executions of the tool.

Accuracy. The tool giving the most accurate result is QUAIL because it supports arbitrary precision. LeakWatch provides an approximated result and therefore is imprecise by definition. Moped-QLeak does not implement arbitrary precision analysis, and consequently suffers from approximation errors. For instance, we found an error in the order of 1 bit on the majority voting protocol with 9 voters and 6 candidates, for which we have the exact result. Also, for the same protocol with 12 voters and 6 candidates Moped-QLeak reported a leakage of negative infinity bits, which we conjecture is caused by approximation and division-by-zero errors in the computation.

Scalability. For small secrets, LeakWatch scales better than the other tools analyzed. In the Smart Grid case study, we managed to analyze the leakage for an aggregation of 150000 houses in less than one hour.However, the returned result is obtained statistically, and varies from one execution to the other.

For large secrets, the winner is Moped-QLeak, as it scales much better than QUAIL on the Smart Grid case study. However, for the voting protocol, QUAIL manages to analyze only two voters less than Moped-QLeak (6 against 8), before approximation issues make Moped-QLeak's results incorrect.

Usability. Since all the tools studied here are academic tools who are still in their early years, usability is not necessarily the main concern of their developers. However, we have found some important discrepancies in this area.

The most usable tool is LeakWatch, especially if the program to analyze is already written in Java. In that case, it is sufficient to annotate the program in order to declare the secrets and the observable values. Furthermore, LeakWatch has a command line option to display the current results based on the traces collected so far, which is convenient when the analysis time is very long.

QUAIL has its own language, which is an imperative WHILE language with arrays and constants. QUAIL allows the explicitly declaration of variables as observable, public, private or secret, with a specific range of allowed values. Furthermore, QUAIL has a command-line option to change the values of constants declared in a program, which comes in handy when performing batch experimentation.

Using Moped-QLeak has been more problematic because of some issues with the Remopla language. In particular, the range of the secrets cannot be determined, instead the program has to raise an `out_of_domain` exception when the values are not in the expected range. Also, all integer variables have the same length, defined in the `DEFAULT_INT_BITS` constant. Finally, some error messages are misleading and slow down the modelling process.

To conclude, Moped-QLeak is the fastest tool, because it uses a suitable data structure (Algebraic Decision Diagrams) for representing the executions. However, this data structure may become a problem with complex program, as shown by the preference ranking example, which Moped-QLeak cannot analyze, contrarily to the other tools. The other tools, QUAIL and LeakWatch are more usable. QUAIL, which also has its own dedicated language, provide some specific constructs for declaring the visibility and range of a variable.

We believe that reimplementing QUAIL with a better data structure for probability distributions, like the ADDs used in Moped-QLeak, would provide a fast and usable tool for performing leakage analysis. The statistical techniques used in LeakWatch should also be integrated to allow approximated results for large instances.

6   Related Tools

We discuss some security-related automated tools and their relation with the work presented in this paper.

The STA tool developed by Boreale et al. [7] is similar in intent to the algorithms we propose, since it also uses symbolic trace analysis. More recent work by Boreale et al. [8] introduces a semiring-based semantics able to perform compositional quantitative analysis of non-deterministic systems, but no tool is available at the moment.

Efficient tools have been developed by Phan and Malacaria for information-theoretical analysis of systems. The tools squifc [25], QILURA [26], and jpf-qif [27] use SMT solving to perform a symbolic analysis of C or Java code and to compute channel capacity of programs, where the channel capacity is the maximum information leakage achievable for any prior distribution over the secret and randomness of the system. Since the tools compute channel capacity and not Shannon leakage of randomized systems, they have not been included in our comparison.

McCamant et al. have obtained interesting results in detecting leakage of information by implicit flow by applying dynamic and quantitative taint analysis techniques [20,23]. Again, their techniques have not been included in this evaluation since they do not compute information-theoretical leakage measures like Shannon and min-entropy leakage.

References

1. Alvim, M.S., Chatzikokolakis, K., Palamidessi, C., Smith, G.: Measuring information leakage using generalized gain functions. In: Chong, S. (ed.) CSF, pp. 265–279. IEEE (2012)
2. Backes, M., Doychev, G., Köpf, B.: Preventing side-channel leaks in web traffic: A formal approach. In: NDSS. The Internet Society (2013)
3. Biondi, F., Legay, A., Malacaria, P., Wąsowski, A.: Quantifying information leakage of randomized protocols. In: Giacobazzi, R., Berdine, J., Mastroeni, I. (eds.) VMCAI 2013. LNCS, vol. 7737, pp. 68–87. Springer, Heidelberg (2013)
4. Biondi, F., Legay, A., Nielsen, B.F., Malacaria, P., Wasowski, A.: Information leakage of non-terminating processes. In: Raman and Suresh [28], pp. 517–529
5. Biondi, F., Legay, A., Traonouez, L.-M., Wąsowski, A.: QUAIL: a quantitative security analyzer for imperative code. In: Sharygina, N., Veith, H. (eds.) CAV 2013. LNCS, vol. 8044, pp. 702–707. Springer, Heidelberg (2013)
6. Boreale, M.: Quantifying information leakage in process calculi. Inf. Comput. **207**(6), 699–725 (2009)
7. Boreale, M., Buscemi, M.G.: Experimenting with STA, a tool for automatic analysis of security protocols. In: SAC, pp. 281–285. ACM (2002)
8. Boreale, M., Clark, D., Gorla, D.: A semiring-based trace semantics for processes with applications to information leakage analysis. Math. Struct. Comput. Sci. **25**(2), 259–291 (2015)
9. Boreale, M., Pampaloni, F.: Quantitative information flow under generic leakage functions and adaptive adversaries. In: Ábrahám, E., Palamidessi, C. (eds.) FORTE 2014. LNCS, vol. 8461, pp. 166–181. Springer, Heidelberg (2014)
10. Bytschkow, D., Quilbeuf, J., Igna, G., Ruess, H.: Distributed MILS architectural approach for secure smart grids. In: Cuéllar [15], pp. 16–29
11. Chadha, R., Mathur, U., Schwoon, S.: Computing information flow using symbolic model-checking. In: Raman and Suresh [28], pp. 505–516
12. Chothia, T., Guha, A.: A statistical test for information leaks using continuous mutual information. In: CSF, pp. 177–190. IEEE Computer Society (2011)

13. Chothia, T., Kawamoto, Y., Novakovic, C.: LeakWatch: estimating information leakage from Java programs. In: Kutyłowski, M., Vaidya, J. (eds.) ICAIS 2014, Part II. LNCS, vol. 8713, pp. 219–236. Springer, Heidelberg (2014)
14. Chothia, T., Kawamoto, Y., Novakovic, C., Parker, D.: Probabilistic point-to-point information leakage. In: CSF, pp. 193–205. IEEE (2013)
15. Cuéllar, J. (ed.): SmartGridSec 2014. LNCS, vol. 8448. Springer, Heidelberg (2014)
16. Denning, D.E.: A lattice model of secure information flow. Commun. ACM 19(5), 236–243 (1976)
17. Esparza, J., Kiefer, S., Schwoon, S.: Abstraction refinement with Craig interpolation and symbolic pushdown systems. J. Satisfiability, Boolean Model. Comput. 5, 27–56 (2008). Special Issue on Constraints to Formal Verification
18. Goguen, J.A., Meseguer, J.: Security policies and security models. In: IEEE Symposium on Security and Privacy, pp. 11–20. IEEE Computer Society (1982)
19. Gray III, J.W.: Toward a mathematical foundation for information flow security. In: IEEE Symposium on Security and Privacy, pp. 21–35 (1991)
20. Kang, M.G., McCamant, S., Poosankam, P., Song, D.: DTA++: dynamic taint analysis with targeted control-flow propagation. In: NDSS. The Internet Society (2011)
21. Köpf, B., Mauborgne, L., Ochoa, M.: Automatic quantification of cache side-channels. In: Madhusudan, P., Seshia, S.A. (eds.) CAV 2012. LNCS, vol. 7358, pp. 564–580. Springer, Heidelberg (2012)
22. Koss, D., Sellmayr, F., Bauereiß, S., Bytschkow, D., Gupta, P.K., Schätz, B.: Establishing a smart grid node architecture and demonstrator in an office environment using the SOA approach. In: SE4SG. ICSE, pp. 8–14. IEEE (2012)
23. Newsome, J., McCamant, S., Song, D.: Measuring channel capacity to distinguish undue influence. In: Chong, S., Naumann, D.A. (eds.) PLAS. ACM (2009)
24. Norris, P.: Electoral Engineering: Voting Rules and Political Behavior. Cambridge University Press, Cambridge (2004). Cambridge Studies in Comparative Politics
25. Phan, Q., Malacaria, P.: Abstract model counting: a novel approach for quantification of information leaks. In: Moriai, S., Jaeger, T., Sakurai, K. (eds.) ASIACCS, pp. 283–292. ACM (2014)
26. Phan, Q., Malacaria, P., Pasareanu, C.S., d'Amorim, M.: Quantifying information leaks using reliability analysis. In: Rungta, N., Tkachuk, O. (eds.) SPIN, pp. 105–108. ACM (2014)
27. Phan, Q., Malacaria, P., Tkachuk, O., Pasareanu, C.S.: Symbolic quantitative information flow. ACM SIGSOFT Softw. Eng. Notes 37(6), 1–5 (2012)
28. Raman, V., Suresh, S.P. (eds.) FSTTCS, vol. 29. LIPIcs. Schloss Dagstuhl - Leibniz-Zentrum fuer Informatik (2014)
29. Rottondi, C., Fontana, S., Verticale, G.: A privacy-friendly framework for vehicle-to-grid interactions. In: Cuéllar [15], pp. 125–138
30. Smith, G.: On the foundations of quantitative information flow. In: de Alfaro, L. (ed.) FOSSACS 2009. LNCS, vol. 5504, pp. 288–302. Springer, Heidelberg (2009)

Family-Based Model Checking Without a Family-Based Model Checker

Aleksandar S. Dimovski[✉], Ahmad Salim Al-Sibahi, Claus Brabrand,
and Andrzej Wąsowski

IT University of Copenhagen, Copenhagen, Denmark
adim@itu.dk

Abstract. Many software systems are variational: they can be configured to meet diverse sets of requirements. Variability is found in both
communication protocols and discrete controllers of embedded systems.
In these areas, model checking is an important verification technique. For
variational models (systems with variability), specialized *family-based*
model checking algorithms allow efficient verification of multiple variants, simultaneously. These algorithms scale much better than "brute
force" verification of individual systems, one-by-one. Nevertheless, they
can deal with only very small variational models.

We address two key problems of family-based model checking. First,
we improve scalability by introducing abstractions that simplify variability. Second, we reduce the burden of maintaining specialized family-based
model checkers, by showing how the presented variability abstractions
can be used to model-check variational models using the standard version of (single system) SPIN. The abstractions are first defined as Galois
connections on semantic domains. We then show how to translate them
into syntactic source-to-source transformations on variational models.
This allows the use of SPIN with all its accumulated optimizations for
efficient verification of variational models without any knowledge about
variability. We demonstrate the practicality of this method on several
examples using both the $\overline{\text{SNIP}}$ (family based) and SPIN (single system)
model checkers.

1 Introduction

Variability is an increasingly frequent phenomenon in software systems. A growing number of projects follow the *Software Product Line* (SPL) methodology [8]
for building a *family* of related systems. Implementations of such systems usually
[1] contain statically configured options (variation points) governed by a *feature
configuration*. A feature configuration determines a single *variant* (product) of
the system family, which can be derived, built, tested, and deployed. The SPL
methodology is particularly popular in the embedded systems domain, where
development and production in lines is very common (e.g., cars, phones) [8].

Danish Council for Independent Research, Sapere Aude grant no. 0602-02327B.

B. Fischer and J. Geldenhuys (Eds.): SPIN 2015, LNCS 9232, pp. 282–299, 2015.
DOI: 10.1007/978-3-319-23404-5_18

Variability plays a significant role outside of the SPL methodology as well. Many communication protocols, components and system-level programs are highly configurable: a set of parameters is decided/implemented statically and then never changes during execution.

These systems interpret decisions over variation point at runtime, instead of statically configuring them. Nevertheless, since the configurations do not normally change during the time of execution, the abstract semantics of highly configurable systems is similar to static SPLs. Thus, systems with variability, i.e. system families, can be conceptually specified using *variational* models.

Since embedded systems, system-level software and communication protocols frequently are safety critical, they require rigorous validation of models, where model-checking is a primary validation technique. Performance of single-variant (single-system) model checking algorithms depends on the size of the model and the size of the specification property [2]. Classical model-checking research provides abstraction and reduction techniques to address the complexity stemming from both the model and the specification [4,13,15]. In most of these works, the generation of the abstract model is based on abstract interpretation theory [11]: the semantics of the concrete model is related with the semantics of its abstract version by using Galois connections. Provided the abstraction preserves the property we want to check, the analysis of the smaller abstract model suffices to decide the satisfaction of the property on the concrete model.

Unfortunately, model checking families of systems is harder than model-checking single systems because, combinatorically, the number of possible variants is exponential in the number of features (aka, configuration parameters). Hence, the "brute force" approach, that applies *single-system* model checking to each individual variant of a *family-based* system, one-by-one, is inefficient. To circumvent this problem, family-based model checking algorithms have been proposed [6,7]. However, efficiency of these algorithms *still* depend on the size of the configuration space (still inherently exponential in the number of configuration parameters). In order to handle variational models efficiently we need abstraction and reduction techniques that address the third issue—the size of the configuration space.

In this paper, we use abstract interpretation to define a calculus of property preserving *variability abstractions* for variational models. Thus, we lay the foundations for *abstract* family-based model checking of variational models. Then, we define source-to-source transformations on the source level of input models, which enable an effective computation of abstract models syntactically from high-level modelling languages. This makes it easier to implement than using the semantic-based abstractions defined for (featured) transition systems [7]. We avoid the need for intermediate storage in memory of the semantics of the concrete variational model. It also opens up a possibility of verifying properties of variational models, so of multiple model variants simultanously, without using a dedicated family-based model checker such as $\overline{\text{SNIP}}$ [6] (overlined purely to avoid confusion with SPIN). We can use variability abstraction to obtain an abstracted family-of-models (with a low number of variants) that can then be model checked via brute force using a single-system model checker (e.g., SPIN [16]).

We make the following contributions:

- **Variability Abstractions:** A class of variability abstractions for featured transition systems, defined inductively using a simple compositional calculus of Galois connections.
- **Soundness of Abstraction:** A soundness result for the proposed abstractions, with respect to LTL properties.
- **Abstraction via Syntactic Transformation:** A syntactic definition of the abstraction operators as source-to-source transformations on variational models. The transformations are shown to have the same effect as applying the abstractions to the semantics of models (featured transitions systems). This allows the application of abstractions in a preprocessing step, without any modifications to the model checking tools.
- **Family-Based Model-Checking w/o a Family-Based Model Checker:** A method for Family-based model-checking using an off-the-shelf model-checker. This method relies on partitioning and abstracting the variational models until the point when they contain no variability. The default highly-optimized implementation of SPIN can be used to verify the resulting abstracted models.
- **Experimental Evaluation:** An experimental evaluation exploring the effectiveness of the above method of family-based model checking with SPIN, as well as the impact of abstractions on the scalability of the state of the art family-based model checker $\overline{\text{SNIP}}$.

This paper targets researchers and practitioners who already use model checking in their projects, but, so far, have only been analyzing one variant at a time. Although designed for SPIN, the proposed rewrite techniques shall be easily extensible to other model checkers, including probabilistic and real-time models. Also the designers of efficient family-based model checkers may find the methodology of applying abstractions ahead of analysis interesting, as it is much more lightweight to implement, yet very effective, as shown in our experiments.

2   Background: Variational Models of Behavior

A common way of introducing variability into modeling languages is superimposing multiple variants in a single model [12]. Following this, Classen et al. present *f*PROMELA [6], an extension of PROMELA with a static configuration-time branching capable of *enabling/disabling* model code in variants. They generalize the semantic model of PROMELA (transition systems) accordingly, including static guard conditions over features on transitions, creating *featured transition systems* (FTS). The guards determine in which variants the transitions appear. The set of legal configurations is encoded in a separate so-called *feature model* [17]. They have also proposed model-checking algorithms for verification of FTSs against LTL properties and implemented them in the $\overline{\text{SNIP}}$ tool[1].

---

[1] https://projects.info.unamur.be/fts/.

Featured Transition Systems (FTS). Let $\mathbb{F} = \{A_1, \ldots, A_n\}$ be a finite set of Boolean variables representing the features available in a variational model. A *configuration* is a specific subset of features $k \subseteq \mathbb{F}$. Each configuration defines a variant of a model. Only a subset $\mathbb{K} \subseteq 2^{\mathbb{F}}$ of configurations are valid. Equivalently, configurations can be represented as formulae (minterms). Each configuration $k \in \mathbb{K}$ can be represented by the term $\bigwedge_{i=1..n} \nu(A_i)$ where $\nu(A_i) = A_i$ if $A_i \in k$, and $\nu(A_i) = \neg A_i$ if $A_i \notin k$. (Since minterms can be bijectively translated into sets of features, we use both representations interchangeably.) In software engineering the set of valid configurations is typically described by a feature model [17], but we disregard syntactic representations of the set $\mathbb{K}$ in this paper.

Example 1. Throughout this paper, we use the beverage VENDINGMACHINE example [7]. It contains the following features: VendingMachine, denoted v, for purchasing a drink which represents a mandatory root feature enabled in all variants; Tea (t), for serving tea; Soda (s), for serving soda; CancelPurchase (c), for canceling a purchase after a coin is entered; and FreeDrinks (f) for offering free drinks. Hence, $\mathbb{F} = \{v, t, s, c, f\}$. In this example, we assume that only configurations in the set $\mathbb{K} = \{\{v, s\}, \{v, s, t, c, f\}, \{v, t, c\}, \{v, t, c, f\}\}$ are valid. The valid configuration $\{v, s\}$ can be expressed as the formula $v \wedge s \wedge \neg t \wedge \neg c \wedge \neg f$.

The behaviour of individual variants is given as transition systems.

Definition 1. *A transition system is a tuple $\mathcal{T} = (S, Act, trans, I, AP, L)$, where S is a set of states, Act is a set of actions, $trans \subseteq S \times Act \times S$ is a transition relation, $I \subseteq S$ is a set of initial states, AP is a set of atomic propositions, and $L : S \to 2^{AP}$ is a labeling function. We write $s_1 \xrightarrow{\lambda} s_2$ when $(s_1, \lambda, s_2) \in trans$.*

An *execution* of a transition system $\mathcal{T}$ is a nonempty, potentially infinite sequence $\rho = s_0 \lambda_1 s_1 \lambda_2 \ldots$ such that $s_0 \in I$ and $s_i \xrightarrow{\lambda_{i+1}} s_{i+1}$ for all $i \geq 0$. The *semantics* of $\mathcal{T}$, written $[\![\mathcal{T}]\!]_{\text{TS}}$, is the set of all executions of $\mathcal{T}$.

Let *FeatExp*($\mathbb{F}$), denote the set of all Boolean constraints over $\mathbb{F}$ generated using the grammar: $\psi ::= true \mid A \in \mathbb{F} \mid \neg\psi \mid \psi_1 \wedge \psi_2$. For a condition $\psi \in$ *FeatExp*($\mathbb{F}$) we write $[\![\psi]\!]$ meaning the set of valid variants that satisfy ψ, i.e. $k \in [\![\psi]\!]$ iff $k \models \psi$ and $k \in \mathbb{K}$, where $\models$ denotes the standard satisfaction of propositional logic. Feature transition systems are basically transition systems appropriately decorated with feature expressions:

Definition 2. *A tuple $\mathcal{F} = (S, Act, trans, I, AP, L, \mathbb{F}, \mathbb{K}, \delta)$ is a feature transition system (FTS) if $(S, Act, trans, I, AP, L)$ is a transition system, $\mathbb{F}$ is the set of available features, $\mathbb{K}$ is a set of valid configurations, and $\delta : trans \to FeatExp(\mathbb{F})$ is a total function labeling transitions with feature expressions.*

The *projection* of an FTS $\mathcal{F}$ onto a variant $k \in \mathbb{K}$, written $\pi_k(\mathcal{F})$, is a transition system $(S, Act, trans', I, AP, L)$, where $trans' = \{t \in trans \mid k \models \delta(t)\}$. Projection is analogous to *preprocessing* of #ifdef statements in C/CPP family-based SPLs and is naturally lifted to *sets* of variants. Given $\mathbb{K}' \subseteq \mathbb{K}$, the projection $\pi_{\mathbb{K}'}(\mathcal{F})$ is the FTS $(S, Act, trans', I, AP, L, \mathbb{F}, \mathbb{K}', \delta)$, where $trans' = \{t \in trans \mid \exists k \in \mathbb{K}'.k \models \delta(t)\}$. The semantics of the FTS $\mathcal{F}$, written $[\![\mathcal{F}]\!]_{\text{FTS}}$, is the union of the behavior of the projections onto all valid variants $k \in \mathbb{K}$,

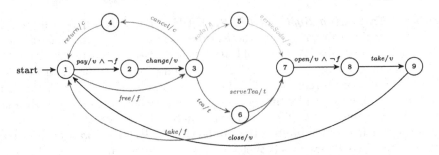

Fig. 1. The FTS of the VENDINGMACHINE.

i.e. $[\![\mathcal{F}]\!]_{\mathrm{FTS}} = \bigcup_{k \in \mathbb{K}} [\![\pi_k(\mathcal{F})]\!]_{\mathrm{TS}}$. The *size* of an FTS [7] is defined as: $|\mathcal{F}| = |S| + |trans| + |expr| + |\mathbb{K}|$, where $|expr|$ is the size of all feature expressions bounded by $O(2^{|\mathbb{F}|} \cdot |trans|)$. In these terms, our abstractions aim to reduce the $|expr|$ and $|\mathbb{K}|$ components of the size $|\mathcal{F}|$.

Example 2. Figure 1 presents an FTS describing the behavior of the VENDING-MACHINE. Each transition is labeled first by an action, and then by the feature expression following a slash. For readability, the transitions included by the same feature have the same color. The transition ③ $\xrightarrow{soda/s}$ ⑤ is enabled by feature s. A basic variant of this machine that only serves soda is defined by the configuration $\{v, s\}$. It accepts payment, returns change, serves a soda, opens the access compartment, so that the customer can take the soda, and closes it again.

The fLTL Logics and Properties. An LTL formula is defined as: $\phi ::= true \mid a \in AP \mid \phi_1 \wedge \phi_2 \mid \neg\phi \mid X\phi \mid \phi_1 U \phi_2$, with the following standard satisfaction semantics defined over an execution $\rho = s_0\lambda_1 s_1\lambda_2 \ldots$ (we write $\rho_i = s_i\lambda_i s_{i+1} \ldots$ for the i-th suffix of ρ):

$$\rho \models true \quad \text{always (for any} \rho)$$
$$\rho \models a \quad \text{iff } a \in L(s_0),$$
$$\rho \models \phi_1 \wedge \phi_2 \quad \text{iff } \rho \models \phi_1 \text{ and } \rho \models \phi_2,$$
$$\rho \models \neg\phi \quad \text{iff not } \rho \models \phi,$$
$$\rho \models X\phi \quad \text{iff } \rho_1 \models \phi,$$
$$\rho \models \phi_1 U \phi_2 \quad \text{iff } \exists k \geq 0: \rho_k \models \phi_2 \text{ and } \forall j \in \{0, \ldots, k-1\}: \rho_j \models \phi_1$$

A TS $\mathcal{T}$ satisfies a formula ϕ, written $\mathcal{T} \models \phi$, iff $\forall \rho \in [\![\mathcal{T}]\!]_{\mathrm{TS}}: \rho \models \phi$. Other temporal operators can be derived as usual: $F\phi = true U \phi$ (means "some Future state, eventually") and $G\phi = \neg F\neg\phi$ (means "Globally, always").

In the variational case, properties may hold only for some variants. To capture this in specifications, fLTL properties are quantified over the variants of interest:

Definition 3. *A feature LTL (fLTL) formula is a pair $[\chi]\phi$, where ϕ is an LTL formula and $\chi \in FeatExp(\mathbb{F})$ is a feature expression. An FTS $\mathcal{F}$ satisfies an fLTL formula $[\chi]\phi$, written $\mathcal{F} \models [\chi]\phi$, iff for all configurations $k \in \mathbb{K} \cap [\![\chi]\!]$ we have that $\pi_k(\mathcal{F}) \models \phi$. An FTS $\mathcal{F}$ satisfies an LTL formula ϕ iff $\mathcal{F} \models [true]\phi$.*

Example 3. Consider the FTS $\mathcal{F}$ in Fig. 1. Suppose that states ⑤ and ⑥ are labeled *selected*, and the state ⑧ is labeled *open*. Consider an example property ϕ that after each time a beverage has been selected, the machine will eventually open the compartment to allow the customer to access his drink: G (*selected* $\implies$ F *open*). The basic VENDINGMACHINE satisfies this property: $\pi_{\{v,s\}}(\mathcal{F}) \models \phi$, while the entire variational model does not: $\mathcal{F} \not\models \phi$. For example, if the feature f is enabled, the state ⑧ is unreachable. At the same time, we have that $\mathcal{F} \models [\neg f]\phi$.

3   Variability Abstractions

We shall now introduce abstractions decreasing the sizes of FTSs, in particular the number of features and the configuration space. We show how these abstractions preserve fLTL properties allowing to speed-up the algorithms for model checking.

A Calculus of Abstractions. For fLTL model checking, variability abstractions can be defined over the set of features $\mathbb{F}$ and the configuration space $\mathbb{K}$ and then lifted to FTSs. This greatly simplifies the definitions. We begin with the complete Boolean lattice of propositional formulae over $\mathbb{F}$: $(FeatExp(\mathbb{F})_{/\equiv}, \models, \vee, \wedge, true, false)$. Elements of $FeatExp(\mathbb{F})_{/\equiv}$ are equivalence classes of propositional formulae ψ obtained by quotienting by the semantic equivalence $\equiv$. The pre-order relation $\models$ is defined as the satisfaction (entailment) relation from propositional logic. (Alternatively, we could work with the set-theoretic definition of propositional formulae and an isomorphic complete lattice of sets of configurations).

Join. This abstraction confounds the control-flow of all configurations of the model, obtaining a single variant that includes all the executions occurring in any variant. The unreachable parts of the variational model that do not occur in any valid variant are eliminated. The information about which states belong to which variants is lost.

Technically, the abstraction collapses the entire configuration space onto a singleton set. Each feature expression ψ in the FTS is replaced with *true* if ψ is satisfied in at least one configuration from $\mathbb{K}$. The set of features in the abstracted model is empty: $\boldsymbol{\alpha}^{\text{join}}(\mathbb{F}) = \emptyset$, and the set of valid configurations is: $\boldsymbol{\alpha}^{\text{join}}(\mathbb{K}) = \{true\}$ if $\mathbb{K} \neq \emptyset$ and $\boldsymbol{\alpha}^{\text{join}}(\mathbb{K}) = \{false\}$ otherwise.

A pair of *abstraction,* $\boldsymbol{\alpha}^{\text{join}} : FeatExp(\mathbb{F}) \to FeatExp(\emptyset)$, and *concretization* functions, $\boldsymbol{\gamma}^{\text{join}} : FeatExp(\emptyset) \to FeatExp(\mathbb{F})$, are specified as follows:

$$\boldsymbol{\alpha}^{\text{join}}(\psi) = \begin{cases} true & \text{if } \exists k \in \mathbb{K}.k \models \psi \\ false & \text{otherwise} \end{cases} \qquad \begin{array}{l} \gamma^{\text{join}}(true) = true \\ \gamma^{\text{join}}(false) = \bigvee_{k \in 2^{\mathbb{F}} \setminus \mathbb{K}} k \end{array}$$

Theorem 1. $\langle FeatExp(\mathbb{F})_{/\equiv}, \models \rangle \xrightarrow[\boldsymbol{\alpha}^{\text{join}}]{\gamma^{\text{join}}} \langle FeatExp(\emptyset), \models \rangle$ *is a Galois connection*[2].

---

[2] $\langle L, \leq_L \rangle \xrightarrow[\alpha]{\gamma} \langle M, \leq_M \rangle$ is a *Galois connection* between complete lattices L and M iff α and γ are total functions that satisfy: $\alpha(l) \leq_M m \iff l \leq_L \gamma(m)$ for all $l \in L, m \in M$.

Ignoring Features. The abstraction $\alpha_A^{\text{fignore}}$ ignores a single feature $A \in \mathbb{F}$ that is not directly relevant for the current analysis. We confound the control flow paths that only differ with regard to A, and we keep the precision with respect to control flow paths that do not depend on A.

To apply this abstraction, we first need to convert the given feature expression ψ into NNF (negation normal form), which contains only $\neg, \wedge, \vee$ connectives and $\neg$ appears only in literals. We write l_A for the literals A or $\neg A$. We write $\psi[l_A \mapsto true]$ to denote the formula ψ where l_A is replaced with $true$.

The abstract sets of features and valid configurations are: $\alpha_A^{\text{fignore}}(\mathbb{F}) = \mathbb{F} \setminus \{A\}$, and $\alpha_A^{\text{fignore}}(\mathbb{K}) = \{k[l_A \mapsto true] \mid k \in \mathbb{K}\}$. The abstraction and concretization functions between $FeatExp(\mathbb{F})$ and $FeatExp(\alpha_A^{\text{fignore}}(\mathbb{F}))$ are defined as:

$$\alpha_A^{\text{fignore}}(\psi) = \psi[l_A \mapsto true] \qquad \gamma_A^{\text{fignore}}(\varphi') = (\varphi' \wedge A) \vee (\varphi' \wedge \neg A)$$

where ψ and φ' are in NNF from.

Theorem 2. $\langle FeatExp(\mathbb{F})_{/\equiv}, \models \rangle \xleftarrow[\alpha_A^{\text{fignore}}]{\gamma_A^{\text{fignore}}} \langle FeatExp(\mathbb{F} \setminus \{A\})_{/\equiv}, \models \rangle$ *is a Galois connection.*

Sequential Composition. The composition of two Galois connections is also a Galois connection [11]. Let $\langle FeatExp(\mathbb{F})_{/\equiv}, \models \rangle \xleftarrow[\alpha_1]{\gamma_1} \langle FeatExp(\alpha_1(\mathbb{F}))_{/\equiv}, \models \rangle$ and $\langle FeatExp(\alpha_1(\mathbb{F}))_{/\equiv}, \models \rangle \xleftarrow[\alpha_2]{\gamma_2} \langle FeatExp(\alpha_2(\alpha_1(\mathbb{F})))_{/\equiv}, \models \rangle$ be two Galois connections. Then $\langle FeatExp(\mathbb{F})_{/\equiv}, \models \rangle \xleftarrow[\alpha_2 \circ \alpha_1]{\gamma_1 \circ \gamma_2} \langle FeatExp(\alpha_2(\alpha_1(\mathbb{F})))_{/\equiv}, \models \rangle$ is defined as: $\alpha_2 \circ \alpha_1(\psi) = \alpha_2(\alpha_1(\psi))$, $\gamma_1 \circ \gamma_2(\psi) = \gamma_1(\gamma_2(\psi))$. We also have $\alpha_2 \circ \alpha_1(\mathbb{F}) = \alpha_2(\alpha_1(\mathbb{F}))$ and $\alpha_2 \circ \alpha_1(\mathbb{K}) = \alpha_2(\alpha_1(\mathbb{K}))$.

Syntactic Sugar. We can define an operation which ignores a *set* of features: $\alpha_{\{A_1,\ldots,A_m\}}^{\text{fignore}} = \alpha_{A_1}^{\text{fignore}} \circ \ldots \circ \alpha_{A_m}^{\text{fignore}}$ and $\gamma_{\{A_1,\ldots,A_m\}}^{\text{fignore}} = \gamma_{A_m}^{\text{fignore}} \circ \ldots \circ \gamma_{A_1}^{\text{fignore}}$.

In the following, we will simply write (α, γ) for any Galois connection $\langle FeatExp(\mathbb{F})_{/\equiv}, \models \rangle \xleftarrow[\alpha]{\gamma} \langle FeatExp(\alpha(\mathbb{F}))_{/\equiv}, \models \rangle$ constructed using the operators presented in this section.

Abstracting FTSs. Given Galois connections defined on the level of feature expressions, available features, and valid configurations, we now induce a notion of abstraction between featured transition systems (FTSs).

Definition 4. *Let* $\mathcal{F} = (S, Act, trans, I, AP, L, \mathbb{F}, \mathbb{K}, \delta)$ *be an FTS,* $[\chi]\phi$ *be an fLTL formula, and* (α, γ) *be a Galois connection.*

- *We define* $\alpha(\mathcal{F}) = (S, Act, trans, I, AP, L, \alpha(\mathbb{F}), \alpha(\mathbb{K}), \alpha(\delta))$, *where* $\alpha(\delta) : trans \to FeatExp(\alpha(\mathbb{F}))$ *is defined as:* $\alpha(\delta)(t) = \alpha(\delta(t))$.
- *We define* $\alpha([\chi]\phi) = [\alpha(\chi)]\phi$.

Example 4. Consider the FTS $\mathcal{F}$ in Fig. 1 with the set of valid configurations $\mathbb{K} = \{\{v, s\}, \{v, s, t, c, f\}, \{v, s, c\}, \{v, s, c, f\}\}$. We show $\alpha^{\text{join}}(\mathcal{F}), \alpha^{\text{join}}(\pi_{[\neg f \wedge s]}(\mathcal{F}))$,

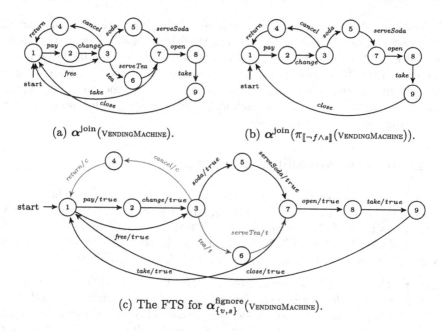

(a) $\alpha^{\text{join}}(\text{VendingMachine})$.

(b) $\alpha^{\text{join}}(\pi_{\llbracket \neg f \wedge s \rrbracket}(\text{VendingMachine}))$.

(c) The FTS for $\alpha^{\text{fignore}}_{\{v,s\}}(\text{VendingMachine})$.

Fig. 2. Various abstractions of the FTS, VendingMachine.

and $\alpha^{\text{fignore}}_{\{v,s,f\}}(\mathcal{F})$ in Fig. 2. Note that $\mathbb{K} \cap \llbracket \neg f \wedge s \rrbracket = \{\{v,s\},\{v,s,c\}\}$, and hence transitions annotated with the feature t (**Tea**) and f (**FreeDrinks**) are not present in $\alpha^{\text{join}}(\pi_{\llbracket \neg f \wedge s \rrbracket}(\mathcal{F}))$. Also note that in the case of $\alpha^{\text{join}}(\mathcal{F})$ and $\alpha^{\text{join}}(\pi_{\llbracket \neg f \wedge s \rrbracket}(\mathcal{F}))$ we obtain ordinary transition systems, since all transitions are labelled with the feature expression *true*.

Property Preservation. We now show that abstracted FTSs have some interesting preservation properties.

Lemma 1. *Let $\chi, \psi_0, \psi_1, \ldots \in FeatExp(\mathbb{F})$, and $\mathbb{K}$ be a set of configurations over $\mathbb{F}$. Let $k \in \mathbb{K} \cap \llbracket \chi \rrbracket$, such that $k \models \psi_i$ for all $i \geq 0$ Then there exists $k' \in \alpha(\mathbb{K}) \cap \llbracket \alpha(\chi) \rrbracket$, such that $k' \models \alpha(\psi_i)$ for all $i \geq 0$.*

By using Lemma 1, we can prove by contraposition the following result.

Theorem 3. (Abstraction Soundness). *Let (α, γ) be a Galois connection.*
$$\alpha(\mathcal{F}) \models [\alpha(\chi)]\phi \implies \mathcal{F} \models [\chi]\phi.$$

It follows from Definition 3 that a family-based model checking problem can be reduced to a number of smaller problems by partitioning the set of variants:

Proposition 1. *Let the subsets $\mathbb{K}_1, \mathbb{K}_2, \ldots, \mathbb{K}_n$ form a partition of the set $\mathbb{K}$. Then: $\mathcal{F} \models [\chi]\phi$ iff $\pi_{\mathbb{K}_i}(\mathcal{F}) \models [\chi]\phi$ for all $i = 1, \ldots, n$.*

Corollary 1. *Let $\mathbb{K}_1, \mathbb{K}_2, \ldots, \mathbb{K}_n$ form a partition of $\mathbb{K}$, and $(\alpha_1, \gamma_1), \ldots, (\alpha_n, \gamma_n)$ be Galois connections. If $\alpha_1(\pi_{\mathbb{K}_1}(\mathcal{F})) \models [\alpha_1(\chi)]\phi \wedge \ldots \wedge \alpha_n(\pi_{\mathbb{K}_n}(\mathcal{F})) \models [\alpha_n(\chi)]\phi$, Then $\mathcal{F} \models [\chi]\phi$.*

The above results show that, *if* we are successfully able to verify an *abstracted* property for an *abstracted* FTS, then the verification also holds for the unabstracted FTS. Note that verifying the abstracted FTS can be a lot (even exponentially) faster. If a counter-example is found in the abstracted FTS, then it may be spurious (introduced due to the abstraction) for some variants and genuine for the others. This can be established by checking which products can execute the found counter-example.

4   High-Level Modelling Languages

It is very difficult to use FTSs to directly model very large systems. Therefore, it is necessary to have a high-level modelling language, which can be used directly by engineers for modelling large systems. fPROMELA is designed for describing variational models; whereas TVL for describing the sets of features and configurations. We present fPROMELA and TVL and show their FTS semantics.

Syntax. fPROMELA is obtained from PROMELA [16] by adding *feature variables*, $\mathbb{F}$, and *guarded statements*. PROMELA is a non-deterministic modelling language designed for describing systems composed of concurrent processes that communicate asynchronously. A PROMELA program, P, consists of a finite set of processes to be executed concurrently. The basic statements of processes are given by:

$$
\begin{aligned}
stm \quad ::= \quad & \texttt{skip} \quad | \quad \texttt{x} := expr \quad | \quad c?x \quad | \quad c!expr \quad | \quad stm_1 \; ; \; stm_2 \quad | \\
& \texttt{if} :: g_1 \Rightarrow stm_1 \; \cdots \; :: g_n \Rightarrow stm_n :: \texttt{else} \Rightarrow stm \; \texttt{fi} \quad | \\
& \texttt{do} :: g_1 \Rightarrow stm_1 \; \cdots \; :: g_n \Rightarrow stm_n \; \texttt{od}
\end{aligned}
$$

where x is a variable, c is a channel, and g_i are conditions over variables and contents of channels. The "if" is a non-deterministic choice between the statements stm_i for which the guard g_i evaluates to *true* for the current evaluation of the variables. If none of the guards $g_1, \ldots, g_n$ are *true* in the current state, then the "else" statement stm is chosen. Similarly, the "do" represents an iterative execution of the non-deterministic choice among the statements stm_i for which the guard g_i holds in the current state. Statements are preceded by a declarative part, where variables and channels are declared.

The features used in an fPROMELA program have to be declared as fields of the special type *features*. The new guarded statement introduced in fPROMELA is of the form: "$\texttt{gd} :: \psi_1 \Rightarrow stm_1 \ldots :: \psi_n \Rightarrow stm_n :: \texttt{else} \Rightarrow stm \; \texttt{dg}$", where $\psi_1, \ldots, \psi_n$ are feature expressions defined over $\mathbb{F}$. The "gd" is a non-deterministic statement similar to "if", except that only features can be used as conditions (guards). Actually, this is the only place where features may be used. (Hence, "gd" in fPROMELA plays the same role as "#ifdef" in C/CPP SPLs [18]).

TVL [5] is a textual modelling language for describing the set of all valid configurations, $\mathbb{K}$, for an fPROMELA program along with all available features, $\mathbb{F}$. A feature model is organized as a tree, whose nodes denote features and edges represent parent-child relationship between nodes. The **root** keyword denotes the root of the tree, and the **group** keyword, followed by a decomposition type "allOf", "someOf", or "oneOf", declares the children of a node. The meaning is that if the parent feature is part of a variant, then "all", "some", or "exactly one" respectively, of its non-optional children have to be part of that variant. The optional features are preceded by the **opt** keyword. Various Boolean constraints on the presence of features can be specified as well.

Example 5. Figure 3 shows a simple *f*PROMELA program and the corresponding TVL model. After declaring feature variables in the *f*PROMELA program in Fig. 3a, a process **foo** is defined. The first **gd** statement specifies that i++ is available for variants that contain the feature A, and **skip** for variants with ¬A. The second **gd** statement is similar, except that the guard is the feature B. The TVL model in Fig. 3b specifies four valid configurations: {Main}, {Main, A}, {Main, B}, {Main, A, B}. If we use the $\overline{\text{SNIP}}$ tool to check the assertion, i ≥ 0, in this example, we will obtain that it is satisfied by all (four) valid variants. If we include the constraint in comments in line 5 of Fig. 3b that excludes the variant: ¬A ∧ ¬B, then the assertion i > 0 will also hold for all (three) valid variants.

Semantics. We now show only the most relevant details of *f*PROMELA semantics. For the precise account of PROMELA semantics the reader is referred to [16]. Each *f*PROMELA program defines a so-called *featured program graph* (FPG), which formalizes the control flow of the program. The FPG represents a program graph [2] (or "finite state automaton" in [16]) in which transitions are explicitly linked with feature expressions. The vertices of the graph are control locations (represented by line numbers in the program) and its transition relation defines the control flow of the program. Each transition has *condition* under which it can be executed, an *effect* which specifies the effect on the set of variables, and a *feature expression* which indicates in which variants this transition is enabled. Thus, transitions are annotated with condition/effect/feature expression. The "gd" statement specifies the control flow and the feature expression part of transitions.

Let V be the set of variables, and $\mathbb{F}$ be the set of features in an *f*PROMELA program. Let $Cond(V)$ denote the set of Boolean conditions over V, and $Assgn(V)$ denote all assignments over V. $Eval(V)$ is the set of all evaluations of V that assign

```
0  typedef features {              0  root Main {
1    bool A; bool B; }             1    group allOf {
2  features f;                     2      opt A,
3  active proctype foo() {         3      opt B
4    int i := 0;                   4    }
5    gd :: f.A ⇒ i++ :: else ⇒ skip dg;    5    // A || B;
6    gd :: f.B ⇒ i++ :: else ⇒ skip dg;    6  }
7    assert(i ≥ 0);
8  }
```

(a) An *f*PROMELA program.   (b) A TVL model.

Fig. 3. A simple *f*PROMELA program and the corresponding TVL model

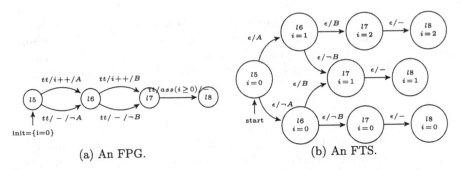

(a) An FPG.   (b) An FTS.

Fig. 4. The semantics of the fPROMELA program in Fig. 3. Note that "lx" refers to the line number x from the program in Fig. 3a, and tt is short for *true*.

concrete values to variables in V. A *featured program graph* over V and $\mathbb{F}$ is a tuple $(Loc, tr, Loc_0, init, \mathbb{K}, fe)$, where Loc is a set of control locations, $Loc_0 \subseteq Loc$ is a set of initial locations, $tr \subseteq Loc \times Cond(V) \times Assgn(V) \times Loc$ is the transition relation, $init \in Cond(V)$ is the initial condition characterising the variables in the initial state, $\mathbb{K}$ is a set of configurations, and $fe : trans \rightarrow FeatExp(\mathbb{F})$ annotates transitions with feature expressions. The *semantics* of an FPG is an *FTS* obtained from "*unfolding*" the graph (see [2, Sect. 2] for details). The unfolded FTS is $(Loc \times Eval(V), \{\epsilon\}, trans, I, Cond(V), L, \mathbb{F}, \mathbb{K}, \delta)$, where the states are pairs of the form (l, v) for $l \in Loc, v \in Eval(V)$; action names are ignored (ϵ is an empty (dummy) action name); $I = \{(l, v) \mid l \in Loc_0, v \models init\}$; $L((l, v)) = \{g \in Cond(V) \mid v \models g\}$; and transitions are defined as: if $(l, g, a, l') \in tr$ and $v \models g$, then $((l, v), \epsilon, (l', apply(a, v))) \in trans$. Here, we write $v \models g$ if the evaluation v makes g *true*, and $apply(a, v)$ is the evaluation obtained after applying the assignment a to v. Given $t \in trans$, let $t' \in tr$ be the corresponding transition of the FPG. Then $\delta(t) = true$ if $fe(t')$ is undefined; and $\delta(t) = fe(t')$ otherwise. Hence, the semantics of an fPROMELA program follows the semantics of PROMELA, just adding feature expression from the FPG to the transitions. For example, in Fig. 4 are shown the FPG and FTS for the family in Fig. 3.

5   Variability Abstraction via Syntactic Transformation

We present the syntactic transformations of fPROMELA programs and TVL models introduced by projection and variability abstractions. Let P represent an fPROMELA program, for which the sets of features $\mathbb{F}$ and valid configurations $\mathbb{K}$ are given as a TVL model T. We denote with $[\![P]\!]_T$ the FTS obtained for this program, as shown in Sect. 4.

Let $\mathbb{K}' \subseteq \mathbb{K}$ be described by a feature expression ψ', i.e. $[\![\psi']\!] = \mathbb{K}'$. The projection $\pi_{[\![\psi']\!]}([\![P]\!]_T)$ is obtained by adding the constraint ψ' in the corresponding TVL model T, which we denote as $T + \psi'$. Thus, $\pi_{[\![\psi']\!]}([\![P]\!]_T) = [\![P]\!]_{T+\psi'}$.

Let (α, γ) be a Galois connection obtained from our calculus in Sect. 3. The abstract $\alpha(P)$ and $\alpha(T)$ are obtained by defining a translation recursively over the structure of α. The function α copies all non-compound basic statements of fPROMELA, and recursively calls itself for all sub-statements of compound statements other than "gd". For example, $\alpha(\texttt{skip}) = \texttt{skip}$ and $\alpha(stm_1;stm_2) = \alpha(stm_1);\alpha(stm_2)$. We discuss the rewrites for "gd" below.

For α^{join}, we obtain a PROMELA (single variant) program $\alpha^{\mathrm{join}}(P)$ where all "gd"-s are appropriately resolved and all features are removed. Thus, $\alpha^{\mathrm{join}}(T)$ is empty. The transformation is

$$\alpha^{\mathrm{join}}(\texttt{gd}::\psi_1 \Rightarrow stm_1 \ldots ::\psi_n \Rightarrow stm_n ::\texttt{else} \Rightarrow stm' \texttt{ dg}) =$$
$$\texttt{if} ::\alpha^{\mathrm{join}}(\psi_1) \Rightarrow \alpha^{\mathrm{join}}(stm_1) \ldots ::\alpha^{\mathrm{join}}(\psi_n) \Rightarrow \alpha^{\mathrm{join}}(stm_n)$$
$$::\alpha^{\mathrm{join}}(\neg(\psi_1 \vee \ldots \psi_n)) \Rightarrow \alpha^{\mathrm{join}}(stm') \texttt{ fi}$$

For $\alpha_A^{\mathrm{fignore}}$, the transformation is

$$\alpha_A^{\mathrm{fignore}}(\texttt{gd}::\psi_1 \Rightarrow stm_1 \ldots ::\psi_n \Rightarrow stm_n ::\texttt{else} \Rightarrow stm' \texttt{ dg}) =$$
$$\texttt{gd}::\alpha_A^{\mathrm{fignore}}(\psi_1) \Rightarrow \alpha_A^{\mathrm{fignore}}(stm_1) \ldots ::\alpha_A^{\mathrm{fignore}}(\neg(\psi_1 \vee \ldots \psi_n)) \Rightarrow \alpha_A^{\mathrm{fignore}}(stm')\texttt{dg}$$

and the feature A is removed from T obtaining a new $\alpha_A^{\mathrm{fignore}}(T)$, when $\mathbb{F}\backslash\{A\} \neq \emptyset$. Otherwise, if $\mathbb{F}\backslash\{A\} = \emptyset$, then $\alpha_A^{\mathrm{fignore}}(P)$ is a PROMELA program and $\alpha_A^{\mathrm{fignore}}(T)$ is empty.

For $\alpha_2 \circ \alpha_1$, we have $\alpha_2 \circ \alpha_1(\texttt{gd}::\psi_1 \Rightarrow stm_1 \ldots \texttt{ dg}) = \alpha_2(\alpha_1(\texttt{gd}::\psi_1 \Rightarrow stm_1 \ldots \texttt{ dg}))$. Similarly, we transform the TVL model T.

Theorem 4. *Let P and T be an fPROMELA program and the corresponding TVL model, and (α, γ) be a Galois connection. We have: $\alpha([\![P]\!]_T) = [\![\alpha(P)]\!]_{\alpha(T)}$.*

6 Evaluation

We now evaluate our variability abstractions. First, we show how variability abstractions can render analysis of previously infeasible model families, feasible. Second, we turn to the main point of this paper: That instead of verifying properties using a family-based model checker (e.g., $\overline{\text{SNIP}}$), we can use variability abstraction to obtain an abstracted family-of-models (with a low number of variants) that can then be model checked using a single-system model checker (e.g., SPIN). By soundness of abstraction, *if* we are able to verify properties on the abstracted model family, we may safely conclude that they also hold on the original (unabstracted) model family. We investigate improvements in *performance* (TIME) and *memory consumption* (SPACE) on the MINEPUMP family-model [7] that comes with the installation of $\overline{\text{SNIP}}$. Finally, we do a case study on the MINEPUMP. We show how various variability abstractions may be tailored for analysis of properties of the MINEPUMP.

All of our abstractions are applied using our fPROMELA RECONFIGURATOR (model-family-*to*-model-family) transformation tool[3] as described in Sect. 5. All

---

[3] The fPROMELA RECONFIGURATOR tool (including all benchmarks) is available from: [http://ahmadsalim.github.io/p3-tool].

	unabstracted			abstracted			improvement	
$|\mathbb{F}|$	$|\mathbb{K}|$	TIME	SPACE	$|\alpha(\mathbb{K})|$	TIME	SPACE	TIME	SPACE
4	16	0.98 s	67 k	1	0.03 s	18 k	33 ×	3.8 ×
7	128	2.96 s	251 k	1	0.04 s	34 k	74 ×	7.4 ×
9	512	6.05 s	523 k	1	0.05 s	57 k	121 ×	9.2 ×
11	2,048	58.55 s	4,585 k	1	0.07 s	114 k	836 ×	40.3 ×
12	4,096	— ⋆crash⋆ —		1	0.09 s	171 k	infeasible → feasible	

Fig. 5. Verifying deadlock absence in MINEPUMP for increasing levels of variability (without vs. with maximal abstraction, $\alpha = \alpha^{\text{join}}$, confounding all configurations).

experiments were executed on a 64-bit Mac OS × 10.10 machine, Intel®Core^{TM} i7 CPU running at 2.3 GHz with 8 GB memory. The performance numbers reported (TIME) constitute the median runtime of five independent executions.

A Characterization of MINEPUMP. The *f*PROMELA MINEPUMP model family contains about 200 LOC and 7 (non-mandatory) independent optional features: Start, Stop, MethaneAlarm, MethaneQuery, Low, Normal, and High, thus yielding $2^7 = 128$ variants. Its FTS has 21,177 states and all variants combined have 889,252 states. It consists of 5 communicating processes: a controller, a pump, a watersensor, a methanesensor, and a user.

From Infeasible to Feasible Analysis via Abstraction. Combinatorially, the number of variant models grows exponentially with the number of features, $|\mathbb{F}|$, which means that there is an inherent exponential blow-up in the analysis time for the brute-force strategy, $\mathcal{O}(2^{|\mathbb{F}|})$. Consequently, for families with high variability, analysis quickly becomes infeasible. They take too long time to analyze.

Let us for a moment focus on (single-system) model checkers which may be applied at the family level by "brute force" model checking *all* variants of a given model family, one by one. As an experiment, we gradually added variability to the family-model in Fig. 3. Already for $|\mathbb{F}| = 11$ (for which $|\mathbb{K}| = 2^{11} = 2,048$ variants), analysis time to check the assertion becomes almost a minute. For $|\mathbb{F}| = 25$, analysis time ascends to almost a year. On the other hand, if we apply the variability abstraction, α^{join} (confounding all configurations), prior to analysis, we are able to verify the same assertion by only one call to SPIN on the *abstracted* model in 0.03 s for $|\mathbb{F}| = 11$ and in 0.04 s for $|\mathbb{F}| = 25$, effectively eliminating the exponential blow up.

Family-Based Model Checking without a Family-Based Model Checker. Recently, researchers have introduced *family-based model-checking* [6] that work at the family level and thus do not explicitly check all variants, one by one. (Analogous endeavors have been undertaken in, for instance, type checking [18], and dataflow analysis [3].) Much effort has been dedicated to speeding up analyses via *improving representation*; in particular, by exploiting information that may be "shared" among multiple configurations via BDDs. In this paper, we propose to speed up analyses via *increasing abstraction* on the configuration space. In fact, increasing abstraction and improving representation are orthogonal; i.e., they may cooperatively speed up analyses even further!

Figure 5 compares the effect (in terms of both TIME and SPACE) of analyzing the original (unabstracted) MINEPUMP vs. analyzing it after it has been variability abstracted using α^{join}. *Unabstracted* means running $\overline{\text{SNIP}}$ on MINEPUMP; whereas *abstracted* means running SPIN on $\alpha^{\text{join}}(\text{MINEPUMP})$. We verify the deadlock freedom property. *Improvement* is the relative comparison of *unabstracted* vs. *abstracted*. TIME is the time to model-check (in seconds) and SPACE is the number of explored states plus the number of re-explored states (which is equivalent to the number of transitions fired). In the case of $\overline{\text{SNIP}}$, the verification time includes the times to parse the fPROMELA program, to build the initial FTS, and to run the verification procedure. In the case of SPIN, we measure the times to generate a process analyser (pan) and to execute it. We do not count the time for compiling pan, as it is due to a design decision in SPIN rather than its verification algorithm. The same measurement technique was used in the experiments in [6,7].

The rows of Fig. 5 represent different versions of MINEPUMP, with increasing levels of variability. The "real" version has $|\mathbb{K}| = 128$ variants. For the $|\mathbb{K}| = 16$ version, we applied a *projection* to keep the four features Start, Stop, MethaneAlarm, and High (eliminating features MethaneQuery, Low, and Normal). For the $|\mathbb{K}| = 512$ version, we turned implementation alternatives (already present in the original MINEPUMP, as comments) into variability choices in the form of two new independent features. Parts of the controller process exists *with* and *without* race conditions (the former in comments); we turned that into an optional feature, RaceCond. Similarly, the watersensor process exists in two versions: *standard* and *alternative* (the latter in comments); we turned that into an optional feature, Standard. For $|\mathbb{K}| = 2,048$ and $|\mathbb{K}| = 4,096$, we inflated variability by adding independent optional features and gd statements to the methanesensor process, preseving the overall behavior of the process (differing only with respect to the value of an otherwise uninteresting local variable, i).

Unsurprisingly, analysis TIME and SPACE increase exponentially with the number of features, $\mathcal{O}(|\mathbb{F}|)$. However, the TIME and SPACE it takes to verify the deadlock absence in the *abstracted* model do not increase significantly with the number of variants, when using the maximal abstraction, α^{join}. For $|\mathbb{K}| = 2,048$ variants, $\overline{\text{SNIP}}$ terminates after almost a minute (checking 4.6 million transitions) whereas calling SPIN on the *abstracted* system obtains the verification results after a mere 0.07 s (visiting only 113,775 transitions). For $|\mathbb{K}| = 4,096$ variants, $\overline{\text{SNIP}}$ *crashes* after 88 s (exploring 6.3 million transitions). SPIN, on the other hand, is capable of analysis the *abstracted* system in 0.09 s (exploring 170,670 transitions).

Devising Abstractions for Properties (A Case Study of* MINEPUMP*).
We start by considering four universal properties, φ_1 to φ_4 (taken from [7], see Fig. 6), that are intended to be satisfied by all variants. By applying the α^{join} abstraction on the system, we can verify those properties efficiently by only *one*

Φ	property
(φ_0)	(GF readCommand) ∧ (GF readAlarm) ∧ (GF readLevel) *Fairness: The system will infinitely often read messages of various types.*
φ_1	*Absence of deadlock.*
φ_2	G (¬pumpOn ∨ stateRunning) *If the pump is switched on, then the controller state is "running".*
φ_3	φ_0 ⇒ (¬GF (¬pumpOn ∧¬methane ∧ highWater)) *Assuming fairness (φ_0), the pump is never indefinitely off when the water level is high and there is no methane.*
φ_4	G ((¬pumpOn ∧ lowWater ∧ F highWater) ⇒ (¬pumpOn U highWater)) *When the pump is off and the water level is low, then the the pump will be switched off until the water level is high again.*
φ_5	¬ (GF pumpOn) *The pump cannot be switched on infinitely often.*
φ_6	φ_0 ⇒ ¬FG (pumpOn ∧ methane) *Assuming fairness (φ_0), the system cannot be in a state where the pump is on indefinitely in the presence of methane.*

Fig. 6. Properties for the MINEPUMP (taken from [7]).

prop- -erty	unabstracted			abstracted			improvement	
	$\|\mathbb{K}\|$	TIME	SPACE	$\|\alpha(\mathbb{K})\|$	TIME	SPACE	TIME	SPACE
φ_1	128	2.96 s	251 k	1	0.04 s	34 k	74 ×	7.4 ×
φ_2	128	4.28 s	326 k	1	0.05 s	34 k	86 ×	9.6 ×
φ_3	128	6.37 s	441 k	1	0.09 s	161 k	71 ×	2.7 ×
φ_4	128	5.98 s	420 k	1	0.05 s	57 k	120 ×	7.3 ×
φ_5	128	3.20 s	207 k	3	0.11 s	12 k	29 ×	16.6 ×
φ_6	128	4.54 s	309 k	4	0.16 s	42 k	28 ×	7.3 ×

Fig. 7. Verification of above MINEPUMP properties using tailored abstractions.

call to SPIN on the *abstracted* family-model, α^{join}(MINEPUMP) which has only one configuration, $|\alpha^{join}(\mathbb{K}_{MINEPUMP})| = 1$. The first four rows of Fig. 7 organizes the results of maximally abstracting the MINEPUMP prior to verification of properties, φ_1 to φ_4. Consistent with our expectations and previous results (cf. Fig. 5), maximal abstraction translates to massive improvements in both TIME and SPACE on a family-model with many variants (here, $|\mathbb{K}| = 128$). In fact, model checking is between 71 and 120 times faster.

We now consider non-universal properties which are *preserved* by some variants and *violated* by others: φ_5 and φ_6 (see Fig. 6). Property φ_5 (concerning the pump being switched on), is violated by all variants, 32 in total, for which Start ∧ High is satisfied (since these two features are required for the pump to be switched on in the first place). Given sufficient knowledge of the system and the property, we can easily tailor an abstraction for analyzing the system more effectively: First, we calculate three projections of the MINEPUMP family-model: $\pi_{\text{Start}\wedge\text{High}}$ (corresponding to the above 32 configurations), $\pi_{\neg\text{Start}}$ (64 configurations), and $\pi_{\neg\text{High}}$ (64 configurations). Second, we apply α^{join} on all three projections. Third and finally, we invoke SPIN three times to verify φ_5 on each of them. For the first abstracted projection, $\alpha^{\text{join}}(\pi_{\text{Start}\wedge\text{High}}(\text{MINEPUMP}))$, SPIN correctly identifies an *"abstract"* counter-example violating the property, that is *shared* by all violating variants. For the remaining abstracted projections, SPIN reports that φ_5 is *satisfied*.

Overall, we can see that our approach is significantly faster. The second-last row of Fig. 7 shows that analysis time drops from 3.20 s when verified with $\overline{\text{SNIP}}$, to 0.11 s when running SPIN "brute-force" on our *three* abstracted projections. The last row shows the results of a similar development for the property, φ_6. It takes 4.54 s using $\overline{\text{SNIP}}$, but may be verified by *four* "brute-force" invocations of SPIN in only 0.16 s. Verification of both properties constitute an almost 30 times speed up (using considerably less memory). Of course, much of the performance improvement is due to the highly-optimized industry-strength SPIN tool (compared to the $\overline{\text{SNIP}}$ research prototype). Previous work attributes a factor of two advantage for (brute force) SPIN over $\overline{\text{SNIP}}$ [7]. However, for models with more variability (larger values of $|\mathbb{F}|$), a constant factor will be dwarfed by the inherent exponential blow up.

We can also use α^{fignore} abstraction to speed up the family-based model checker. For the property φ_5, we call $\overline{\text{SNIP}}$ on $\alpha^{\text{fignore}}_{\mathbb{F}\setminus\{\text{Start},\text{High}\}}(\text{MINEPUMP})$, and we obtain the same counter-examples as in the unabstracted case for the variants in Start $\wedge$ High. However, the verification time is reduced from 3.20 to 0.97 s, and the number of examined transitions is reduced from 207, 377 to 54,376.

In conclusion, by exploiting high-level knowledge of a family-model and property, we may carefully devise variability abstractions that are able to verify nontrivial properties in only a few calls to SPIN.

7   Related Work

Abstractions for Family-Based Model Checking. *Simulation-based abstraction* of family-based model checking was introduced in [9]. The concrete FTS is related with its abstract version by defining a *simulation* relation on the level of states (as opposed to Galois connections here). Several abstract (and thus smaller) models are induced by studying quotients of concrete FTSs under such a simulation relation. Any behaviour of the concrete FTS model can be reproduced in its abstraction, and therefore the abstraction preserves satisfiability of LTL formulae. Only states and transitions that can be simulated are reduced by this approach. However, this approach [9] results in small model reductions and only marginal efficiency gains of verifications times (the evaluation reports reductions of 8–9 %). Since abstractions are applied directly on FTSs, the computation time for calculating abstracted FTSs takes about 10 % of the overall verification time.

Variability-aware abstraction procedures based on counterexample guided abstraction refinement (CEGAR) have been proposed in [10]. Abstractions are introduced by using existential F-abstraction functions, and simulation relation is used to relate different abstraction levels. Three types of abstractions are considered: *state abstractions* that only merge states, *feature abstractions* that only modify the variability information, and *mixed abstractions* that combine the previous two types. Feature abstractions [10] are similar to ours since they also aim to reduce variability specific information in SPLs. However, there are many differences between them. Different levels of precision of feature abstractions in [10] are defined by simply enriching (resp., reducing) the sets of variants for which transitions are enabled. In contrast, our variability abstractions are capable to change not only the feature expression labels of transitions but also the sets of available features and valid configurations. Moreover, the user can use those abstractions to express various verification scenarios for their families. While the abstractions in [10] are applied on feature program graphs, we apply our abstractions as preprocessor transformations directly on high-level programs thus avoiding to generate any intermediate concrete model in the memory.

Family-Based Static Analysis. Various lifted techniques have been proposed, which *lift* existing analysis and verification techniques to work on the level of families, rather than on the level of single programs/systems. This includes lifted type checking [18], lifted data-flow analysis [3], lifted model checking [6,7], etc.

A formal methodology for systematic derivation of lifted data-flow analyses for program families with #ifdef-s is proposed in [19]. The method uses the calculational approach to abstract interpretation of Cousot [11] in order to derive a directly operational lifted analysis. In [14], an expressive calculus of variability abstractions is also devised for deriving abstracted lifted data-flow analyses. Such variability abstractions enable deliberate trading of precision for speed in lifted analysis. Hence, they tame the exponential blow-up caused by the large number of features and variants in an program family. Here, we pursue this line of work by adapting variability abstractions to lifted model checking as opposed to data-flow analysis in [14]. Moreover, the abstractions in [14] are directed at reducing the configuration space $|\mathbb{K}|$ since the elements of the property domain are $|\mathbb{K}|$-sized tuples, whereas the abstractions defined here aim at reducing the space of feature expressions since the variability-sensitive information in FTSs, fLTL formulae, and *f*PROMELA programs is encoded by using feature expressions.

8   Conclusion

We have proposed variability abstractions to derive abstract model checking for families of related systems. The abstractions are applied before model generation directly on *f*PROMELA programs. The evaluation confirms that interesting properties can be efficiently verified in this way by only a few calls to SPIN. Given a system with variability and a property, an interesting direction for future work would be to devise algorithms for automatic generation of suitable abstractions.

References

1. Apel, S., Batory, D.S., Kästner, C., Saake, G.: Feature-Oriented Software Product Lines - Concepts and Implementation. Springer, Heidelberg (2013)

2. Baier, C., Katoen, J.: Principles of model checking. MIT Press, Cambridge (2008)
3. Brabrand, C., Ribeiro, M., Tolêdo, T., Borba, P.: Intraprocedural dataflow analysis for software product lines. In: Hirschfeld, R., Tanter, É., Sullivan, K.J., Gabriel, R.P. (eds.) Proceedings of the 11th International Conference on Aspect-oriented Software Development, AOSD 2012, pp. 13–24. ACM (2012)
4. Clarke, E.M., Grumberg, O., Long, D.E.: Model checking and abstraction. ACM Trans. Program. Lang. Syst. **16**(5), 1512–1542 (1994)
5. Classen, A., Boucher, Q., Heymans, P.: A text-based approach to feature modelling: Syntax and semantics of TVL. Sci. Comput. Program. **76**(12), 1130–1143 (2011)
6. Classen, A., Cordy, M., Heymans, P., Legay, A., Schobbens, P.: Model checking software product lines with SNIP. STTT **14**(5), 589–612 (2012)
7. Classen, A., Cordy, M., Schobbens, P., Heymans, P., Legay, A., Raskin, J.: Featured transition systems: Foundations for verifying variability-intensive systems and their application to LTL model checking. IEEE Trans. Softw. Eng. **39**(8), 1069–1089 (2013)
8. Clements, P., Northrop, L.: Software Product Lines: Practices and Patterns. Addison-Wesley, Boston (2001)
9. Cordy, M., Classen, A., Perrouin, G., Schobbens, P., Heymans, P., Legay, A.: Simulation-based abstractions for software product-line model checking. In: Glinz, M., Murphy, G.C., Pezzè, M. (eds.) 34th International Conference on Software Engineering, ICSE 2012, pp. 672–682. IEEE (2012)
10. Cordy, M., Heymans, P., Legay, A., Schobbens, P., Dawagne, B., Leucker, M.: Counterexample guided abstraction refinement of product-line behavioural models. In: Cheung, S., Orso, A., Storey, M.D. (eds.) Proceedings of the 22nd ACM SIG-SOFT International Symposium on Foundations of Software Engineering, (FSE-22), pp. 190–201. ACM (2014)
11. Cousot, P.: The calculational design of a generic abstract interpreter. In: Broy, M., Steinbrüggen, R. (eds.) Calculational System Design. NATO ASI Series F. IOS Press, Amsterdam (1999)
12. Czarnecki, K., Antkiewicz, M.: Mapping features to models: a template approach based on superimposed variants. In: Glück, R., Lowry, M. (eds.) GPCE 2005. LNCS, vol. 3676, pp. 422–437. Springer, Heidelberg (2005)
13. Dams, D., Gerth, R., Grumberg, O.: Abstract interpretation of reactive systems. ACM Trans. Program. Lang. Syst. **19**(2), 253–291 (1997)
14. Dimovski, A., Brabrand, C., Wąsowski, A.: Variability abstractions: Trading precision for speed in family-based analyses. In: 29th European Conference on Object-Oriented Programming ECOOP 2015 (2015)
15. Gallardo, M., Martínez, J., Merino, P., Pimentel, E.: aspin: a tool for abstract model checking. STTT **5**(2–3), 165–184 (2004)
16. Holzmann, G.J.: The SPIN Model Checker - primer and reference manual. Addison-Wesley, Boston (2004)
17. Kang, K.C., Cohen, S.G., Hess, J.A., Novak, W.E., Peterson, A.S.: Feature-Oriented Domain Analysis (FODA) feasibility study. Carnegie-Mellon University Software Engineering Institute, Technical report (1990)
18. Kästner, C., Apel, S.: Type-checking software product lines - A formal approach. In: 23rd IEEE/ACM International Conference on Automated Software Engineering (ASE) 2008, pp. 258–267. IEEE (2008)
19. Midtgaard, J., Dimovski, A.S., Brabrand, C., Wasowski, A.: Systematic derivation of correct variability-aware program analyses. Sci. Comput. Program. **105**, 145–170 (2015)

IC-Cut: A Compositional Search Strategy for Dynamic Test Generation

Maria Christakis[1][✉] and Patrice Godefroid[2][✉]

[1] Department of Computer Science, ETH Zurich, Zürich, Switzerland
`maria.christakis@inf.ethz.ch`
[2] Microsoft Research, Redmond, USA
`pg@microsoft.com`

Abstract. We present IC-Cut, short for "Interface-Complexity-based Cut", a new compositional search strategy for systematically testing large programs. IC-Cut dynamically detects function interfaces that are simple enough to be cost-effective for summarization. IC-Cut then hierarchically decomposes the program into units defined by such functions and their sub-functions in the call graph. These units are tested independently, their test results are recorded as low-complexity function summaries, and the summaries are reused when testing higher-level functions in the call graph, thus limiting overall path explosion. When the decomposed units are tested exhaustively, they constitute verified components of the program. IC-Cut is run dynamically and on-the-fly during the search, typically refining cuts as the search advances.

We have implemented this algorithm as a new search strategy in the whitebox fuzzer SAGE, and present detailed experimental results obtained when fuzzing the ANI Windows image parser. Our results show that IC-Cut alleviates path explosion while preserving or even increasing code coverage and bug finding, compared to the current generational-search strategy used in SAGE.

1 Introduction

Systematic dynamic test generation [7,14] consists of symbolically executing a program dynamically, while collecting constraints on inputs from branch statements along the execution. These constraints are systematically negated and solved with a constraint solver to infer variants of the previous inputs, which will exercise alternative execution paths of the program. The process is systematically repeated with the goal of exploring the entire set (in practice, a subset) of all feasible execution paths of the program. This approach to automatic test case generation has been implemented in many popular tools over the last decade, such as EXE [8], jCUTE [21], Pex [23], KLEE [6], BitBlaze [22], and Apollo [2], to name a few. Although effective in detecting bugs, these testing tools have never

---

M. Christakis—The work of this author was mostly done while visiting Microsoft Research.

B. Fischer and J. Geldenhuys (Eds.): SPIN 2015, LNCS 9232, pp. 300–318, 2015.
DOI: 10.1007/978-3-319-23404-5_19

been pushed toward program verification of a large and complex application, i.e., toward proving that the application is free of certain classes of errors.

We have recently used the whitebox fuzzer SAGE [16] to show how systematic dynamic test generation can be extended toward program verification of the ANI Windows image parser [10]. In this previous work, we limit path explosion in the parser with user-guided program decomposition and summarization [1,12]. In particular, we *manually* identify functions for summarization whose input/output interfaces with respect to higher-level functions in the call graph are not too complex, so that the logic encoding of their summaries remains simple. Indeed, we find that it is common for functions to return a single "success" or "failure" value. If "failure" is returned, the higher-level function typically terminates. If "success" is returned, parsing proceeds with new chunks of the input, that is, completely independently of the specific path taken in the function being summarized. We, therefore, decompose the program at very few interfaces, of functions that parse independent chunks of the input and return a single "success" or "failure" value.

Based on these previous insights, we now define a new compositional search strategy for *automatically* and dynamically discovering simple function interfaces, where large programs can be effectively decomposed. IC-Cut, short for "Interface-Complexity-based Cut", tests the decomposed program units independently, records their test results as low-complexity function summaries (that is, summaries with simple logic encoding), and reuses these summaries when testing higher-level functions in the call graph, thus limiting overall path explosion. IC-Cut runs on-the-fly during the search to incrementally refine interface cuts as the search advances. In short, IC-Cut is inspired by compositional reasoning, but is only a search strategy, based on heuristics, for decomposing the program into independent units that process different chunks of the input. We, therefore, do not perform compositional verification in this work, except when certain particular restrictions are met (see Sects. 3.4 and 4).

The main contributions of this paper are:

- We present an attractive and principled alternative to ad-hoc state-of-the-art search heuristics for alleviating path explosion.
- As our experiments show, IC-Cut preserves or even increases code coverage and bug finding in significantly less time, compared to the current generational-search strategy of SAGE.
- IC-Cut can identify which decomposed program units are exhaustively tested and, thus, *dynamically verified*.

This paper is organized as follows. In Sect. 2, we recall basic principles of systematic dynamic test generation and whitebox fuzzing, and give an overview of the SAGE tool used in this work. Section 3 explains the IC-Cut search strategy in detail. In Sect. 4, we present our experimental results obtained when fuzzing the ANI Windows image parser. We review related work in Sect. 5 and conclude in Sect. 6.

2   Background

We consider a sequential deterministic program P, which is composed of a set of functions and takes as input an input vector, that is, multiple input values. The determinism of the program guarantees that running P with the same input vector leads to the same program execution.

We can systematically explore the state space of program P using *systematic dynamic test generation* [7,14]. Systematic dynamic test generation consists of repeatedly running a program both concretely and symbolically. The goal is to collect symbolic constraints on inputs, from predicates in branch statements along the execution, and then to infer variants of the previous inputs, using a constraint solver, in order to steer the next execution of the program toward an alternative program path.

Symbolic execution means executing a program with symbolic rather than concrete values. A symbolic variable is, therefore, associated with each value in the input vector, and every constraint is on such symbolic variables. Assignment statements are represented as functions of their (symbolic) arguments, while conditional statements are expressed as constraints on symbolic values. Side-by-side concrete and symbolic executions are performed using a concrete store M and a symbolic store S, which are mappings from memory addresses (where program variables are stored) to concrete and symbolic values, respectively. For a program path w, a *path constraint* ϕ_w is a logic formula that characterizes the input values for which the program executes along w. Each symbolic variable appearing in ϕ_w is, thus, a program input. Each constraint is expressed in some theory[1] T decided by a constraint solver, i.e., an automated theorem prover that can return a satisfying assignment for all variables appearing in constraints it proves satisfiable.

Whitebox fuzzing is an application of systematic dynamic test generation for detecting security vulnerabilities. In particular, *whitebox file fuzzing* explores programs that take as input a file, all bytes of which constitute the input vector of the program. SAGE [16] is a whitebox file fuzzing tool for security testing, which implements systematic dynamic test generation and performs dynamic symbolic execution at the x86 binary level. It is optimized to scale to very large execution traces (billions of x86 instructions) and programs (like Excel). Notably, SAGE is credited to have found roughly one third of all the security bugs discovered by file fuzzing during the development of Microsoft's Windows 7 [5].

Obviously, testing and symbolically executing *all* feasible program paths is not possible for large programs. Indeed, the number of feasible paths can be exponential in the program size, or even infinite in the presence of loops with an unbounded number of iterations. In practice, this *path explosion* is alleviated using *heuristics* to maximize code coverage as quickly as possible and find bugs faster in an incomplete search. For instance, SAGE uses a *generational-search strategy* [16], where all constraints in a path constraint are negated one by one (by the Z3 theorem prover [11]) in order to maximize the number of new tests

---

[1] A theory is a set of logic formulas.

generated per symbolic execution. This search strategy is combined with simple heuristics that guide the search toward least covered parts of the search space and prune the search space using *flip count limits* and *constraint subsumption* (see Sects. 3.3 and 4). Other related industrial-strength tools like Pex [23] use similar techniques. In this paper, we explore a different approach to alleviate path explosion.

3 The IC-Cut Search Strategy

In this section, we present the IC-Cut search algorithm, precisely define the low-complexity function summaries of IC-Cut, and discuss its correctness guarantees and limitations.

3.1 Algorithm

Algorithm 1 presents the IC-Cut search strategy. IC-Cut consists of three phases, which are overlapping: learning, decomposition, and matching.

Learning. The learning phase of IC-Cut runs the program under test on a set of seed inputs. The goal is to learn as much of the call graph of the program. As a result, the larger this set, the more detailed is the global view that IC-Cut has of the program, and the fewer new functions are discovered in the next phase.

On line 2 of Algorithm 1, function CREATECALLGRAPH returns the call graph of the program that is learned, dynamically and incrementally, by running the program on the seed inputs. Each node in the call graph represents a function of the program, and contains the function name and one seed input that steers execution of the program through this function. Each edge (f, g) in the call graph denotes that function f calls function g. Note that we assume no recursion.

Handling recursion is conceptually possible [12]. In practice, it is not required for the application domain of binary image parsers. Recursion in such parsers is very rare due to obvious performance, scalability, and reliability reasons, which is why we do not address it in this work.

Decomposition. During the decomposition phase, IC-Cut fuzzes (that is, explores using dynamic symbolic execution) one function at a time, starting at the bottom of the learned call graph, and potentially records the function test results as a low-complexity summary (that is, a summary with a simple logic encoding, as defined in Sect. 3.2). This is done in function EXPLORE of Algorithm 1, which is called on line 4 and takes as arguments the call graph cg, the program under test p, and an empty map from call-graph nodes to function summaries *summaries*.

Algorithm 1. The IC-Cut search algorithm.

```
 1  function IC-CUT(p, seeds)
 2    cg ← CREATECALLGRAPH(p, seeds)
 3    summaries ← {}
 4    EXPLORE(cg, p, summaries)

 6  function EXPLORE(cg, p, summaries)
 7    workQueue ← GETLEAVES(cg)
 8    while ISNOTEMPTY(workQueue) do
 9      f ← PEEK(workQueue)
10      cg′, summaries ← PROCESS(f, p, summaries)
11      if cg′ == cg then
12        workQueue ← DEQUEUE(workQueue)
13        predecessors ← GETPREDECESSORS(f, cg)
14        workQueue ← ENQUEUE(predecessors, workQueue)
15      else
16        newFunctions ← GETNEWFUNCTIONS(cg, cg′)
17        workQueue ← ADDFIRST(newFunctions, workQueue)
18        cg ← cg′

20  function PROCESS(f, p, summaries)
21    seed ← GETSEED(f)
22    interface, cg′ ← FUZZ(f, p, seed, summaries)
23    if ISSUMMARIZABLE(interface) then
24      summary ← GENERATESUMMARY(interface)
25      summaries ← PUTSUMMARY(f, summary, summaries)
26    return cg′, summaries
```

In particular, IC-Cut selects a function from the bottom of the call graph that has not been previously fuzzed. This is shown on line 7 of Algorithm 1, in function EXPLORE, where we create a $workQueue$ of the call graph leaf-nodes, and on line 9, where a function f is selected from the front of the $workQueue$. The selected function is then tested independently (in function PROCESS) to determine whether its interface is simple enough to be cost-effective for summarization. To test the selected function, IC-Cut chooses an appropriate seed input, which in the previous phase has been found to steer execution of the program through this function (line 21 of Algorithm 1). Subsequently, on line 22, IC-Cut fuzzes the program starting with this seed input, using dynamic symbolic execution.

However, while fuzzing the program, not all symbolic constraints that IC-Cut collects may be negated; we call the constraints that may be negated *open*, and all others *closed*. Specifically, the constraints that are collected until execution encounters the *first* call to the selected function are closed. Once the function is called, the constraints that are collected until the function returns are open. As soon as the function returns, symbolic execution terminates. This means that IC-Cut fuzzes only the selected function and for a single calling context of the program. Note that the function is fuzzed using a *generational search*.

While fuzzing the selected function, IC-Cut dynamically determines the complexity of its interface, as defined in Sect. 3.2. If the function interface is simple enough to be cost-effective for summarization (line 23 of Algorithm 1), the test results of the function are recorded as a summary. On line 24, we generate the function summary, and on line 25, we add it to the *summaries* map. Note that function PROCESS describes our algorithm in a simplified way. If a function interface is found to be suitable for summarization, IC-Cut actually records the summary *while* fuzzing the function. If this is not the case, IC-Cut aborts fuzzing of this function. How summaries are generated is precisely documented in Sect. 3.2.

It is possible that new functions are discovered during fuzzing of the selected function, i.e., functions that do not appear in the call graph of the learning phase. When this happens, IC-Cut updates the call graph. Of course, these new functions are placed lower in the call graph than the currently-fuzzed function, which is their (direct or indirect) caller. IC-Cut then selects a function to fuzz from the bottom of the updated call graph.

This is shown on lines 11–18 of Algorithm 1. If no new functions are discovered during fuzzing of the selected function (line 11), we remove this function from the *workQueue*, and add its predecessors in the call graph at the end of the *workQueue* (lines 12–14). When IC-Cut explores these predecessors, their callees will have already been fuzzed. If, however, new functions are discovered (lines 15–16), we add these functions at the front of the *workQueue* (line 17), and update the call graph (line 18). Note that when new functions are discovered, IC-Cut aborts exploration of the currently-fuzzed function; this is why this function is not removed from the *workQueue* on line 17.

The above process highlights the importance of the set of seed inputs in the learning phase: the better this set is in call-graph coverage, the less time is spent on switches between the decomposition and learning phases of IC-Cut.

Matching. In general, summaries can be reused by callers to skip symbolic execution of a summarized callee and, hence, alleviate path explosion caused by inlining the callee, i.e., by re-exploring all callee paths.

The matching phase decides whether a recorded summary may be reused when testing higher-level functions in the call graph. This is why function FUZZ of Algorithm 1 (line 22) takes the *summaries* map as argument. On the whole, FUZZ explores (using dynamic symbolic execution) one function at a time, records its interface, and reuses previously-computed summaries.

In our context, while fuzzing a higher-level function in the decomposition phase, the exploration might come across a call to a function for which a summary has already been computed. Note, however, that this summary has been computed for a particular calling context. Therefore, the matching phase determines whether the encountered calling context of the function matches (precisely defined in Sect. 3.2) the old calling context for which the summary has been computed. If this is the case, it is guaranteed that all execution paths of the function for the encountered calling context are described by the recorded summary. Consequently, the summary may be reused, since no execution paths of the function will be missed. If, on the other hard, the calling contexts do not match, the called function is fuzzed as part of the higher-level function (that is, it is inlined to the higher-level function) as if no summary had been recorded, to avoid missing execution paths or generating false alarms. In other words, IC-Cut allows that a function is summarized only for a single calling context, and summary reuse must be calling-context specific.

3.2   Function Summaries

Before describing which constraints on interface complexity a function must satisfy to be summarized, we first precisely define function inputs and outputs.

Function Inputs and Outputs

- An *input* i_f of function f is any value that is read and tested by f. In other words, the value of i_f is not only read in f, but also affects which execution path of the function is taken at runtime.
- An input i_f of f is *symbolic* if it is a function of any whole-program inputs; otherwise, i_f is *concrete*.
- A *candidate output* co_f of function f is any value that is written by f.
- An *output* o_f of function f is any candidate output of f that is tested later in the program.

Consider program P below, which expects two non-negative inputs a and b:

```
int is_less(int x, int y) {
  if (x < y)
    return 1;
  return 0;
}

void P(int a, int b) {
  if (is_less(a, 0) || is_less(b, 0))
    error();
  ...
}
```

For both calling contexts of function is_less in program P, is_less has one symbolic input (that is, a or b), one concrete input (that is, 0), and one output (which is 0 or 1 and tested by the if-statement in P).

Generating Summaries. In compositional symbolic execution [1,12], a summary ϕ_f for a function f is defined as a logic formula over constraints expressed in a theory T. Summary ϕ_f may be computed by symbolically executing all paths of function f, generating an input precondition and output postcondition for each path, and gathering all of these path summaries in a disjunction.

Precisely, ϕ_f is defined as a disjunction of formulas ϕ_{w_f} of the form

$$\phi_{w_f} = pre_{w_f} \wedge post_{w_f}$$

where w_f denotes an intra-procedural path in f, pre_{w_f} is a conjunction of constraints on the inputs of f, and $post_{w_f}$ a conjunction of constraints on the outputs of f. For instance, a summary ϕ_f for function is_less is

$$\phi_f = (x < y \wedge ret = 1) \vee (x \geq y \wedge ret = 0)$$

where ret denotes the value returned by the function. This summary may be reused across different calling contexts of is_less. In practice, however, these disjunctions of conjunctions of constraints can become very large and complex, thus making summaries expensive to compute. For this reason, IC-Cut generates only low-complexity function summaries for specific calling contexts.

For a given calling context, a function f is summarized by IC-Cut only if the following two conditions are satisfied:

- All symbolic inputs of f are unconstrained, that is, they are completely independent of the execution path taken in the program until function f is called. In particular, the symbolic inputs of f do not appear in any of the closed constraints collected before the call to f. Therefore, the input precondition of f must be true.
- Function f has at most one output o_f.

If the above conditions are not satisfied, function f is inlined to its calling contexts (that is, not summarized). As an example, consider again program P. For the first calling context of function is_less in P (that is, is_less(a, 0)), the symbolic input of is_less is unconstrained, and the function has exactly one output. As a result, is_less is summarized by IC-Cut for this *first* calling context, as described in Sect. 3.1.

As a consequence of these conditions, the summaries considered in this work have a single precondition on all symbolic inputs, which is true, and a single precondition on all concrete inputs, which is of the form

$$\bigwedge_{0 \leq j < N} i_j = c_j$$

where i_j is a concrete input, c_j a constant representing its concrete value, and N the number of concrete inputs. Moreover, the summaries in this work have no output postconditions, as explained later in this section. As a result, when IC-Cut generates a summary for a function f, it actually records a precondition of the above form on all concrete inputs of f; this precondition also represents the current calling context of f. In this paper, we abuse terminology and call such preconditions "summaries", although we do not record any disjunctions or postconditions. For example, in the program P above, IC-Cut generates the following summary for the first calling context of function is_less

$$y = 0$$

which denotes that all inputs of is_less except for y are symbolic and unconstrained, and that y is a concrete input whose value is 0 in the particular calling
context. This summary indicates that function is_less has been fuzzed for a
calling context in which x may take any value, while y must have the value 0.

Reusing Summaries. While fuzzing a higher-level function in the decomposition phase of IC-Cut, the exploration might come across a call to a function
for which a summary has already been generated. Then, the matching phase
determines if this summary may be reused by checking whether the new calling
context of the function matches, i.e., is equally or more specific than, the old
calling context for which the summary has been recorded (see Sect. 3.1).

- The new calling context is *as specific* as the old calling context only if (1) the
  function inputs that are symbolic and unconstrained in the old calling context
  are also symbolic and unconstrained in the new calling context, and (2) all
  other function inputs are concrete and have the same values across both calling
  contexts, except in the case of non-null *pointers* whose concrete values may
  differ since dynamic memory allocation is nondeterministic (see Sect. 3.4 for
  more details).
- The new calling context is *more specific* than the old calling context only
  if (1) the function inputs that are concrete in the old calling context are
  also concrete in the new calling context and have the same values (except in
  the case of non-null pointers), and (2) one or more function inputs that are
  symbolic and unconstrained in the old calling context are either symbolic and
  constrained in the new calling context or they are concrete.

Recall that, in our previous example about program P, IC-Cut records a summary for the first calling context of function is_less in P. This summary is then
reused in the second calling context of is_less in P (that is, is_less(b, 0)),
which is as specific as the first.

After having described *when* a recorded summary may be reused, we now
explain *how* this is done. When the matching phase of IC-Cut determines that
a function summary matches a calling context of the function, the following two
steps are performed:

1. The function is executed only concretely, and not symbolically, until it returns.
2. The function candidate outputs are associated with fresh symbolic variables.

Step (1) is performed because all execution paths of the function have already
been explored when testing this function independently for an equally or more
general calling context. Step (2) is used to determine whether the function has
at most one output, as follows.

When testing a function f for a given calling context, we can determine all
values that are written by f, which we call *candidate outputs*. Yet, we do not
know whether these candidate outputs are tested later in the program, which
would make them *outputs* of f. Therefore, when reusing a summary of f, we
associate fresh symbolic variables with all of its candidate outputs. We expect

that at most one of these candidate outputs is ever tested later in the program. If this condition is not satisfied, the summary of f is invalidated. In this case, the higher-level function that reused the summary of f is tested again, but this time, f is inlined to its calling contexts instead of summarized.

When reusing the summary of function is_less in program P, we associate a symbolic variable with the function's only candidate output, its return value. This symbolic variable is tested by function P, in the condition of the if-statement, thus characterizing the return value of is_less as a function output.

3.3 Input-Dependent Loops

We use constraint subsumption [16] to automatically detect and control input-dependent loops. Subsumption keeps track of the constraints generated from a given branch instruction. When a new constraint c is generated, SAGE uses a fast syntactic check to determine whether c implies or is implied by a previous constraint, generated from the same instruction during the execution, most likely due to successive iterations of an input-dependent loop. If this is the case, the weaker (implied) constraint is removed from the path constraint.

In combination with subsumption, which eliminates the weaker constraints generated from the same branch, we can also use *constraint skipping*, which never negates the remaining stronger constraints injected at this branch. When constraint subsumption and skipping are both turned on, an input-dependent loop is concretized, that is, it is explored only for a fixed number of iterations.

3.4 Correctness

We now discuss the correctness guarantees of the IC-Cut search strategy. The following theorems hold assuming symbolic execution has perfect precision, i.e., that constraint generation and solving are sound and complete for all program instructions.

We define an *abort-statement* in a program as any statement that triggers a program error.

Theorem 1 *(Soundness). Consider a program P. If IC-Cut reaches an abort, then there is some input to P that leads to an abort.*

Proof Sketch. The proof is immediate by the soundness of dynamic symbolic execution [12,14]. In particular, it is required that the summaries of IC-Cut are not over-approximated, but since these summaries are computed using dynamic symbolic execution, this is guaranteed. □

Theorem 2 *(Completeness). Consider a program P. If IC-Cut terminates without reaching an abort, no constraints are subsumed or skipped, and the functions whose summaries are reused have no outputs and no concrete non-null pointers as inputs, then there is no input to P that leads to an abort.*

Proof Sketch. The proof rests on the assumption that any potential source of incompleteness in the IC-Cut summarization strategy is conservatively detected. There are exactly two sources of incompleteness: (1) constraint subsumption and skipping for automatically detecting and controlling input-dependent loops, and (2) reusing summaries of functions that have a single output and concrete non-null pointers as inputs.

Constraint subsumption and skipping remove or ignore non-redundant constraints from the path constraint to detect and control successive iterations of input-dependent loops. By removing or ignoring such constraints, these techniques omit certain execution paths of the program, and are therefore incomplete.

When reusing the summary of a function with a single output, certain execution paths of the program might become infeasible due to the value of its output. As a result, IC-Cut might fail to explore some execution paths. On the other hand, summaries of functions with no outputs are completely independent of the execution paths taken in the program. Therefore, when such summaries are reused, no paths are ever missed. Note that by restricting the function outputs to at most one, we set an upper bound to the number of execution paths that can be missed, that is, in comparison to reusing summaries of functions with more than one output.

When reusing the summary of a function that has concrete non-null pointers as inputs, execution paths that are guarded by tests on the values of these pointers might be missed, for instance, when two such pointers are compared for aliasing. This is because we ignore whether the values of such inputs actually match the calling context where the summary is reused, to deal with the nondeterminism of dynamic memory allocation.

The program units for which the exploration of IC-Cut is complete and does not lead to an abort are dynamically verified.   □

3.5   Limitation: Search Redundancies

It is worth emphasizing that IC-Cut may perform redundant sub-searches in two cases: (1) partial call graph, and (2) late summary mismatch, as detailed below. However, as our evaluation shows (Sect. 4), these limitations seem outweighed by the benefits of IC-Cut in practice.

Partial Call Graph. This refers to discovering functions during the decomposition phase of IC-Cut that do not appear in the call graph built in the learning phase. Whenever new functions are discovered, fuzzing is aborted in order to update the call graph, and all test results of the function being fuzzed are lost.

Late Summary Mismatch. Consider a scenario in which function `foo` calls function `bar`. At time t, `bar` is summarized because it is call-stack deeper than `foo` and the interface constraint on `bar`'s inputs is satisfied. At time $t + i$, `foo` is explored while reusing the summary for `bar`, and `bar`'s candidate outputs are associated with symbolic variables. At time $t + i + j$, while still exploring foo, the interface constraint on bar's outputs is violated, and thus, the summary of bar is invalidated. Consequently, fuzzing of foo is aborted and restarted, this time by inlining bar to its calling context in foo.

4 Experimental Evaluation

In this section, we present detailed experimental results obtained when fuzzing the ANI Windows image parser, which is available on every version of Windows.

This parser processes structured graphics files to display "ANImated" cursors and icons, like the spinning ring or hourglass on Windows. The ANI parser is written mostly in C, while the remaining code is written in x86 assembly. It is a large benchmark consisting of thousands of lines of code spread across hundreds of functions. The implementation involves at least 350 functions defined in five Windows DLLs. The parsing of input bytes from an ANI file takes place in at least 110 functions defined in two DLLs, namely, in user32.dll, which is responsible for 80 % of the parsing code, and in gdi32.dll, which is responsible for the remaining 20 % [10].

Our results show that IC-Cut alleviates path explosion in this parser while preserving or even increasing code coverage and bug finding, compared to the current generational-search strategy used in SAGE. Note that by "generational-search strategy used in SAGE", we mean a monolithic search in the state space of the entire program.

For our experiments, we used five different configurations of IC-Cut, which we compared to the generational-search strategy that is implemented in SAGE. All configurations are shown in Table 1. For each configuration, the first column of the table shows its identifier and whether it uses IC-Cut. Note that configurations A–E use IC-Cut, while F uses the generational-search strategy of SAGE. The second column shows the maximum runtime for each configuration: configurations A–E allow for a maximum of three hours to explore each function of

Table 1. All configurations used in our experiments; we used five different configurations of IC-Cut (A–E), which we compared to the generational-search strategy of SAGE (F).

Configuration		Maximum runtime	Summarization at maximum runtime	Constraint subsumption	Constraint skipping	Flip count limit
ID	IC-Cut					
A	✓	3h/function		✓	✓	
B	✓	3h/function		✓	✓	✓
C	✓	3h/function	✓	✓	✓	
D	✓	3h/function		✓		
E	✓	3h/function	✓	✓		
F		48h		✓		✓

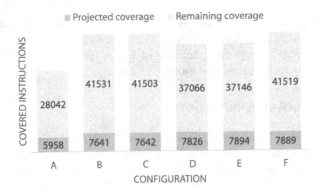

Fig. 1. The instructions of the ANI parser that are covered by each configuration. The projected instruction coverage is critical for bug finding.

the parser (since the exploration is per function), while F allows for a total of 48 h to explore the entire parser (since the exploration is whole program). The four rightmost columns of the table indicate whether the following options are turned on:

– *Summarization at maximum runtime*: Records a summary for the currently-fuzzed function when the maximum runtime is exceeded if no conditions on the function's interface complexity have been violated;
– *Constraint subsumption*: Eliminates weaker constraints implied by stronger constraints generated from the same branch instruction, most likely due to successive iterations of an input-dependent loop (see Sect. 3.3);
– *Constraint skipping*: Does not negate stronger constraints that imply weaker constraints generated from the same branch instruction (see Sect. 3.3);
– *Flip count limit*: Establishes the maximum number of times that a constraint generated from a particular program instruction may be negated [16].

Note that F is the configuration of SAGE that is currently used in production.

Figure 1 shows the instructions of the ANI parser that are covered by each configuration. We partition the covered instructions in those that are found in `user32.dll` and `gdi32.dll` (projected coverage), and those that are found in the other three DLLs (remaining coverage). Note that the instructions in `user32.dll` and `gdi32.dll` are responsible for parsing *untrusted* bytes and are, therefore, critical for bug finding. As shown in Fig. 1, configuration E, for which options "summarization at maximum runtime" and "constraint subsumption" are turned on, achieves the highest projected coverage. Configuration D, for which only "constraint subsumption" is turned on, achieves a slightly lower coverage. This suggests that summarizing when the maximum runtime is exceeded helps in guiding the search toward new program instructions; in particular, it avoids repeatedly exploring the code of the summarized functions. In contrast, configurations A–C, for which "constraint skipping" is turned on, achieve the lowest projected coverage. This indicates that testing input-dependent loops for more than just a single number of iterations is critical in increasing coverage.

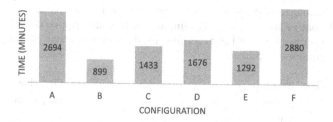

Fig. 2. The time it takes for each configuration to stop exploring the ANI parser.

Figure 2 shows the time (in minutes) it takes for each configuration to stop exploring the ANI parser. Note that configuration B stops in the smallest amount of time (approximately 15 h); this is because too many constraints are pruned due to options "constraint subsumption", "constraint skipping", and "flip count limit", which are turned on. D achieves almost the same projected coverage as F (Fig. 1) in much less time, indicating that ad-hoc heuristics such as flip count limits are no longer necessary with IC-Cut. Configuration E, which achieves the highest projected coverage, stops exploring the parser in the second smallest amount of time, that is, in approximately 21.5 h—roughly 55 % faster than the generational-search strategy used in production (configuration F).

In this amount of time, configuration E also detects the largest number of unique first-chance exceptions in the ANI parser. This is shown in Fig. 3, which presents how many unique exceptions are detected by each configuration. A first-chance exception is an exception (similar to an assertion violation) thrown at runtime (by the operating system) during program execution, but caught by the program using a C/C++ try/catch-mechanism (see [10]). Note that the nine exceptions found by configuration E are a superset of all other exceptions detected by the remaining configurations.

In summary, configuration E detects more unique exceptions than all other configurations combined. Compared to configuration F (generational search), E finds more exceptions (Fig. 3) and achieves the same projected instruction coverage (Fig. 1) in less than half the time (Fig. 2). E is the most effective configuration against path explosion.

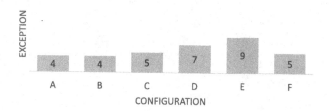

Fig. 3. The number of unique exceptions that are detected by each configuration.

Table 2. Performance of the winner-configuration E when the maximum runtime per function of the parser is one minute, 90 min, and three hours, respectively. Performance is measured in terms of covered instructions, total exploration time of the parser, and detected first-chance exceptions.

Maximum runtime	Coverage		Total time (in minutes)	First-chance exceptions	
	projected	remaining		unique	duplicate
1 min	5,421	36,250	23	0	0
90 min	7,896	37,183	683	8	7
3 h	7,894	37,146	1292	9	10

Table 2 shows how the winner-configuration E performs when the maximum runtime per function of the parser is one minute, 90 min, and three hours, respectively. Performance is measured in terms of covered instructions, total exploration time of the parser, and detected first-chance exceptions. As shown in the table, IC-Cut performs better than configuration F even for a maximum runtime of 90 min per function: there is a noticeable improvement in projected code coverage and bug finding, which is achieved in approximately eleven hours (roughly 76% faster than configuration F). This is a strong indication of how much the summarization strategy of IC-Cut can alleviate path explosion.

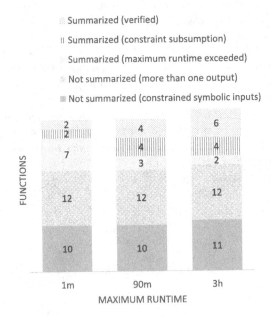

Fig. 4. How many functions are explored by the winner-configuration E when the maximum runtime per function of the parser is one minute, 90 min, and three hours, respectively. Only functions for which SAGE generated symbolic constraints are shown.

Figure 4 shows the number of functions that are explored by the winner-configuration E when the maximum runtime per function of the parser is one minute, 90 min, and three hours, respectively. This figure shows only functions for which SAGE generated symbolic constraints. The functions are grouped as follows: exhaustively tested and summarized, summarized despite constraint subsumption or an exceeded runtime, not summarized because of multiple outputs or constrained symbolic inputs. The functions in the first group constitute verified program components (according to Theorem 2), highlighting a *key originality of IC-Cut*, namely, that it can dynamically verify sub-parts of a program during fuzzing. As expected, the larger the maximum runtime, the more functions are discovered, the fewer functions are summarized at maximum runtime, and the more functions are verified. Interestingly, the functions that are not summarizable because of multiple outputs or constrained symbolic inputs are identified immediately, even for a maximum runtime of one minute per function.

We also used IC-Cut to fuzz other image parsers, namely, GIF and JPEG. Unfortunately, our prototype implementation could not handle the size of these larger parsers. However, preliminary experiments showed that our restrictions for summarization on function interfaces apply to both GIF and JPEG. For instance, when running on GIF with a time-out of three hours per function, 16 out of 140 functions (with symbolic constraints) were summarized. When running on JPEG with the same time-out, 27 out of 204 functions were summarized.

5   Related Work

Automatic program decomposition for effective systematic dynamic test generation [9] is not a new idea. Moreover, compositional symbolic execution [1,12] has already been shown to alleviate path explosion. However, when, where, and how compositionality is most effective in practice is still an open problem.

Algorithms for automatic program summarization have been proposed before [1,12,18]. SMART [12] tests all program functions in isolation, encodes their test results as summaries expressed using input preconditions and output postconditions, and then reuses these summaries when testing higher-level functions. Demand-driven compositional symbolic execution [1] generates partial summaries that describe only a subset of all paths in a function and can be expanded lazily. SMASH [18] computes both may and must information compositionally using both may and must summaries. IC-Cut is inspired by this compositional reasoning and summarization although it does not generate full-fledged function summaries. Instead, IC-Cut records a single precondition on all concrete function inputs without disjunctions or postconditions. In contrast to SMART, IC-Cut generates summaries only for functions with low interface complexity. Similarly to demand-driven compositional symbolic execution, our summaries are partial in that they describe a single calling context. Furthermore, when testing a function in isolation, the closed symbolic constraints that IC-Cut collects before the first call to the function are similar to the lazily-expanded dangling nodes in the demand-driven approach.

Other closely related techniques [3, 4, 19, 20] can be considered as approximations of sub-program summarization. Dynamic state merging and veritesting [3, 19] merge sub-program searches, and RWset [4] prunes searches by dynamically computing variable liveness. Information partitions [20] are used to identify "non-interfering" input chunks such that symbolically solving for each chunk while keeping all other chunks fixed to concrete values finds the same bugs as symbolically solving for the entire input. Similarly to these techniques, our work also approximates sub-program summarization. Moreover, IC-Cut is closely related to reducing test inputs using information partitions. Both techniques exploit independence between different parts of the program input. However, IC-Cut does not require that the input is initially partitioned, and avoids the overhead of dynamically computing data and control dependencies between input chunks.

Overall, our algorithm does not require any static analysis and uses very simple summaries, which are nevertheless sufficient to significantly alleviate path explosion. As a result, it is easy to implement on top of existing dynamic test generation tools. Our purely dynamic technique can also handle complicated ANI code patterns, such as stack-modifying, compiler-injected code for structured exception handling, and stack-guard protection, which most static analyses cannot handle. Furthermore, a static over-approximation of the call graph might result in testing more functions than necessary and for more calling contexts. With an over-approximation of function interfaces, we would summarize fewer functions, given the restrictions we impose on function inputs and outputs, thus fighting path explosion less effectively.

In addition to our low-complexity function summaries, SAGE implements other specialized forms of summaries, which deal with floating-point computations [13], handle input-dependent loops [17], and can be statically validated against code changes [15].

6   Concluding Remarks

We have presented a new search strategy inspired by compositional reasoning at simple function interfaces. However, we do not perform compositional verification in this work, except when certain restrictions are met (Theorem 2 and Sect. 4).

IC-Cut uses heuristics about interface complexity to discover, dynamically and incrementally, independent program units that process different chunks of the input vector. Our search strategy is sound for bug finding, while limiting path explosion in a more principled and effective manner than in the current implementation of SAGE, with its simple, yet clever, search heuristics. Indeed, compared to the generational-search strategy of SAGE, our experiments show that IC-Cut preserves code coverage and increases bug finding in significantly less exploration time.

IC-Cut generates low-complexity summaries for a single calling context of functions with unconstrained symbolic inputs and at most one output. Our previous work on proving memory safety of the ANI Windows image parser [10] shows that such simple interfaces exist in real, complex parsers, which is why we chose the above definition. However, our definition could be relaxed to allow for more than one calling context or function output, although our experiments show that this definition is already sufficient for large improvements. We leave this for future work. We also leave for future work determining how suitable such a definition is for application domains other than that of binary image parsers.

References

1. Anand, S., Godefroid, P., Tillmann, N.: Demand-driven compositional symbolic execution. In: Ramakrishnan, C.R., Rehof, J. (eds.) TACAS 2008. LNCS, vol. 4963, pp. 367–381. Springer, Heidelberg (2008)
2. Artzi, S., Kiezun, A., Dolby, J., Tip, F., Dig, D., Paradkar, A.M., Ernst, M.D.: Finding bugs in web applications using dynamic test generation and explicit-state model checking. TSE **36**, 474–494 (2010)
3. Avgerinos, T., Rebert, A., Cha, S.K., Brumley, D.: Enhancing symbolic execution with veritesting. In: Proceedings of ICSE, pp. 1083–1094. ACM (2014)
4. Boonstoppel, P., Cadar, C., Engler, D.: RWset: attacking path explosion in constraint-based test generation. In: Ramakrishnan, C.R., Rehof, J. (eds.) TACAS 2008. LNCS, vol. 4963, pp. 351–366. Springer, Heidelberg (2008)
5. Bounimova, E., Godefroid, P., Molnar, D.A.: Billions and billions of constraints: whitebox fuzz testing in production. In: Proceedings of ICSE, pp. 122–131. ACM (2013)
6. Cadar, C., Dunbar, D., Engler, D.R.: KLEE: unassisted and automatic generation of high-coverage tests for complex systems programs. In: Proceedings of OSDI, pp. 209–224. USENIX (2008)
7. Cadar, C., Engler, D.: Execution generated test cases: how to make systems code crash itself. In: Godefroid, P. (ed.) SPIN 2005. LNCS, vol. 3639, pp. 2–23. Springer, Heidelberg (2005)
8. Cadar, C., Ganesh, V., Pawlowski, P.M., Dill, D.L., Engler, D.R.: EXE: automatically generating inputs of death. In: Proceedings of CCS, pp. 322–335. ACM (2006)
9. Chakrabarti, A., Godefroid, P.: Software partitioning for effective automated unit testing. In: Proceedings of EMSOFT, pp. 262–271. ACM (2006)
10. Christakis, M., Godefroid, P.: Proving memory safety of the ANI Windows image parser using compositional exhaustive testing. In: D'Souza, D., Lal, A., Larsen, K.G. (eds.) VMCAI 2015. LNCS, vol. 8931, pp. 373–392. Springer, Heidelberg (2015)
11. de Moura, L., Bjørner, N.S.: Z3: an efficient SMT solver. In: Ramakrishnan, C.R., Rehof, J. (eds.) TACAS 2008. LNCS, vol. 4963, pp. 337–340. Springer, Heidelberg (2008)
12. Godefroid, P.: Compositional dynamic test generation. In: Proceedings of POPL, pp. 47–54. ACM (2007)
13. Godefroid, P., Kinder, J.: Proving memory safety of floating-point computations by combining static and dynamic program analysis. In: Proceedings of ISSTA, pp. 1–12. ACM (2010)
14. Godefroid, P., Klarlund, N., Sen, K.: DART: directed automated random testing. In: Proceedings of PLDI, pp. 213–223. ACM (2005)

15. Godefroid, P., Lahiri, S.K., Rubio-González, C.: Statically validating must summaries for incremental compositional dynamic test generation. In: Yahav, E. (ed.) Static Analysis. LNCS, vol. 6887, pp. 112–128. Springer, Heidelberg (2011)
16. Godefroid, P., Levin, M.Y., Molnar, D.A.: Automated whitebox fuzz testing. In: Proceedings of NDSS, pp. 151–166. The Internet Society (2008)
17. Godefroid, P., Luchaup, D.: Automatic partial loop summarization in dynamic test generation. In: Proceedings of ISSTA, pp. 23–33. ACM (2011)
18. Godefroid, P., Nori, A.V., Rajamani, S.K., Tetali, S.: Compositional may-must program analysis: unleashing the power of alternation. In: Proceedings of POPL, pp. 43–56. ACM (2010)
19. Kuznetsov, V., Kinder, J., Bucur, S., Candea, G.: Efficient state merging in symbolic execution. In: Proceedings of PLDI, pp. 193–204. ACM (2012)
20. Majumdar, R., Xu, R.-G.: Reducing test inputs using information partitions. In: Bouajjani, A., Maler, O. (eds.) CAV 2009. LNCS, vol. 5643, pp. 555–569. Springer, Heidelberg (2009)
21. Sen, K., Agha, G.: CUTE and jCUTE: concolic unit testing and explicit path model-checking tools. In: Ball, T., Jones, R.B. (eds.) CAV 2006. LNCS, vol. 4144, pp. 419–423. Springer, Heidelberg (2006)
22. Song, D., et al.: BitBlaze: a new approach to computer security via binary analysis. In: Sekar, R., Pujari, A.K. (eds.) ICISS 2008. LNCS, vol. 5352, pp. 1–25. Springer, Heidelberg (2008)
23. Tillmann, N., de Halleux, J.: Pex–white box test generation for .NET. In: Beckert, B., Hähnle, R. (eds.) TAP 2008. LNCS, vol. 4966, pp. 134–153. Springer, Heidelberg (2008)

Author Index

Printed in the United States
By Bookmasters